| DATE DUE | | | |
|---|---|---|---|
| | | | |
| | | | |
| | | | |
| | | | |
| | | | |
| | | | |
| | | | |
| | | | |
| | | | |
| | | | |
| | | | |

GAYLORD M-2                                    PRINTED IN U.S.A.

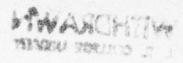

*Chronicles of the*
*First Planters of the Colony of*
*Massachusetts Bay*
*1623–1636*

# Chronicles of the
# First Planters of the Colony of
# Massachusetts Bay
## 1623–1636

## BY ALEXANDER YOUNG

DA CAPO PRESS • NEW YORK • 1970

A Da Capo Press Reprint Edition

*974.402*

*. Yo 8c*

*70755*

*July, 1970*

This Da Capo Press edition of *Chronicles of the First Planters of the Colony of Massachusetts Bay, 1623–1636*, is an unabridged republication of the first edition published in Boston in 1846.

*Library of Congress Catalog Card Number 71-87668*

SBN 306-71759-X

Published by Da Capo Press
A Division of Plenum Publishing Corporation
227 West 17th Street
New York, N. Y. 10011

Manufactured in the United States of America

# CHRONICLES

OF

# THE FIRST PLANTERS

OF

# THE COLONY OF MASSACHUSETTS BAY,

FROM 1623 TO 1636.

NOW FIRST COLLECTED FROM ORIGINAL RECORDS AND CONTEMPORANEOUS
MANUSCRIPTS, AND ILLUSTRATED WITH NOTES.

By ALEXANDER YOUNG.

*Sicut patribus, sit Deus nobis.*

BOSTON:
CHARLES C. LITTLE AND JAMES BROWN.
MDCCCXLVI.

BOSTON:
PRINTED BY FREEMAN AND BOLLES,
DEVONSHIRE STREET.

TO

THE HONORABLE

# LEMUEL SHAW, LL. D.

CHIEF JUSTICE OF THE COMMONWEALTH OF MASSACHUSETTS,

THIS VOLUME

IS RESPECTFULLY INSCRIBED

BY

HIS FRIEND AND PASTOR.

# PREFACE.

THE unexpected favor with which the publication of the "Chronicles of the Pilgrim Fathers of the Colony of Plymouth," was received, whilst it furnished gratifying proof of a growing interest in the early annals of New-England, encouraged the editor to enter into the collateral but broader field of the Colony of Massachusetts Bay, and to gather up here the scattered sheaves of a no less abundant harvest. The present volume, it is believed, will be found to contain every authentic document relating to the planting of the Colony of Massachusetts, from its first faint dawnings in 1623 to the full sunrise of 1636, with the single exception of Winthrop's History, to which it may be considered an introduction or supplement. Its chief and peculiar value, as well as that of its predecessor, consists in the fact that it imbodies the earliest materials for the History of our Commonwealth, written by men who lived at the time, on the spot, and were personally engaged in the transactions which they record. Such documents can never become obsolete, can never be superseded by subsequent narratives, however eloquent or beautiful, but must always be appealed to as the solid groundwork of our history. In the estimation of not a few, the severe and simple beauty of their Doric structure outvies the florid ornaments of more stately and ambitious edifices.

The numerous references in the Notes, though to some they may appear unnecessary, will enable the reader to verify my statements, and will point him to the sources of additional information. The former volume of Chronicles is included among the works referred to, to save the necessity of repeating what has already been said.

No nation or state has a nobler origin or lineage than Massachusetts. My reverence for the character of its founders constantly rises with the closer study of their lives, and a clearer insight into their principles and motives. Much as has been said in commendation of them, their worth has never been overrated, and we should never be tired of recounting their virtues. "Vestra autem pietas, viri exules, quæ maluit patriam quam Evangelium deserere, commodisque carere temporariis quam permisceri sacris a Christo alienis, egregiam sane meretur laudem."

ALEXANDER YOUNG.

Boston, June 1, 1846.

# CONTENTS.

# WHITE'S BRIEF RELATION.

THE PLANTERS PLEA. Or the Grovnds of Plantations Examined, and vsuall Objections answered. Together with a manifestation of the causes mooving such as have lately vndertaken a Plantation in NEVV-ENGLAND : For the satisfaction of those that question the lawfulnesse of the Action. 2 Thess. v. 21. *Prove all things, and holde fast that which is good.* LONDON. Printed by *William Iones.* 1630. sm. 4to. pp. 88.

# CHAPTER I.

## A BRIEF RELATION OF THE OCCASION OF PLANTING OF THIS COLONY.

THE ensuing faithful and unpartial narration of the CHAP. first occasions, beginning, and progress of the whole I. work, is laid before the eyes of all that desire to receive satisfaction, by such as have been privy to the very first conceiving and contriving of this project of planting this Colony,[1] and to the several passages that have happened since ; who also, in that they relate, consider they have the searcher of all hearts and observer of all men's ways witness of the truth and falsehood that they deliver.

About ten years since, a company of English, 1620. part out of the Low Countries, and some out of London and other parts, associating themselves into one body, with an intention to plant in Virginia, in their passage thither being taken short by the wind, in the Nov. depth of winter, the whole ground being under snow, 9. Old were forced with their provisions to land themselves style.

[1] This fact gives to the Narrative the sanction of the highest authority.

CHAP. in New-England, upon a small bay beyond Matta-
I.
~~~~ chusets,[1] in the place which they now inhabit, and
1620. call by the name of New Plymouth.[2]  The ground
Dec.
11.  being covered a foot thick with snow, and they being
without shelter, and having amongst them divers
women and children, no marvel if they lost some[3] of
their company; it may be wondered how they saved
the rest.  But notwithstanding this sharp encounter
at the first, and some miscarriages afterward, yet,
conceiving God's providence had directed them unto
that place, and finding great charge and difficulty in
removing, they resolved to fix themselves there; and
being assisted by some of their friends in London,[4]
having passed over most of the greatest difficulties
that usually encounter new planters, they began to
subsist at length in a reasonably comfortable manner; being, notwithstanding, men but of mean and
weak estates of themselves ;[5] and after a year's experience or two of the soil and inhabitants, sent home
tidings of both, and of their well-being there, which

---

[1] It seems to us somewhat strange to speak of Plymouth as on a "small bay beyond Massachusetts." But for some time after the first settlement of the country, the name Massachusetts was usually confined to the territory lying around Boston harbour, from Nahant to Point Alderton.  See Savage's Winthrop, i. 27, 121.

[2] We find here no allusion whatever to the alleged treachery of the captain of the Mayflower, who is said by Morton in his *New-England's Memorial*, p. 34, to have been bribed by the Dutch to carry that vessel north of their plantation on Hudson's river.  See this charge examined in the Chronicles of the Pilgrim Fathers of the Colony of Plymouth,

by the editor of this volume, p. 101, note [2].

[3] Before the first of April, that is, in less than four months, forty-four of the hundred persons who constituted the company, died.  See Chronicles of Plymouth, p. 198.

[4] Some of these friends in London were also interested in the Massachusetts Company ; such as John White, Thomas Goffe, Samuel Sharpe, John Revell, and John Pocock.  See the Collections of the Massachusetts Historical Society, iii. 48.

[5] With the exception of Winslow and Standish, the first settlers of Plymouth Colony were, in point of family and property, much inferior to those of Massachusetts.

occasioned other men to take knowledge of the place,
and to take it into consideration.[1]

About the year 1623, some western merchants,
who had continued a trade of fishing for cod and bar-
tering for furs in those parts for divers years before,[2]
conceiving that a Colony planted on the coast might
further them in those employments, bethought themselves how they might bring that project to effect,
and communicated their purpose to others, alleging
the conveniency of compassing their project with a
small charge, by the opportunity of their fishing
trade, in which they accustomed to double-man
their ships, that, by the help of many hands, they
might despatch their voyage and lade their ship
with fish while the fishing season lasted ; which
could not be done with a bare sailing company.
Now it was conceived that, the fishing being ended,
the spare men that were above their necessary sailors, might be left behind with provisions for a year ;
and when that ship returned the next year, they
might assist them in fishing, as they had done the
former year ; and, in the mean time, might employ
themselves in building, and planting corn, which,
with the provisions of fish, fowl and venison, that the
land yielded, would afford them the chief of their
food. This proposition of theirs took so well, that

---

[1] The publication in London, in
1622, of Bradford and Winslow's
Journal, and in 1624, of Winslow's
Good News from New-England, undoubtedly did much to draw the at-
tention of the people of England to
the subject of colonizing the northern part of this continent. See both
of these documents in the Chronicles
of Plymouth, pp. 109 and 269.

[2] In the year 1620 there went six
or seven ships from the west of
England to fish on the northeastern
coasts of New-England ; in 1621,
ten or twelve ; in 1622, thirty-five ;
in 1623, about forty ; and in 1624,
about fifty. See Prince's Annals,
pp. 157, 185, 201, 210, 224, (8vo.
ed. Boston, 1826.)

CHAP.
I.
1623.

it drew on divers persons to join with them in this project ; the rather because it was conceived that not only their own fishermen, but the rest of our nation that went thither on the same errand, might be much advantaged, not only by fresh victual, which that Colony might spare them in time, but withal, and more, by the benefit of their ministers' labors, which they might enjoy during the fishing season ; whereas otherwise, being usually upon those voyages nine or ten months in the year, they were left all the while without any means of instruction at all.[1] Compassion towards the fishermen, and partly some expectation of gain, prevailed so far that for the planting of a Colony in New-England there was raised a stock of more than £3000, intended to be paid in in five years, but afterwards disbursed in a shorter time.

How this stock was employed, and by what errors and oversights it was wasted, is, I confess, not much pertinent to this subject in hand. Notwithstanding, because the knowledge thereof may be of use for other men's direction, let me crave leave, in a short digression, to present unto the reader's view the

---

[1] " There were more than a few attempts of the English to people and improve the parts of New-England which were to the northward of New Plymouth. But the designs of those attempts being aimed no higher than the advancement of some worldly interests, a constant series of disasters has confounded them, until there was a plantation erected upon the nobler designs of Christianity. And that plantation, though it has had more adversaries than perhaps any one upon earth, yet, having obtained help from God, it continues to this day. There have been very fine settlements in the northeast regions ; but what is become of them ! I have heard that one of our ministers, once preaching to a congregation there, urged them to approve themselves a religious people from this consideration, that otherwise they would contradict the main end of planting this wilderness. Whereupon a well-known person, then in the assembly, cried out, ' Sir, you are mistaken. You think you are preaching to the people at the Bay. Our main end was to catch fish.' " Mather's Magnalia, i. 61, (Hartford ed. 1820.)

whole order of the managing of such moneys as were
collected, with the success and issue of the business
undertaken.

The first employment, then, of this new raised
stock was in buying a small ship of fifty tons, which
was, with as much speed as might be, despatched
towards New England upon a fishing voyage ; the
charge of which ship, with a new suit of sails, and
other provisions to furnish her, amounted to more
than £300. Now by reason the voyage was undertaken too late, she came at least a month or six
weeks later than the rest of the fishing ships that
went for that coast ; and by that means wanting fish
to make up her lading, the master thought good to
pass into Mattachusets Bay,[1] to try whether that
would yield him any ; which he performed, and
speeding there better than he had reason to expect,
having left his spare men behind him in the country
at Cape Anne, he returned to a late and consequently
a bad market in Spain, and so home. The charge of
this voyage, with provision for fourteen spare men
left in the country, amounted to above £800, with
the £300 expended upon the ship, mentioned before.
And the whole provenue, besides the ship, which
remained to us[2] still, amounted not to above £200.
So the expense, above the return of that voyage,
came to £600, and upwards.

The next year was brought to the former ship a
Flemish fly-boat,[3] of about a hundred and forty tons ;

[1] See note [1] on page 4.
[2] From this expression, *us*, it
would seem that the author of this
paper, White, was one of the adventurers.
[3] The Half-Moon, in which Henry

CHAP.
I.

1624.

which being unfit for a fishing voyage, as being built merely for burthen, and wanting lodging for the men which she needed for such an employment, they added unto her another deck, (which seldom proves well with Flemish buildings,) by which means she was carved so high that she proved walt,[1] and unable to bear any sail; so that before she could pass on upon her voyage, they were fain to shift her first, and put her upon a better trim, and afterwards, that proving to little purpose, to unlade her, and take her up and fur her. Which notwithstanding it were performed with as much speed as might be, yet the year was above a month too far spent before she could despatch to set to sea again. And when she arrived in the country, being directed by the master of the smaller ship, upon the success of his former year's voyage, to fish at Cape Anne, not far from Mattachusets Bay,[2] sped very ill, as did also the smaller ship that led her thither, and found little fish; so that the greater ship returned with little more than a third part of her lading, and came back (contrary to her order, by which she was consigned to Bourdeaux,) directly for England; so that the Company of Adventurers was put to a new charge to hire a small ship to carry that little quantity of fish she brought home to market.

The charge of this voyage, with both the ships,

Hudson discovered the noble river now called by his name, and explored it above Albany, was a fly-boat or yacht of eighty tons. See Moulton's History of the State of New York, pp. 202, 245, and Brodhead's Address before the New York Hist. Society, p. 14.

[1] Walt, crank. A ship is said to

walt, when she has not her due ballast, that is, not enough to enable her to bear her sails or keep her stiff. Hubbard, in his History of New England, p. 322, speaking of Lamberton's ill-fated ship, says that she "was ill built, very walt-sided."

[2] See note [1] on page 4.

amounted to about £2200; whereof £800 and up- CHAP.<br>I.
ward must be accounted for the building and other
charges about the greater ship. By these two ships 1624.
were left behind in the country about thirty-two
men, the charges of whose wages and provision
amounted to at the least £500 of the sum formerly
mentioned. The provenue of both the voyages that
year exceeded not the sum of £500, at the most.

The third year, 1625, both ships, with a small 1625.
vessel of forty tons, which carried kine[1] with other
provisions, were again set to sea upon the same
voyage, with the charge of £2000, of which sum the
Company borrowed and became indebted for £1000,
and upwards. The great ship, being commanded by
a very able master, having passed on about two
hundred leagues in her voyage, found herself so
leaky by the carpenter's fault, (that looked not well
to her calking,) that she bare up the helm and returned for Weymouth, and having unladen her provisions and mended her leak, set herself to sea again,
resolving to take advice of the wind whether to pass
on her former voyage, or to turn into Newfoundland;
which she did, by reason that the time was so far
spent that the master and company despaired of doing any good in New-England, where the fish falls
in two or three months sooner than at Newfoundland.
There she took fish, good store, and much more than
she could lade home. The overplus should have
been sold and delivered to some sacke or other sent
to take it in there, if the voyage had been well man-

---

[1] The first cattle, a bull and three heifers, were brought to Plymouth in March, 1624, by Edward Wins- low. See Prince's Annals, p. 225. (8vo. ed. Boston, 1826.)

aged.  But that could not be done, by reason that the ship, before she went, was not certain where to make her fish.  By this accident it fell out that a good quantity of the fish she took was cast away, and some other part was brought home in another ship.

At the return of the ships that year, fish, by reason of our wars with Spain, falling to a very low rate, the Company endeavoured to send the greater ship for France.  But she being taken short with a contrary wind, in the west country, and intelligence given in the mean time that those markets were overlaid, they were enforced to bring her back again, and to sell her fish at home as they might.  Which they did, and with it the fish of the smaller ship, the New-England fish about ten shillings the hundred by tale, or thereabout, the Newfoundland fish at six shillings four pence the hundred ; of which was well nigh eight pence the hundred charge raised upon it after the ship's return.  By this reason the fish, which at a market in all likelihood might have yielded well nigh £2000, amounted not, with all the provenue of the voyage, to above £1100.

Unto these losses by fishing, were added two other no small disadvantages ; the one in the country by our land-men, who being ill chosen and ill commanded, fell into many disorders, and did the Company little service ; the other by the fall of the price of shipping, which was now abated to more than the one half ; by which means it came to pass, that our ships, which stood us in little less than £1200, were sold for £480.

The occasions and means then of wasting this stock are apparently these : first, the ill choice of the place

for fishing. The next, the ill carriage of our men at
land, who having stood us in two years and a half in
well nigh £1000 charge, never yielded £100 profit.
The last, the ill sales of fish and shipping. By all
which the Adventurers were so far discouraged, that
they abandoned the further prosecution of this de- 1626.
sign, and took order for the dissolving of the company on land, and sold away their shipping and other
provisions.

Two things withal may be intimated by the way;
the first, that the very project itself of planting by
the help of a fishing voyage, can never answer the
success that it seems to promise; which experienced
fishermen easily have foreseen beforehand, and by that
means have prevented divers ensuing errors. Whereof, amongst divers other reasons, these may serve for
two; first, that no sure fishing-place in the land is
fit for planting, nor any good place for planting found
fit for fishing, at least near the shore; and, secondly,
rarely any fishermen will work at land, neither are
husbandmen fit for fishermen but with long use and
experience. The second thing to be observed is,
that nothing new fell out in the managing of this
stock, seeing experience hath taught us that, as in
building houses, the first stones of the foundation are
buried under ground and are not seen, so in planting
colonies, the first stocks employed that way are consumed, although they serve for a foundation to the
work.

But to return to our former subject, from which
we digressed. Upon the manifestation of the Western Adventurers' resolution to give off their work,

CHAP.
I.

1626.

most part of the land-men, being sent for, returned. But a few of the most honest and industrious resolved to stay behind, and to take charge of the cattle sent over the year before ; which they performed accordingly. And not liking their seat at Cape Anne, chosen especially for the supposed commodity of fishing, they transported themselves to *Nahum-Keike*,[1] about four or five leagues distant to the south-west from Cape Anne.

Some then of the Adventurers, that still continued their desire to set forward the plantation of a Colony there, conceiving that if some more cattle were sent over to those few men left behind, they might not only be a means of the comfortable subsisting of such as were already in the country, but of inviting some other of their friends and acquaintance to come over to them, adventured to send over twelve kine and bulls more ; and conferring casually with some gentlemen of London,[2] moved them to add unto them as many more. By which occasion, the business came

1627.

to agitation afresh in London, and being at first approved by some and disliked by others, by argument

---

[1] The author, White, in another part of his work, after referring to the opinion held by some that the Indians might formerly have had some intercourse with the Jews, observes, " Howsoever it be, it falls out that the name of the place which our late Colony hath chosen for their seat, proves to be perfect Hebrew, being called *Nahum Keike*, by interpretation, *The Bosom of Consolation*." Cotton Mather also says, " Of which place I have somewhere met with an odd observation, that the name of it was rather Hebrew than Indian ; for *Nahum* signifies Comfort, and *Keik* signifies a Haven ; and our English not only found it a haven of comfort, but happened also to put a Hebrew name upon it ; for they called it Salem, for the peace which they had and hoped in it ; and so it is called unto this day." Mather probably derived this whimsical etymology from Scottow, who says, " Its original name was called *Naumkek*, the Bosom of Consolation, being its signification, as the learned have observed." See Planter's Plea, p. 14, Mather's Magnalia, i. 63, and Joshua Scottow's Narrative of the Planting of the Massachusetts Colony, p. 51, (Boston, 1694.)

[2] Their names will appear hereafter in the records of the Company.

and disputation it grew to be more vulgar ; insomuch CHAP.
that some men showing some good affection to the I.
work, and offering the help of their purses if fit men 1627.
might be procured to go over, inquiry was made
whether any would be willing to engage their persons in the voyage. By this inquiry it fell out that
among others they lighted at last on Master ENDE-
COTT,[1] a man well known to divers persons of good
note, who manifested much willingness to accept of
the offer as soon as it was tendered ; which gave
great encouragement to such as were upon the point
of resolution to set on this work of erecting a new
Colony upon the old foundation. Hereupon divers
persons having subscribed for the raising of a reasonable sum of money, a patent was granted with large
encouragements every way by his most excellent
Majesty.[2] Master Endecott was sent over Governor, 1628.
assisted with a few men, and arriving in safety there June
in September, 1628,[3] and uniting his own men with Sept.
those which were formerly planted in the country 6.
into one body, they made up in all not much above
fifty or sixty[4] persons.

[1] "A fit instrument to begin this
wilderness-work, of courage bold,
undaunted, yet sociable, and of a
cheerful spirit, loving and austere,
applying himself to either, as occasion served." Edward Johnson's
Wonderworking Providence, ch. ix.
(London, 1654.)

[2] "Deputy governor Dudley, Mr.
Hubbard, and others, wrongly place
Mr. Endicott's voyage after the
grant of the royal charter, whereas
he came above eight months before." The patent of the Massachusetts Company was confirmed by
the king, Charles I. March 4, 1629.
Edward Johnson says it was "procured by advice of one Mr. White,
an honest counsellor-at-law, as also

furthered by the honored Mr. Richard Bellingham." A previous patent had been obtained from the
Council for New England, March
19, 1628. It was under this that
Endicott came out, and not under
the broad seal of England, as erroneously stated by Gov. Bradford,
Secretary Morton, and Edward Johnson. See Prince's Annals, pp. 249,
250, 254 ; Mass. Hist. Coll. xii. 63 ;
and Morton's New-England's Memorial, p. 137, (Davis's edition, Boston, 1826.)

[3] This was the *first* emigration
under the authority of the Massachusetts Company.

[4] It will be seen from Higginson's
Narrative, in a subsequent part of

His prosperous journey, and safe arrival of himself and all his company, and good report which he sent back of the country, gave such encouragement to the work, that more adventurers joining with the first undertakers, and all engaging themselves more deeply for the prosecution of the design, they sent over the next year about three hundred persons more,[1] most servants, with a convenient proportion of rother-beasts,[2] to the number of sixty or seventy, or thereabout, and some mares and horses ; of which the kine came safe for the most part, but the greater part of the horses died, so that there remained not above twelve or fourteen alive.

By this time the often agitation of this affair in sundry parts of the kingdom, the good report of Captain Endecott's government, and the increase of the Colony, began to awaken the spirits of some persons of competent estates,[3] not formerly engaged.   Considering that they lived either without any useful employment at home, and might be more serviceable in assisting the planting of a Colony in New-England, [they] took at last a resolution to unite themselves for the prosecution of that work.   And, as it usually falls out, some other of their acquaintance, seeing such men of good estates[3] engaged in the voyage,

this volume, that on his arrival at Salem in June, 1629, he found there about a hundred persons with Endicott.

[1] This was the *second* emigration, under Higginson. He says, " We brought with us about two hundred passengers and planters more."

[2] Cows, oxen. " The old Saxon word *hrutan* signifies to snort, snore, or rout in sleeping. To rowt or rawt is to low like an ox or cow. Hence also the Saxon *hruther*, bos, a rother-beast." Ray's North Coun-

try Words, p. 51, and Richardson's Eng. Dict. under *Rout*.

[3] Winthrop, Isaac Johnson, Saltonstall, Dudley, Cradock, the Vassals, and most of the Massachusetts Company, were men of " good " and " competent estates." Winthrop had an estate of six or seven hundred pounds a year, and Johnson's interest in the New-England adventure was six hundred pounds. See Hutchinson's History of the Colony of Massachusetts Bay, i. 14, 16. (London, 1760.)

some for love to their persons, and others upon other CHAP.<br>I.
respects, united unto them ; which together made up
a competent number, (perhaps far less than is re- 1630.
ported,) and embarked themselves for a voyage to April.
New-England, where I hope they are long since
safely arrived.[1]

This is an unpartial though brief relation of the
occasion of planting of this Colony. The particulars
whereof, if they could be entertained, were clear
enough to any indifferent judgment, that the suspi-
cious and scandalous reports raised upon these gentlemen and their friends, (as if, under the color of
planting a Colony, they intended to raise and erect a
seminary of faction and separation,) are nothing else
but the fruits of jealousy of some distempered mind,
or, which is worse, perhaps, savor of a desperate
malicious plot of men ill affected to religion, endeavouring, by casting the undertakers into the jealousy
of State, to shut them out of those advantages which
otherwise they do and might expect from the countenance of authority. Such men would be intreated to
forbear that base and unchristian course of traducing
innocent persons under these odious names of Separatists[2] and enemies to the Church and State, for fear
lest their own tongues fall upon themselves by the
justice of His hand who will not fail to clear the in-
nocency of the just, and to cast back into the bosom
of every slanderer the filth that he rakes up to throw
in other men's faces. As for men of more indiffe-

---

[1] This was the *third* or great em- paratists. For the difference be-
igration, under Winthrop. tween the two, consult the Chroni-
[2] The first planters of Massachu- cles of Plymouth, pp. 398, 414–17.
setts were Nonconformists, not Se-

rent and better tempered minds, they would be seriously advised to beware of entertaining and admitting,
much more countenancing and crediting such un-
charitable persons as discover themselves by their
carriage, and that in this particular, to be men ill
affected towards the work itself, if not to religion, at
which it aims, and consequently unlikely to report
any truth of such as undertake it.[1]

[1] The PLANTERS' PLEA, from which this chapter is extracted, was printed in London in 1630, soon after the sailing of Winthrop's fleet, as appears from page 15. It has generally been ascribed to the Rev. John White, of Dorchester, England, of whom some account will be given hereafter. The copy which I use, and which formerly belonged to Increase Mather, has on the title-page, in his hand-writing, " Mr. White, of Dorchester, Author."— This may be considered good authority, as Increase Mather probably derived his information from his father, Richard, who came over in 1635, or from some other of the first settlers. The work is an original, contemporaneous authority, of the highest value, as it contains facts relating to the earliest attempts at settlement in Massachusetts Bay, which can be found nowhere else, and these facts furnished by the persons who were themselves engaged as adventurers in these attempts. See page 3. In his Preface the author says, " The reader is intreated to observe that the particulars of this small pamphlet being all ranged under these two heads, matters of *fact* or of opinion, in the former the author sets down his *knowledge*, and consequently what he resolves to justify."

In the Preface to John Cotton's sermon, entitled " God's Promise to his Plantation," delivered just before the departure of Winthrop's company, I. H. (which I suppose to be the initials of John Humphrey, who, though chosen Deputy Governor of the Colony, remained behind, and did not come over till July 1634,) says, " Ere long, (if God will,) thou shalt see a larger declaration of the first rise and ends of this enterprise, and so clear and full a justification of this design, both in respect of that warrant it hath from God's word, and also in respect of any other ground and circumstance of weight that is considerable in the warrant of such a work, as (I hope) there will easily be removed any scruple of moment which hitherto hath been moved about it." The Planters' Plea corresponds to this description, and I have no doubt is the work which the writer intended to announce.

The Planters' Plea appears to have been unknown to our historians. Neither Mather, Prince, Hutchinson, Bancroft, nor Grahame make any use or mention of it. Hubbard may have had it ; but I think he derived his knowledge of the first settlement of the Colony from Conant and his companions.

# HUBBARD'S NARRATIVE.

# CHAPTER II.

## THE DISCOVERY AND FIRST PLANTING OF THE MASSACHUSETTS.

SEVERAL mariners and persons skilled in navigation, (whether employed by others in a way of fishing and trading, or to satisfy their own humors in making further and more exact discoveries of the country, is not material,) had some years before looked down into the Massachusetts Bay.[1] The inhabitants of New Plymouth had heard the fame thereof, 1621. and in the first year after their arrival there took an Sept. occasion to visit it,[2] gaining some acquaintance with the natives of the place, in order to future traffic with them. For which purpose something like a habitation was set up at Nantasket,[3] a place judged then

---

[1] Capt. John Smith appears to have been the first navigator, of whom we have any account, that penetrated to the bottom of Massachusetts Bay. This was in 1614. He says, "The country of the Massachusetts is the paradise of all those parts; for here are many isles all planted with corn, groves, mulberries, salvage gardens, and good harbours." Mass. Hist. Coll. xxvi. 118.

[2] Gov. Bradford says, "We returned with a considerable quantity of beaver and a good report of the place, *wishing we had been seated there.*" See the original Journal of the expedition in the Chronicles of Plymouth, pp. 224–229.

[3] A peninsula at the entrance of Boston harbour, now called Hull, which name it received from the General Court in 1644. See Savage's note on Winthrop, ii. 175.

CHAP.  most commodious for such an end.   There Mr. Ro-
II.
——  ger Conant, with some few others, after Mr. Lyford
and Mr. Oldham were, for some offence, real or supposed, discharged from having anything more to do
1624. at Plymouth,[1] found a place of retirement and reception for themselves and families for the space of a
year and some few months, till a door was opened
for them at Cape Anne, a place on the other side the
Bay, (more convenient for those that belong to the
tribe of Zebulon than for those that chose to dwell
in the tents of Issachar,) whither they removed
1625. about the year 1625.   And after they had made
another short trial thereof, for about a year's contin-
1626. uance, they removed a third time down a little lower
towards the bottom of the Bay, being invited by the
accommodations which they either saw or hoped to
find on the other side of a creek near by, called

---

[1] John Lyford came over to Plymouth in the spring of 1624, and
John Oldham in August, 1623. Robert Cushman, in a letter dated London, Jan. 24, 1624, writes, " We
send a preacher, though not the
most eminent, for whose going Mr.
Winslow and I gave way, to give
content to some at London." Gov.
Bradford speaks of " the minister, Mr. John Lyford, whom a
faction of the adventurers send to
hinder Mr. Robinson." Lyford
wrote home to the adverse part of
the adventurers in 1624, counselling
them that " the Leyden company,
Mr. Robinson and the rest, must still
be kept back, or else all will be spoiled." " Lyford," says Bradford,
" soon joins with Oldham, and they
fall a plotting both against our
church and government, draw a
company apart, set up for themselves, and he would administer the
sacrament to them by his Episcopal
calling. Upon this the Governor calls
a Court, and charges Lyford and Oldham with plotting against us. Oldham being outrageous, would have
raised a mutiny ; but his party
leaves him, and the Court expels
them the colony." Edward Winslow, the agent of the Plymouth Colony in England, afterwards made
such disclosures there respecting
Lyford as confounded the party
among the merchant adventurers
who adhered to him, and he was
judged unfit for the ministry. " By
this, (says Prince,) it seems as if the
Rev. Mr. White and the Dorchester
gentlemen had been imposed upon
with respect to Lyford and Oldham,
and had sent invitations to them before this discovery." A minute account of this affair, which appears
to justify the Plymouth people, may
be seen in Morton's Memorial, pp.
111-122. See also Prince's Annals,
pp. 226-232, and Chronicles of Plymouth, p. 476.

Naumkeag, which afforded a considerable quantity CHAP.
of planting land near adjoining thereto. Here they II.
took up their station, upon a pleasant and fruitful
neck of land, environed with an arm of the sea on
each side, in either of which vessels and ships of
good burthen might safely anchor. In this place,
(soon after by a minister,[1] that came with a company 1629.
of honest planters, called Salem, from that in Psalm
lxxvi. 2,) was laid the first foundation on which the
next colonies were built.

Notwithstanding the many adventures which had
hitherto been made, by sundry persons of estate and
quality, for the discovery and improvement of this
part of America, called New-England, nothing could
as yet be settled by way of planting any colony upon
the coast, with desirable success, save that of New
Plymouth.[2] As for the rest of the plantations, they
were like the habitations of the foolish, as it is in Job,
Job, cursed before they had taken root. v. 3.

But the vanishing of all the forementioned attempts did but make way for the settling the Colony
of the Massachusetts ; and this was the occasion
thereof.

As some merchants from the west of England had
for a long time frequented the parts about Mun-

[1] Francis Higginson, who says in
his Journal, " When we came first
to Naimkecke, *now* called Salem."
Roger Conant, the founder of it, expressly disclaims having had " any
hand in naming that town." See
Mass. Archives, Towns. i. 217.

[2] These abortive attempts to plant
colonies in New-England, were, (1.)

The Plymouth Company's in 1607,
near the mouth of the Kennebec ;
(2.) Weston's at Wessagusset
(Weymouth) in 1622 ; (3.) Robert
Gorge's at the same place in 1623 ;
(4.) David Thomson's at the mouth
of the Piscataqua in 1623 ; and (5.)
Captain Wollaston's at Quincy in
1625.

CHAP. higgon,[1] for the taking of fish,[2] &c., so did others,
II.
especially those of Dorchester, make the like attempt
upon the northern promontory of the Massachusetts
Bay, in probability first discovered by Capt. Smith,
1614. before or in the year 1614, and by him named Tra-
gabizanda,[3] for the sake of a lady from whom he received much favor while he was a prisoner among
the Turks; by whom also the three small islands at
the head of the Cape were called the Three Turks'
Heads.   But neither of them glorying in these Ma-
hometan titles, the promontory willingly exchanged
its name for that of Cape Anne, imposed, as is said,
by Capt. Mason,[4] and which it retaineth to this day,
in honor of our famous Queen Anne, the royal con-
sort of King James; and the three other islands are
now known by other names.[5]

Here did the foresaid merchants first erect stages
whereon to make their fish, and yearly sent their
ships thither for that end for some considerable time,
until the fame of the Plantation at New Plymouth,
with the success thereof, was spread abroad through
all the western parts of England so far, as that it
began to revive the hopes of some of those merchants
who had not long before adventured their estates to
promote so honorable a design as was the planting

---

[1] See Chronicles of Plymouth Colony, page 182, note [4], and Williamson's History of Maine, i. 61.

[2] " It is well known, before our breach with Spain, (1624,) we usually sent out to New-England yearly forty or fifty sail of ships of reasonable good burthen for fishing only." Planters' Plea, p. 23. See also note on p. 5.

[3] See Hillard's Life of Smith in Sparks's American Biography, ii. 191–194, 197, and Mass. Hist. Coll. xxvi. 97, 118, 120.

[4] This is a mistake. The name was altered by Prince Charles, in honor of his mother, Anne of Denmark. See Mass. Hist Coll. xxvi. 97, 99, and xxiii. 20.

[5] They are now called Straitsmouth island, Thacher's island, and Milk island.

and peopling this new world;[1] although, finding CHAP.
hitherto but small encouragement that way, they <sub>II.</sub>
were ready to withdraw their hands.

On this consideration it was, that some merchants
and other gentlemen about Dorchester did, about
the year 1624, at the instigation of Mr. White, the 1624.
famous preacher of that town, upon a common stock,
together with those that were coming to make fish,
send over sundry persons, in order to the carrying
on a Plantation at Cape Anne, conceiving that planting on the land might go on equally with fishing on
the sea in those parts of America.

Mr. John Tylly[2] and Mr. Thomas Gardener[3] were
employed as overseers of that whole business;
the first with reference to the fishing, the other with
respect to the planting on the main land, at least for
one year's time; at the end of which Mr. White, 1625.
with the rest of the Adventurers, hearing of some
religious and well-affected persons, that were lately
removed out of New Plymouth, out of dislike of their
principles of rigid Separation, — of which number
Mr. ROGER CONANT[4] was one, a religious, sober, and

---

[1] In 1623, thirteen of the Company of Adventurers in England, writing to their brethren at New Plymouth, tell them, "Let it not be
grievous to you that you have been
instruments to break the ice for
others who come after you. The
honor shall be yours to the world's
end." Bradford in Prince, p. 220.

[2] John Tylley was admitted a
freeman March 4, 1635. See Savage's Winthrop, ii. 365.

[3] Thomas Gardner removed to
Salem with Conant, was admitted a
freeman May 17, 1637, and was a
member of the General Court the
same year. Compare Farmer's Genealogical Register of the first set-

tlers of New-England, with Savage's Winthrop, ii. 367.

[4] ROGER CONANT, to whom belongs the high honor of being the
first planter of the Colony of Massachusetts Bay, was born at Budleigh,
near Sidmouth, in the county of
Devon, in the year 1593, as we infer from the record in the parish register of East Budleigh, which
states that he was baptized April 9,
1593. He was probably the son of
William Conant, who, as appears
from the same register, was married
Nov. 26, 1588. We have no account of the time or manner in which
Roger Conant came over to New-
England. Christopher Conant was

CHAP.
  II.
~~~
1625.

prudent gentleman, yet surviving about Salem till the year 1680, wherein he finished his pilgrimage, having a great hand in all these forementioned transactions about Cape Anne, — they pitched upon him, the said Conant, for the managing and government of all their affairs at Cape Anne. The information he had of him, was from one Mr. Conant, a brother of his, and well known to Mr. White; and he was so well satisfied therein, that he engaged Mr. Humphrey, the treasurer of the joint Adventurers, to write to him in their names, and to signify that they had chosen him to be their governor in that place, and would commit unto him the charge of all their affairs, as well fishing as planting. Together with him, likewise, they invited Mr. Lyford, lately dismissed from Plymouth, to be the minister of the place; and Mr. Oldham, also discharged on the like account

one of the passengers in the Anne, which arrived at Plymouth in 1623. But I find no evidence in Gov. Bradford or Morton, or in any of the Plymouth records or authorities, to confirm the statement here made by Hubbard, that Roger Conant was once a resident in that colony, and was expelled from it with Lyford and Oldham. Still it may have been so ; and Hubbard may have got his information from Conant himself. The same mystery hangs over his arrival and early residence here, as over Walford, Blackstone, and Maverick. They all probably came over in some of the fishing-vessels that were constantly hovering on the coast. He was admitted a freeman of the Colony May 18, 1631, and was a representative from Salem in the first Court of Deputies, held in 1634. In 1636, he received from that town a grant of two hundred acres of land at the head of Bass river, in what is now the town of Beverly, on which he settled, and in 1671, the General Court made him a grant of two hundred acres more, on the ground of his being "an ancient planter." He died Nov. 19, 1679, in the 87th year of his age. Hutchinson says, " He is always spoken of as a person of worth. The superior condition of the persons who came over with the charter cast a shade upon him, and he lived in obscurity. Governor's Island, in Boston harbour, [on which is now Fort Warren,] was formerly called Conant's island." Conant had four sons. Roger, the second, was the first child born in Salem, and on that account received from the town, in 1640, a grant of twenty acres of land. See Mass. Hist. Coll. xxvii. 250–255, xxviii. 306 ; Savage's Winthrop, i. 130, ii. 362 ; Stone's Hist. of Beverly, p. 18; and Hutchinson's Hist. of Mass. i. 7.

from Plymouth, was invited to trade for them with the Indians. All these three at that time had their dwelling at Nantasket. Mr. Lyford accepted, and came along with Mr. Conant. Mr. Oldham liked better to stay where he was for a while, and trade for himself, and not become liable to give an account of his gain or loss. But after a year's experience, the Adventurers, perceiving their design not like to answer their expectation, at least as to any present advantage, threw all up; yet were so civil to those that were employed under them, as to pay them all their wages, and proffered to transport them back whence they came, if so they desired.

It must here be noted, that Mr. Roger Conant, on the foresaid occasion made the superintendent of their affairs, disliked the place as much as the Adventurers disliked the business; and therefore, in the mean while, had made some inquiry into a more commodious place near adjoining, on the other side of a creek, called Naumkeag,[1] a little to the westward, where was much better encouragement as to the design of a Plantation, than that which they had attempted upon before at Cape Anne; secretly conceiving in his mind, that in following times (as since is fallen out) it might prove a receptacle for such as upon the account of religion would be willing to begin a foreign Plantation in this part of the world; of which he gave some intimation to his friends in England. Wherefore that reverend person, Mr. WHITE, (under God, one of the chief founders of

CHAP.
II.

1625.

1626.

---

[1] Capt. John Smith writes this Naemkeck, Naemkecke, and Naimkeck. See note on page 12, and Mass. Hist. Coll. xxvi. 97, 107, 118 and xxiii. 22, 31.

CHAP. the Massachusetts Colony in New-England,)[1] being
II.
~~~ grieved in his spirit that so good a work should be
1626. suffered to fall to the ground by the Adventurers
thus abruptly breaking off, did write to Mr. Conant
not so to desert the business, faithfully promising
that if himself, with three others, (whom he knew to
be honest and prudent men, viz. John Woodberry,
John Balch,[2] and Peter Palfreys,[3] employed by the

[1] JOHN WHITE, "usually called," says Anthony Wood, " patriarch of Dorchester, or patriarch White," was born at Stanton St. John in Oxfordshire, in 1575, and was educated first at Winchester, and then at New College, Oxford, of which he was fellow. In 1605 he became rector of Trinity parish in Dorchester. Wood says, " He was for the most part of his time a moderate Puritan, and conformed to the ceremonies of the Church of England before and when Archbishop Laud sat at the stern." On the breaking out of the civil wars, he sided with the popular party ; and his house and library having been plundered by the royalists under Prince Rupert, he came to London, and was made minister of the Savoy parish. In 1643 he was chosen one of the Assembly of Divines at Westminster, and " showed himself one of the most learned and moderate among them, and his judgment was much relied on therein." Soon after he was appointed rector of Lambeth, in Surrey. When the civil wars were over, he returned to Dorchester, and in 1647 was chosen warden of New College, but declined the honor. He died suddenly July 24, 1648, in his 74th year, and was buried July 21, in the porch of St. Peter's in Dorchester. Wood says, " He was a person of great gravity and presence, and had always influence on the Puritanical party, near to and remote from him, who bore him more respect than they did to their diocesan." Fuller,

in his Worthies, says that " he had a patriarchal influence both in Old and New England." Callender, in his Historical Discourse on Rhode Island, calls him " the father of the Massachusetts Colony." His name will often occur hereafter in the meetings of the Massachusetts Company in London. See Wood's Athen. Ox. iii. 236, (ed. Bliss) ; Fuller's Worthies of England, ii. 233 ; Hutchins's History of Dorset, i. 390 ; Mass. Hist. Coll. xxviii. 306 ; and Rhode Island Hist. Coll. iv. 67.

[2] John Balch is said to have come from Bridgewater, in Somersetshire. He was made a freeman May 18, 1631. In 1636, he received, at the same time with Conant, a grant of two hundred acres of land at the head of Bass river, near the present residence of Mr. John Bell, in Beverly, where he died in 1648. He was an intelligent, exemplary, and useful citizen. He had two wives, Margaret and Agnes, and three sons, the second of whom, John, married Mary, the daughter of Roger Conant, and was drowned in crossing the ferry to Beverly, Jan. 16, 1662. See Farmer's Gen. Register, and Stone's Hist. of Beverly, p. 23.

[3] Peter Palfrey was admitted a freeman May 18, 1631. In May, 1632, when each town in the Colony chose two men to advise with the Governor and Assistants at the next Court about raising a public stock — the " embryo of a parliament," as Savage calls it — Palfrey was joined with Conant in this trust. In 1635,

Adventurers,) would stay at Naumkeag, and give CHAP.
II.
timely notice thereof, he would provide a patent for
them, and likewise send them whatever they should 1626.
write for, either men, or provision, or goods wherewith to trade with the Indians. Answer was returned, that they would all stay on those terms, entreating that they might be encouraged accordingly. Yet
it seems, before they received any return according
to their desires, the three last mentioned began to
recoil, and repenting of their engagement to stay at
Naumkeag, for fear of the Indians and other inconveniences, resolved rather to go all to Virginia ;
especially because Mr. Lyford, their minister, upon
a loving invitation, was thither bound.[1] But Mr.
Conant, as one inspired by some superior instinct,
though never so earnestly pressed to go along with
them, peremptorily declared his mind to wait the
providence of God in that place where now they
were, yea, though all the rest should forsake him,[2]

he was a deputy from Salem in the second General Court. In 1636, with the other first planters, he received a grant of two hundred acres of land on Bass river. In 1653 he removed to Reading, where he died Sept. 15, 1663. His estate was apprized at £84 10s. His wife's name was Edith, and he had a son Jonathan, and three daughters, Jehodan, Remember, and Mary. Descendants of this worthy planter remain in Salem, and the present Secretary of the Commonwealth, John Gorham Palfrey, claims him as his ancestor. See Farmer's Register, Savage's Winthrop, ii. 362, and Prince's Annals, p. 394.

[1] "And there shortly dies." — Bradford, in Prince, p. 245.

[2] In the Archives of the Commonwealth there is preserved a petition, in his own hand-writing, "of Roger Conant of Bass River, alias Beverly," dated May 28, 1671. In that petition he says, that he "hath been a planter in New-England forty years and upwards, being one of the first, if not the very first, that resolved and made good any settlement, under God, in matter of plantation, with my family, in this Colony of the Massachusetts Bay, and have been instrumental both for the founding and carrying on of the same ; and when, in the infancy thereof, it was in great hazard of being deserted, I was a means, through grace assisting me, to stop the flight of those few that then were here with me, and that by my utter denial to go away with them, who would have gone either for England, or mostly for Virginia, but

CHAP. not doubting, as he said, but if they departed, he
II.
should soon have more company. The other three,
observing his confident resolution, at last concurred
1627. with him, and soon after sent back John Woodberry[1]
for England to procure necessaries for a Plantation.

But that God, who is ready to answer his people
before they call, as he had filled the heart of that good
man, Mr. Conant, in New-England, with courage and
resolution to abide fixed in his purpose, notwithstanding all opposition and persuasion he met with to the
contrary, had also inclined the hearts of several others
in England to be at work about the same design. For
about this time the Council established at Plymouth for
the planting, ruling, ordering and governing of New-
England,[2] had, by a deed indented under the common
1628. seal, bearing date March 19, 1627, bargained and sold

thereupon stayed to the hazard of
our lives." In the same petition he
says that he " was the first that had
a house in Salem," that " those that
were then with him were all from
the western part of England," and
that he himself was " born at Budleigh, a market-town in Devonshire,
near unto the sea." See Mass. Archives, Towns, i. 217. The petition is printed entire in Mass. Hist.
Coll. xxvii. 252.

[1] John Woodbury is said to have
come from Somersetshire, in England. He was made a freeman May
18, 1631, and in 1635 was chosen,
with Palfrey, a deputy to the General Court, and again in 1638. In
1636, in connection with Conant,
Balch, and Palfrey, he received
from the town a grant of two hundred acres of land on Bass river.
" He was an energetic, faithful and
worthy man, and took an active part
in the settlement and transactions of
the Colony. He died in 1641, having lived to see his perils, sufferings
and toils contribute to prepare a refuge for his countrymen." His
wife's name was Agnes, and his
son, Humphrey, born in 1609, came
to Salem with his father in 1628,
and was living in 1681. The home-
stead has remained in the family
since the first settlement. All bearing the name of Woodbury in New-
England probably descend from John
or his brother William. See Farmer's Register and Stone's History of
Beverly, pp. 21–23.

[2] On the 3d of Nov. 1620, King
James signed a patent by which the
adventurers to the northern colony
of Virginia between forty and forty-
eight degrees north, were incorporated as " The Council established at
Plymouth, in the county of Devon,
for the planting, ruling, ordering
and governing of New-England in
America." This is the great civil
basis of the future patents and plantations that divide the country. See
the patent in Hazard's Collection of
State Papers, i. 103.

unto some knights and gentlemen about Dorchester, CHAP. II.
namely, Sir Henry Roswell, Sir John Young, knights,
Thomas Southcoat, John Humphry, John Endicot, 1628.
and Simon Whetcomb,[1] gentlemen, that part of New-
England that lies between Merrimack and Charles
river, in the bottom of the Massachusetts Bay. And
not long after, by the means of Mr. White, the foresaid gentlemen were brought into acquaintance with
several other religious persons of like quality in and
about London, such as Mr. Winthrop, Mr. Johnson,
Mr. Dudley, Mr. Cradock, and Mr. Goffe, and Sir
Richard Saltonstall; who being first associated to
them, at last bought of them all their right and interest in New-England aforesaid; and consulting
together about settling some Plantation in New-England upon the account of religion, where such as
were called Nonconformists might, with the favor
and leave of the King, have a place of reception if
they should transport themselves into America,
there to enjoy the liberty of their own persuasion in
matters of worship and church discipline, without
disturbance of the peace of the kingdom, and without
offence to others not like-minded with themselves,
did at the last resolve, with one joint consent, to
petition the King's Majesty to confirm unto the forenamed and their associates, by a new grant or patent,
the tract of land in America forementioned; which
was accordingly obtained.[2]

---

[1] " It is very likely the three persons first named in this grant had nothing more in view by the purchase than a settlement for trade with the natives, or for fishery, or for other advantageous purposes. As soon as a colony for religion was projected, we hear no more of them. The other three remained." Hutchinson's Hist. Mass. i. 9.

[2] " Some of the principal of the liberal speakers in parliament being committed to the Tower, others to other prisons, this took away all

Soon after, the Company, having chosen Mr. Cradock, Governor, and Mr. Goffe, Deputy Governor,
with several others for Assistants, sent over Mr. Endicot, in the year 1628, to carry on the Plantation
of the Dorchester agents at Naumkeag, or Salem,
and make way for the settling of another Colony in
the Massachusetts. He was fully instructed with
power from the Company to order all affairs in the
name of the Patentees, as their agent, until themselves should come over ; which was at that time
intended, but could not be accomplished till the
year 1630. With Mr. Endicot, in the year 1628,
came Mr. Gotte,[1] Mr. Brakenberry,[2] Mr. Daven-

hope of reformation of Church government from many not affecting
Episcopal jurisdiction, nor the usual
practice of the common prayers of
the Church, whereof there were
several sorts, though not agreeing
among themselves, yet all of like
dislike of those particulars. Some
of the discreeter sort, to avoid what
they found themselves subject unto,
made use of their friends to procure
from the Council for the Affairs of
New-England to settle a colony
within their limits ; to which it
pleased the thrice-honored Lord of
Warwick to write to me, then at
Plymouth, to condescend that a patent might be granted to such as
then sued for it. Whereupon I
gave my approbation so far forth as
it might not be prejudicial to my son
Robert Gorges's interests, whereof
he had a patent under the seal of
the Council. Hereupon there was
a grant passed as was thought reasonable. But the same was after
enlarged by his Majesty, and confirmed under the great seal of England ; by the authority whereof the
undertakers proceeded so effectually,
that in a very short time numbers
of people of all sorts flocked thither
in heaps." Sir Ferdinando Gorge,
in Mass. Hist. Coll. xxvi. 80.

[1] "Mr." Charles Gott was admitted
a freeman May 18, 1631, and was a
representative from Salem in the
General Court in 1635. He was a
deacon of the Church there; and the
selectmen of the town, on June 25,
1638, voted to him and John Horne
five acres of land, which was long
known as the Deacons' Marsh. It
was situated in South Fields, near
Castle Hill. He removed to Wen-
ham, which he represented in 1654,
and died in 1667 or 1688. A letter
written by him to Gov. Bradford,
July 30, 1629, giving an account of
the choice of Skelton and Higginson
as pastor and teacher of the church
at Salem, is contained in Mass. Hist.
Coll. iii. 67. It appears by this letter that he and his wife had both
been at Plymouth ; and from this
fact I am almost tempted to believe
that he arrived there, and did not
come with Endicott in the Abigail.
See Farmer's Register and Felt's
Annals of Salem, i. 183.

[2] Richard Brackenbury took the
oath of freeman May 14, 1634, and
in 1636 received a grant of seventy-
five acres of land. He was one of
the early settlers of Beverly, and
died there in 1685, aged 85. See
Farmer's Gen. Register, and Stone's
Beverly, p. 24.

port,[1] and others ;[2] who, being added to Capt. Trask[3] CHAP. and John Woodberry, (that was before this time re- turned with a comfortable answer to them that sent 1628. him over,) went on comfortably together to make pre- paration for the new Colony that were coming over ; the late controversy that had been agitated with too much animosity betwixt the forementioned Dorches- ter planters and their new agent, Mr. Endicot, and his company then sent over, being by the prudent moderation of Mr. Conant, agent before for the Dor- chester merchants, quietly composed ;[4] that so *meum* and *tuum*, that divide the world, should not disturb the peace of good Christians, that came so far to

[1] Richard Davenport was admitted a freeman Sept. 3, 1634, and was a representative in 1637 from Salem, where he resided till 1642. He was ensign-bearer at the time that Endicott cut the cross out of the King's colors, was a. lieutenant in the Pequot war, in which he was dangerously wounded, and afterwards was captain of the castle in Boston harbour, where he was killed by lightning, July 15, 1665, aged 59. See Farmer's Register, Savage's Winthrop, i. 146, 192, 233, and Mass. Hist. Coll. xviii. 146, 236.

[2] The omission here of the name of the Spragues, (Ralph, Richard, and William,) invalidates the assertion of Felt that they "were among the emigrants who came in the Abigail," with Endicott, and confirms the construction put by Gov. Everett on the statement in the Charlestown records, that "they arrived at Salem at their own charge," that is, as "independent adventurers, not members of Gov. Endicott's Company." See Felt's Salem, p. 44, and Edward Everett's Address at Charlestown on the anniversary of the arrival of Gov. Winthrop, p. 19.

[3] "Mr." William Trask desired to

be made freeman on the 19th of October, 1630. He represented Salem five years, from 1635 to 1639. In January, 1636, he received from that town, at the same time with Conant, Palfrey, Woodbury, and Balch, a grant of two hundred acres of land on Bass river. He was a captain under Stoughton in the Pequot war, and died in 1666. It would appear from the text that he was one of Conant's company, and not, as Felt says, "among the emigrants who came in the Abigail," with Endicott. See Farmer's Register, Stone's Beverly, p. 20, Felt's Salem, p. 44, and Mass. Hist. Coll. xviii. 146, 147, 236.

[4] White alludes to this controversy between the old planters under Conant and the new comers with Endicott, when in speaking of the change of name from Nahumkeik to Salem, he says that it was done "upon a fair ground, in remembrance of a *peace* settled upon a conference at a general meeting between them and their neighbours, after expectance of some dangerous jar." See page 12, and Planters' Plea, p. 14. See also what Hubbard says, Mass. Hist. Coll. xv. 113.

CHAP. provide a place where to live together in Christian
II.
amity and concord.

1628.    In the same year were sent over several servants
upon the joint stock of the Company, who, arriving
there in an uncultivated desert, for want of wholesome diet and convenient lodgings, were many of
them seized with the scurvy and other distempers,[1]
which shortened many of their days, and prevented
many of the rest from performing any great matter of
labor that year for advancing the work of the Plantation. Yet was the good hand of God upon them so
far, as that something was done which tended to advantage ; nor was, upon that account, an evil report
brought upon the place by any of them, so as to dis-
courage others from coming after them.

During this whole lustre of years, from 1625, there
was little matter of moment acted in the Massachusetts, till the year 1629, after the obtaining the patent ; the former years being spent in fishing and
trading by the agents of the Dorchester merchants
and some others of the west country.

1625.    In one of the fishing voyages about the year 1625,
under the charge and command of one Mr. Hewes,
employed by some of the west country merchants,
there arose a sharp contest between the said Hewes
and the people of New Plymouth, about a fishing-stage,
built the year before about Cape Anne by Plymouth
men, but was now, in the absence of the builders

---

[1] " Upon which," says Governor
Bradford, " Mr. Endicott, hearing
we at Plymouth have a very skilful
doctor, namely, Mr. Fuller, sends
to our governor for him, who forthwith sends him to their assistance."
Endicott writing to Bradford from
Salem, May 11, 1629, says, " I acknowledge myself much bound to
you for your kind love and care in
sending Mr. Fuller amongst us."
See Prince's Annals, p. 253, Morton's Memorial, p. 144, and Chronicles of Plymouth, p. 223.

made use of by Mr. Hewes his company; which the CHAP.
other, under the conduct of Capt. Standish, very II.
eagerly and peremptorily demanded.  For the Com- 1625.
pany of New Plymouth, having themselves obtained
a useless patent for Cape Anne about the year 1623,[1] 1623.
sent some of the ships, which their Adventurers employed to transport passengers over to them, to make
fish there; for which end they had built a stage
there in the year 1624.[2]  The dispute grew to be 1624.
very hot, and high words passed between them;
which might have ended in blows, if not in blood and
slaughter, had not the prudence and moderation of
Mr. Roger Conant, at that time there present, and
Mr. Peirce's[3] interposition, that lay just by with his
ship, timely prevented.  For Mr. Hewes had barri-
cadoed his company with hogsheads on the stage-
head, while the demandants stood upon the land, and
might easily have been cut off.  But the ship's crew,
by advice, promising to help them build another, the
difference was thereby ended.[4]  Capt. Standish had

[1] Robert Cushman, writing to
Gov. Bradford from London, Jan.
24, 1624, says, "We have taken a
patent for Cape Ann." Prince's
Annals, p. 226.

[2] Christopher Levett, who was on
the coast of New-England in 1624,
says, that "the people of New Plymouth have begun a new plantation
at Cape Ann; but how long it will
continue, I know not;" and Capt.
John Smith, writing in 1624, says,
"At Cape Ann there is a plantation begun by the Dorchester men,
which they hold of those of New
Plymouth; who also by them have
set up a fishing-work." See Mass.
Hist. Coll. xxviii. 181, and Prince's
Annals, pp. 227, 228, 230.

[3] Capt. William Peirce, whose
name will frequently occur in these

Chronicles, and who "deserves honorable mention among the early na-
vigators between Old England and
New." See Savage's valuable note
on Winthrop, i. 25, to which nothing can be added.

[4] Gov. Bradford gives a different
version of this affair.  He says that
"some of Lyford and Oldham's
friends in the company of the merchant adventurers in London, set
out a ship a fishing, and getting the
start of ours, they take our stage
and other provisions made for fishing
at Cape Ann the year before, to
our great charge, and refuse to restore it without fighting; upon
which we let them keep it, and our
Governor sends some planters to
help the fishermen build another."
And in a letter to the Council for

CHAP.
II.
1625.

been bred a soldier in the Low Countries, and never entered the school of our Saviour Christ, or of John Baptist, his harbinger ; or, if he was ever there, had forgot his first lessons, to offer violence to no man, and to part with the cloak rather than needlessly contend for the coat, though taken away without order. A little chimney is soon fired ; so was the Plymouth captain, a man of very little stature, yet of a very hot and angry temper. The fire of his passion soon kindled, and blown up into a flame by hot words, might easily have consumed all, had it not been seasonably quenched.[1]

In transactions of this nature were the first three years spent in making way for the planting of the Massachusetts.[2]

New-England, dated June 28, 1625, he writes, "We are now left and forsaken of our adventurers, who have not only cast us off, but entered into particular course of trading, and have by violence and force taken at their pleasure our possession at Cape Ann." See Prince's Annals, p. 233, and Mass. Hist. Coll. iii. 38.

[1] This account of Standish is graphic, but flippant and unjust. Judge Davis remarks, " It does not appear that his conduct was reprehensible. He acted under authority, and was sent to enforce a manifest right." Belknap says, "The best apology for Captain Standish is, that as a soldier he had been accustomed to discipline and obedience ; that he considered himself as the military servant of the Colony, and received his orders from the Governor and people. Sedentary persons are not always the best judges of a soldier's merit or feelings. Men of his own profession will admire the courage of Standish, his promptitude and decision in the execution of his orders.

No one has ever charged him either with failure in point of obedience or of wantonly exceeding the limits of his commission. If the arm of flesh was necessary to establish the rights and defend the lives and property of colonists, in a new country, surrounded with enemies and false friends, certainly such a man as Standish, with all his imperfections, will hold a high rank among the worthies of New-England." See Morton's Memorial, p. 126, Belknap's American Biography, ii. 330, and Chronicles of Plymouth, p. 125.

[2] WILLIAM HUBBARD, from whose History of New-England this Chapter is taken, was born in England in 1621, and came to this country with his father in 1635. He was one of the first class that graduated at Harvard College, in 1642, and about the year 1657 was settled in the ministry at Ipswich, where he died Sept. 14, 1704, at the age of 83. His History of New-England was completed in 1680, to which time it is brought down, but contains few

facts after 1650. In 1682, the General Court of Massachusetts granted him fifty pounds "as a manifestation of thankfulness" for his work. It remained in manuscript till 1815, when it was published by the Massachusetts Historical Society in the 15th and 16th volumes of their Collections. The manuscript was of great use to Mather, Prince, and Hutchinson, and until it was printed was held in high estimation as an original authority for our early history. But the collation of it with the complete edition of Gov. Winthrop's History of New-England, published by Mr. Savage in 1825, disclosed the source whence Hubbard had derived his facts, and even his language through successive pages. He seems to have sustained the same literary relation to Winthrop, that Secretary Morton did to Gov. Bradford, that of a close but not very accurate copyist. A just estimate of the value of his History is given by Mr. Savage in his note on Winthrop, i. 297.

The most original and valuable part of Hubbard's History is unquestionably this very Chapter, in which he gives us a statement of facts in relation to the first settlements at Cape Ann and Salem, which can be found nowhere else. Now from whom did he obtain these facts? Most probably from Roger Conant, the father of the Colony, of whom he was a contemporary and neighbour. Living at Ipswich, he must have been acquainted with this prominent old planter, who resided but a few miles from him, at Bev-

erly, and who survived till 1679. Some of the facts which he relates he could hardly have obtained from any other source; as for instance, Mr. White's acquaintance with Conant's brother, his procuring Mr. Humphrey to write to Conant, and his subsequently writing to him l imself "not to desert the business." The manner too in which Hubbard speaks of Conant, indicates one with whom he was personally acquainted, and for whose character and intellect he felt the highest respect. He speaks of him as " that good man," as " a religious, sober and prudent gentleman," and in a particular emergency, as "one inspired by a superior instinct." In another part of his History he mentions "a strange impression on the mind of Roger Conant to pitch upon Naumkeag." Now the fact of such " inspiration" and " impression" could have been derived only from Conant's own mouth. We may therefore consider that in this Chapter we have Roger Conant's own narrative, as taken down by Hubbard in the conversations which he held with him when collecting the materials for his History.

I have copied this Chapter from Hubbard's MS., preserved in the archives of the Massachusetts Historical Society, and have thus been enabled to correct several errors in the printed volume of the History. See Hutchinson's Mass. ii. 147, and Farmer's Memorials of the Graduates of Harvard College, pp. 12–17, and Holmes's Annals of América, i. 490. (2d ed.)

THE COMPANY'S RECORDS.

# CHAPTER III.

## RECORDS OF THE GOVERNOR AND COMPANY OF THE MASSACHUSETTS BAY IN NEW-ENGLAND.

[Prefixed to the Records of the Company are certain memoranda, in the handwriting of Washburne, their first Secretary, of articles to be procured and sent over for the use of the Plantation at Naumkeak, and of the new Colony to be planted in Massachusetts Bay. They are preserved here as antique curiosities, showing us how the planters were furnished with arms, clothing, and provisions.]

*[To be] cast in to the ballast of the ships.*[1]

2 loads of chalk,
10 thousand of bricks,[2] and
5 chaldron of sea-coals,[3]
   Nails,
   Iron, 1 ton,
   Steel, 2 fagots,[4]
   Lead, 1 fodder,[5]

[1] The names of these ships were the Talbot, the George, the Lion's Whelp, the Four Sisters, and the Mayflower. They carried out Higginson and his company, and sailed in April and May.

[2] To build furnaces, fire-places, and chimneys.

[3] For the use of the smiths.

[4] A term for a parcel of small bars of steel, weighing 120 pounds.

[5] From the Dutch *fuder*, a cartload. It relates properly to lead, and Ray says it signifies a certain weight, viz. eight pigs, or 1600 pounds. But Bailey and Dyche both say that the weight varies in different places, in London 1956

Red lead, 1 barrel,

Salt, sail-cloth, copper.

Francis Johnson.[1]

RapheWhite, at corner of Philpot Lane, for aqua-vitæ.[1]

---

*Apparel for* 100 *Men.*

400 pair of shoes,

300 pair of stockings, whereof 200 pair Irish, about 13*d.* a pair, (Mr. Deputy,)[2] 100 pair of knit stockings, about 2*s.* 4*d.* a pair, (Mr. Treasurer,)[2]

10 dozen pair of Norwich garters,[3] about 5*s.* a dozen pair,

400 shirts,

200 suits doublet and hose, of leather, lined with oiled-skin leather, the hose and doublet with hooks and eyes,

100 suits of Northern dussens, or Hampshire kerseys, lined, the hose with skins, the doublets with linen of Guildford,[4] or Gedlyman serges, 2*s.* 10*d.* to 3*s.* a yard, 4½ to 5 yards a suit, at the George, in Southwark,

400 bands,[5] 300 plain falling bands, 100 [ [6] ] bands,

---

pounds, at Newcastle 2100, in Derbyshire 2400, sometimes more, sometimes less, according to the custom of the several liberties where it is melted or made. See Tyrwhitt's Chaucer, v. 94, and Ray's North Country Words, p. 31.

[1] These are memoranda in the margin.

[2] I suppose the Deputy Governor and the Treasurer were to provide these arti les.

[3] At this time the stockings were gartered beneath the knee, and the garters fastened in a large bow or rosette on one side. See the History of British Costume, in the Library of Entertaining Knowledge, xxiv. 275.

[4] A town in Surrey, formerly celebrated for its manufactures.

[5] The great stiff ruffs of Queen Elizabeth's time were exchanged in James's reign for wide horizontal collars and broad falling bands. To these succeeded the small Geneva bands, like those worn by clergymen, which have since been superseded by stocks and neckcloths. See British Costume, pp. 274, 305.

[6] Illegible.

100 waistcoats of green cotton, bound about with red tape,

100 leather girdles,[1]

100 Monmouth caps,[2] about 2s. a piece,

100 black hats, lined in the brims with leather,

500 red knit caps, milled, about 5d. apiece,

200 dozen hooks and eyes, and small hooks and eyes for mandilions,

16 dozen of gloves, whereof 12 dozen calf's leather, and 2 dozen tanned sheep's leather, and 2 dozen kid,

Ells sheen[3] linen for handkerchers,

½ a deker[4] of leather, of the best bend[5] leather,

50 mats to lie under 50 beds aboard ship,

50 rugs,

50 pair of blankets, of Welsh cotton,

100 pair of sheets,

50 bed-ticks and bolsters, with wool to put them in, Scotch ticking,

Linen for towels, and tablecloths, and napkins,

Sea chests,

3 c. Poppering hops, and 1 c. particular.

---

16th March. Agreed the apparel to be 100 mandilions,[6] lined with white cotton, 12d. a yard,

---

[1] Girdles performed the office of our modern suspenders.

[2] " The best caps," says Fuller, " were formerly made at Monmouth, where the *Cappers' Chapel* doth still remain." They were formerly much worn, particularly by soldiers.

" Wearing leeks in their Monmouth caps."

Shakspeare's Hen. V. Act iv. Sc. 7, Fuller's Worthies, ii. 116, (4to ed.)

[3] Fair, shining.

[4] A dicker is a term used by the tanners to express a quantity consisting of ten hides. See Bailey and Dyche.

[5] Sole leather, cut from the best part of the hide — a technical word, still in use among leather-dealers.

[6] A soldier's garment, a loose cassock or sack covering the whole

breeches and waistcoats, and 100 leather suits, doublets and breeches, of oiled leather, 100 pair breeches of leather,[1] drawers to serve to wear with both their other suits.

[Send to] Sherbrooke by to-morrow in the afternoon.

Proclamation to hinder the selling guns and gun-powder.

[Nu]mber of cattle,

[Have] Blood here to help them.[2]

---

*To provide to send for New-England.*

MINISTERS,

Patent, under seal,

A Seal,[3]

Men skilful in making of pitch, of salt,

Vine-planters,

Wheat, rye, barley, oats, a hogshead of each in the ear ; beans, pease, stones of all sorts of fruits, as peaches, plums, filberts, cherries ; pear, apple, quince kernels ; pomegranates, woad seed, saffron heads, liquorice seed, (roots sent, and madder roots,) potatoes, hop roots, hemp seed, flax seed, against

---

of the body, and usually without sleeves.

" Thus put he on his arming truss, fair
   shoes upon his feet,
About him a mandilion, that did with
   buttons meet,
Of purple, large, and full of folds,
   curl'd with a warmful nap,
A garment that 'gainst cold in nights
   did soldiers use to wrap."

Chapman's Homer, Iliad, book x. ;
Hist. of British Costume, p. 267.

[1] On account of its durability, leather was for a long time the ordinary material for clothing among the common people of England. The leather breeches have come down to our own day.

[2] Memoranda, written in the margin.

[3] This seal was of silver, as will be seen hereafter.

winter, coneys, currant plants, tame turkeys, shoes, CHAP.
III.
linen cloth, woollen cloth, pewter bottles, of pints
and quarts, brass ladles and spoons, copper kettles, 1629.
of [illegible] making, without bars of iron about them,
oiled skins of leather, madder seeds.

---

### 23d February, 1628.

This day, delivered a warrant to Mr. George Har- Feb.
23.
wood, Treasurer, to pay [Mr.] Barnard Michell one
hundred pounds, in part of the freight of the [Abi-
gail,] Henry Gauden, master, from Weymouth to
Nahumkeke, the goods shipped [per bill] of lading
dated 20th June last, being per bill of lading $46\frac{1}{2}$
tons [of goods,] beside the charge of Captain John
Endecott, his wife, and [blank] persons of his company, their passage and diet.

26th. William Sherman hath liberty for fourteen 26.
days to fetch his vines in Northampton, near [torn
off] ferry.

---

### 26th February, 1628.

*Necessaries conceived meet for our intended voyage for
New-England, to be prepared forthwith.*

For our five pieces of ordnance, long since bought
and paid for, Mr. John Humphry is entreated and
doth promise forthwith to cause them to be delivered
to Samuel Sharpe, who is to take care for having fit
carriages made for them.

### Arms for 100 Men.

3 drums, to each two pair of heads,
2 ensigns,

CHAP.
III.

1629.
Feb.
26.

2 partisans,[1] for captain and leftenant,

3 halberds,[2] for three sergeants,

80 bastard muskets, with snaphances,[3] four foot in the barrel, without rests,

6 long fowling-pieces, with musket bore, six and a half foot long,

4 long fowling-pieces, with bastard musket bore, five and a half foot long,

10 full muskets, four foot barrel, with matchcocks and rests,[4]

90 bandoleers,[5] for the muskets, each with a bullet bag,

10 horn flasks, for the long fowling-pieces, to hold two pound apiece, and

100 swords, and belts,

60 corselets,[6] and 60 pikes, 20 half pikes,

---

[1] A variety of the pike or spontoon, introduced in Henry the Eighth's time. Its blade was broader than that of the pike, and that part of it which was near the staff was formed in the manner of a crescent. It is still carried by the yeomen of the guard.

" Shall I strike at it with my partisan ?"

Shakspeare, Hamlet, Act i. Sc. 1 ; See Meyrick, ii. 285.

[2] A weapon consisting of a staff about five feet long, with a steel head, in the shape of an axe, formerly carried by the sergeants of foot and artillery. See Crabbe's Technological Dictionary.

[3] The snaphance was the Dutch name for the firelock. It differed from the modern firelock in the hammer not forming the covering of the pan. See Meyrick, iii. 101.

[4] On account of the heaviness of the long matchlock muskets, a rest was used, which was a staff, on the top of which was a kind of fork to receive the musket, and at the bottom a sharp iron ferule, for sticking it into the ground. Meyrick. iii. 41.

[5] Bandoleers were little cylindrical wooden boxes, covered with leather, each containing one charge of powder for a musket, to facilitate the loading of the piece. Twelve of them were suspended to a belt worn over the left shoulder; and at the bottom of the belt, at the right hip, were hung the bullet bag and priming box. These little cases were sometimes made of tin. They were used till the close of the 17th century, when they were superseded by the cartridge and cartridge-box. See Meyrick, iii. 77, British Costume, p. 273.

[6] "A kind of armour chiefly worn by pikemen. Strictly speaking, the word *corselet* means only that part which covered the *corse* or body; but was generally used to express the whole suit, under the term of a corselet furnished or complete, which included the head-piece and gorget, the back and breas s, with skirts of iron, called tasses, hanging over the

12 barrels powder, $\begin{cases} 8 \text{ barrels for the fort,} \\ 4 \quad \text{``} \quad \text{for small shot,} \end{cases}$

Shot, 1 lb. to a bandoleer,

8 pieces of land ordnance for the fort, whereof 5 already provided,

namely $\begin{cases} 2 \text{ demi-culverins,}^1 \text{ 30 cwt. apiece,} \\ 3 \text{ sakers,}^2 \text{ each weighing 25 cwt.} \end{cases}$

to provide $\begin{cases} 1 \text{ whole culverin,}^3 \text{ as long as may be,} \\ 2 \text{ small pieces, iron drakes,} \end{cases}$

For great shot, a fit proportion to the ordnance,

A seine, being a net to fish with.

———

*For the Talbot,*[4] *if* 100 *passengers and* 35 *mariners, three months, the mariners accounted double.*[5]

45 tuns beer, whereof 6 tuns 4s. $\Big\}$ beer,
        39 tuns 6s. $\Big\}$ ,

Malaga and Canary casks, 16s. a tun,

6 tuns of water,

12 m. of bread, after $\frac{3}{4}$ c. to a man,

22 hogsheads of beef,

40 bushels pease, a peck a man the voyage,

20 bushels oatmeal,

4 c. haberdine,[6] 62 cople each c. — (each cople makes 11 pound) — and half a pound a man per day,

8 dozen pounds of candles,

thighs." Meyrick's Ancient Armour, iii. 21.

[1] A piece of cannon four inches in diameter in the bore, and carrying a ball of 9½ pounds. See Meyrick, iii. 65, 70.

[2] A smaller piece of artillery, 3½ inches in the bore, weight of shot 5½ pounds. Meyrick, ibid.

[3] A cannon 5½ inches in the bore, weight of metal 4500 pounds, weight of shot 17½ pounds.

[4] The Talbot was a ship of 300 tons.

[5] Because they must be supplied with provisions for the return voyage.

[6] Salted cod-fish.

2 tierces of beer vinegar,

1½ bushels mustard seed,

20 gallons oil Gallipoli,[1] or Majorca, two quarts a man,

2 firkins of soap,

2 rundlets Spanish wine, 10 gallons apiece,

4 thousand of billets,[2]

10 firkins of butter,

10 c. of cheese,

20 gallons aqua-vitæ.

---

### 26th February, 1628.

Agreed with John Hewson to make eight pair of welt neat's leather shoes, crossed on the outside with a seam, to be substantial, good over leather, of the best, and two soles, the inner sole of good neat's leather, and the outer sole of tallowed backs,[3] to be two pair of ten inches, two pair of eleven inches, two pair of twelve inches, and two pair of thirteen inches' size.

The proportions we intend is,

1 of 10 inches, ⎫
3 of 11 inches, ⎪
3 of 12 inches, ⎬ 2s. 7d.
1 of 13 inches, ⎭

2 of  8 inches, ⎫
2 of  9 inches, ⎬ 2s. 4d.

And he to refer it to the Company whether to allow 1d. per pair more.

---

[1] Gallipoli, a sea-port in the kingdom of Naples, on the Gulf of Taranto, is the chief mart of the oil produced in this region.

[2] Of firewood, to be used on shipboard.

[3] Hides, dressed with tallow instead of oil.

2d *March*, 1628.  Present,

THE GOVERNOR,  MR. ADAMS,
THE DEPUTY,  MR. NOELL,
MR. WRIGHT,  MR. WHETCOMBE,
MR. VASSALL,  MR. PERRY,
MR. HARWOOD,  MR. HUSON.[1]
MR. COULSON,

This day James Edmonds, a sailor, fisher, and a cooper, was propounded to serve the Company ; as also Sydrach Miller, a cooper and a cleaver ; who demanding £45 for him and his man the first year, £50 a year the second and third year, and Edmonds's demands being £10 the first year, £15 the second, and £20 the third year, both held too dear for the Company to be at charges withal.

Also, for Mr. Malbon, it was propounded, he having skill in iron works, and willing to put in £25 in stock, it should be accepted as £50, and his charges to be borne out and home from New-England ; and upon his return, and report what may be done about iron works, consideration to be had of proceeding therein accordingly, and further recompense, if there be cause to entertain him.

Touching making of salt, it was conceived fit that commodity should be reserved for the general stock's benefit ; yet with this proviso, that any planter or brother of the Company should have as much as he might any way have occasion to make use of, at as cheap rate as themselves could make it ; provided,

[1] " This is the first account of names set down at their meetings, in the Massachusetts Court Records. By Governor is doubtless meant Mr. Cradock, and by Deputy Governor, Mr. Goff ; who seem to be chose to those offices by virtue of their patent from the New-England Council." Prince, p. 254. What precedes seems to be the notes and memoranda of Washburne, the Secretary.

CHAP.
III.

1629.
March
2.

if the Company be not sufficiently provided for themselves, then particular men may have liberty to make for their own expense and use any way, but not to transport nor sell.

Touching John Oldham,[1] the Governor was ordered to confer with him upon any indifferent course that might not be prejudicial to the Company.

Also, it being propounded by Mr. Coney,[2] in behalf of the Boston men,[3] (whereof divers had promised,

[1] Oldham, after his expulsion from Plymouth with Lyford in the summer of 1624, retired, as we have seen, to Nantasket. Returning in the spring of 1625, without leave, he was ejected a second time from the colony in a summary and ignominious manner. After declining, the same year, the invitation of the Dorchester adventurers, to trade for them with the Indians, he sailed in 1626 for Virginia, and on his voyage being delivered from extreme danger, he becomes penitent, and "after carries himself fairly to us," says Bradford, "and we give him liberty to come and converse with us when he pleases." After this reconciliation, so great was the confidence of the Plymouth people in him, that in June, 1628, when Morton, the rioter of Merry Mount, was arrested and sent prisoner to England, he was committed to Oldham's custody. At this time he seems to be prosecuting his own private affairs. See Prince's Annals, pp. 231, 236, 252; Morton's Memorial, p. 120; Mass. Hist. Coll. iii. 63.

[2] This was probably the "Mr. Thomas Cony," who at an assembly held at the Guildhall of the borough of Boston on the 22d July, 1633, communicated to the mayor and burgesses an intimation from the Bishop of Lincoln, that Mr. John Cotton, late vicar of Boston, had resigned his vicarage on the 8th of that month. For this as well as for many other new facts illustrative of our early

annals, we are indebted to Mr. Savage's filial pilgrimage to our fatherland, the fruits of which he has embodied in his delightful Gleanings for New-England History, contained in Mass. Hist. Coll. xxviii. 243–348. See particularly page 343.

[3] It is gratifying to find "the Boston men" so early engaged in the work. "Lincolnshire," says Hutchinson, "contributed greatly, and more of our principal families derive their origin from thence than from any part of England, unless the city of London be an exception." Among the prominent Boston men, who came to this country, besides Cotton, were Thomas Dudley, Richard Bellingham, John Leverett, with his father Thomas, William Coddington, and Atherton Hough. The three first named were governors of Massachusetts, and Coddington was the father and governor of Rhode Island. Hough was mayor of the borough in 1628, Bellingham was recorder from 1625 to 1633, and Thomas Leverett was an alderman. The Rev. Samuel Whiting, who had been minister of Skirbeck church, less than a mile from Boston, and was afterwards the minister of Lynn, in our Colony, had a father and brother both mayors of the borough. Under these circumstances it is not surprising that the name of the native place of so many of the prominent colonists should have been given to the peninsula which even then to their imagination "presaged some sumptu-

though not in our book underwritten, to adventure £400 in the joint stock,) that now their desire was that ten persons of them might underwrite £25[1] a man in the joint stock, they withal promising with these ships to adventure in their particular above £250 more, and to provide able men to send over for managing the business ; which, though it be prejudicial to the general stock, by the abatement of so much money thereout, yet appearing really to conduce more to the good of the Plantation, which is most desired, it was condescended unto.

ous city." It was probably for this reason, and not for the one commonly assigned, viz. out of respect for Mr. Cotton, who did not come over till three years afterwards, that at a Court of Assistants held at Charlestown, Sept. 7, 1630, it was "ordered that Trimountain shall be called Boston." See Hutchinson's Hist. of Mass. i. 18, Mass. Hist. Coll. xxviii. 343, and Snow's History of Boston, pp. 32, 33.

Boston is a borough town in Lincolnshire, 116 miles north of London, and 36 south-east of Lincoln, situated on both sides of the river Witham, five miles from the sea. It sends two members to Parliament. The parish church in which Cotton preached, built in 1309, is 382 feet in length by 99 in breadth, and the tower is 262 feet in height, and resembles that of the cathedral at Antwerp. It forms a conspicuous landmark for sailors, being visible at sea for forty miles. "Among the parish churches of England," said Edward Everett, in his beautiful

Address at Plymouth, Dec. 22,1845, " there is not a finer than the church at Boston, almost a cathedral in size, and unsurpassed by any of its class in the beauty of its architecture. I went many miles out of my way to behold this venerable pile ; and while I mused beneath its arches, ascended its grand tower, and stood before the altar at which Cotton ministered, I gained new impressions of the Christian heroism, the spiritual grandeur of the men, who turned their backs on all this sacred grandeur and beauty, as well as on all the comforts and delights of civilized life, that they might freely worship God in cabins and garrets, under exile and penury in the old world, and in face of the gaunt terrors of this unsubdued wilderness." See Thompson's Hist of Boston, in Lincolnshire, and the Parliamentary Gazetteer of England, i. 229.

[1] Prince, quoting this record, page 254, says, £10 a man — one of the very few errors that I have detected in the accurate Annalist.

*The 3d March*, 1628. Present,

THE GOVERNOR,         MR. NOELL,

MR. DEPUTY,         MR. SHARPE.

MR. WRIGHT,

It was at present debated how some good course might be settled for the division of the lands, and that all men intending to go in person or to send over, might underwrite and seal some instrument to be made, whereby every man to be tied to such Orders as shall be agreed upon here ; and that a copy of this agreement be sent to Dorchester,[1] for all men to underwrite and seal, that intend to take their passage in the Lion's Whelp,[2] or else order to be taken that the ships proceed without them.

Mr. Samuel Sharpe, with whom there hath been an agreement made in the behalf of the Company to give him £10 per year for three years, to have the oversight of the ordnance to be planted in the fort to be built upon the Plantation, and what else may concern artillery business to give his advice in ; but for all other employments was left to be entertained by any particular brethren of the Company, who for other occasions had entertained him already, and held not fit to be at further charge in that kind. The said Sharpe is also entertained to oversee the [servants] and employments of certain particular[3]

---

[1] Dorchester, which may be considered the cradle of the Massachusetts Colony, is a borough town in Dorsetshire, on the southern bank of the river Frome, 120 miles from London, and having in 1831 a population of 3033. It is under the government of a mayor, and sends two members to Parliament. Trinity Church, in which patriarch White preached, was pulled down in 1824, and a new church erected on the site. See Parl. Gaz. of England, i. 602.

[2] The Lion's Whelp was a vessel of 120 tons.

[3] Sharpe was Cradock's agent, as will be seen hereafter.

men of the Company. But for the general,[1] present- CHAP. III.
ed a bill for three drums and other particulars,
amounting to five pounds, nineteen shillings ; which 1629.
the Treasurer hath order to pay.

---

*The 5th March,* 1628. Present, March 5.

| | |
|---|---|
| THE GOVERNOR, | MR. WRIGHT, |
| MR. DEPUTY, | MR. NOWELL, |
| MR. TREASURER, | MR. WHITE, |
| SIR RICHARD SALTONSTALL, | MR. WHETCOMBE. |
| CAPT. VENN, | |

A new proposition being made in the behalf of Mr. Oldham to be entertained by this Company, it was deferred to further consideration.

Also, John Washburne being propounded for Secretary to the Company, it was conceived fit to entertain him, but deferred till another [time.]

A proposition being made by Sir William Brereton[2] to the Governor, of a patent granted him of

---

[1] The general stock, the Company's concern.

[2] Captain Robert Gorges, son of Sir Ferdinando, obtained a patent from the Council of Plymouth, dated Dec. 13, 1622, ten miles in breadth and thirty miles into the land, on the northeast side of Massachusetts Bay. On the death of Robert, his patent descended to his brother John, who by a deed dated Jan 10, 1629, conveyed to Sir William Brereton, of Handforth, in the county of Chester, Bart., and his heirs, " all the land in breadth lying from the east side of Charles river to the easterly part of the cape called Nahant, and all the lands lying in length twenty miles northeast into the main land from the mouth of the said Charles river, lying also in length twenty miles into the main land northeast from the said cape Nahant." Now the grant made by the Plymouth Council to the Massachusetts Company, March 19, 1628, covered this same territory, and also the tract granted by John Gorges to John Oldham ; and hence the disputes of the Company with Brereton and Oldham. It appears that Brereton sent over several families and servants, who possessed and improved large tracts of the said land, and made several leases. He seems to have been preparing to come over himself, but on the breaking out of the civil wars, taking the popular side, he found employment in the Long Parliament and the army, and was at the head of the forces that reduced Chester. See Mass. Archives, Lands, i. 1 ;

lands in the Massachusetts Bay by Mr. John Gorges, and that if this Company would make him a promise, so as he consent to underwrite with this Company, it might not be prejudicial to his patent, it was resolved this answer should be given him, namely, that if he please to underwrite with us without any condition whatsoever, but to come in as all other adventurers do, he should be welcome upon the same conditions that we have.

A proposition being made to entertain a surgeon for the Plantation, Mr. [blank] Pratt[1] was propounded as an able man, upon these conditions, namely, that £40 should be allowed him, viz. for his chest £25, the rest for his own salary for the first year, provided he continues three years, the Company to be at charge of transporting his wife and a [servant,] and to have £20 a year for the other two years, and to build him a house at the Company's charge, and to allot him a hundred acres of ground. But if he stay but one year, then the Company to be at charge

Hutchinson's Mass. i. 6, 18; Hazard's State Papers, i. 152; and Mass. Hist. Coll. xxvi. 75.

[1] Pratt's name was John. He settled at Newtown, or Cambridge, but removed to Connecticut in 1636. In Nov. 1635, he was cited before the Court of Assistants for a letter which he had written to England, "wherein he raised an ill report of this country." He made an equivocal and rather unsatisfactory apology, which is printed at length in Mass. Hist. Coll. xvii. 126. In Nov. 1644, he sailed from Boston with his wife, for Malaga, in a new ship of 400 tons, which was lost on the coast of Spain, and they were both drowned. Governor Winthrop says, "This man was above sixty years old, an experienced surgeon, who had lived in New-England many years, and was of the first church at Cambridge in Mr. Hooker's time, and had good practice, and wanted nothing. But he had been long discontented, because his employment was not so profitable to himself as he desired, and it is like he feared lest he should fall into want in his old age, and therefore he would needs go back into England, (for surgeons were then in great request there by occasion of the wars,) but God took him away childless." See Savage's Winthrop, i. 173, ii. 239, and Hutchinson's Collection of Papers, p. 166.

of his bringing back for England, and he to leave his CHAP.
servant and the chest for the Company's service.

Agreed with Robert Morley, servant to Mr. An- 1629.
drew Mathewes, late barber surgeon, to serve the March
Company in New-England, for three years ; the first
year to have 20 nobles,[1] the second year [30, and
the third] year 20 marks,[2] to serve as a barber and
a surgeon, on all occasions belonging to his calling
to any of this Company that are planters, or their
servants ; and for his chest and all in it, whereof he
hath given an inventory, [if, on the] sight of it, it be
approved, five pounds is [to be allowed] and paid to
him for it, and the same to be fo[rthwith paid.]

The business concerning the division of the lands,
propounded the 3d of this month, was again taken
into consideration, and it was resolved that Captain
Waller, Captain Venn, Mr. Eaton, and Mr. Adams,
Mr. Whetcombe, Mr. Wright, Mr. Vassall, Mr.
Treasurer, with the Governor, and Deputy, shall
consider seriously of the business, calling to their
assistance Mr. Graves, Mr. Sharpe, or any other,
and to set down in writing what course they conceive fit to be held herein, whereby an equality may
be held, to avoid all contention 'twixt the adventurers ; and Tuesday morning appointed for the committees to meet about this business.

[At] this Court also Mr. Thomas Graves was propounded to go over with the ships now bound for
New-England, to have his charges borne out and
home ; and being a man experienced in iron works,

---

[1] A noble is an old English coin,    13s. 4d., just twice as much as the
worth about 6s. 8d.                     noble.
[2] A mark is an old coin, worth

CHAP. III.

~~~

1629.
March
5.

in salt works, in measuring and surveying of lands, and in fortifications, &c., in lead, copper, and alum mines, having a charge of wife, five children, a man and maid-servant; after some conference with him, he tendering his employment, to go and return with one of our ships, to the Company's discretion for his salary in that time, it was thought fit that he should consider 'twixt this and to-morrow what to demand in case he do return presently with the ships he should take his passage in; and what his demands would be if the Company should continue him there, and be at charges of the transportation of his wife and family thither in their next ships, if he take liking to continue in New-England.

Mr. John Malbon[1] being also desired to be here, after conference had with him touching the proposition made in his behalf the 2d of this month, he was wished to consider what further proposition he would make, that the Company might take it into consideration.

## The 6th March, 1628.

6.

Agreed with Mr. Thomas Steevens, armourer in Buttolph Lane, for twenty arms, viz. corselet, breast, back, culet, gorget, tasses,[2] and head-piece[3] to each, varnished all black, with leathers and buckles, at

---

[1] Not Oldham, as Felt has it in his Annals, i. 64.

[2] Defensive armour: the *culet*, or guarde de reins, for the lower part of the body, the *gorget* for the neck, and the *tasses* for the front part of the thighs. These last were appendages to the ancient corselet, consisting of skirts, made of overlapping plates, fastened to the cuirass with hooks, and reaching down to the middle of the thigh. See Meyrick's Ancient Armour, and Grose's Military Antiquities.

[3] The head-pieces were probably *morions*, circular scull-caps, with a rim round them.

17*s.* each armour, excepting four which are to be CHAP.
with close head-pieces, and these four armours at III.
24*s.* apiece, to be delivered all by the 20th of this 1629.
month ; whereof one left now for a sample, 6.
March

Agreed with John Wise, shoemaker in Mark Lane,
for

| | | |
|---|---|---|
| 1 dozen pair shoes, of tens | | |
| 3 dozen " " of 11 | | at 2*s.* 7*d.* a pair, |
| 3 dozen " " of 12 | | |
| 1 dozen pair of 13 | | |
| 1 dozen pair of 8 | | at 2*s.* 5*d.* a pair, |
| 1 dozen pair of 9 | | |

10 dozen pair, to be delivered by the 20th of
this month.

---

### *The 9th March,* 1628.

This day John Washborne is entertained for Secre- 9.
tary for one whole year, to enter the courts, to keep
the Company's accounts, to make warrant for all
moneys to be brought in or paid out, and to give notice at every meeting of such as are backward in payment of their subscriptions ; as also for all provision
to be made ready, to call upon such as have the
charge thereof, whereby the ships now bound for
New-England[1] may be despatched by the 25th of this
month, at furthest. His salary for this year is to be
[torn off], he, in the premises and the office of a Secretary, to perform [his] faithful, diligent and true endeavours, whereunto [he] doth fully [consent and]
agree. JOHN WASHBORNE.[2]

[1] With Higginson's company.  [2] The original is Washburne's own
signature.

Agreed with John Gace, of London, turner, for forty bandoleers,[1] to be made of neat's leather, broad girdles, each with twelve charges, whereof one a priming [box, the boxes] of wood, covered with black leather, at 2s. apiece, to be delivered next meeting, the boxes to be for bastard musket size, excepting ten for full musket size ; and those to be marked M, the other for bastard muskets, B.

Moreover, agreed with him for ten dozen of shovels and spades, at eighteen shillings the dozen, of three several sizes, whereof the smallest proportion to be of the smallest sizes ; and three spades and three shovels left here for samples.

This day these things were ordered to be provided by these men, for 120 men's provisions.

Mr. Thomas Hewson, $\begin{cases} \text{120 flitches bacon,} \\ \text{120 gallons sweet oil,} \end{cases}$

Mr. Deputy, $\begin{cases} \text{150 quarters of meal,} \\ \text{30 quarters of pease, at 26s.} \\ \text{15 q'rs of groats, at 4s. full dried,} \\ \text{20 firkins of butter, 17s.} \\ \text{60 quarters of malt, 17s. 6d.} \\ \text{30 c. of cheese.} \end{cases}$

10.     *This 10th March,* 1628, I, Thomas Graves, of Gravesend, in the county of Kent, gent., and by my profession skilful and experienced in the discovery and finding out of iron mines, as also of lead, copper, mineral salt, and alum,[2] in fortifications of all sorts, according to the nature of the place, in surveying of

---

[1] See note on page 44.
[2] Alum. So says Prince, quoting the Records. The word is now
obliterated in the MS.

buildings and of lands, and in measuring of lands, in CHAP. III.
describing a country by map, in leading of water
[courses] to proper uses for mills or other uses, in 1629.
finding out all sorts of limestones and materials for March 10.
buildings, in manufacturing, &c., have this present
day agreed to serve the New-England Company, and
in their employment to take my passage for New-
England, in such ship as they shall appoint me; and
during my stay there, according to the conditions
hereafter expressed, to do my true and uttermost
endeavour, in all or any the particulars above mentioned, for the most good and benefit of the said
Company; and I do hereby faithfully promise to do
my uttermost endeavour for the discovery of aught
that may be beneficial to the Company, and not to
conceal aught from them whom I shall be enjoined to
reveal the same unto, that may tend or conduce to
the good and profit of the said Company. Neither
that I shall[1] or disclose aught that they shall enjoin
me to keep secret, to any man whomsoever; but in
all things to bend my uttermost skill and ability to
do the Company the best, true, and faithful service I
may or can perform.

In consideration whereof, the said Company are to
bear all my charges by sea into New-England, together with my charges during my stay in their employments in New-England, and my charges at sea
in my return home, apparel only excepted, which is
to be always at my own charge. And it is agreed
moreover, that from the time of my first landing in
New-England, to the time of the return from thence

---

[1] A word seems to have been accidentally omitted.

for London of such ships as shall be sent from London next after Michaelmas next, and in which I shall take my passage for London, that there shall be allowed unto me five pounds for each month that I shall continue in New-England, as aforesaid, for my salary or wages, but nothing to be allowed [for] my charges during the time of my being at sea outward and home ; with this further proviso, that in case the said Company, [after I] shall have continued six or eight months in the country [aforesaid], shall desire my continuance in [the same for] three years from the time of my f [irst arrival], I will and do hereby [torn off] thereof. [And the said Company, in case it be] their intent to retain me in their service to the end of three years, do hereby promise to be at the charge of the transportation into New-England of my wife, five children, a boy and a maid servant, and withal to build me a convenient house for myself and my said family at their charges, and thereto to assign me one hundred acres of land, and to have part thereof planted at the Company's charge, against the coming of my family, whereby they may subsist ; till I shall be possessed of my family, to perform the same, or otherwise to allow me some competency of necessary victuals for the subsistence of me and my family till the next season of planting and reaping after their arrival. And it is further agreed, that if I continue in the Company's employments for three years, the payment of five pounds per month for my salary is to be utterly void; and my yearly allowance in money, from the time of my first arrival in New-England to the end of three years, to be after the rate of fifty pounds by the year ; provided always,

that my said family going over as aforesaid, there CHAP.
shall be such a proportion of land allowed me for
them hereafter as if they had now taken their passage 1629.
with me in the ships now bound for New-England. March 10.
And for further recompense for my true and faithful
endeavours in the said Company's employments,
(which I do promise, with God's assistance, to perform truly and sincerely, to the best of my ability
and understanding,) I do and shall refer myself
wholly to the Company's discretion, as my true endeavours and the success thereof, through God's
mercy, shall encourage them to do.

In witness of all the premises, I have hereunto set
my hand and seal this present 10th day of March,
anno 1628, in London.

THO. GRAVES.[1] [Seal.]

Witness hereunto,
GEORGE HARWOOD,
JOHN VENN.

----

The 10th March, 1628. Present,

| | |
|---|---|
| THE GOVERNOR, | MR. EATON, |
| MR. DEPUTY, | MR. ADAMS, |
| CAPT. VENN, | MR. WHETCOMB, |
| MR. TREASURER, | MR. HUTCHINS. |
| MR. VASSALL, | |

A proposition was made this day by Samuel Sharpe,
who was formerly entertained to do his endeavour in
the Company's employments concerning artillery
business, (as appeareth the 3d of this month,) that
all or the better part of his salary might be paid him

----

[1] Graves's signature is in his own handwriting.

now, to provide him apparel withal; and if he should happen to die before he had deserved it, his said apparel should satisfy it. Upon debate whereof, it was thought fit that twenty pounds should be paid him; and this to be the Treasurer's warrant for payment thereof, upon his salary of £10 a year, for three years; I say, twenty pounds, to be paid him presently.

This day being appointed to take into consideration touching the division of the lands in New-England, where our first Plantation shall be, it was, after much debate, thought fit to refer this business to the Governor, and a committee to be chosen to that purpose to assist him; and whatsoever they shall do herein, that to stand for good.

This day order was given to the Treasurer for payment of twenty pounds more to Mr. John Humphry towards charges of our patent;[1] and this to be his warrant for the payment thereof.

Captain Venn,[2] Mr. Eaton, Mr. Samuel Vassall, and Mr. Nowell, and Mr. Whetcombe, or any three of them, are intreated once more to confer with Mr.

---

[1] The patent had been obtained, by the solicitation of Lord Viscount Dorchester, March 4, 1629. Chalmers prints a copy of the docket of the grant to Sir Henry Rosewell and others, and remarks, " The following paper demonstrates that what was so strongly asserted during the reign of Charles II., to prove that the Charter was surreptitiously obtained, is unjust." See page 29, and Chalmers's Political Annals, pp. 136, 147, 148.

[2] Mr. John Venn, commonly called Captain or Colonel Venn, was a distinguished citizen of London, and is commemorated by Clarendon as " leading the city after him in seditious remonstrances." Hutchinson says, " he was in the design from the beginning, and intended to have removed, but never did. Upon the change of affairs in England, he made a figure there, being one of the members for the city in the Long Parliament, and among the most active in the opposition to the Court, and was one of the King's judges." He was one of the ten, Pym and Hambden being two others, whom Charles charged with high treason. See Clarendon's Hist. of the Rebellion, ii. 10, 91, iii. 618, (Oxford ed. 1826), and Hutchinson's Mass. i. 18.

John Oldham [to see what] accommodation may be CHAP.<br>III. made 'twixt the Company and him, that [their differ-<br>ences may be accomm]odated.

1629.

---

12*th March*, 1628.   Present,

| Mr. Whetcomb,         | Mr. Treasurer, |
| Sir Richard Saltonstall, | Mr. Nowell. |

John Browne, gent., and Mr. Samuel Browne, of  March<br>Roxwell, in Essex, [proposing] to take their passage   12.<br>in the Company's ships for New-England, at their<br>own charge, and intending to plant there, it is agreed<br>by these [present,] that for their passage and diet<br>they shall pay five pounds [each] ; and that for their<br>encouragement, land shall be allotted to them [there]<br>as if they had subscribed fifty pounds in the general<br>stock, [and to have the same] privileges as others<br>that are in the patent do.

John Browne,<br>Samuel Browne.[1]

Richard Claydon,[2] aged thirty-four years, or there-<br>abouts, carpenter, who being desirous to transport<br>himself, his wife, one daughter of [torn off] years<br>old, his sister of fourteen years old, his brother Bar-<br>naby C[laydon,] aged twenty-three years, and his<br>brother-in-law Thomas Hanscombe, aged [torn off],<br>for New-England, in the Company's ships, it is pro-<br>mised [this] day, that he being able to furnish £40<br>towards the charges of him and his, what shall be

---

[1] These signatures are in their own handwriting.

[2] It appears from a marginal note, that Claydon was of Bedfordshire, parish of Sutton.

wanting the Company will [furnish] ; upon this condition, that upon their arrival in New-England, what
he shall be indebted to the Company shall be paid
by the labor of himself, and his two servants or brothers aforesaid, allowing them all three 3s. the day
for so long time [until] they have paid this debt,
and in that time finding [these] three persons diet at
the Company's charge, and whilst [he is] earning
out this debt to instruct any of the Company's servants in the trade of a ploughwright.  And there is
land to be [allotted] to him and his, as is usual, by
the Company's orders, to those that transport themselves.  Written this 12th March, 1628.

RICHARD CLAYDON.[1]

Cannot go this voyage.

---

### The 16th March, 1628.

16.    Bespoken of Mr. Durbridge, at 2s. 7d. a pair, 6
dozen pair of shoes, to be delivered this week, viz.

(4 pair delivered.)

1 dozen pair of tens,
2 dozen pair of 11,
2          of 12,
1 dozen pair of 13.

---

### The 16th March, 1628.

Bespoke of Mr. Mayo, at 10½d. per yard for beds
and bolsters,

20 bedticks, (Scotch ticking, ¾ broad,) $2\frac{1}{16}$ long,
and 1½ yards broad, 11 yards each bed and bolster.

---

[1] Claydon's signature, and his " Cannot go this voyage," are in
his own handwriting.

Bespoke the day abovesaid, of Robert Harret, 8
dozen pair neat's leather shoes,

1 dozen 10,⎫
3 dozen 11, ⎬ at 2s. 7d. per pair, to be good
3 dozen 12, | liquored neat's leather, ac-
1 dozen 13,⎭ cording to the pattern.

---

*Estimate of* 100 *men, charge of them and their provisions, with others noted,*

| | | |
|---|---:|---:|
| 100 men, their charge, £15 a man . . . | | £1500 |
| Freight of the ship Talbot, 5 months, £80 | | |
| per month . . . . . . . . | 400 ⎱ | 750 |
| Victuals and wages 32 men, £70 a month, 350 ⎰ | | |
| The Lion's Whelp set to sea . . . . . | | 500 |
| 20 cows and bulls, £4 apiece . . . | 80 ⎫ | |
| 10 mares and horses, £6 apiece . . | 60 ⎬ | 610 |
| Charges of these . . . . . . . . | 470 ⎭ | |
| | | £3360 |

---

Agreed with [illegible] Churchill for 100 swords, with [torn out] blades, at 4s. 6d. apiece, to have all chapes,[1] and 10 short swords, at 2s. apiece, and Polonia hilts, at 3s 4d., as many as we like, to be delivered within eight days.

---

Bought of Felix Boreman, dwelling in Fleet Lane.

14 swords, at 4s. 6d apiece ⎫
7 ditto, at 3s. apiece ⎬ £4 12s.
4 ditto, at 2s. apiece ⎭
‾‾
25 swords.

---

[1] Chape is the little thin plate of silver, iron or brass, at the point of the scabbard of a sword.

CHAP.
III.

1629.
March
16.

Agreed with Mr. Raphe White, in Philpot Lane,[1] for 12 gallons aqua-vitæ, 2s. 6d. a gallon.

12 sides of bacon, delivered by John Gladwing, at Mr. Goff's, of 74½ stone, each stone 8 lbs., at 2s. 5d. a stone.

### 17th March, 1628.

17.

A warrant was made for payment of £120 to Mr. Nathaniel Wright, for so much paid by him to Mr. Jarvis Kirk, Mr. William Barkley, and Mr. Robert Charlton, for the ship.

Also, to pay for iron and steel.

Also, to pay for buhrs[2] to make mill-stones, 110, 2s. apiece, bought of Edward Casson, of London, merchant tailor, . . £11 0 0

14 c. of plaster of Paris, 18d. per c. . 1 1 0

And porterage, weighing the plaster, and casting out of the buhrs, 12d. and 23d. . 3 0

£12 4 0

### The 19th of March, 1628.

19.

A warrant was made for payment of twelve pounds and twelve shillings unto Mr. Gawen Helme and Thomas Brickhed for two coppers[3] for the Lion's Whelp. I say for £12 12s. 0d.

---

[1] See page 40.

[2] "This is a hard, siliceous stone, remarkable for its cellular structure, containing always a greater or less number of irregular cavities. Hence its surface, however worn and levelled, is always rough. This property renders buhrstone an invaluable material for millstones. When it is not found of sufficient size for this use, small pieces of it are fitted together, cemented, and bound with an iron hoop." This stone abounds at Epernay, in France. It has also been discovered within ten or twelve miles of Zanesville, Ohio, of a quality equal if not superior to the best French buhr, and in great abundance. See Bigelow's Technology, p. 13, (ed. 1829,) and Dr. Frederick Hall's Letters from the West, (1840) p. 70.

[3] Boilers, to cook in.

*The* 19*th of March,* 1628.

A warrant was made for payment of eighteen pounds unto Mr. [blank] Browne, and is for one bale of French cloth, for the Lion's Whelp. I say £18.

---

*The* 19*th of March,* 1628.

A warrant was made for payment of twenty-five pounds, fifteen shillings, unto Mr. John White, of Redding, for thirty quarters of malt, to go in the ships. I say £25 15s. 0d.

---

23*d of March,* 1628. Present,[1]

| | |
|---|---|
| THE GOVERNOR, | MR. HUMFREY, |
| MR. DEPUTY, | WILLIAM VASSALL, |
| SIR RICHARD SALTONSTALL, | MR. WHETCOMB, |
| MR. DAVENPORT, | MR. NOWELL. |
| CAPT. VENN, | |

At this meeting intimation was given by Mr. Nowell, by letters from Mr. Isaac Johnson, that one Mr. HIGGESON, of Leicester, an able minister, proffers to go to our Plantation ; who being approved for a reverend, grave minister, fit for our present occasions, it was thought by these present to entreat Mr. John Humfry to ride presently to Leicester,[2] and, if Mr. Higgeson may conveniently be had to go this present voyage, that he should deal with him ; first, if his remove from thence may be without scandal to that people, and approved by the consent of some of the best affected among them, with the approbation

---

[1] This line, torn off from the top of the leaf, is restored from Prince, p. 256.

[2] Leicester is 97 miles from London.

CHAP. of Mr. Hildersham,[1] of Ashby-de-la-Zouch; secondly,
III.
——— that in regard of the shortness of the time, the Com-
1629. pany conceive it would be best, if he so thought
March
23. good, to leave his wife and family till towards Bar-
tholomew, for their better accommodation. Yet if it
should be held inconvenient, that may be referred to
himself to take [his wife and] two children with him;
thirdly, that for his entertainment, the Company
[torn off.] [2]

April          30th April, 1629.[3]
30.
It is further ordered by these present, that the
Governor, the Deputy, and Council aforesaid, or the

[1] Arthur Hildersham, *Malleus He-reticorum*, as he was called, *Mauler of Heretics*, as old Fuller would render it, was, according to Echard, "a great and shining light of the Puritan party, and justly celebrated for his singular learning and piety." He was born at Stetchworth, in Cambridgeshire, Oct. 6, 1563, and was educated at Christ's College, Cambridge. In 1593, he was presented by his kinsman, the Earl of Huntingdon, to the benefice of Ashby-de-la-Zouch, 18 miles from Leicester, where he preached 43 years. In the course of that time he was four times silenced and restored. In 1615 he was committed to the Fleet prison by the High Commission, where he remained three months. In 1616 that execrable Court again proceeded against him, fined him £2000, excommunicated him, degraded him from the ministry, and ordered him to be again imprisoned. Foreseeing the danger, however, he concealed himself and escaped. In 1625 he was restored to his living; but when Laud was in power, he was again silenced, and was not restored till a few months before his death, which took place March 4, 1632, when he was in the 69th year of his age. His character and writings were held in high esteem by the fathers of New-England. "It is affirmed," says Hubbard, "that Mr. Hildersham advised Mr. Higginson and other ministers looking this way, to agree upon their form of church government before they came away from England." See Fuller's Worthies, i. 164, and Church Hist. iii. 370; Neal's Puritans, ii. 245; Brook's Lives of the Puritans, ii. 376–388; Echard's Hist. of England, p. 451, (ed. 1720); Nichols's Hist. of Leicestershire, ii. 622; Mass. Hist. Coll. xv. 118.

[2] A leaf of the MS. is here missing. Hubbard, p. 121, and Prince, p. 257, both appear to have had it. I have endeavoured in vain to supply this deficiency by procuring an ancient copy of these Records now existing in England. Prince quotes from the Records under April 16, "Sixty women and maids, 26 children, and 300 men, with victuals, arms, apparel, tools, 140 head of cattle, &c., in the Lord Treasurer's warrant (to go to New-England.)"

[3] The first part of the Record of this meeting is wanting. It appears from Prince, p. 258, who had it, that at this meeting they chose Mr.

major part of them, shall make choice of a Secretary, CHAP.<br>III. and such other Officers as shall in their discretions seem requisite and needful for the peaceable and 1629. quiet government of the Plantation ; and shall frame April<br>30. such oaths, and administer the same to every [one] of them for the execution of his place and office for the year ensuing next after they shall have taken [the said] oaths, as they in their discretions, or the greater number of them, shall think good.

And it is ordered, that the said Governor, Deputy, Council, and other Officers aforesaid, shall be established and continue in their said several places for one whole year, or until this Court shall think fit to choose others in the place or places of them, or any of them ; and in case of death, &c.

It is further ordered, that the said Governor, Mr. Endecott, [or his Deputy,] and the said Council, being chosen as aforesaid, and having taken their oaths respectively to their places, or the greater number of them, (whereof the Governor or Deputy to be always one,) at any of their meetings, (which the said Governor, at his discretion, or in his absence the Deputy, is hereby authorized to appoint, as oft as there shall be occasion,) shall have full power and authority, and they are hereby authorized by power derived from his Majesty's letters patent, to make, ordain, and establish all manner of wholesome and reasonable orders, laws, statutes, ordinances, directions and instructions, not contrary to the laws of the realm of England, for the present government of

Endicott Governor of the Plantation, and Messrs. Higginson, Skelton, Bright, John and Samuel Brown, Thomas Graves, and Samuel Sharp, to be of his Council.

CHAP. III. our Plantation, and the inhabitants residing within the limits of our Plantation ; a copy of all which orders is from time to time to be sent to the Company in England.[1]

1629. April 30.

It is ordered by these presents, that a copy of the Acts and Orders[2] made this present day for settling the government in the Plantation of the Massachusetts Bay aforesaid, shall be fairly engrossed, and sent under the Company's seal, subscribed by the Governor and Deputy, by the speediest[3] conveyance for New-England that can be had.

All this confirmed by erecting of hands.

Mr. Walgrave, Mr. Pelham, and Mr. Humphry, and Mr. Nowell, are entreated to frame the form of the oath for the Governor, Mr. Endicott, and also for his Deputy, and for the Council,[4] which shall be sent over and be administered to them in New-England.

———

*Thursday, the 7th May,* 1629.    Present,

May 7.

| | |
|---|---|
| THE GOVERNOR, | MR. COULSON, |
| MR. DEPUTY, | MR. NOWELL, |
| MR. ALDERSEY, | MR. HUMPHRY, |
| MR. ADAMS, | MR. THO. PULYSTON. |
| MR. HUTCHINS, | |

The last Court was read, and confirmed by these present.

---

[1] Some words in this and the preceding paragraph, torn off or obliterated in the manuscript, I have been enabled to restore from the "Form of Government," sent over to Endicott, and which embodies the substance and often the language of this day's record.

[2] These Acts and Orders for the settling the Government, will be found in a subsequent part of this volume.

[3] They wished to anticipate Oldham in his contemplated settlement in Massachusetts Bay. For this purpose the Company's instructions to Endicott were despatched by the George about a fortnight before the sailing of the other ships which carried out Higginson and his company.

[4] These oaths will also be found in a subsequent part of this volume.

A form of an oath for the Governor beyond the CHAP.<br>III.
seas, and of an oath for the Council there, was drawn
and delivered to Mr. Humphry to show the Council.[1] 1629.

Letters are to be written about lands to be allotted May 7.
to each adventurer.

Also, about Mr. Fra. Webb's business for a
mill, &c.

To have those punished beyond seas that sell
guns.

To have some men's lands laid together.

---

*The 11th of May,* 1629.  Present this day,  11

| | |
|---|---|
| Mr. Deputy, | Mr. Humfreys, |
| Mr. Treasurer, | Mr. Vassall, |
| Sir Richard Saltonstall, | Mr. Peters,[2] |
| Mr. Adams, | Mr. Pinchon, |
| Mr. Nowell, | Mr. Whyte. |
| Mr. Hutchins, | |

This day Mr. Oldham propounded unto Mr. White,
that he would have his patent examined ; and it is
agreed by the Court not to have any treaty with him
about it, by reason it is thought he doth it not out of
love, but out of some sinister respect.

A warrant delivered unto Mr. Seale for ten dozen
and two hats, at 2s. per dozen, for the sum of 20s. 4d.

---

[1] The Privy Council.
[2] This was the celebrated Hugh
Peters. He was in the Company as

early as May 30, 1628. See Hutchinson's Mass. i. 9.

CHAP.
III.

1629.

May
13.

*The* 13*th of May,* 1629.[1]   Present this day,

| | |
|---|---|
| THE GOVERNOR, | MR. PINCHON, |
| MR. DEPUTY, | MR. HUTCHINS, |
| MR. TREASURER, | MR. HEWSON, |
| MR. GLOVER, | MR. BACKHOUSE, |
| SIR RICHARD SALTONSTALL, | MR. BALLARD, |
| MR. ADAMS, | MR. CROWTHER, |
| MR. OFFIELD, | MR. WHICHCOTE, |
| MR. WHETCOMBE, | MR. WHITE, |
| MR. FOXCROFT, | MR. PETERS, |
| MR. VASSALL, | MR. CRANE, |
| MR. PERRY, | MR. HUMPHRY. |
| MR. NOWELL, | |

Delivered a warrant unto Richard Bowry for twelve pounds, £12, as $\frac{2}{3}$ parts of £18, the other $\frac{1}{3}$ being to be paid for the Governor, and is for his apprentice, Robert Seale, his time.

Mr. Matthew Cradock is this day chosen by the consent of the generality of the Company to be Governor to the New-England Company for the year following ; Mr. Thomas Goffe,[2] Deputy ; also, Mr. George Harwood,[3] Treasurer to the said Company.

---

[1] " Hubbard styles this the second court of election, when by the royal charter it is the first; though by virtue of the former patent from the New-England Council, it seems the Company had chosen a governor, &c. the year before." Prince, Annals, p. 260 ; Hubbard, in Mass. Hist. Coll. xv. 122.

[2] Goffe was a London merchant, and had been previously engaged in furthering the Colony at New Plymouth. His name occurs frequently in Winthrop's Journal. See Mass. Hist. Coll. iii. 48.

[3] I find the name of George Harwood, citizen of London, in the list of the twelve *feofees* into whose hands was paid the money raised in 1624 for buying up impropriations and supporting " lecturers " or preachers in destitute places in England. Two other members of the Massachusetts Company, John White, the lawyer, and the Rev. John Davenport, afterwards of New Haven and Boston, were among these feofees. They were suppressed and ruined by Laud in 1633. A good account of their purpose may be found in Carlyle's Cromwell, i. 50, 70, 88, (Am. edit.) See Brook's Lives of the Puritans, i. 75, and Neal's Hist. of the Puritans, ii. 248.

The Assistants being this day to be chosen, two CHAP. III. of the former Assistants, mentioned in the patent, viz. Mr. John Endecott and Mr. John Browne being 1629. out of the land, the other sixteen were confirmed, May 13. viz. Sir Richard Saltonstall, Mr. Isaac Johnson, Mr. Samuel Aldersey, Mr. John Venn, Mr. John Humphry, Mr. Symon Whetcombe, Increase Nowell, Richard Perry, Nathaniel Wright, Samuel Vassall, Theophilus Eaton, Thomas Adams, Thomas Hutchins, George Foxcroft, William Vassall, and William Pinchion; and to make up the number of eighteen, Mr. John Pocock and Mr. Christopher Coulson were chosen Assistants. And of these all, excepting Mr. Isaac Johnson, Samuel Aldersey, John Venn, Nathaniel Wright, Samuel Vassall, Theophilus Eaton and Christopher Coulson, took their oaths appertaining.

William Burges, Humphry Lewis, John Washborne, and Lawrence Roe, being all put in election for the place of Secretary, by a free election, Mr. William Burges was chosen Secretary for the year ensuing.[1]

Humphry Seale chosen and sworn Beadle.

It is this day ordered, that whensoever any Court of Assistants shall be summoned, whosoever of the Assistants comes not, 'twixt 25 March and 29 of September, before eight of the clock in the morning, and from 29 September to 25 March, before 9 of the clock in the morning, shall forfeit twelve pence for every such offence; and if he come not within two hours after either of the said hours respectively, then two shillings for every default each man to forfeit

---

[1] Washburne, I suspect, was superseded on account of his illegible chirography. He certainly deserved to be.

and pay; and for want of payment within [blank] days, after demand made by the officer of the Company, the fine double to be set upon his account; always [provided, upon the pleasure] of the Governor, Deputy, or a lawful expression of approbation, [a line or two torn off.]

It is also agreed, that for any that shall have private conference after the Court is summoned, by the Governor or his Deputy knocking of the hammer thrice on the table, to sit down and attend the Court, that sixpence by every person for every such offence shall be paid.

It is agreed, that three pounds shall be paid John Washbourne for his pains as Secretary to the Company for the time past.

---

*The Names of the Governor, Deputy, Treasurer, and Assistants, for the year* 1629, *and other Officers.*

MR. MATTHEW CRADOCK, *Governor.*
MR. THOMAS GOFFE, *Deputy.*
MR. GEORGE HARWOOD, *Treasurer.*

| | |
|---|---|
| SIR RICHARD SALTONSTALL, | MR. SAMUEL VASSALL, |
| MR. ISAAC JOHNSON, | MR. THEOPHILUS EATON, |
| MR. SAMUEL ALDERSEY, | MR. THOMAS ADAMS, |
| MR. JOHN VENN, | MR. THOMAS HUTCHINS, |
| MR. JOHN HUMFREY, | MR. GEORGE FOXCROFT, |
| MR. SYMON WHETCOMBE, | MR. WILLIAM VASSALL, |
| MR. INCREASE NOWELL, | MR. WILLIAM PINCHION, |
| MR. RICHARD PERRY, | MR. JOHN POCOCK, |
| MR. NATHANIEL WRIGHT, | MR. CHRISTOPHER COWLSON. |

*Assistants.*

WILLIAM BURGIS, *Secretary.*
HUMPHREY SEALE, *Beadle.*

*At a Court of Assistants, on Monday, the 18th of May,* CHAP.
     1629. Present,   III.

1629.

| | |
|---|---|
| MR. GOVERNOR, | MR. THOMAS ADAMS, |
| MR. DEPUTY, | MR. SYMON WHETCOMBE, |
| SIR R. SALTONSTALL, | MR. RICHARD PERRY, |
| MR. GEORGE HARWOOD, *Treasurer,* | MR. JOHN POCOCK, |
| MR. JOHN HUMPHREY, | MR. GEORGE FOXCROFT. |

May 18.

William Burgis, chosen by the last General Court to be Secretary for the year ensuing, was now admitted and sworn accordingly; upon the salary of twenty marks from the day he was chosen, for the said year.

The Acts made at a Court the 30th of April last, for choosing and establishing a Governor, Deputy, Council, and other Officers in New-England, was now read; and this Court thought fit to add thereunto, that they shall be established in their said several places for one whole year, or till such time as the Company here shall think fit to choose others in the places of them, or any of them; and that in case any of them shall depart this life before the expiration of the time they were so chosen for, that the Governor or Deputy and Council, at an ample Court assembled, shall have power to nominate and choose fit person or persons to succeed him or them so deceased in the said place or places for the residue of the time unexpired.

Upon motion made for allotment of land to the several adventurers and planters,[1]

Mr. Humphreys and Mr. Adams are desired to meet and consider what provisions are fit to be now

---

[1] There appears to be something omitted here.

sent over to Captain John Indicott and his family, and to provide the same accordingly.

The names of all the adventurers to be now sent over, with the several sums by them underwritten; and it is ordered that the Governor and Council there shall have power to allot unto every particular adventurer that shall desire the same by himself or his assignees, two hundred acres of land upon the sum of £50 adventure in the general stock in this first dividend, and proportionably for more or less according to their several adventures; and Mr. Governor, Deputy, Mr. Whyte, and Mr. Adams, and Mr. Whetcombe are to meet at Mr. Governor's house[1] to-morrow morning at six of the clock to advise and conclude of this business.

---

19. *The 19th of May*, 1629. [Present,]

MR. GOVERNOR,        MR. WHETCOMBE,
MR. WHYTE,          MR. ADAMS.

Concerning the allotment of land to those persons as are adventurers in the common stock, it is thought fit that letters be written to the Governor to set out and allot unto them after the proportion of two hundred acres of land for £50 adventure, and after that rate for more or less, to the intent to build their houses and to improve their labors thereon. And if within ten days after their arrival, and demand made by any particular adventurer in the common stock, or his servant for him, the same be not so allotted,

---

[1] Governor Cradock's house was in St. Swithin's Lane, near London Stone.

that each man, being an adventurer, is hereby permitted free liberty to build in any place where himself shall think most convenient, with reservation
not to build or manure that already built on or manured ; provided that if the plot of ground whereon
the town is intended to be built be set out, and it be
publicly known to be intended for that purpose, that
then no man shall presume to build his house anywhere else, (unless it be in the Massachusetts Bay,[1]
and there according to such directions as shall be
thought meet for that place.)   But in case his allotment be not set out within the town where he shall
build, and having, in his own name or in the behalf
of his master, made request to the Governor to have
the same assigned to him, if it be not done within
ten days after his arrival, it shall be free for any in
such case, being an adventurer in the common stock,
to build his house within the aforesaid plot of ground,
set out for the town to be built on, and to impale to
his own use proportionable to half an acre of ground
for £50 adventure in the common stock ; unless a
greater or lesser proportion be formerly determined
of by the Governor and Council ; in which case that
proportion is to be made use of and appropriated to
each man within the liberties of the plot set out for
the town to be built on.   And it is ordered, that
conveyance be made in the Company's name, with
the common seal of the Company to it, to any that
shall desire it, for each man's peaceable enjoying of
that land he holds, at the charge of the Company.

It is further thought fit and ordered, that all such

---

[1] See note [1] on page 4.

CHAP.
III.

1629.
May
19.

persons as go over at their own charge, and are adventurers in the common stock, shall have lands
allotted to them for themselves and their families
forthwith, fifty acres of land for each person ; but
being no adventurers in the common stock, shall
have fifty acres of land for the master of the family,
and such a proportion of land more, if there be cause,
as, according to their charge and quality, the Governor and Council of New-England shall think necessary for them, whereby their charge may be fully
and amply supported ; unless it be to any with whom
the Company in London shall make any other particular agreement, to which relation is to be had in
such case.   And for such as transport servants, land
shall be allotted for each servant, fifty acres to the
master ; which land the master is to dispose of at his
discretion, in regard the servants' transportation,
wages, &c., is at the master's charge.

21.  *A Court of Assistants, on Thursday the 21st of May,*
*1629.   Present,*

| | |
|---|---|
| MR. GOVERNOR, | MR. BILSON, |
| MR. GOFF, *Deputy,* | MR. THOMAS HUSON, |
| MR. HARWOOD, *Treasurer,* | MR. INCREASE NOELL, |
| MR. ADAMS, | MR. HUMPHREY, |
| MR. WHICHCOYTE, | CAPT. WALLER, |
| MR. FOXCROFT, | MR. HUTCHINS. |
| MR. EATON, | |

Mr. Eaton took the oath of Assistant.   And he
is desired to accompany Mr. Humphrey to Mr. Whyte,
the counsellor, to be satisfied concerning the administering oaths to the Governor and Council in New-

England. Mr. Whetcombe is also desired to be with CHAP.
them.

III.

May
21.

The Court of the 18th of May was now read, as also
the Order conceived by Mr. Governor and others
concerning the allotment of lands, and a part of the
letter[1] formerly written in this particular was confirmed ; whereunto this Court thought fit to add, —
If within ten days after the arrival of these ships, and
demand made by any person, adventurer in the common stock, or his or their servant, of their allotment
of land, the same not being done, that then each person be permitted to seat himself and build his house
in a convenient place not formerly built [upon] nor
manured, and enclose the same to his or their use,
not exceeding the one half of that proportion which
by the former order of this Court is allowed ; and
when the dividend is made, to be free to make his
choice within the said allotment, if he dislike that he
had formerly chosen.

It is thought fit that the Secretary draw out at
large the Orders[2] concerning the establishment of
the Governor and Council in New-England, as also
the Order[2] made concerning the allotment of lands ;
and Mr. Governor, Mr. Deputy, Mr. Treasurer, Mr.
Adams, Mr. Eaton, Mr. Hutchins, Mr. Nowell, Mr.
Whetcombe, Mr. William Vassall, or any four of
them, whereof the Governor or Deputy to be always
one, are desired and appointed to meet and resolve
of these Orders, and to affix the Company's seal
thereunto ; as also for preparing letters to be now

---

[1] The letter here referred to was
one written to Endicott on the 17th
and 21st of April. It will be found

in a subsequent part of this volume.
[2] These Orders will be found in a
subsequent part of this volume.

CHAP.
III.

1629.

written, and to resolve and determine of all other business requisite for despatching of these ships.[1]

---

May
22.

*A Meeting at the Governor's house on Friday, the 22d of May, 1629.  Present,*

Mr. GOVERNOR,

DEPUTY,

Mr. ADAMS,

Mr. HUMPHREY.

The Orders drawn for the establishment of the Governor, Deputy, and Council, and other Officers in the Plantation at the Mattachusetts Bay in New-England, as also the Orders for the dividing and allotment of land there to the adventurers and others, were now read, advised on, corrected, and concluded on, &c. ; together with the General Letter from the Company here to the Governor and Council there.[2] All which are appointed to be fairly engrossed, and the said Orders to be sealed with the common seal of the Company, and sent over upon the ships now ready to depart for New-England.

---

June
11.

*A General Court the 11th of June, 1629.  Present,*

| | |
|---|---|
| Mr. GOVERNOR, | Mr. WILLIAM VASSALL, |
| Mr. DEPUTY, | Mr. WEBB, |
| Mr. HARWOOD, *Treasurer*, | Mr. HUMFREY, |
| Mr. ADAMS, | Mr. CRANE, |
| Mr. JOHN VENN, | Mr. PULLISTON, |
| Mr. BACKHOUSE, | Mr. FOXCROFT. |

This Court was appointed to take consideration of

---

[1] These ships were, the May-flower, the Four Sisters of 400 tons, and the Pilgrim. They sailed about the end of this month.

[2] This is their Second Letter to Endicott, dated May 18th. It will appear hereafter.

raising of moneys for payment of divers debts and CHAP.
III.
bills ; and thereupon an estimate was made of what
was owing, per severals' bills, and which are of ne- 1629.
June
cessity to be presently paid. 11.

That another day be appointed, and the whole
Company to be summoned by tickets, which is
thought fit to be on Wednesday next.

Mr. Godden,[1] master of the ship [blank], made
demand of freight pretended to be due unto him for
his last voyage ; but he not expressing a certain sum,
this Assembly think fit to defer him till the next
Court ; and in the mean time he is desired to bring
in a note of what is due, as also to give security to
the Company to free them from any further demands, &c., and thereupon a final conclusion thereof
to be made.

---

*A General Court at the Deputy's house on Wednesday,
the 17th of June, 1629. Present,* 17.

| | |
|---|---|
| Mr. GOVERNOR, | Mr. COOKE, |
| Mr. DEPUTY, | Mr. CLARKE, |
| SIR R. SALTONSTALL, | Mr. BALLARD, |
| Mr. GEORGE FOXCROFT, | Mr. PULISON, |
| Mr. RICHARD PERRY, | Mr. WALGRAVE, |
| Mr. ADAMS, | Mr. BACKHOUSE, |
| Mr. WHITCOMBE, | Mr. DAVIS, |
| Mr. POCOCKE, | Mr. EDMUND WHYTE, |
| Mr. JOHNSON, | CAPT. WALLER, |
| Mr. NOELL, | CAPT. VENN, |
| Mr. HARWOOD, *Treasurer*, | Mr. DAVIS,[2] |
| Mr. WHYTE, | Mr. THOMAS ANDREWS, |
| Mr. PELHAM, | Mr. ALDERSEY. |

---

[1] Henry Gauden was master of the Abigail, the ship that carried over Endicott and his company. See p. 43.

[2] Mr. Davis's name was probably repeated by mistake.

CHAP.
III.

1629.

June
17.

Mr. [blank] Johnson[1] sworn an Assistant of this Company, being chosen thereunto at a Court the 13th of May, 1629.

Mr. Governor moved that a course might be settled for bringing in of moneys, and

Mr. Treasurer returned a note concerning the Leicestershire men.

It was propounded,

> To increase their former subscriptions,
>
> To invite others to underwrite,
>
> To borrow money for a time to supply the occasions,
>
> To take up money at interest,
>
> That those here present do furnish [£]200 or [£]100 apiece, to have allowance for it.

The Court taking into consideration the necessity of a present supply of the sum of £1500, for discharging of debts and bills, and that the moneys underwritten by the adventurers, and not yet brought in, nor not likely to be brought in, in convenient time for satisfaction of those debts and bills which are of necessity to be presently paid ; upon several propositions made, it is desired and concluded on, that those of the Company here present would each of them voluntarily lend such a sum of money as he shall think fit, for advancing the sum wanting, and to have the common seal of the Company for the repayment thereof, according to the time for which he or they so lend the same; and also that the Secretary be appointed to go to such others of the Company not present as Mr. Governor shall name, to intimate

---

[1] This was Isaac Johnson, already mentioned on pp. 65 and 72. Some account of him will be given hereafter.

the same unto them, and to desire them to underwrite what sums they will lend for this occasion,
according as many of the Company here present
have done. And it is ordered that the common seal
of the Company be given to them, and all others
that will lend, for repayment thereof at such time as
they shall desire the same.

Names of those in Court that underwrit to lend.

| | | | |
|---|---|---|---|
| Sir R. Saltonstall, | £100 | Sym. Whetcombe, | £25 |
| Mr. Governor, | 150 | Tho. Hutchins, | 25 |
| Mr. Deputy, | 50 | Edw. Cooke, | 50 |
| [Richard] Perry, | 25 | Dan. Ballard, | 25 |
| [Thomas] Adams, | 50 | Edm. Whyte, | 20 |
| Increase Noell, | 25 | Joseph Caron,[1] | 25 |
| George Harwood, | 50 | [Samuel] Aldersey, | 50 |
| Richard Whyte, | 25 | Tho. Andrews, | 25 |
| Mr. Clark, | 25 | | |

Auditors appointed for auditing the accounts, viz.
Mr. Symon Whetcombe, Mr. Nathaniel Wright, Mr.
Noell, Mr. Perry, Mr. Crane, Mr. Clarke, Mr. Eaton,
and Mr. Andrews ;[2] these eight, or any four or more
of them, to meet at a convenient time and place to
audit the accounts.

A Committee for reducing of all former Orders
into a method, viz. the Governor, Mr. Whyte, Mr.
Davenport, Mr. Johnson, Capt. Waller, Capt. Venn,

---

[1] Probably the same person who signed the instructions to Endicott, May 30, 1628, and who is there called Joseph Caxon. See Hutchinson's Mass. i. 9.

[2] Thomas Andrews was a London merchant, living in Bowe Lane, and was mayor of the city in 1551. He was one of the adventurers that were interested in the Plymouth Colony. He is not to be confound-ed with Richard, probably his brother, a haberdasher at the Mermaid in Cheapside, who was also interested in the Plymouth adventure, and was an eminent benefactor of the Massachusetts Colony, having sent them sixteen heifers and upwards of £500 in money. See Mass. Hist. Coll. iii. 48, xxi. 22, and Savage's Winthrop, i. 136, 374, ii. 75, 212, 342.

CHAP.
III.

1629.
June
17.

Mr. Aldersey, Mr. Adams, Mr. Wright, and Mr. Darby, they or any four of them, and to present the same to the next General Court, to be ratified and confirmed, in part or in whole, as shall be then thought fit ; which are then by the Secretary to be entered into a fair book to be kept for that purpose, according to the usage and custom of other Companies.

July
28.

*A General Court holden for the Company of the Matta-chusetts Bay, in New-England, at Mr. Deputy's house, on Tuesday the 28th of July, 1629.* Present,

MR. MATTHEW CRADOCK, *Governor,*
MR. THOMAS GOFF, *Deputy,*
MR. GEORGE HARWOOD, *Treasurer,*

| | |
|---|---|
| MR. THOMAS ADAMS, | MR. SAMUEL VASSALL, |
| MR. NATHANIEL WRIGHT, | MR. JOSEPH BRADSHAWE, |
| MR. THEOPHILUS EATON, | MR. BURNELL, |
| MR. RICHARD PERRY, | MR. REVELL, |
| MR. INCREASE NOELL, | MR. DANIEL BALLARD, |
| MR. SYMON WHETCOMBE, | MR. SPURSTOWE, |
| MR. JOHN POCOCK, | MR. THOMAS HEWSON, |
| MR. [CHRISTOPHER] COLSON, | MR. WOODGATE, |
| MR. [THOMAS] HUTCHINS, | MR. WEBB, |
| MR. WILLIAM PINCHON, | MR. CRANE, |
| *Assistants.* | *Generality.* |

The business treated on at the last meeting was now read ; and thereupon the accounts of Mr. Governor, Mr. Deputy, and Mr. Treasurer, being now presented to this Court, the Auditors formerly appointed for auditing the Company's accounts were now desired to meet and peruse and audit these accounts ; which they have agreed to do to-morrow in the afternoon.

It was moved by Mr. Governor, that a ship of four CHAP.
hundred tons and of good force being now to be sold,
should be bought for the Company's use, upon their 1629.
general stock ; or that some particular members of July
28.
the Company would undertake to buy the said ship,
in regard the Company are not now in cash ; and
that the Company will not only employ that ship,
but take other ships of them of less defence, for
transport of their cattle and all other commodities,
from time to time, so long as they shall be willing to
furnish such shipping. Whereupon Mr. Governor
declared that he was willing to take $\frac{1}{8}$ part of the
said ship, or under,

| And did write | $\frac{1}{8}$ part, | Mr. Revell, | $\frac{1}{16}$ |
|---|---|---|---|
| Mr. Deputy, | $\frac{1}{16}$ | Mr. Aldersey, | $\frac{1}{16}$ |
| Mr. Adams, | $\frac{1}{8}$ | Mr. Milburne, | $\frac{1}{8}$ |
| Mr. Wright, | $\frac{1}{8}$ | Mr. Huson, | $\frac{1}{16}$ |
| Mr. Eaton, | $\frac{1}{16}$ | The Company, | $\frac{1}{8}$ |
| Mr. Whetcombe, | $\frac{1}{16}$ | &c. | |

A letter[1] of the 27th of May from Mr. John Endecott was now read ; wherein, amongst other things,
he complains of the profane and dissolute living of
divers of our nation, former traders to those parts,
and of their irregular trading with the Indians,[2] contrary to his late Majesty's Proclamation,[3] desiring
that the Company would take the same into their
serious consideration, and to use some speedy means

---

[1] This letter, unfortunately, is
not preserved.
[2] Endicott probably had in view
Morton, of Mount Wollaston, who
is said to have been the first in these
parts to sell guns and ammunition
to the Indians, and to teach them
their use. See Morton's Memorial,
p. 138.

[3] This proclamation, prohibiting
interloping and disorderly trading to
New-England in America, was issued by James I. on the 6th of November, 1622. It is printed in Rymer's Fœdera, xvii. 416, and in
Hazard's State Papers, i. 151.

here for reformation thereof. Whereupon the Pro-

clamation made in anno 1622 was read, and it is

thought fit that suit be made to his Majesty or the

Lords[1] for renewing thereof, with addition of such beneficial clauses as shall be needful for reforming so great and unsufferable abuses ; and Mr. Governor, Mr. Aldersey, Mr. Wright, and Mr. Eaton, are desired to repair to the Lord Keeper[2] and Mr. Secretary Coke[3] to acquaint their Honors herewith, and afterwards a petition to be presented to the Council Board accordingly.[4]

A note of divers propositions offered to the consideration of this Company by one John Betts was read, pretending that he is able to discover divers things for the good and advancement of the Plantation, and the benefit of this Company. Whereupon some of those here present were desired to inquire further of him, not only of his ability, but of his deportment in his life and conversation, and then the Company to treat with him as they shall think fit.

Also, Mr. Webb moved concerning a Frenchman, being a physician, and otherwise well qualified, who is desirous to go over to live upon the Company's Plantation, and gave good commendations both of his sufficiency and of his godly life and conversation ;

---

[1] Of the Privy Council.

[2] Lord Coventry, late Sir Thomas, was at this time lord keeper of the great seal of England. See Clarendon's Hist. of the Rebellion, i. 80.

[3] Sir John Coke ; not, as might at first be supposed, Edward, the famous Coke upon Littleton, who was then in his 81st year. See Clarendon's Rebellion, i. 113, and Miss Aikin's Charles I. i. 361.

[4] In compliance with this petition, a new proclamation was issued by Charles I. on the 24th of November, 1630, forbidding the disorderly trading with the salvages in New-England in America, especially the furnishing the natives in those and other parts of America by the English with weapons and habiliments of war. See it in Rymer's Fœdera, xix. 210, and in Hazard's State Papers, i. 311.

and of one Mr. Gardner, an able and expert man in
divers faculties ; who are to be further inquired of
and treated with, against the next meeting of the
Company.

It is also thought fit and ordered, that letters be
written to those in the country to pay in what they
are behind upon their subscriptions ; and that some
tradesmen here in London that have occasion to
travel into any of those parts, be desired to receive
the money on the Company's behalf.

And lastly, Mr. Governor read certain propositions conceived by himself,[1] viz. That for the
advancement of the Plantation, the inducing and
encouraging persons of worth and quality to trans-
plant themselves and families thither, and for other
weighty reasons[2] therein contained, to transfer the
government of the Plantation to those that shall
inhabit there, and not to continue the same in subor-
dination to the Company here, as now it is. This
business occasioned some debate ; but by reason of
the many great and considerable consequences thereupon depending, it was not now resolved upon, but
those present are desired privately[3] and seriously to
consider hereof, and to set down their particular
reasons in writing *pro et contra*, and to produce the
same at the next General Court ; where they being
reduced to heads, and maturely considered of, the
Company may then proceed to a final resolution

---

[1] Let it be noted, that Cradock
was at the bottom of this move-
ment.

[2] What these other weighty reasons were, we are left to conjecture.
Considerations of a religious nature
it would not, perhaps, have been

prudent or safe to mention at that
time.

[3] Privately, secretly. This is
noteworthy. They doubtless apprehended that measures might be taken
to defeat their purpose, should it become known to those in authority.

CHAP.
III. thereon.    And in the mean time they are desired to
carry this business secretly,[1] that the same be not
1629. divulged.

———

*A General Court holden at Mr. Deputy's house, the 28th*
*of August,* 1629.    Present,

Aug.
28.

| | |
|---|---|
| Mr. Goff, *Deputy,* | Mr. Nowell, |
| Mr. Harwood, *Treasurer,* | Mr. Foxcroft, |
| Sir Richard Saltonstall, | Mr. Whyte, |
| Mr. Johnson, | Mr. Cooke, |
| Mr. Davenport, | Mr. Ballard, |
| Mr. Humfreys, | Mr. Wright, |
| Mr. Adams, | Mr. Whetcombe, |
| Capt. Venn, | Mr. Smith, |
| Mr. Pocock, | Mr. Revell, |
| Mr. Perry, | Mr. Davis, |
| Mr. Colston, | Mr. Eaton, |
| Mr. Pinchion, | Mr. Colbrand. |
| Mr. Wm. Vassall, | |

Mr. Deputy acquainted this Court, that the especial cause of their meeting was to give answer to
divers gentlemen, intending to go into New-England, whether or no the chief government of the
Plantation, together with the patent, should be settled in New-England, or here.[2]    Whereupon it was
ordered, that this afternoon Mr. Wright, Mr. Eaton,
Mr. Adams, Mr. Spurstowe, and such others as they

———

[1] See note [3] on preceding page.

[2] Only two days before, namely, on the 26th of August, a mutual agreement had been made and signed at Cambridge, by Saltonstall, Winthrop, Johnson, Dudley, Humphrey, Nowell, Pynchon, Thomas Sharpe, William Vassall, and others, that they would embark with their families for the Plantation in New-England, by the first of March next, to inhabit and continue there, provided that before the last of September next the whole government, together with the patent for the said Plantation, be first, by an order of Court, legally transferred and established to remain with them and others who shall inhabit upon the said Plantation.

should think fit to call unto them, whether they were CHAP. III. of the Company or not, to consider of arguments against the settling of the chief government in New-England ; and on the other side, Sir Richard Saltonstall, Mr. Johnson, Capt. Venn, and such others as they should call unto them, to prepare arguments for the settling of the said government in New-England ; and that to-morrow morning, being the 29th of August, at 7 of the clock, both sides should meet and confer and weigh each other's arguments, and afterwards at 9 of the clock, (which is the time appointed of meeting for a General Court,) to make report thereof to the whole Company, who then will determine this business.

1629.
Aug.
28.

---

*A General Court at Mr. Deputy's house, the 29th of August,* 1629.  Present,

29.

| | |
|---|---|
| Mr. Deputy, | Mr. Harwood, *Treasurer,* |
| Sir Richard Saltonstall, | Mr. Perry, |
| Mr. Johnson, | Mr. Foxcroft, |
| Mr. Davenport, | Mr. Davis, |
| Mr. Aldersey, | Mr. Ironsyde, |
| Mr. Humfrey, | Mr. Pinchon, |
| Capt. Waller, | Mr. William Vassall, |
| Capt. Venn, | Mr. Rowe, |
| Mr. Adams, | Mr. Ballard, |
| Mr. Eaton, | Mr. Nowell, |
| Mr. Samuel Vassall, | Mr. Webb, |
| Mr. Wright, | Mr. Whetcombe, |
| Mr. Colston, | Mr. Colbrand. |
| Mr. Pocock, | |

This day the Committees which were appointed to meet yesterday in the afternoon to consider of arguments *pro et contra* touching the settling of the gov-

CHAP.
III.

1629.

Aug.
29.

ernment of the Company's Plantation in New-England, being according to the order of the last Court, met together, debated their arguments and reasons on both sides ; where were present many of the Assistants and Generality ; and after a long debate, Mr. Deputy put it to the question, as followeth :

As many of you as desire to have the patent and the government of the Plantation to be transferred to New-England, so as it may be done legally, hold up your hands. So many as will not, hold up your hands.

When, by erection of hands, it appeared by the general consent of the Company, that the government and patent should be settled in New-England, and accordingly an Order to be drawn up.[1]

---

Sept.
19.

*A General Court holden at Mr. Deputy's house, the 19th of Sept. 1629.  Present,*

MR. MATTHEW CRADOCK, *Governor*,       MR. COLSON,

MR. THOMAS GOFF, *Deputy*,                    MR. PINCHON,

MR. GEORGE HARWOOD, *Treasurer*,       MR. HUTCHINS,

MR. SPURSTOWE,                                       MR. PERRY,

MR. POCOCK,                                              MR. WHETCOMBE,

MR. WRIGHTE,                                            and others.

---

[1] It has been justly remarked that a transaction similar to this in all its circumstances, is not easily to be met with in story. It certainly stands alone in the history of English colonization. The power of the Corporation to make the transfer has been seriously doubted and even denied. It is evident from the Charter, that the original design of it was to constitute a corporation in England like that of the East India and other great Companies, with powers to settle plantations within the limits of the territory, under such forms of government and magistracy as should be fit and necessary. But the boldness of the step is not more striking than the silent acquiescence of the King in permitting it to take place. See the whole matter discussed in Grahame's History of the United States, i. 221–224 ; Robertson's History of America, ch. x. ; Chalmers's Political Annals, p. 151 ; Hutchinson's Mass. i. 13 ; and Story's Commentaries on the Constitution, i. 50.

At this Court letters[1] were read from Capt. Endi- CHAP.
cott and others from New-England. And whereas a
difference hath fallen out betwixt the Governor there 1629.
and Mr. John and Samuel Browne, it was agreed by Sept. 19.
the Court, that for the determination of those differences, Mr. John and Samuel Browne might choose
any three or four of the Company on their behalf, to
hear the said differences, the Company choosing as
many.[2] Whereupon the said Mr. John and Samuel
Browne made choice of Mr. Samuel Vassall,[3] and
Mr. William Vassall, Mr. Symon Whetcombe, and

[1] These letters are unfortunately missing.

[2] This certainly seems to be a very fair course of proceeding towards the Brownes, whose case will be more circumstantially stated hereafter. And yet Chalmers says, "When the persons who had been thus expelled, arrived in England, they naturally applied to the Governor and Company for reparation of their wrongs; but it appears not from their records that they ever received any redress. The insolence of contempt was superadded to the injustice of power. — The General Court was at that time too much occupied in preparing for an important change, to attend to the first duty of all rulers, to give protection to the injured." Chalmers's Political Annals, p. 146.

[3] Samuel Vassall was the son of the gallant John Vassall, an alderman of London, who in 1588, at his own expense fitted out and commanded two ships of war against the Spanish Armada. Samuel was likewise an alderman of London, and an eminent merchant, and represented that city in two successive Parliaments, in 1640 and 1641. In 1628 he was the first who refused to submit to the tax of tonnage and poundage, for which his goods were seized and his person imprisoned by the Star Chamber Court. In July, 1641,

Parliament voted him £10,445 12s. 2d. for the damages he had thus sustained, and resolved that he should be further considered for his imprisonment and personal sufferings. He was one of the 300 members who signed the protestation to support the liberty of Parliament, and subscribed £1200 against the rebels in Ireland, his name appearing at the head of the list. In 1643 he took the covenant, and in 1646 was appointed one of the commissioners for the kingdom of England for the conservation of the peace with Scotland. He never came over to this country, and I have not been able to ascertain when he died. His son John settled in Jamaica, and John's grandson, Florentius Vassall, Esq., of London, in 1766 sent over a marble monument in honor of his great-grandfather, Samuel, which was set up in King's Chapel, in Boston, where it is still to be seen. From the inscription on this monument I have derived the greater part of the preceding account. The late Lord Holland married Elizabeth, a grand-daughter of Florentius Vassall. See Greenwood's Hist. of King's Chapel, pp. 131, 207; Burke's Hist. of the Commoners of Great Britain, i. 499; Rushworth's Hist. Coll. i. 641, Appendix, p. 57; and Mass. Hist. Coll. xxviii. 294.

CHAP.
III.

1629.
Sept.
19.

Mr. William Pinchion ; and for the Company there were chosen Mr. John Whyte, Mr. John Davenport, Mr. Isaac Johnson, and Mr. John Wynthropp ; who, with the Governor or Deputy, are to determine and end the business the first Tuesday in the next term ; and if any of the aforenamed parties be absent, others to be chosen by either [of the] parties in their stead.

For the unlading of the ships now come, viz. the Lion's Whelp and the Talbot, it was desired that the Governor and Deputy would take such order therein as they should think fit.

And lastly for the five boys returned from New-England upon the Talbot, it is to be advised on what course to be taken for their punishment, either by procuring Mr. Recorder his warrant, by complaining to the Judge of the Admiralty, or otherwise.

---

29. *A General Court holden at Mr. Deputy's house, on Tuesday, the 29th of Sept. 1629.   Present,*

| | |
|---|---|
| MR. MATTHEW CRADOCK, *Governor,* | MR. ANDREWS, |
| MR. THOMAS GOFF, *Deputy,* | MR. ROE, |
| CAPT. WALLER, | MR. REVELL, |
| CAPT. VENN, | MR. HUSON, |
| MR. NATHANIEL WRIGHT, | MR. WEBB, |
| MR. THOMAS ADAMS, | MR. WOODGATE, |
| MR. GEORGE FOXCROFT, | MR. PULISTON, |
| MR. RICHARD PERRY, | MR. BATEMAN, |
| MR. NOWELL, | MR. WYNCHE. |
| MR. SYMON WHETCOMBE, | |

At this Court were read the Orders made the 28th and 29th of August last, concerning the transferring of the patent and government of the Plantation into

New-England.   But that business being of great and CHAP.
weighty consequence, is thought fit to be deferred
for determination until Sir Richard Saltonstall, Mr. 1629.
Johnson, and other gentlemen be come up to Lon-    Sept.
don, and may be here present ; and in the mean     29.
time it was propounded that a committee should be
appointed,

To prepare the business ;

To take advice of learned counsel whether the
same may be legally done or no ;

By what way or means the same may be done, to
correspond with and not to prejudice the government here ;

To consider of the time when it will be fit to do it ;

To resolve on whom to confer the government ;
and divers other circumstances material to be resolved on, &c.

The next thing taken into consideration was the
letters from Mr. John and Samuel Browne to divers
of their private friends here in England, whether the
same should be delivered or detained, and whether
they should be opened and read, or not.   And for
that it was to be doubted by probable circumstances,
that they had defamed the country of New-England,
and the Governor and government there, it was
thought fit that some of the said letters should be
opened and publicly read, which was done accordingly ; and the rest to remain at Mr. Deputy's house,
and the parties to whom they are directed to have
notice, and Mr. Governor, Mr. Deputy, Mr. Treasurer, and Mr. Wright, or any two of them, are entreated to be at the opening and reading thereof, to
the end the Company may have notice, if aught be

CHAP.
III.
1629.
Sept.
29.

inserted therein which may be prejudicial to their government or Plantation in New-England. And it is also thought fit that none of the letters from Mr. Samuel Browne shall be delivered, but kept to be made use of against him as occasion shall be offered.

The business of clearing the two ships[1] lately come home, paying and discharging the men, and housing the goods, is recommended to the care of Mr. Deputy, who hath undertaken the same.

It is also thought fit and ordered, that the Secretary shall write out a copy of the former grant to the Earl of Warwick and others,[2] which was by them resigned to this Company, to be presented to his Lordship, he having desired the same.

The Governor moved to know the resolution of the Company concerning buying the ship Eagle; and it was concluded on, as formerly, that the said ship should be bought by those hereafter named, viz.

| | | | |
|---|---|---|---|
| The Governor, | $\frac{1}{8}$ | Mr. Revell, | $\frac{1}{16}$ |
| The Deputy, | $\frac{1}{16}$ | Mr. Aldersey, | $\frac{1}{16}$ |
| Mr. Adams, | $\frac{1}{8}$ | Mr. Milburne, | $\frac{1}{16}$ |
| Mr. Wright, | $\frac{1}{8}$ | Mr. Huson, | $\frac{1}{16}$ |
| Mr. Eaton, | $\frac{1}{16}$ | The Company, | $\frac{1}{8}$ |
| Mr. Whetcombe, | $\frac{1}{16}$ | | |

And Mr. Governor is desired to go on and conclude the bargain upon such terms as he can. And it was

[1] The Lion's Whelp and the Talbot. See page 90.

[2] This was the grant made March 19, 1628, by the Council for the Affairs of New-England to Sir Henry Roswell and his associates, and by them transferred to the Massachusetts Company. Sir Robert Warwick was a member of that Council, and a stanch friend of the New-England Colonies. Winthrop says in his Journal, July 9, 1634, that he "received a letter from the Earl of Warwick, wherein he congratulated the prosperity of our Plantation, and encouraged our proceedings, and offered his help to further us in it." See pp. 28–30, and Savage's Winthrop, i. 137.

further thought fit and resolved on, that this ship, CHAP. being of good force, and bought for the safety and honor and benefit of the Plantation, shall always be 1629. preferred in that voyage before any other ship,[1] and Sept. 29. to have some consideration in her freight above other ships accordingly.

It is also thought fit, for the present raising of money, that sale be made of the beaver skins; and to that purpose a rate was now set upon them of 20s. per pound. And Mr. Nathaniel Wright being here present, is to have time till to-morrow to accept of them at that rate, or to return his answer; and in the mean time the skins not to be sold under that rate, the sale of them being referred to . Mr. Governor and Mr. Deputy.

Also some speech was had concerning the delivery of the petition to the Lords of the Council. But this is deferred till their Lordships' coming to London.

Mr. Treasurer and Mr. Adams are desired to make an abstract of those who are behind with their subscriptions, to the end some course may be taken to call in for those moneys.

For the twelve cows, and three calves, and two mares, and two foals, it is thought fit that they be forthwith sold, rather than kept at charges all this winter; which is recommended to the care of Mr. Bateman and Mr. Huson.

Also concerning the five boys returned in the Talbot, Mr. Whetcombe and Mr. Noell are desired to acquaint Sir Henry Martyn with their misdemeanour,

---

[1] Her name was afterwards changed to the Arbella, in honor of the Lady Arbella, daughter of the Earl of Lincoln, and wife of Isaac Johnson, Esq., one of the Assistants of the Massachusetts Company. See Edward Johnson's Hist. of New-England, in Mass. Hist. Coll. xii. 79.

CHAP.
III.

1629.

Sept.
29.

and to advise what punishment may be inflicted upon them, and how the Company may be legally discharged of them.

Upon the desire of Mr. John and Samuel Browne, it is thought fit and ordered, that they should have a copy of the accusation sent from New-England against them, to the end they may be the better prepared to make answer thereunto.

Mr. Wright is desired to take care of the sale of the clapboard and other wood.

Also, letters from Robert Moulton, the shipwright, and from the coopers and cleavers of wood, consisting of divers particulars, were now read ; which are to be abbreviated, and fitting answers to be made unto them, by the return of the next ships to New-England.

Oct.
15.

*A General Court at the Deputy's house, on Thursday, the 15th of October*, 1629. Present,

| | |
|---|---|
| Mr. Matthew Cradock, *Governor*, | Mr. George Foxcroft, |
| Mr. George Harwood, *Treasurer*, | Mr. Increase Noell, |
| Sir Richard Saltonstall, | Mr. Ballard, |
| Mr. John Davenport, | Mr. Revell, |
| Mr. Isaac Johnson, | Mr. Dudley, |
| Mr. Samuel Aldersey, | Mr. Winthrop, |
| Mr. John Humfry, | Mr. Webb, |
| Mr. Nathaniel Wright, | Mr. Huson, |
| Mr. John Venn, | Mr. Young, |
| Mr. Thomas Adams, | Mr. Whichcoyte, |
| Mr. William Vassall, | Mr. Crane, |
| Mr. Symon Whetcombe, | Mr. Owen Roe,[1] |
| Mr. William Pinchion, | Mr. Ford, |

With divers others of the *Generality*.

---

[1] Owen Rowe was a silk-mercer in London. " In the beginning of the Rebellion," says Anthony Wood, " being a violent Covenanter, and

The especial and only occasion of this meeting
being to consider and resolve of the settling the
trade in New-England, (now upon transferring the
government thither,) for the encouragement as well
of the adventurers in the joint stock here, as of those
who already are, and of others who intend to go over
in person to be planters there, and for their mutual
correspondency and behoof, and the advancement of
the Plantation to the end which was at first intended;
the Court took the same into due and mature consideration; and after a long debate, and sundry opinions given, and reasons why the joint stock, (which
had borne the brunt of the charge hitherto, and was
likely to bear much more,) should have certain commodities appropriate thereunto, for reimbursement
and defrayment thereof, and divers objections being
made to those reasons, all which was largely discussed and well weighed, the Court, in conclusion,

afterwards an Independent, he was by Cromwell's interest made a prime officer (lieutenant colonel, I think) in the militia of London, and became a firebrand in that city, and an enemy to its ancient civil government. In 1648 he was nominated one of the King's judges, sat on the bench when he was several times before them, stood up as consenting when sentence was passed for severing his head from his body, and at length set his hand and seal to the warrant for his execution. About that time he was made keeper of the maga-zines and stores, and received £5000 to buy arms. In 1659, July 7, he was constituted colonel of the mili-tia of the said city by the Rump Parliament, and was then in great favor with them. But in the year after, when his Majesty was restor-ed, and a proclamation thereupon was issued out for all such persons that had sat in judgment on King Charles I. to come in, he surrendered himself; so that after his trial had passed in the sessions-house in the Old-Bailey, he was condemned to perpetual imprisonment, and his es-tate confiscated. What became of him afterwards, I know not." He was scout-master general in Crom-well's army, and being in his suite when he visited Oxford, in May, 1649, he received from the Univer-sity, with his other chief officers, the honorary degree of Master of Arts. In this way we get the above lean but authentic sketch of him from crabbed Anthony. There is a letter of Rowe's to Governor Win-throp, dated Feb. 18, 1636, in which he expresses his desire and intention to come to Massachusetts, where it appears he had cattle and desired a farm. See Wood's Fasti Oxon. ii. 136, (ed. Bliss) ; Carlyle's Crom-well, i. 296, 364 ; Hutchinson's Col-lection, p. 59.

for accommodation of both parts, fell upon a moderation,[1] as followeth, viz.

That the Company's joint stock shall have the
trade of beaver and all other furs in those parts
solely, for the term of seven years from this day, for
and in consideration of the charge that the joint stock
hath undergone already, and is yet annually to bear,
for the advancement of the Plantation.

That for the charge of fortifications, the Company's joint stock to bear the one half, and the planters
to defray the other, viz. for ordnance, munition,
powder, &c.    But for laborers in building of
forts, &c. all men to be employed in an equal proportion, according to the number of men upon the
Plantation, and so to continue until such fit and
necessary works be finished.

That the charge of the ministers now there or that
shall hereafter go to reside there, as also the charge
of building convenient churches, and all other public
works upon the Plantation, be in like manner indifferently borne, the one half by the Company's joint
stock for the said term of seven years, and the other
half by the planters.

That the ordnance already provided for fortification be rated as they cost, as also all powder and
munition whatsoever concerning arms, so as the same
be delivered there for public use; and this to be
accounted as part of the joint stock of the Company.

All which being several times read, was by Mr.
Governor put to the question, and by general consent, by erection of hands, was agreed and concluded
on, and ordered accordingly.

[1] That is, compromise.

And forasmuch as by [a] former Order the patent CHAP. III. and government is to be transferred to New-England, a Committee is appointed, part of the adventurers here, and part of those that intend to go over, viz.

1629. Oct. 15.

| | |
|---|---|
| MR. DAVENPORT, | SIR RICHARD SALTONSTALL,[1] |
| MR. WRIGHT, | MR. JOHNSON, |
| MR. PERRY, | MR. WINTHROP, |
| CAPT. WALLER, | MR. HUMFRY, |
| CAPT. VENN, | MR. DUDLEY, |
| MR. ADAMS, | MR. VASSALL, |
| MR. WHETCOMBE, | MR. PINCHON, and |
| MR. YOUNG, | MR. DOWNING.[2] |
| MR. SPURSTOWE, and | |
| MR. REVELL. | |

Who are desired to meet to-morrow morning, to confer of and draw fit and convenient clauses to be inserted in Articles of Agreement, which may be commodious for either part, and to prepare the same for a Court of Assistants, appointed that afternoon to determine thereof.

[1] Those in the second column, I suppose, intended to go over.

[2] Emanuel Downing was of the Inner Temple, and married a sister of Governor Winthrop. He came over, I suppose, in 1638, for I find it stated in the Colony Records, that on the 14th of December of that year, "Mr. Endicott and Mr. John Winthrop, Jr. had order to give Mr. Emanuel Downing the oath of freedom." He resided at Salem, which he represented five years in the General Court. He, and not Calibute Downing, (as is erroneously stated by Anthony Wood,) was the father of the notorious Sir George Downing. Simon Bradstreet, an Assistant, and afterwards Governor of the Colony, married a daughter of Emanuel Downing. See Wood's Athen. Oxon. iii. 108, (ed. Bliss) ; Hutchinson's Mass. 18, 111 ; Winthrop's N. E. i. 49, 100, ii. 240, 369.

*A Court of Assistants at the Deputy's house, on Friday,*
*the 16th of October, 1629.   Present,*

1629.
Oct.
16.

Mr. Matth. Cradock, *Governor,*

Sir Richard Saltonstall,

Mr. Isaac Johnson,

Mr. Dudley,

Mr. John Humfry,

Mr. William Vassall,

Mr. Revell,

Mr. George Foxcroft,

Mr. Adams,

Mr. G. Harwood, *Treasurer,*

Mr. Winthrop,

Mr. Huson,

Mr. Whetcombe,

Mr. Perry,

Mr. Pocock,

Mr. Spurstowe,

Mr. Pinchon,

Capt. Venn,

Mr. Samuel Vassall.

This Court was appointed to treat and resolve, upon the transferring of the government to New-England, what government shall be held at London, whereby the future charge of the joint stock may be cherished and preserved, and the body politic of the Company remain and increase ;

What persons shall have the charge of the managing of the joint stock both at London and in New-England ; wherein it is conceived fit that Capt. Endecott continue the government there, unless just cause to the contrary.

These and other things were largely discussed ; and it was thought fit and natural that the government of persons be held there, the government of trade and merchandises to be here.

That the joint stock being mutual, both here and there, that some fit persons be appointed for managing thereof in both places.

But for that there is a great debt owing by the joint stock, it was moved that some course might be taken for clearing thereof before the government be

transferred ; and to this purpose it was first thought CHAP.
III.
fit that the accounts should be audited, to see what
the debt is. But the business not admitting any such 1629.
delay, it was desired that Mr. Governor and Mr. Oct.
16.
Treasurer would meet to-morrow, and make an estimate of the debts, and prepare the same against a
meeting to be on Monday next, to determine this
question.

The ship Eagle is to be freighted from Bristol.

Lastly, letters were read and signed to Mr. Endecott, Mr. Skelton, and Mr. Higgison, as appears by
the entries of them in the book of copies of letters.[1]

---

*A Meeting at Mr. Deputy's house, on Monday, the* 19*th
of October,* 1629. Present, 19.

| | |
|---|---|
| MR. MATTHEW CRADOCK, *Governor,* | MR. FOXCROFT, |
| MR. GEORGE HARWOOD, *Treasurer,* | SIR R. SALTONSTALL, |
| MR. NATHANIEL WRIGHT, | MR. ISAAC JOHNSON, |
| CAPT. VENN, | MR. DAVENPORT, |
| MR. PINCHON, | MR. WHYTE, the preacher, |
| MR. WILLIAM VASSALL, | MR. WHYTE,[2] the counsellor, |
| MR. HUSON, | MR. WYNTHROPP, |
| MR. NOELL, | MR. DUDLEY. |
| MR. ADAMS, | |

The occasion of this meeting being to resolve of
the alteration of the government, and therein to con-

---

[1] These letters, in the handwriting of Burgess, the Secretary, are
preserved in the first book of Deeds
in the Registry of Suffolk. The
MS. is probably a part of the original Letter-Book here referred to.
They will be found in another part
of this volume.

[2] This was probably the Mr.
White, described by Clarendon as
"a grave lawyer, but notoriously
disaffected to the Church," who was
chairman of the parliamentary committee on religion in 1640. See
Clarendon's Rebellion, i. 348.

sider how the debts upon the joint stock shall be first discharged, and how the same shall be hereafter managed ; and herein what was formerly treated on was again related. And for that divers questions will arise to be determined in this business, which will take up much time, and cannot be so conveniently done at a Court, it was thought fit that certain committees be appointed, on either part, to meet and make propositions each to other, and set the same down in writing ; and if they can, to agree and conclude of a fit end to be made for the good of the Plantation; and if any differences happen which they cannot agree on, that then the same be referred to the umpirage and determination of some of the preachers, to be chosen to that purpose ; who are desired to set down in writing what they shall think in conscience is fit to be done indifferently for the good of the work and the encouragement both of planters and adventurers. And to this purpose, Articles between the planters and adventurers for performance of what shall be determined, was now drawn by Mr. Whyte, the counsellor, read and approved, and are to be presented to-morrow at a General Court, to be ratified, and then sealed ; and at that Court the Governor and Assistants to be chosen for the government in New-England.

*A General Court holden at Mr. Goff, the Deputy's house,
on Tuesday, the 20th of October, 1629.  Present,*

| | |
|---|---|
| Mr. Matthew Cradock, *Governor,* | Mr. Davenport, ⎫ clerks,[1] |
| Sir Richard Saltonstall, | Mr. Whyte, ⎭ |
| Mr. Isaac Johnson, | Mr. Winthrop, |
| Capt. John Venn, | Mr. Dudley, |
| Mr. [Samuel] Aldersey, | Mr. Puliston, |
| Mr. Nathaniel Wright, | Mr. Ballard, |
| Mr. George Harwood, *Treasurer,* | Mr. Job Bradshaw, |
| Mr. John Humfry, | Mr. Cooke, |
| Mr. William Vassall, | Mr. Revell, |
| Mr. William Pinchon, | Capt. Waller, |
| Mr. George Foxcroft, | Mr. Ballard,[2] |
| Mr. Increase Noell, | Mr. Woodgate, |
| Mr. Christopher Colson, | Mr. Stephens, |
| Mr. Richard Perry, | Mr. Francis Flyer, |
| Mr. Thomas Adams, | Mr. Spurstowe, |
| Mr. John Pocock, | Mr. Huson, |
| Mr. Thomas Hutchins, | Mr. Roe, |
| | Mr. Webb, |

*Assistants.*        With some others of the *Generality.*

Mr. Governor caused to be read the Order formerly
made concerning the buying of the ship Eagle;
and desired to know the pleasure of the Court for
confirmation thereof.  Whereupon some debate being had, the Order was well approved of; but for
that it is wished that the gentlemen that are to go
over should have the ⅛ part of the said ship which
was formerly allotted to the Company, (the Company
being out of cash, and for other reasons,) they not
having notice thereof till now, desired time till the
afternoon to consider thereof, and to give their an

---

[1] Clergymen.
[2] Mr. Ballard's name is probably repeated by mistake.

swer ; which was condescended unto, and the same
is then to be determined accordingly.

After which Mr. Governor acquainted those present, that the especial occasion of summoning this Court was for the election of a new Governor, Deputy, and Assistants, the government being to be transferred into New-England, according to the former Order and resolution of the Company. But before the Court proceeded to the said election, certain Articles of Agreement, conceived at a meeting yesterday between the adventurers here at home and the planters that are to go over, as well for the managing and settling of the joint stock, as for reconciling of any differences that may happen upon this change of government, was now read, and recommended to the Court for their approbation, and for the nomination and appointment of a competent number of committees, to meet and treat and resolve of these businesses. The Articles themselves were approved of, and five committees on either part were thereupon chosen, viz. Sir Richard Saltonstall, Mr. Winthrop, Mr. Dudley, Mr. Johnson, and Mr. Humfry, for the planters ; and for the adventurers was chosen Mr. Governor, Mr. Aldersey, Mr. Wright, Mr. Hutchins, and Capt. Venn. And in case the said committee, or the greater number of them, should differ in any one or more particulars, and not agree thereon, there was chosen for umpires Mr. Whyte, the counsellor, Mr. Whyte, of Dorchester, and Mr. Davenport,[1] to whom the decision and de-

---

[1] John Davenport was born in 1597, at Coventry, of which city his father was mayor. He was educated at Oxford, where he received the degrees of A. M. and B. D. He became a noted preacher among the Puritans, and at length minister of St. Stephen's, Coleman-street,

termination of all such differences is referred, accord- CHAP.<br>III.
ing to the tenure of the said Articles of Agreement.
And it being further taken into consideration, that in 1629.<br>Oct.<br>20.
regard of the shortness of the time limited to the
committees, many things of weight and consequence
in this so great a business may either not be at all
thought on, or otherwise left unresolved, by them
and the said umpires, it is therefore thought fit by
this Court that the said committee and umpires shall
continue till the end of this term ; and whatsoever
material things for the good of the Plantation shall in
that time be treated on and resolved by them, the
same to be as valid and effectual as if it had been
done before the expiration of the time limited by the

---

London. About the year 1627, he was appointed one of the *feoffees* for buying in of impropriations ; concerning which see note [3] on page 70. Being persecuted by the prelates for his nonconformity, and a warrant having been issued by the High Commission to summon him before them, he resigned his benefice Dec. 18, 1633, and fled into Holland. Archbishop Laud says in his annual account to the King, dated Jan. 2, 1634, " Since my return out of Scotland, Mr. John Davenport, vicar of St. Stephen's in Coleman-street, whom I used with all moderation, and about two years after thought I had settled his judgment, [not quite, my Lord !] having him then at advantage enough to have put extremity upon him, but forbore it, hath now resigned his vicarage, declared his judgment against conformity with the Church of England, and is since gone (as I hear) to Amsterdam." Here he preached for some time to the English congregation ; but on the breaking out of the civil wars, he returned to England, as other Nonconformists did, and had a ben- efice bestowed on him. Not being entirely satisfied, however, with the proceedings there, he yielded to the urgent letters of John Cotton, and came over to New-England in June, 1637, with Theophilus Eaton, who had been one of his parishioners in London, and Edward Hopkins, and with them laid the foundations of the Colony of New Haven in 1638. In 1668, in his 71st year, he removed to Boston to become the pastor of the First Church, and died there in 1670. He was buried by the side of Cotton, and near to Governor Winthrop, in the northern corner of King's Chapel grave-yard. Increase Mather wrote some account of his life. See Wood's Athen. Oxon. iii. 889, (ed. Bliss) ; Newcourt's Repertorium, i. 537 ; Laud's Troubles and Trial, pp. 348, 526 ; Mather's Magnalia, i. 226, 292-302 ; Winthrop's N. England, i. 227 ; Hutchinson's Mass. i. 82, 115, 215 ; Emerson's Hist. of the First Church in Boston, pages 110-124 ; Prof. Kingsley's Cent. Discourse, pp. 12, 62 ; Leonard Bacon's Historical Discourses, pp. 75-155.

Articles. And it was further thought fit that all such others of the Company as will, may from time to time have access to the said committee, to propound such things as they conceive beneficial for the business, or to present their opinions in writing, but not to debate with them for interrupting their proceedings.

All which being put to the question, was approved of, and by erection of hands ordered accordingly.

And now the Court proceeding to the election of a new Governor, Deputy, and Assistants, which, upon serious deliberation, hath been and is conceived to be for the especial good and advancement of their affairs ; and having received extraordinary great commendations of Mr. JOHN WYNTHROP,[1] both for

[1] Of JOHN WINTHROP, the first Governor of the Massachusetts Colony, the narrow limits of a Note will not permit us to speak adequately or worthily ; and we must therefore refer those who wish to know the particulars of his life and understand his character, to the memoir in Belknap's Am. Biog. ii. 337–358, to the account given by Mather, in the Magnalia, i. 108–120, and to his own Journal, or History of New-England, (with Savage's invaluable notes,) and his admirable letters appended to both volumes of that work. Suffice it now to say, that he was born at Groton, in Suffolk, Jan. 12, 1588, · and was descended from an ancient and honorable family. He was bred to the law, as his ancestors had been before him, one of them, Adam Winthrop, having been an eminent lawyer in the reign of Henry VIII. Such was the gravity and steadiness of his character, that, at the early age of eighteen, he was made a justice of the peace. " He had an estate of six or seven hundred pounds a year, which he turned into money, and embarked his all to promote the settlement of New-England. It is a very full evidence of the esteem in which he was held, that, when many gentlemen of character, some of them of noble alliance, were concerned in the same undertaking with him, he, by a general voice, was placed at their head." He says himself, " I was first chosen to be Governor without my seeking or expectation, there being then divers other gentlemen who, for their abilities every way, were far more fit." He was eleven times chosen Governor, and spent his whole estate in the public service. His son John, and his grandson, Fitz-John, (who was a captain in Col. Read's regiment at the Restoration in 1660,) were successively governors of Connecticut Colony, and Wait Still, another grandson, was chief justice of Massachusetts. Stephen, another son of the elder Winthrop, went to England in 1645 or 1646, had the command of a regiment, and succeeded Harrison in his major-generalship, was a member of Parliament for Scotland in 1656, and was

his integrity and sufficiency, as being one every CHAP.
[way[1]] well fitted and accomplished for the place of III.
Governor, did put in nomination for that place the 1629.
said Mr. John Winthrop, Sir Richard Saltonstall, Oct.
Mr. Isaac Johnson, and Mr. John Humfry; and the 20.
said Mr. Winthrop was with a general vote and full
consent of this Court, by erection of hands, chosen
to be Governor for the ensuing year, to begin on
this present day; who was pleased to accept thereof,
and thereupon took the oath to that place appertaining.

much trusted by the Protector. The family, in every generation, have occupied high stations, and been deservedly held in great respect in New-England. Its character is now worthily sustained by the Hon. Robert C. Winthrop, who represents the city of Boston in the Congress of the United States. Gov. Winthrop was in his 43d year when he sailed for New-England. He died March 26, 1649, in the 62d year of his age, and was buried, April 3d, in the northern corner of the King's Chapel burial-ground, in Boston. His son John, governor of Connecticut, was interred in the same tomb in April, 1676. "The Green," the Governor's town lot, included the land now owned by the Old South Church in Washington-street, and his house stood about opposite School-street. Prince, the Annalist, who died in 1758, says that Winthrop "deceased in the very house I dwell in." It was a two-story building, of wood, and remained till it was destroyed by the British troops for fuel in 1775. The Governor's portrait, an original painting, hangs in the Senate Chamber of Massachusetts. — "Sept. 6, 1631, there is granted to Mr. Governor, 600 acres of land, near his house at Mistick." This was then and has ever since been called the Tenhills Farm. April 3, 1632, Conant's Island, in Boston harbor, on which

Fort Warren is built, was granted to him, and the name was changed to the Governor's Garden. "Nov. 7, 1632, there is about fifty acres of meadow ground granted to John Winthrop, Esq., present Governor, lying between Cobbett's house and Wanottymies' river;" and, March 4, 1634, the wear at Mistick was granted to him and Matthew Cradock, of London. — It is much to be regretted that Gov. Winthrop's "larger discourse of all things," mentioned in a letter to his wife, July 16, 1630, and twice afterwards referred to in his letters to his son, July 23 and Aug. 14, is lost. It may have contained interesting statements, not included in his Journal or History. — In his magnanimity, disinterestedness, and moderation, in his mingled firmness of principle and mildness of temper, in his harmonious character, consistent life, and well-balanced mind, the Father of Massachusetts reminds us of the great "Father of his country," and is the only name in our history worthy to stand as a parallel to WASHINGTON. See Mass. Col. Records, in MS., i. 82, 85, 95, 131; Hutchinson's Mass. i. 14, 151; Savage's Winthrop, i. 64–68, 126, 318, 396; ii. 338, 357, 372, 373, 376; Thurloe's State Papers, v. 366.

[1] This word seems to have been accidentally omitted.

CHAP.
III.

1629.
Oct.
20.

In like manner, and with like free and full consent, Mr. John Humfry[1] was chosen Deputy Governor, and

| | |
|---|---|
| SIR RICHARD SALTONSTALL, | MR. THOMAS SHARPE, |
| MR. ISAAC JOHNSON, | MR. JOHN REVELL, |
| MR. THOMAS DUDLEY, | MR. MATTHEW CRADOCK, |
| MR. JOHN ENDECOTT, | MR. THOMAS GOFF, |
| MR. INCREASE NOELL, | MR. [SAMUEL] ALDERSEY, |
| MR. WILLIAM VASSALL, | MR. JOHN VENN, |
| MR. WILLIAM PINCHON, | MR. NATHANIEL WRIGHT, |
| MR. SAMUEL SHARPE, | MR. THEOPHILUS EATON, and |
| MR. EDWARD ROSSITER, | MR. THOMAS ADAMS, |

were chosen to be Assistants. Which said Deputy,

---

[1] John Humphrey, it will be recollected, was one of the six original patentees to whom the grant of Massachusetts Bay was made by the Council of Plymouth. See page 29. He was also one of the original patentees of the Colony of Connecticut. It will be seen presently, that he stayed behind, and did not come over with Winthrop, as he intended. He married Susan, daughter of Thomas, the third Earl of Lincoln, and brought her with their children to Massachusetts in 1632, and settled at Swampscot, in Lynn. In expectation of his arrival, he was chosen an Assistant, and continued to be re-elected to that office as long as he remained in the Colony. John Cotton, in a letter to Lord Saye and Sele, written in 1636, says, "Mr. Humfrey was chosen for an Assistant (as I hear) before the Colony came over hither; and though he be not as yet joined into church fellowship (by reason of the unsettledness of the congregation where he liveth,) yet the Commonwealth do still continue his magistracy to him, as knowing he waiteth for opportunity of enjoying church fellowship shortly." He was admitted to the church in Salem Jan. 16, 1638. Upon an invitation from Lord Say, he intended, in the year 1640, to have removed to the Bahama Islands; but the island of Providence being taken by the Spaniards, he abandoned that design. Soon after, having met with great losses by fire, and his estate being much impaired, he sold his farm at Swampscot to Lady Moody, (for nine or eleven hundred pounds, says Lechford,) and returned to England October 26, 1641. This estate probably included the 500 acres given him by the General Court May 6, 1635, in fulfilment of the resolve passed Nov. 7, 1632, by which "it is referred to Mr. Turner, Peter Palfry and Roger Conant to set out a proportion of land in Saugus to John Humfry, Esq." Winthrop speaks of him as "a gentleman of special parts of learning and activity, and a godly man, who had been one of the first beginners in the promoting of this Plantation, and had labored very much therein." A letter of his to Winthrop, dated Sept. 4, 1646, is preserved in Hutchinson's Collection, p. 159. See Mass. Col. Records, in MS., i. 95, 149; Winthrop's N. E., i. 75, 332, ii. 13, 26, 46; Hutchinson's Mass. i. 15, 493, 498; Mass. Hist. Coll. xxiii. 97; Hazard's State Papers, i. 318; Trumbull's Connecticut, i. 495.

and the greatest part of the said Assistants, being CHAP. present, took the oaths to their said places appertaining respectively.

*A Court of Assistants, at Mr. Goff's house, on Friday, the 20th of November, 1629. Present,*

| | |
|---|---|
| Mr. John Wynthrop, *Governor*, | Mr. Thomas Goff, |
| Mr. John Humfry, *Dep. Gov.* | Mr. William Pinchion, |
| Sir Richard Saltonstall, | Mr. [Christopher] Colson, |
| Mr. Thomas Dudley, | Mr. Matthew Cradock, |
| Mr. Thomas Adams, | Mr. George Harwood, |
| Mr. Nathaniel Wright, | Mr. John Revell, |
| Mr. [Thomas] Hutchins, | Mr. Increase Noell. |

The especial occasion of this meeting was to advise of a course for bringing in of moneys for payment of mariners' wages, freight of ships, and other debts. And thereupon Mr. Cradock acquainted those present what sums he had disbursed for account of the Company, and what more was owing for mariners' wages upon the ships Talbot, Mayflower, and Four Sisters,[1] and for the freight of those ships, amounting to £1200 and upwards; which the Court think fit and order to be first paid before any other debts. And Mr. Governor desiring to have power from the Court to grant warrants for payment of moneys, as was formerly accustomed, the same was condescended unto; and a warrant was now made and signed by the Governor and Deputy, directed to Mr. Harwood, the Treasurer, for payment of [£]800 to Mr. Cradock, so soon as money shall come to his hands.

---

[1] Which had lately returned from New-England, having carried over Higginson and his company.

CHAP.
III.

1629.
Nov.
20.

Some debate was had concerning Mr. John and Samuel Browne's complaining that their goods, praised[1] in New-England, are undervalued, and divers things omitted to be praised ;[1] wherein they desire to have relief, and justice done. It is thereupon thought fit, that if they can produce proof thereof, then they are to be relieved here ; otherwise, the same is to be suspended, and all the objections they can make to be taken notice of and recommended to Mr. Governor, to be considered of and determined after his arrival in New-England, when he may hear the praisers' answers to those objections ; and in the mean time Mr. Cradock to pay the money charged upon him for the same.

Mr. Beecher, master of the ship Talbot, desired to have in a bond, which he entered into, to Mr. Pratt[2] for wages or allowance to a chirurgeon for the Lion's Whelp, who was to have 2s. 6d. for every person in the ship, according to an agreement made with them ; the number of the persons being about 125, of which Mr. Beecher had formerly delivered a particular note to Mr. Goff. The Court conceiving the said allowance to be exorbitant, and more than is usual in like cases, do desire that the chirurgeon be appointed to be here the next General Court, and then such conclusion is to be made with him as shall be fit.

Lastly, Mr. Smith, the accomptant, attended them with their accounts ; and after perusal thereof, it appearing that divers were behind with their whole subscriptions or part thereof, it was thought fit that,

---

[1] Appraised.      [2] See note [1] on page 52.

for the present supply of moneys, tickets should be CHAP.<br>III.
sent unto them to desire them to send in the sums
by them underwritten ; to which purpose a list of 1629.
their names and sums was now drawn out, and tick- Nov.<br>20.
ets are forthwith to be made accordingly.

---

*A General Court on Wednesday, the 25th of November,*   25.
          1629.   Present,

| | |
|---|---|
| Mr. John Winthrop, *Governor,* | Mr. Matthew Cradock, |
| Mr. John Humfry, *Deputy,* | Capt. Waller, |
| Sir Richard Saltonstall, | Mr. Whyte, |
| Mr. Isaac Johnson, | Mr. Davenport, |
| Mr. Thomas Adams, | Mr. Huson, |
| Mr. Nathaniel Wright, | Mr. Backhouse, |
| Mr. Theophilus Eaton, | Mr. Foxcroft, |
| Mr. William Pinchion, | Mr. Woodgate, |
| Capt. Venn, | Mr. Bradshaw, |
| Mr. Increase Noell, | and others. |

A letter[1] of the 5th of September from Mr. Ende-
cot, the Governor, and others in New-England, was
now read ; as also Mr. Governor acquainted those
present with certain testimonies sent over against one
William Rovell, master of a ship of [blank], concerning some insolent and misbeseeming speeches uttered
by him in contempt of the Company's privileges and
government ; which is to be taken into further consideration, and be proceeded against, when other
certificates are come, which are expected, concerning that business.

    This day being one one of the four quarter days
appointed by the Charter for keeping a General

---

[1] This letter is not preserved.

Court, the general business of the Plantation should
have been treated on. But by reason of the small
appearance, and shortness of time, nothing was done
therein. Only the Governor made relation of the
proceedings of the joint committee concerning the
settling of the joint stock ; that notwithstanding
there had been all good concordancy and fair proceedings between them, yet by reason of the greatness of the business and the smallness of the supplies,
they could not bring the same to a wished effect, but
only had reduced it to certain propositions, to be
represented to the consideration of the Company to
receive their resolution therein.

The accomptant having made an estimate of the
accounts, the joint stock appears to be in arrear
£3000, and upwards. Towards which £3000 there
is [£]1900 in subscriptions not yet brought in, and
about 8 or £900 upon freight of ships.

There will be a necessity for supply of necessaries
for the Company's servants,    .   .   £2000[1]

For merchandises for trade,    .   .   500

For munition and artillery for fortification, 500

So as there being an inevitable necessity of [a]
supply of money, either to revive the old stock or to
raise a new, the propositions were now expressed, viz.

1. That all the former adventurers should double
their former subscriptions.

2. That the servants, cattle, and all merchandises
or provisions belonging to the joint stock, should be
sold, and the underwriters be paid their proportions of what shall accrue or arise thereof.

---

[1] Felt, Annals of Salem, i. 141, errs in making this £1000.

3. Or lastly, that the old stock be put over to cer- CHAP. III.
tain undertakers, upon such conditions as can be ——
agreed on, and they to go on with the work and 1629. Nov.
manage the business, to bear all charges, and to 25.
stand to profit and loss, and to pay the underwriters
their principal by them brought, at the end of seven
years ; and this to be understood not to exclude any
who have affection to this business, but that they may
come in under those undertakers for such sums as
they shall think fit to adventure ; but that for the
better furtherance and facilitating the business, the
same to be managed by few hands. And for the encouragement of such undertakers, the committee
have thought of certain inducements, viz.

That they shall have

The one half of the beaver ;

The sole making of salt ;

The sole transportation of passengers, — servants
and goods to be transported at reasonable rates;

To be allowed a reasonable profit upon all such
provisions as they shall keep in magazine there for
the use and relief of the inhabitants.

All which premises the Governor recommended
to the consideration of those present. But by reason
of the small appearance, nothing could be determined ; and therefore a special Court is appointed for
this purpose on Monday next, and the whole Company to be summoned by tickets to be present.

Lastly, upon the motion of Mr. Whyte, to the end
that this business might be proceeded in with the
first intention, which was chiefly the glory of God,
and to that purpose that their meetings might be

CHAP. sanctified by the prayers[1] of some faithful ministers
III.
—⁓— resident here in London, whose advice would be
1629. likewise requisite upon many occasions, the Court
Nov.
25. thought fit to admit into the freedom of this Company[2] Mr. John Archer[3] and Mr. Philip Nye,[4] ministers here in London, who being here present kindly
accepted thereof. Also Mr. Whyte did recommend
unto them Mr. Nathaniel Ward,[5] of Standon.

[1] This shows the antiquity of the practice, still observed in Massachusetts, of opening the meetings of the Legislature, or General Court, with prayer.

[2] This admission of freemen was authorized by the Charter of the Company, and was a practice long observed in the Colony. The Charter provides, that "the Governor and Company shall have full power and authority to choose, nominate and appoint such and so many as they shall think fit, and that shall be willing to accept the same, to be *free* of the said Company and Body, and them into the same to admit."

[3] I can find no account of John Archer in Newcourt's Repertorium Ecclesiasticum, nor in any of the ecclesiastical registers. I doubt therefore whether he was a minister of London. There may be an error perhaps in the Christian name.

[4] Philip Nye was born in 1596, and was educated at Magdalen Hall, Oxford, where he took the degree of A. M. in 1622. In 1630, according to Anthony Wood, he was curate of St. Michael's church in Cornhill, London. In 1633 he fled from Laud's persecutions into Holland, and became minister of a church at Arnheim, where he remained till the end of 1640, at the opening of the Long Parliament, when he returned to England. In 1643 he was appointed one of the Assembly of Divines, and the same year was sent by the Parliament into Scotland, with Sir Henry Vane, jr. and Stephen Marshall, whose daughter he

had married, as commissioners to ask for assistance and expedite the Covenant. He was one of the chaplains who attended the commissioners to Charles I. in the Isle of Wight in December, 1647, and was made one of the *Triers* of preachers in 1653. He was the principal person in managing the meeting of the Congregational Churches at the Savoy, by the Protector's order, held Oct. 12, 1658. At the Restoration in 1660, it was debated in Parliament whether he should be excepted from the bill of indemnity, and his life was spared solely on condition that he should never hold any office, civil, ecclesiastical, or military. He died in 1672, aged 76. See Wood's Athen. Oxon. iii. 963, Fasti, i. 386, 406 ; Clarendon's Rebellion, iv. 153.

[5] Nathaniel Ward, the eccentric and facetious author of "The Simple Cobbler of Agawam in America," was the son of John Ward, a celebrated Puritan divine, and was born at Haverhill, in Suffolk, of which town his father was minister, about the year 1570. He was entered at Emanuel College, Cambridge, in 1596, and took the degree of A. M. in 1603. He was originally intended for the law ; but travelling on the continent, he fell in at Heidelberg with the learned David Paræus, by whom his mind was turned to theology. On his return to England, he became preacher at St. James's, Duke's Place, London, in 1626, and afterwards was rector of Standon Massye, in Essex, 16

*A General Court at Mr. Goff's house, on Monday, the*
*last of November*, 1629. Present,

Mr. JOHN WINTHROP, *Governor,*

Mr. JOHN HUMFRY, *Deputy,*

Mr. GEORGE HARWOOD, *Treasurer,*

| | |
|---|---|
| SIR RICHARD SALTONSTALL, | MR. THOMAS ADAMS, |
| MR. ISAAC JOHNSON, | MR. THEOPHILUS EATON, |
| MR. THOMAS GOFF, | MR. INCREASE NOELL, |
| MR. THOMAS DUDLEY, | MR. JOHN REVELL, |
| MR. NATHANIEL WRIGHT, | MR. WILLIAM PINCHON, |
| MR. MATTHEW CRADOCK, | *Assistants.* |

With many of the *Generality.* — 25.

It was propounded to the Court that whereas the joint stock was engaged to the value of £2500, present debt, and there was necessarily required £1500

miles from London, where he felt the iron hand of the intolerant Laud. There is extant a letter of his, written to John Cotton, Dec. 13, 1631, in which he says, " I was yesterday convented before the bishop, I mean to his court, and am adjourned to the next term. I expect measure hard enough, and must furnish apace with proportionable armor." Having been excommunicated and deprived of his clerical office for nonconformity, he came over to Massachusetts in 1634, and was soon chosen pastor of the church in Ipswich, from which office he was discharged at his own request in 1636. In 1641 he was chosen by the freemen of the Colony, without the consent of the Governor and magistrates, to preach the Election Sermon. At the request of the General Court he composed " The Body of Liberties," which in Dec. 1641, was adopted by them, and was the first Code of Laws established in New-England. Winthrop, in recording this transaction, says that Ward " had been formerly a student and practiser in the course of the common law ; " and the learn-ed editor of the Code remarks that " The Body of Liberties exhibits throughout the hand of the practised lawyer, familiar with the principles and the securities of English liberty." In 1647 he returned to England, and became minister of Shenfield, in Essex, where he died, aged about 83. Fuller places him among the learned writers of Emanuel College, Cambridge, and also mentions him in his Worthies of England, ii. 344. " The Simple Cobbler of Agawam," by which he is now best known, was written in this country, and printed at London in 1647, and reprinted at Boston in 1686 and again in 1843. A good account of it and its author may be seen in the Monthly Anthology, vi. 341. Mr. Savage speaks of it as a " work very attractive for its humor, and curious for its execrable spirit." See Col. Records, i. 217, 317, MS. ; Mather's Magnalia, i. 470 ; Hutchinson's Mass. i. 120 ; Winthrop's N. E. i. 154, 322, ii. 35, 55 ; Mass. Hist. Coll. xiv. 2, xxviii. 190–237, 248, 9 ; Newcourt's Repertorium, i. 917, ii. 545.

present disbursement for maintenance of the servants
now in the Plantation, and for commodities for truck
1629. and munition, that the adventurers would be pleased
Nov.
30. to double their former subscriptions. Which being
not assented unto by the Court, it was propounded
and agreed by general consent, that ten persons
should be chosen, five of the adventurers, and five of
the planters, who should take the joint stock at the
true value, and take upon them the engagements and
other charges ; for which there should be appropriated to the joint stock, for seven years, these privileges which follow, viz.

    1. Half the trade of the beavers, and all other furs,

    2. The sole making of salt,

    3. The furnishing of a magazine at set rates,

    4. The sole transportation of passengers and goods
        at certain rates.

For which end there was a committee appointed
to value the joint stock, viz. Mr. White,[1] of Dorchester, Mr. Thomas Goff, Mr. Webb, Mr. Increase Noell ; who taking upon them the charge of the said
Dec.
1. business, did the next day (the Court then sitting
upon adjournment,) make certificate of their proceedings to this effect, viz.

That whereas divers sums had been disbursed in
public charges, as transporting of ministers and their
families, ammunition, &c., which were not now to
be valued to the undertakers, as being to remain

---

[1] Here we take leave of the venerable patriarch of Dorchester, and
have only to regret that he never
came over to see the Colony, in
whose welfare he took so early and
deep an interest. Although he lived
at a distance of 120 miles from London, it has been seen that he frequently came up to attend the Courts
of the Company. See an account of
him on page 26.

always to the Plantation ; and whereas many of the CHAP.<br>III.
servants, which were transported at extraordinary
charge, do not prove so useful as was expected, and 1629.
so will not yield the undertakers any such benefit as Dec.<br>1.
may answer their charge ; divers of the cattle and
provisions likewise miscarrying, through want of experience in the beginning of such a work, they could
not find the said stock to remain clear and good (the
debts discharged) above one third part of the whole
sum which hath been adventured from the first to
this present day ; which value, upon due examination and long debate, was allowed by all the Court.

Whereupon it was propounded and agreed by the
whole Court, that the old adventurers, (in lieu of this
abatement of two-thirds of their adventures,) should
have an addition of a double proportion of land, according to the first proportion of two hundred acres
for £50 ; and that they should have liberty to put in
what sums they pleased to be added to their former
adventures, so as they subscribed the same before
the first day of January now next following ; and
such as live in the country, remote from the city of
London, to enter their subscriptions before the second of February next ; and that any of the said
adventurers may take out their adventures after the
aforesaid rate ; and further, that it should be lawful
for all other persons (with consent of any three of
the undertakers) to put in what sums of money they
please, to be traded in the joint stock, (upon such
allowance to the common stock for public uses, in
regard that they shall bear no part in the former
losses,) as the said adventurers, or three of them,
shall agree with them for, from time to time ; and

CHAP.
III.

1629.
Dec.
1.

that all adventurers shall pay in their adventures in such time and manner as shall be agreed between them and the said undertakers, or any three of them. It was also agreed by the Court, that in regard the undertakers should bear the greatest charge and burthen, and all other adventurers should have equal part of the gain, if any did proceed, that therefore they should have £5 in the hundred clear gains of the said joint stock, both in and out, all charges being deducted.

And that the joint stock being thus managed, at the end of seven years, (to be accounted from this day,) as well the said stock, as the proceed and profit thereof, to be divided to every man proportionably, according to his adventure ; and all the said privileges then to cease, and all persons to be at liberty to dispose of their parts in the joint stock at their own pleasures.[1]

Hereupon the Court thought fit to desire the gentlemen hereunder named to undertake the joint stock upon the terms before propounded, viz.

MR. JOHN WINTHROP, *the Gov.*
SIR RICHARD SALTONSTALL, Knt.
ISAAC JOHNSON, ESQ.
MR. THOMAS DUDLEY,
MR. JOHN REVELL,

MR. MATTHEW CRADOCK,
MR. NATHANIEL WRIGHT,
MR. THEOPHILUS EATON,
MR. THOMAS GOFF,
MR. JAMES YOUNG.

Which gentlemen, upon much entreaty of the Court, did accept of the said charge, and accordingly were chosen to be undertakers, to have the sole

---

[1] "We have no account of any dividend ever made, nor indeed of any trade ever carried on for the Company." Hutchinson, i. 13.

managing of the joint stock, with all things incident
thereunto, for the space of seven years ; as is aforesaid.

And it was agreed to desire and nominate Mr. Aldersey to be Treasurer for the said Company ; and
that all moneys which shall come in to the joint stock,
or that shall be given to the common stock, shall be
paid unto him, and to be issued out upon warrant
under the hands of the said undertakers, or any three
of them, as occasion shall require.

It was also ordered by the Court, that the undertakers should provide a sufficient number of ships, of
good force, for transporting of passengers, at the rate
of £5 a person, and £4 a ton for goods ; which shall
be ready to set sail from London by the first day of
March ; and that if any passengers be to take ship
at the Isle of Wight, the ships shall stop there twenty-four hours ; and that all such as intend to pass
over shall give in their names, with 40s. towards
their freight, to one of the said undertakers abiding
in London, in the Michaelmas term before, and shall
deliver their goods on shipboard before the 20th of
February following ; and shall give security for the
rest of their freight, as they can agree with the said
undertakers, either for money to be paid here, or for
commodity to be delivered in the Plantation.

Further it was agreed, that for the transportation
of children, this rate shall be kept, viz. sucking children not to be reckoned ; such as under four years
of age, three for one ; under eight, two for one ;
under twelve, three for two. And that a ship of
200 tons shall not carry above 120 passengers complete ; and so of other ships, after the same propor-

tion. And for goods homewards, the freight shall be, for beavers £3 per ton, and for other commodities 40s. per ton ; and such as will have their goods assured, shall pay £5 per c.

Concerning the magazine, it is likewise agreed, that the undertakers should furnish the Plantation with all such commodities as they shall send for ; and the planters to take them off and retail them at their pleasure, allowing the undertakers £25 in the hundred above all charges, and the planters to have liberty to dispose of their part of the beavers at their own will ; and every man may fetch or send for any commodity for his own use, where or how he please, so as he trade not with interlopers, so long as he may be furnished sufficiently by the adventurers at the rates aforesaid.

Lastly, it is ordered, that in regard this Court could not set down particular direction for everything which may be fit to be considered and provided for in all or any of the matters aforesaid, therefore the said undertakers should have power to meet and consult about the premises ; and what orders and directions they, or the greater number of them, shall set down, shall be accounted legal, and to be duly observed, until it shall be thought fit by this Court to alter or determine the same.

Provided always, that if those that intend to inhabit upon the Plantation shall, before the first of January next, take upon them all the said engagements and other charges of the joint stock, then the power and privileges of the undertakers to determine, and all the trade, &c. to be free.

*A General Court, holden at Mr. Goff's house, on the* CHAP.
*15th of December,* 1629. Present,

III.

1629.

MR. JOHN HUMFRY, *Deputy,* Dec.

| | | |
|---|---|---|
| SIR RICHARD SALTONSTALL, | MR. WILLIAM PINCHION, | 15. |
| MR. MATTHEW CRADOCK, | MR. INCREASE NOELL, | |
| MR. NATHANIEL WRIGHT, | CAPT. VENN, | |
| MR. JOHN REVELL, | MR. THOMAS ADAMS, | |
| MR. GEORGE HARWOOD, | *Assistants.* | |

With divers of the *Generality.*

Mr. Deputy caused to be read the Acts and Orders made at the last General Court of the 30th of
November; which being of great consequence, as
namely for settling the joint stock, and managing of
the whole business, it was desired the same should
receive confirmation by this Court. Upon debate
whereof, some exceptions were taken by those who
had doubled their adventures, conceiving themselves
to be wronged in having both their sums drawn down
to so low a rate as one third part; alleging that the
second sum was paid in upon a proposition of trade,
which went not forward, and not as unto the joint
stock for the Plantation.

This business received a large discussion, and
Capt. Waller and Mr. Vassall were content to give
the first £50 to the Plantation, so as their other £50
might go on wholly in this new stock. But forasmuch as this concerned divers others who were in
the same case, and that it could not be done without
alteration of the Act made the 30th of November,
which was done by a General Court, upon mature
and deliberate consideration, and that the undertakers would not continue their said undertaking but

CHAP.
III.
1629.
Dec.
15.

upon the same conditions, which were then propounded and concluded on,

This Court, in conclusion, put it to the question, and by erection of hands every particular of the former Court was ratified and confirmed. And the matter in difference with them who had doubled their adventures being no more to each of them than between £50 and £33 6s. 8d., was by mutual consent referred to the three ministers here present, Mr. Davenport, Mr. Nye, and Mr. Archer, who are to reconcile the same between the new undertakers and them.

1630.
Feb.
10.

*A General Court, holden at Mr. Goff's house, on Wednesday, the 10th of February, 1629. Present,*

MR. JOHN WINTHROP, *Governor,*
MR. JOHN HUMFRY, *Deputy,*

| | |
|---|---|
| MR. ISAAC JOHNSON, | MR. INCREASE NOELL, |
| MR. MATTHEW CRADOCK, | MR. NATHANIEL WRIGHT, |
| MR. THEOPHILUS EATON, | MR. JOHN REVELL, |
| MR. THOMAS ADAMS, | MR. WILLIAM PINCHON, |
| MR. GEORGE HARWOOD, | |

With many others of the *Generality.*

Forasmuch as the furtherance of the Plantation will necessarily require a great and continual charge, which cannot with convenience be defrayed out of the joint stock of the Company, which is ordained for the maintenance of the trade, without endangering the same to be wasted and exhausted, it was therefore propounded that a common stock should be raised from such as bear good affection to the Plantation and the propagation thereof, and the same to be employed only in defrayment of public charges, as maintenance of ministers, transportation of poor fam-

ilies, building of churches[1] and fortifications, and all
other public and necessary occasions of the Plantation. And the Court do think fit and order that two
hundred acres of land shall be allotted for every £50,
and so proportionably for what sums shall be brought
in by any to this purpose. And Mr. George Harwood is chosen Treasurer for this account of the
common stock, which he accepted of; who is to receive all such money as shall be by any sent in, and
to issue out the same upon warrant under the hands
of any two or more of the undertakers. And it is
further agreed on and ordered, that an Order be
drawn up and published under the seal of the Company, to signify and declare to what uses all such
moneys as are given to the common stock shall be
employed, and what land shall be allotted to each
man that gives thereunto, as well for their satisfaction as the encouragement of others to so laudable
and charitable a work ; and it was further taken into
consideration, and ordered, that this allotment or
division of land shall not prejudice the right of any
the adventurers who are to have land, and have not
yet the same allotted out unto them, nor unto those
whose land is already set out according to the
former order and direction of this Court. Yet,
nevertheless, it is further agreed, that if for good
and weighty reasons, and for the benefit of the Plantation in general, there shall be occasion to alter any

---

[1] Thus houses of public worship
are also called *churches*, at the Court
held Oct. 15th of the preceding year.
See page 96. The word *meeting-*
*house* was a later innovation, which
sprang up in this country, and
ought to have been long ago suppressed.

CHAP.  particular man's allotment, the said party is to have
III.
~~~~  such due recompense for the same as, in the wisdom
1630.  of the Governor and Company, there resident, shall
Feb.  be thought reasonable and expedient.
10.

Motion was made on the behalf of Sir William
Brewerton,[1] who, by virtue of a late patent pretends
right and title to some part of the land within the
Company's privileges and Plantation, in New-England ; yet nevertheless he is content (intends)[2] not
to contest with the Company, but desires that a proportionable quantity of land might be allotted unto
him for the accommodation of his people and servants now to be sent over. Which request the
Court taking into due consideration, do not think fit
to enter into any particular capitulation with him
therein, nor to set out any allotment of land for him
more than the six hundred acres he is to have by
virtue of his adventure in the joint stock, nor to acknowledge anything due unto him as of right, by
virtue of his said patent, nor to give any consideration in case he should relinquish his pretended right;
but they are well content he should join with them
in the prosecution of this business, according to their
Charter, and do promise in the mean time, that such
servants as he shall send over to inhabit upon the
Plantation, shall receive all courteous respect, and
be accommodated with land, and what else shall be
necessary, as other the servants of the Company.
Which answer was delivered unto those that were
sent from him ; and the Court desired also that Capt.

---

[1] See note [2] on page 51.

[2] In the original MS. thus— $\frac{\text{intends}}{\text{is content.}}$

Waller and Mr. Eaton[1] would signify the Company's
affection and due respect unto him, he having written
to them about this business.

A writing of grievances of Mr. Samuel and John
Browne was presented to this Court, wherein they
desire recompense for loss and damage sustained by
them in New-England ; which this assembly taking
into consideration, do think fit that upon their sub-
mitting to stand to the Company's final order for
ending of all differences between them, (which they
are to signify under their hands,) Mr. Wright and
Mr. Eaton are to hear their complaint, and to set
down what they in their judgments shall think requisite to be allowed them for their pretended damage
sustained, and so to make a final end with them accordingly.

Mr. Roger Ludlowe[2] was now chosen and sworn

---

[1] Theophilus Eaton, the father of
the Colony of New-Haven, was
born about the year 1590, at Stony
Stratford, in Oxfordshire, of which
place his father was the minister.
He was educated at Coventry,
whither his father had removed,
and at school formed an intimate
acquaintance and friendship with
John Davenport, son of the mayor
of the city, whose parishioner he
afterwards became in London, and at
whose instigation he came to New-
England. Eaton was a wealthy
London merchant, largely engaged
in business, and deputy-governor of
the company of merchant adventurers that carried on the Baltic trade.
So great was his judgment and experience, gained by travel and practice in affairs, that he was sent by
Charles I. as his agent to the court
of Denmark. In company with Davenport he arrived at Boston, June
26, 1637, and on the 30th of March,
1638, they sailed with their associ-

ates for the place which they afterwards called New-Haven. On the
25th of October, 1639, he was chosen governor of the infant Colony,
to which office he was annually re-
elected till his death, Jan. 7, 1658, a
period of more than eighteen years.
See Hubbard's Hist. N. E. 317, 329 ;
Mather's Magnalia, i. 136 ; Winthrop's Hist. i. 228, 237, 259, 405 ;
Trumbull's Connecticut, i. 95–100,
231 ; Kingsley's Cent. Discourse at
New-Haven, pp. 11, 75 ; and Bacon's Hist. Discourses, pp. 109, 354.

[2] Roger Ludlow was the brother-
in-law of Endicott, and came over
with the west-country people, Rossiter, Warham, Maverick, Roger
Clap, &c., in the Mary & John,
which sailed from Plymouth March
20, and arrived at Nantasket May 30,
thirteen days before Winthrop's arrival at Salem. He was one of the
first settlers of Dorchester, and was
re-elected Assistant until 1634, when
he was chosen Deputy Governor.

CHAP.
III.
an Assistant in the room of Mr. Samuel Sharpe, who by reason of his absence had not taken the oath.

1630.
Feb.
19.
And lastly, upon the petition of Humphry Seale, the beadle of this Company, the Court were content and agreed to give him twenty nobles for his year's salary ending at Christmas last ; which is to be paid by Mr. Aldersey, the Treasurer, out of the joint stock.[1]

In the Colony Records, under date Nov. 7, 1632, it is stated, "There is one hundred acres of land granted to Mr. Roger Ludlowe, to enjoy to him and his heirs forever, lying betwixt Musquantum Chapel and the mouth of Naponsett." He removed with the first emigrants to Windsor, in Connecticut, of which town he may be considered the founder ; in 1636 was chosen an Assistant of that Colony, and in 1639 Deputy Governor, to which office he was several times re-elected. In 1637 he was out in the Pequot war, with Stoughton and Mason, in pursuit of Sassacus. In 1639 he removed to Fairfield, and in 1654 went to Virginia, where it is supposed he died. Trumbull says, " He appears to have been distinguished for his abilities, especially his knowledge of the law, and the rights of mankind. He rendered most essential services to this Commonwealth ; was a principal in forming its original civil constitution, and the compiler of the first Connecticut Code, adopted in 1649, and printed at Cambridge in 1672. For jurisprudence, he appears to have been second to none who came into New-England at that time. Had he possessed a happier temper, he would probably have been the idol of the people, and shared in all the honors which they could have given him." See Mass. Col. Rec. i. 95, MS. ; Trumbull's Connecticut, i. 64, 103, 109, 177, 218 ; Hubbard's N. E., p. 165 ; Hutchinson's Mass. i. 35, 43, 98 ; Winthrop's N. E., i. 28, 132, 233, 235.

[1] Here Secretary Burgess's record ends. He stayed behind, and never came over. The remainder of the Records is in the handwriting of Simon Bradstreet, who was the first Secretary after their arrival in New-England. See Ed. Johnson, in Mass. Hist. Coll. ii. 87, and Col. Rec. MS. i. 55.

*At a Meeting of Assistants at Southampton,*[1] *March* CHAP.
18*th*, 1629. Present, III.

1630.

| MR. GOVERNOR, | MR. HUMFREY, | March |
| SIR RICHARD SALTONSTALL, | MR. NOWELL, | 18. |
| MR. JOHNSON, | MR. PINCHION, | |
| MR. DUDLEY, | MR. GOFFE. | |

It was ordered, and concluded, by erection of
hands, that Sir Brian Janson, Kt.,[2] Mr. William
Coddington, and Mr. Simon Bradstreet,[3] gentlemen,

---

[1] Southampton is situated at the head of an estuary running up from the Isle of Wight, called the Southampton Water. It was from this same port that the Pilgrims sailed in the Mayflower and Speedwell, in July, 1620. See Chronicles of the Pilgrims, p. 89.

[2] Governor Winthrop, writing to his son John "from aboard the Arbella, riding at the Cowes, March 22, 1630," says, "There is newly come into our Company, and sworn an Assistant, one Sir Brian Janson, of London, a man of good estate, and so affected with our society, as he hath given £50 to our common stock, and £50 to the joint stock." Winthrop's Hist. N. E., i. 367.

[3] Simon Bradstreet was the youngest of the Assistants who came over with Winthrop, being at this time only 27 years of age. He was born in March, 1603, at Horbling, in Lincolnshire, of which town his father was a Nonconformist minister, and was educated at Emanuel College, Cambridge, of which his father had been one of the first fellows, and there took the degree of A. B. in 1620 and of A. M. in 1624. He was for some time steward of the Earl of Lincoln, and afterwards served the Countess of Warwick in the same capacity. Before leaving England, he married Ann, daughter of Thomas Dudley, another of the Assistants, she being at this time only 16 years of age, and after her death he married the sister of Sir George Downing. He served the Colony as Assistant, Secretary, Agent in England in 1662, Commissioner for the United Colonies, and Governor, in 1679, when in his 76th year. After the deposition of Andros, in 1689, he was chosen President of the Council of Safety, when in his 87th year, and then again Governor, which office he held till the arrival of Sir William Phips with the new charter in 1692. He lived to be the Nestor of New-England, having been born at the beginning of the century in 1603, and wanting but three years of completing it. He died March 27, 1697, at Salem. The Latin inscription on his monument is printed in Mass. Hist. Coll. vi. 288. "Oct. 3, 1632, there is sixty acres of meadow ground granted to Simon Bradstreet in the marsh ground against the Oyster Bank;" and May 14, 1634, five hundred acres more are granted to him. See Col. Rec. i. 93, 118, MS.; Mather's Magnalia, i. 126; Hutchinson's Mass. i. 18, 219, 323, 382, ii. 13, 105; Mass. Hist. Coll. xxviii. 247, 249.

CHAP.
III.

1630.
March
18.

shall be chosen in the rooms and places of Assistants of Mr. Nathaniel Wright, merchant, Mr. Theophilus Eaton, and Mr. Thomas Goffe, of London, merchants.

Sir Brian Janson was sworn an Assistant before the Governor and Mr. Dudley the same day.[1]

---

23.

## March 23d, 1629.

Mr. William Coddington, Mr. Simon Bradstreet, and Mr. Thomas Sharpe, being formerly chosen Assistants, did now take the oath of Assistants before the Governor, Mr. Dudley, and other Assistants.

[1] Joshua Scottow, in his "Narrative of the Planting of the Massachusetts Colony, anno 1628," printed at Boston in 1694, says, page 13, "Some of their choice friends, as the Reverend Mr. Cotton and others, went along with them from Boston, in Lincolnshire, to Southampton, where they parted, and he preached his farewell sermon." This information he may have received from the venerable Simon Bradstreet, to whom he dedicates his book, and who was then living at the advanced age of 91. We know that Cotton did deliver a sermon, entitled "God's Promise to his Plantations," in 1630, and that it was printed the same year; but whether it was preached at Boston to his parishioners who were then coming over, (among whom were Dudley and Coddington,) or at Southampton, may be a question. That it was at the latter place, as stated by Scottow, is rendered probable by a statement of Dr. Samuel Fuller, the physician of New-Plymouth, who, writing to Governor Bradford from Charlestown, June 28, 1630, soon after the arrival of Winthrop's fleet, says, "Here is a gentleman, one Mr. Coddington, a Boston man, who told me that Mr. Cotton's charge at Hampton was, that they should take advice of them at Plymouth, and should do nothing to offend them." See pp. 16 and 48, and Mass. Hist. Coll. iii. 75.

Hubbard states, p. 125, we know not on what authority, that "Mr. John Winthrop, the Governor of the Company, at a solemn feast amongst many friends a little before their last farewell, finding his bowels yearn within him, instead of drinking to them, by breaking into a flood of tears himself, set them all a weeping, with Paul's friends, while they thought of seeing the faces of each other no more in the land of the living." Mather, in the Magnalia, i. 69, mentions the same circumstance, deriving it, doubtless, from Hubbard's MS. See also Ed. Johnson's Hist. N. E., ch. 12.

"Here is a fleet of fourteen sail, furnished with men, women, children, all necessaries, men of handicrafts, and others of good condition, wealth and quality, to make a firm Plantation in New-England, between 42 and 48, north latitude; but stay at Southampton and thereabouts till May, to take 260 kine, with other live cattle, &c." Howes, Continuation of Stow's Annals, quoted in Prince, p. 270.

*At a Court of Assistants aboard the Arbella,*[1] *March* CHAP.
23, 1629. Present, III.

1630.
MR. JOHN WINTHROP, *Governor,*     MR. WILLIAM CODDINGTON,     March
SIR RICHARD SALTONSTALL,           MR. THOMAS SHARPE,        23.
MR. ISAAC JOHNSON,                 MR. WILLIAM VASSALL,
MR. THOMAS DUDLEY,             MR. SIMON BRADSTREET.

Mr. John Humfrey, (in regard he was to stay behind in England,) was discharged of his Deputy-ship, and Mr. Thomas Dudley chosen Deputy in his place.[2]

[1] The Arbella, formerly the Eagle, a ship of 350 or 400 tons, manned with 52 seamen and 28 pieces of cannon, was at this time riding at Cowes, a well-known anchoring-ground near the Isle of Wight, and in the vicinity of Portsmouth. Here she remained till Monday, the 29th, when she proceeded to Yarmouth. See note [1] on page 93, and Winthrop's Hist. i. 1, 367.

[2] This is the last record of the Massachusetts Company in England. Winthrop, with a fleet of four ships, the Arbella, the Talbot, the Ambrose, and the Jewel, sailed from Cowes, March 29, and from Yarmouth, in the Isle of Wight, April 8. Passing through the Needles, on the 9th they were off Portland, and on the 10th over against Plymouth, and in sight of the Lizard. On the 11th they passed Scilly, and took their departure. They made land on the American coast June 6, were within sight of Cape Ann on the 11th, cast anchor inside of Baker's island on the 12th, where they remained over Sunday, and on the 14th warped ship into the inner harbour of Salem. Winthrop kept a minute journal of the voyage, which is printed at the beginning of his History. The fleet that brought over Winthrop's company consisted of fifteen ships, and the number of persons was not far from 1500. " What must we think,"

says Hutchinson, i. 19, " of persons of rank and good circumstances in life bidding a final adieu to all the conveniences and delights of England, their native country, and exposing themselves, their wives and children, to inevitable hardships and sufferings, in a long voyage across the Atlantic, to land upon a most inhospitable shore, destitute of any kind of building to secure them from the inclemency of the weather, and of most sorts of food to which they had been always used at their former home? The sickness and mortality which prevailed the first winter, they did not foresee." A nobler body of men never left their native soil to colonize a new land. What does Bancroft mean (Hist. U. S. ii. 455,) by " the Puritan felons that freighted the fleet of Winthrop"? Let him who would understand the character of these men, read the admirable Address delivered by Gov. Everett at Charlestown in 1830, on the Second Centennial Anniversary of the arrival of Gov. Winthrop.— It was in reference to the persecution and exile of such men, that Milton, writing in 1641, said, " What numbers of faithful and freeborn Englishmen, and good Christians, have been constrained to forsake their dearest home, their friends and kindred, whom nothing but the wide ocean, and the savage deserts of America, could hide and shelter from the fury of the bishops. O if we could but see the shape of our dear mother England, as poets are wont to give a personal form to what they please, how would she appear, think ye, but in a mourning weed, with ashes upon her .head, and tears abundantly flowing from her eyes, to behold so many of her children exposed at once, and thrust from things of dearest necessity, because their conscience could not assent to things which the bishops thought indifferent? Let the astrologer be dismayed at the portentous blaze of comets and impressions in the air, as foretelling troubles and changes to States ; I shall believe there cannot be a more ill-boding sign to a nation, (God turn the omen from us !) than when the inhabitants, to avoid insufferable grievances at home, are enforced by heaps to forsake their native country." Prose Works, i. 37, (Symmons's ed.)

These RECORDS of the Governor and Company of the Massachusetts Bay in New-England, before the bringing over of the Charter by Gov. Winthrop, now for the first time printed from the original manuscript in the archives of the Common-

wealth, are for the most part, in good order and preservation. This is especially true of by much the larger and more important portion of them, kept after the organization of the Government and the choice of Officers, May 13, 1629, when William Burgess was chosen Secretary, whose handwriting is very distinct and legible. The preceding portion, kept by the first Secretary, John Washburn, who wrote an execrable hand, is considerably mutilated on the edges, particularly the lower edge, by the constant wear and tear of two hundred years and more. One leaf, too, at least, if not more, is missing, as stated on page 66. Still, torn and tattered though it be, it is a most interesting and invaluable relic ; and the Record, taken as a whole, constitutes an authentic history, such as no other Colony, ancient or modern, possesses, of its origin and foundation. The copy of this Record in the Land Office is inaccurate and worthless. Great pains have been taken to secure entire correctness in the copy from which this is printed, by a minute and patient collation of it with the original manuscript, at long intervals of time, and by different eyes and hands.

# GOV. CRADOCK'S LETTER

TO

# CAPTAIN ENDICOTT.

# CHAPTER IV.

WORTHY SIR AND MY LOVING FRIEND,

ALL due commendations premised to yourself and second self, with hearty well-wishes from myself and many others, well-willers and adventurers in this our Plantation, to yourself and the rest of your good company, of whose safe arrival being now thoroughly informed by your letters, bearing date the 13th September last, which came to my hands the 13th this instant February, we do not a little rejoice ; and to hear that my good cousin, your wife, were perfectly recovered of her health, would be acceptable news to us all ; which God grant, in his good time, that we may.[1]

Meanwhile I am, in the behalf of our whole Company, (which are much enlarged since your depart-

CHAP.
IV.

1629.
Feb.
16.

---

[1] She did not live long ; for we find by Gov. Winthrop's Journal, that Endicott was married again, August 18, 1630, to Elizabeth Gibson. The unscrupulous Morton, in his New English Canaan, chap. 18, intimates that the first wife was killed by the quackery of Dr. Fuller, the physician of New Plymouth, who we know visited Salem on professional duty in the time of prevailing sickness there. "Dr. Noddy did a great cure for Capt. Littleworth. He cured him of a disease called a wife." See note on page 32, and Winthrop's N. E., i. 30.

ure out of England,)[1] to give you hearty thanks for
your large advice contained in this your letter, which
I have fully imparted unto them, and farther to cer-
tify you that they intend not to be wanting by all
good means to further the Plantation. To which
purpose, (God willing,) you shall hear more at [large
from] them, and that speedily ; there being one ship
bought for the Company,[2] of 100[3] tons, and two
others hired, of about 200 tons each of them, one of
19, the other of 20[4] pieces of ordnance ; besides, not
unlike but one other vessel shall come in company
with these ; in all which ships, for the general
stock and for particular adventures, there is likely
to be sent thither 'twixt 2 and 300 persons, (we
hope to reside there,) and about 100 head of cattle.
Wherefore, as I wrote you in a letter[5] sent by Mr.
Allerton,[6] of New-Plymouth, in November last, so
the desire of the [Company] is, that you would endeavour to get convenient housing fit to lodge as
many as you can against they do come ; and withal
what beaver, or other commodities, or fish, (if you
have the means to preserve it,) can be gotten ready
to return in the foresaid ships ; likewise wood, if no
better lading be to be had ; that you would endeavour to get in readiness what you can, whereby our
ships, whereof two are to return back directly hither,

---

[1] Endicott left England about June
20, 1628. His instructions were
dated London, May 30. See pp. 13,
30, 43 ; Prince's Annals, p. 249 ;
Hutchinson's Mass. i. 9.

[2] This was the Lion's Whelp, a
vessel of 120 tons.

[3] This is obliterated in the MS.
I have restored it from Prince, Annals, p. 253, who quoted the letter

before it was mutilated. Felt, Annals
of Salem, i. 47, errs in saying 200.

[4] Erased in the MS., but restored
from Prince. Felt, ibid. errs in
calling it 10.

[5] This letter has not been preserved.

[6] See an account of Isaac Allerton in the Chronicles of Plymouth,
p. 195.

may not come wholly empty.   There hath not been
a better time for the sale of timber these two seven
years than at present, and therefore pity it is these
ships should come back empty, if it might be made
ready that they need not stay for it; otherwise, men's
wages and victuals, together with the ships', will
quickly rise too high, if to be reladen with wood,
and that the same be not ready to put aboard as soon
as the ships are discharged of their outward lading.
I wish also that there be some sassafras[1] and sarsa-
parilla sent us, as also good store of sumach, if there
to be had, as we are informed there is.   The like do
I wish for a ton weight at least of silk grass, and of
aught else that may be useful for dying, or in physic;
to have some of each sent, and advice given withal
what store of each to be had there, if vent may be
found here for it.   Also I hope you will have some
good sturgeon in a readiness to send us, and if it be
well cured, 2 or 300 firkins thereof would help well
towards our charge.

We are very confident of your best endeavours for
the general good, and we doubt not but God will in
mercy give a blessing upon our labors; and we trust
you will not be unmindful of the main end of our
Plantation, by endeavouring to bring the Indians to
the knowledge of the Gospel; which that it may be
the speedier and better effected, the earnest desire
of our whole Company is, that you have a diligent
and watchful eye over our own people, that they live
unblamable and without reproof, and demean themselves justly and courteous towards the Indians,
thereby to draw them to affect our persons, and con-

---

[1] See Chronicles of Plymouth, p. 130, note [3].

CHAP.
IV.
1629.
Feb.
16.

sequently our religion ; as also to endeavour to get some of their children to train up to reading and consequently to religion, whilst they are young ; herein to young or old to omit no good opportunity that may tend to bring them out of that woful state and condition they now are in ; in which case our predecessors in this our land sometimes were, and, but for the mercy and goodness of our good God, might have continued to this day. But God, who out of the boundless ocean of his mercy hath showed pity and compassion to our land, he is all-sufficient, and can bring this to pass which we now desire, in that country likewise. Only let us not be wanting on our parts, now we are called to this work of the Lord's ; neither, having put our hands to the plough, let us look back, but go on cheerfully, and depend upon God for a blessing upon our labors ; who by weak instruments is able, (if he see it good,) to bring glorious things to pass. Be of good courage, go on, and do worthily, and the Lord prosper your endeavour.

It is fully resolved, by God's assistance, to send over two ministers, at the least, with the[1] ships now intended to be sent thither. But for Mr. Peters,[2]

[1] " At the least, with the " is restored from Prince.

[2] Hugh Peters, (or Peter, as he himself uniformly spelt his name,) was born at Fowey, in Cornwall, in 1599, and was educated at Trinity College, Cambridge, where he took the degree of A. M. in 1622. Upon leaving the University he came to London, and was appointed lecturer at St. Sepulchre's. Towards the close of 1629, when Laud, (" our great enemy," as Winthrop calls him, ii. 31,) began his persecution of the Puritans, he went to Holland, and became pastor of an Independent Church at Rotterdam, having for a colleague the celebrated Dr. William Ames, whose wife and children, after his death in 1633, came to New-England, bringing with them his valuable library. Peters was one of the earliest members of the Massachusetts Company. In May, 1628, he subscribed £50 to the joint stock of the Plantation, and he was one of the fourteen who signed the first instructions to Endi-

he is now in Holland, from whence his return hither CHAP.
I hold to be uncertain. Those we send you, shall
be by the[1] approbation of Mr. White, of Dorchester, 1629.
and Mr. Davenport. For whatsoever else you have Feb.
given advice, care shall be taken, (God willing,) to

cott, Sept. 13, 1628. It appears from pages 69 and 70, that he attended the courts of the Company held on the 11th and 13th of May, 1629, three months after the date of this letter. Of course he must have come over, for a season, from Holland. After remaining six years in that country he came to New-England Oct. 6, 1635. Gov. Winthrop, speaking of his arrival, says, "amongst others came Mr. Peter, pastor of the English church in Rotterdam, who, being persecuted by the English ambassador — who would have brought his and other churches to the English discipline — and not having had his health these many years, intended to advise with the ministers here about his removal." Dec. 21, 1636, he took charge of the Church in Salem, being the fourth minister, Higginson and Skelton having died, and Roger Williams having left in Nov. 1635. Winthrop calls him "a man of a very public spirit and singular activity for all occasions," and says that "he went from place to place laboring, both publicly and privately, to raise up men to a public frame of spirit." In 1641, Aug. 3, he was sent with Thomas Weld, the minister of Roxbury, as agent of the Colony to attend to its interests in the mother country, and "to congratulate the happy success there." Neither of them returned. During the civil wars Peters made himself active and conspicuous. In 1641 he was "chaplain to the train," and secretary to Cromwell. In 1649 he was chaplain to the Parliamentary forces sent against the rebels in Ireland, and one of the *Triers* of preachers, and in 1651 was one of the commissioners for amending the laws. At the Re-

storation he was apprehended as a regicide, although he had not been one of the King's judges, was tried, condemned, and executed Oct. 16, 1660. After his death, his wife, whom he had married in New-England, and who had been insane, returned to this Colony, and was supported by a collection of £30 a year until 1671. Gov. John Winthrop, of Connecticut, married a daughter of Hugh Peters. — The common accounts we have of Peters, Vane, Cromwell, and their associates, are from the pens of bigoted royalists and churchmen, like Clarendon. A new and more favorable view of Cromwell has recently been given to the world by the ingenious editor of his Letters and Speeches. I have been favored with the perusal, in manuscript, of a very able vindication of the character of Hugh Peters, from the pen of a recent successor of his in the First Church in Salem, the Rev. Charles W. Upham, of whose Life of Sir Henry Vane, in the fourth volume of Sparks's American Biography, Mr. Grahame, the historian of the United States, remarks, "New-England has now repaid Vane's noble devotion by the best memoir of that great man, that has ever been given to the world." It is hoped that Mr. Upham's Life of Hugh Peters may soon be published. See Winthrop's Hist. i. 65, 169, 173, 176, ii. 24, 25, 31; Hutchinson's Mass., i. 9, 98; Carlyle's Cromwell, i. 164, 186, 370; Mass. Hist. Coll., vi. 250–254, 285, xxviii. 248; Monthly Repository, (London,) xiv. 525–532, 602–607; Peters's Last Legacy to his Daughter, (1661,) p. 99.
[1] "Shall be by the" also restored from Prince.

CHAP.
IV.

1629.

Feb.
16.

perform the needful, as near as we can, and the times will permit; whereof also you may expect more ample advertisement in their General Letter,[1] when God shall send our ships thither.

The course you have taken in giving our countrymen their content in the point of planting tobacco there for the present, (their necessity considered,) is not disallowed ; but we trust in God, other means will be found to employ their time more comfortable and profitable also in the end ; and we cannot but generally approve and commend their good resolution to desist from the planting thereof, whenas they shall discern how to employ their labors otherwise ; which we hope they will be speedily induced unto, by such precepts and examples as we shall give them.

And now minding to conclude this, I may not omit to put you in mind, however you seem to fear no enemies there, yet that you have a watchful eye for your own safety, and the safety of all those of our nation with you, and not to be too confident of the fidelity of the salvages. It is [a proverb trite] as true, " the burnt child dreads the fire." Our countrymen have suffered by their too much confidence in Virginia.[2] Let us by their harms learn to beware ; and as we are commanded to be innocent as doves, so withal we are enjoined to be wise as serpents. The God of heaven and earth preserve and keep you

---

[1] The General Letter from the Governor and Company to Endicott is printed immediately after this letter of Cradock's.

[2] He probably alludes to the massacre in Virginia, on the 22d of March, 1622, when, at mid-day, the Indians, by a preconcerted signal, fell upon the English settlements there, and killed 347 persons. See Smith's Virginia, ii. 64–79, (Richmond ed.) ; Stith's Virginia, pages 208–213; and Grahame's Hist. U. S. i. 74–79, (2d ed.)

from all foreign and inland enemies, and bless and CHAP.<br>IV.
prosper this Plantation, to the enlarging of the kingdom of Jesus Christ ; to whose merciful protection I 1629.<br>Feb.
recommend you and all your associates there, known 16.
or unknown ; and so till my next, which shall be,
(God willing,) by our ships, who I make account will
be ready to set sail from here about the 20th of this
next month of March,[1] I end ; and rest,

Your assured loving friend and cousin,

MATTHEW CRADOCK.[2]

*From my house in Swithen's Lane,[3] near London Stone,*
  *this 16th February, 1628, stilo Angliæ.[4]*

---

[1] The ships did not actually sail till the middle of April.

[2] MATTHEW CRADOCK, the first Governor of the Massachusetts Company, was a wealthy London merchant, and, it will be recollected, was usually the highest in all subscriptions for the good of the Colony. He owned the Ambrose and the Jewel, two of the ships in Winthrop's fleet, and went to the Isle of Wight to take leave of the emigrants. On his leaving the Arbella on the 29th of March, " the captain gave him a farewell with four or five shot." He came aboard the same vessel again at Yarmouth, April 6, and on his taking leave, " the captain gave him three shot out of the steerage for a farewell." He never came over to New-England ; but he continued to take an interest in the Colony, and befriended it essentially at home. He had an agent and servants here, and capital engaged in fishing and trading. He had a house at Marblehead and another at Ipswich, and employed fishermen at both places. His name frequently occurs in the Records of the Colony. At a Court held at Watertown, March 8, 1631, " it was ordered that Thomas Fox, servant to Mr. Cradock, shall be whipped." Nov. 7, 1632, " Mr. Matthew Cradock is

fined £4 for his men being absent from training divers times." At a Court held March 4, 1634, " the wear at Mistick is granted to John Winthrop, Esq., present Governor, and to Mr. Matthew Cradock, of London." March 4, 1635, " All the ground, as well upland as meadow, lying and being betwixt the lands of Mr. Nowell and Mr. Wilson on the east, and the partition betwixt Mistick bounds on the west, bounded with Mistick river on the south and the rocks on the north, is granted to Mr. Matthew Cradock, merchant, to enjoy to him and his heirs forever." This farm was within the present town of Malden, opposite Winthrop's farm at Tenhills. William Wood, who was here in 1633, says in his New-England's Prospect, chap. x., " On the east side (of Mistick river) is Mr. Cradock's plantation, where he hath impaled a park, where he keeps his cattle till he can store it with deer. Here likewise he is at charges of building ships. The last year one was upon the stocks of 100 tons. That being finished, they are to build one twice her burden." He was a member of Parliament from the city of London in 1640. He left a claim upon the Colony, which in 1648 amounted to £679 6s. 4d.

CHAP. His widow, Rebecca, márried the
IV.   Rev. Benjamin Whitchcot, D. D.
~~~   His son or grandson was a dissent-
1629. ing minister at Wickambrook in
1690.   A descendant, George Cradock, was an inhabitant of Boston in
the middle of the last century.  See
Col. Rec. i. 68, 95, 108, 143 ; Winthrop's Hist. i. 2, 4, 60, 124, ii. 25 ;
Hutchinson's Mass. i. 18, 22 ; Felt,
Annals of Salem, i. 56.
   [3] It will be observed that he does
not say, *St.* Swithin's.   On St.
Swithin's Lane and London Stone,
see Stow's Survey of London, p. 416
and 420, (ed. 1618.)  St. Swithin's
Lane goes from near the junction of
Cornhill and Lombard street to Cannon street.  It is the street next
east of Walbrook, and parallel to it.
   [4] That is, old style, by which the
year began on the 25th of March.

The Julian year, and the new or
Gregorian style, were not adopted
by law in England and her depend-
encies till 1752.
   This letter must have been
brought over by some fishing-vessel,
for we know of no ship of the
Company's sailing from England
to Salem till the middle of April,
when the George Bonaventure
brought the First General Letter of
Instructions to Endicott.  The original letter lies loose in the first
volume of the Colony Records,
where it has probably lain for more
than two hundred years.  Like the
volume itself, it is in a tattered condition ; and it is a marvel that it
exists at all.  Several words, now
torn off, I have restored from a copy
made twenty-seven years ago, when
the letter was less mutilated.

# THE COMPANY'S INSTRUCTIONS

TO

# ENDICOTT AND HIS COUNCIL.

# CHAPTER V.

THE COMPANY'S FIRST GENERAL LETTER OF INSTRUC-
TIONS TO ENDICOTT AND HIS COUNCIL.

LAUS DEO![1]

*In Gravesend, the 17th of April, 1629.*

LOVING FRIENDS,

WE heartily salute you. We have received your letter[2] of the 13th of September, by which we take notice of your safe arrival, blessing God for it. We have formerly requested Mr. Cradock, our Governor, to write you of the receipt thereof, and give advice how we purposed to proceed in setting forward our Plantation ; whose letters, if they be come to your hands, (as we hope they are,) will put life into your affairs, and encourage you to provide for the entertainment of such as are now coming.

Since your departure we have, for the further strengthening of our grant from the Council at Plymouth, obtained a confirmation of it from his Majesty

---

[1] A not unusual mode of commencing a letter at the time this was written. See Carlyle's Cromwell, i. 132.

[2] This letter has not been preserved.

CHAP.
V.

1629.

April
17.

by his letters patents under the broad seal of England ;[1] by which said letters patents we are incorporated into a body politic, with ample power to govern and rule all his Majesty's subjects that reside within the limits of our Plantation, as by the duplicate[2] thereof, under the broad seal, which we have delivered to Mr. Sharpe to be delivered to you, doth fully appear.

And for that the propagating of the Gospel is the thing we do profess above all to be our aim in settling this Plantation, we have been careful to make plentiful provision of godly ministers; by whose faithful preaching, godly conversation, and exemplary life, we trust not only those of our own nation will be built up in the knowledge of God, but also the Indians may, in God's appointed time, be reduced to the obedience of the Gospel of Christ.[3]    One of them is well known to yourself, viz. Mr. Skelton,[4] whom we

---

[1] The original Charter, with the broad seal appendant, which was brought over by Gov. Winthrop, is carefully preserved in a glass case in the office of the Secretary of State, at the State House in Boston.  It is distinctly and beautifully engrossed on parchment, and has on it the head of the sovereign by whom it was granted, Charles I.  That this is the original, and not a copy, is proved by the fact that on it is the following certificate of Gov. Cradock having taken his oath of office before Sir Charles Cæsar, Master in Chancery.  " Prædictus Matthæus Cradocke juratus est de fide et obedientiâ Regi et successoribus suis, et de debitâ exequutione officii Gubernatoris juxta tenorem præsentium, 18° Martii, 1628, coram me, Carolo Cæsare, Milite, in Cancellariâ Magistro.

CHAR. CÆSAR."

[2] This duplicate of the Charter is preserved in the Athenæum at Salem.  The party-colored string, by which the royal seal was appended, remains, but the seal itself is gone.

[3] Cradock, in his letter to Endicott, mentions this as "the main end of the Plantation," and the Charter also avers, that " to win and invite the natives of the country to the knowledge and obedience of the only true God and Saviour of mankind and the Christian faith, in our royal intention, and the adventurers' free profession, is the principal end of this Plantation."

[4] Samuel Skelton was educated at Clare Hall, Cambridge, where he took the degree of A. B. in 1611, and of A. M. in 1615. He is said by Mather to have come from Lincolnshire ; but as it is here related that Endicott " formerly received much good by his ministry," it is

have the rather desired to bear a part in this work, CHAP.
for that we are informed yourself have formerly re-  V.
ceived much good by his ministry ; he cometh in the 1629.
George Bonaventure, Master Thomas Cox.  Another April 17.
is Mr. Higgeson,[1] a grave man, and of worthy commendations ; he cometh in the Talbot.  The third is
Mr. Bright,[1] some times trained up under Mr. Davenport, who cometh in the Lion's Whelp.  We pray
you, accommodate them all with necessaries as well
as you may, and in convenient time let there be
houses built them, according to the agreement[2] we
have made with them, copies whereof, as of all others
we have entertained, shall be sent you by the next
ships, time not permitting it now.  We doubt not
but these gentlemen, your ministers, will agree lovingly together ;[3] and for cherishing of love betwixt
them, we pray you carry yourself impartially to all.

more probable that he was of Dorsetshire, from which county Endicott came.  Nothing is known of his
history whilst in England.  Arriving at Naumkeak on the 24th of
June, he was, on the 20th of July,
chosen and ordained pastor of the
church there ; and from this circumstance it has been inferred that he
was older than Higginson, who at
the same time was chosen and ordained teacher.  He died at Salem
August 2, 1634.  Edward Johnson,
who was one of Winthrop's company, and may have known him person lly, describes him, in his quaint
way, as " a man of a gracious
speech, full of faith, and furnished
by the Lord with gifts from above
to begin this great work of His,
that makes the whole earth to ring
again at the present day."  It is a
little remarkable that we have no
further accounts of him from the
writers of that or the succeeding age.
"July 3, 1632, there is another neck
of land, lying about three miles from
Salem route, about 200 acres, granted to Mr. Samuel Skelton, called by
the Indians Wahquack.  Also there
is granted to Mr. Skelton one acre
of land on which his house standeth,
and ten acres more in a neck of land
abutting on the south river, and
upon Mr. Higgenson's ground on
the west.  Likewise there is granted to Mr. Skelton two acres more
of ground lying in Salem, abutting
on Capt. Endicott's ground on the
south."  See Col. Rec. i. 90, MS.;
Winthrop, i. 137 ; Mather, i. 331 ;
Mass. Hist. Coll. iii. 67. xii. 71,
xxviii. 248.

[1] Some account of Higginson and
Bright will be given hereafter, under
the date when the former died, and
the latter returned home.

[2] This agreement is preserved,
and is printed in a subsequent part
of this volume.

[3] Bright did not agree very well
with his colleagues, and returned to
England in little more than a year.

CHAP.
V.
——
1629.
April
17.
For the manner of the exercising their ministry, and teaching both our own people and the Indians, we leave that to themselves, hoping they will make God's word the rule of their actions, and mutually agree in the discharge of their duties. And because their doctrine will hardly be well esteemed whose persons are not reverenced, we desire that both by your own example, and by commanding all others to do the like, our ministers may receive due honor.

We have, in prosecution of that good opinion we have always had of you, confirmed you Governor of our Plantation, and joined in commission with you the three ministers, namely, Mr. Francis Higgonson, Mr. Samuel Skelton, and Mr. Francis Bright; also Mr. John and Mr. Samuel Browne, Mr. Thomas Graves, and Mr. Samuel Sharpe; and for that we have ordered that the body of the government there shall consist of thirteen persons, we are content the old planters [1] that are now there within our Plantation and limits thereof, shall choose two of the discreetest and judicial men from amongst themselves to be of the government, that they may see we are not wanting to give them fitting respect, in that we would have their consent, (if it may be,) in making wholesome constitutions for government : always provided, that none shall be chosen, or meddle in their choice, but such as will live amongst us and conform themselves to our government. But if they shall refuse to perform this our direction, then we

---

[1] The old planters were Conant, Palfrey, Woodbury, Balch, and their associates, who had been induced by the Dorchester adventurers to settle at Cape Ann, and afterwards removed to Naumkeag. See pp. 12, 22–28.

hereby authorize you and those nominated to be of the Council aforesaid, to nominate and elect two such men as in your opinions you shall hold meet for that place and office ; and for the other three which will be wanting to make up the full number of thirteen, (which we have styled the Council of the Mattachusetts Bay,) we hereby authorize [you,] with the aforenamed seven persons, to choose and nominate them out of the whole body of the Company, as well of those that are there, as of those that are to come now, not doubting but, all partiality set apart, you will make choice of such men as may be most useful and careful to advance the general good of our Plantation.

And that it may appear, as well to all the world, as to the old planters themselves, that we seek not to make them slaves, (as it seems by your letter some of them think themselves to be become by means of our Patent,[1]) we are content they shall be partakers of such privileges as we, from his Majesty's especial grace, with great cost, favor of personages of note, and much labor, have obtained ; and that they shall be incorporated into this Society, and enjoy not only those lands which formerly they have manured, but such a further proportion as by the advice and judgment of yourself, and the rest of the Council, shall be thought fit for them, or any of them. And besides, it is still our purpose that they should have some benefit by the common stock, as

---

[1] Conant and his associates, as was very natural, appear to have been jealous of the new comers who had arrived with Endicott, and probably did not like it that their authority was to be superseded by his government, and their little plantation absorbed by his Colony. The Massachusetts Company seem to have treated the old planters with great consideration and kindness. See page 31.

CHAP.
V.

1629.
April
17.

was by your first commission[1] directed and appointed ; with this addition, that if it be held too much to take thirty per cent. and the freight of the goods for and in consideration of our adventure and disbursement of our moneys, to be paid in beaver at six shillings per pound, that you moderate the said rate, as you with the rest of the Council shall think to be agreeable to equity and good conscience. And our further orders is, that none be partakers of any the aforesaid privileges and profits, but such as be peaceable men, and of honest life and conversation, and desirous to live amongst us, and conform themselves to good order and government.

And as touching the old planters, their earnest desire for the present to continue the planting of tobacco, (a trade by this whole Company generally disavowed, and utterly disclaimed by some of the greatest adventurers amongst us, who absolutely declared themselves unwilling to have any hand in this Plantation if we intended to cherish or permit the planting thereof, or any other kind, than for a man's private. use, for mere necessity,) we are of opinion the old planters will have small encouragement to that employment ; for we find here, by late experience, that it doth hardly produce the freight and custom ; neither is there hope of amendment, there being such great quantities made in other places, that ere long it is like to be little worth. Nevertheless, if the old planters, (for we exclude all others,) conceive that they cannot otherwise provide for their livelihood, we leave it to the discretion of

[1] Endicott's first instructions were dated London, May 30, 1628. See Hutchinson's Mass. i. 9.

yourself and the Council there, to give way for the CHAP.<br>V.
present to their planting of it in such manner and
with such restrictions as you and the said Council 1629.
shall think fitting ; having an especial care, with as April<br>17.
much conveniency as may be, utterly to suppress the
planting of it, except for mere necessity.  But, however, we absolutely forbid the sale of it, or the use
of it, by any of our own or particular men's servants,
unless upon urgent occasion, for the benefit of health,
and taken privately.

Mr. John Oldham[1] came from New-England not
long before your arrival there, by whom we have had
no small distraction in our business, having been cast
behind at the least two months' time in our voyage,[2]
through the variety[3] of his vast conceits of extraordinary gain of three for one propounded to us, to be
made and raised in three years, if he might have the
managing of our stock, preferring to be contented
for his own employment, so he might have the overplus of the gains.  With whom, after long time spent
in sundry treaties,[4] finding him a man altogether
unfit for us to deal with, we have at last left him to
his own way ; and, as we are informed, he with some
others are providing a vessel, and is minded, as soon
as he can despatch, to come for New-England, pretending to settle himself in Mattachusetts Bay, claim-

---

[1] Oldham left New-England in
June, 1628, and Endicott left England June 20, and arrived at Naumkeak Sept. 6.  Of course they must
have crossed each other on the Atlantic.  See pp. 20, 43, and Mass.
Hist. Coll. iii. 63, and Prince's Annals, p. 249.

[2] This was the voyage of the
George, the Talbot, and the Lion's
Whelp, the ships that brought out

Higginson, Skelton, Samuel Sharpe,
and their company.  It appears from
page 43, that the Company were
preparing for this voyage as early as
Feb. 26 ; yet the ships did not sail
till after the middle of April.

[3] So in the manuscript ; but no
doubt an error of the Secretary, in
copying, for *vanity*.

[4] See pp. 48, 51, 61, 69.

ing a title and right by a grant from Sir Ferdinando Gorge's son,[1] which we are well satisfied by good counsel is void in law. He will admit of no terms of agreement, unless we will leave him at liberty to trade for beaver with the natives; which we deny to the best of our own planters. Neither is he satisfied to trade himself, with his own stock and means, which we conceive is so small that it would not much hinder us, but he doth interest other men, who, for aught we know, are never likely to be beneficial to the planting of the country; their own particular profits, (though to the overthrow of the general Plantation,) being their chief aim and intent.

Now, as we shall unwillingly do any act in debarring such as were inhabitants before us of that trade, as in conscience they ought to enjoy, so shall we as unwillingly permit any to appropriate that to their own private lucre which we, in our religious intentions, have dedicated to the common charge of building houses for God's worship, and forts to defend such as shall come thither to inhabit.[2] We fear that as he hath been obstinate and violent in his opinions here, so he will persist and be ready to draw a party to himself there, to the great hindrance of the common quiet. We have therefore thought fit to give you notice of his disposition, to the end you may beware how you meddle with him; as also that you may use the best means you can to settle an agreement with the old planters, so as they may not hearken to Mr. Oldham's dangerous though vain propositions. We find him a man so affected to his own opinion,

[1] See note [2] on page 51.          [2] See page 96.

as not to be removed from it, neither by reason nor CHAP. V.
any persuasion ; and, unless he may bear sway, and
have all things carried to his good liking, we have 1629.
little hope of quiet or comfortable subsistence where April 17.
he shall make his abode. And therefore, if you shall
see just cause, we hereby require you and the Council there to exercise that power we have, (and our
privileges will bear us out in it,[1]) to suppress a mischief before it take too great a head. Not that we
would wrong him, or any man that will live peaceably within the limits of our Plantation ; but as the
preservation of our privileges will chiefly depend,
under God, upon the first foundation of our government, so if we suffer so great an affront as we find is
intended towards us, by the proceedings of Mr. Oldham and his adherents, in our first beginnings, we
may be sure they will take heart and be emboldened
to do us a far greater injury hereafter. And therefore we pray you and the Council there to advise
seriously together for the maintenance of our privileges and peaceable government ; which if it may be
done by a temperate course, we much desire it,
though with some inconvenience, so as our government and privileges be not brought in contempt,
wishing rather there might be such a union as might
draw the heathen by our good example to the embracing of Christ and his Gospel, than that offence
should be given to the heathen, and a scandal to our

---

[1] By the Charter it was provided, that " all officers employed by the Company in the government of the Plantation, shall have full and abso-lute power and authority to correct, punish, govern and rule all persons as shall at any time hereafter inhabit within the precincts and parts of New-England aforesaid, according to the orders and instructions of the Company, not being repugnant to the laws and statutes of the realm of England." See the Charter in Haz-ard, i. 239 ; Hutchinson's Coll. p. 1.

CHAP.  religion, through our disagreement amongst our-
V.
∽∽∽ selves.

1629.     But if necessity require a more severe course,
April
17.   when fair means will not prevail, we pray you to
deal as in your discretions you shall think fittest for
the general good and safety of the Plantation, and
preservation of our privileges.[1] And because we
would not omit to do anything which might strengthen
our right, we would have you (as soon as these ships,
or any of them, arrive with you, whereby you may
have men to do it,) send forty or fifty persons to
Mattachusetts Bay,[2] to inhabit there ; which we pray
you not to protract, but to do it with all speed ; and
if any of our Company in particular shall desire to
settle themselves there, or to send servants thither,
we desire all accommodation and encouragement
may be given them thereunto, whereby the better to
strengthen our possession there against all or any that
shall intrude upon us, which we would not have you
by any means to give way unto ;[3] with this caution,
notwithstanding, that for such of our countrymen as
you find there planted,[4] so as they be willing to live
under [our] government, you endeavour to give them

---

[1] These instructions seem to approve and justify Endicott's attack
upon Morton's riotous company at
Mount Wollaston, soon after his
arrival in the preceding year. See
Hubbard's N. E., p. 104 ; Morton's
Memorial, pp. 138, 141, note, where
the chronology is set right.

[2] See note [1] on page 4.

[3] All this shows the anxious desire and settled determination of the
Company to anticipate Oldham, and
by preoccupying the ground, to get
the exclusive possession of Massachusetts Bay ; by which was then

understood only the territory bordering on Boston harbour, from Nahant
to Point Alderton. Naumkeak was
not included in it.

[4] The planters in Massachusetts
Bay at this time were William
Blackstone at Shawmut, (Boston),
Thomas Walford at Mishawum,
(Charlestown), Samuel Maverick
at Noddle's Island, (East Boston),
and David Thompson, at Thompson's Island, near Dorchester. How
or when they came there, is not
known. See Johnson, Hist. N. E.,
ch. 17.

all fitting and due accommodation as to any of our- CHAP.
selves ; yea, if you see cause for it, though it be with ˅.
more than ordinary privileges in point of trade. 1629.

Mr. Ralph Smith,[1] a minister, hath desired passage April 17.
in our ships ; which was granted him before we
understood of his difference in judgment in some
things from our ministers. But his provisions for
his voyage being shipped before notice was taken
thereof, through many occasions wherewith those
intrusted with this business have been employed, and
forasmuch as from hence it is feared there may grow
some distraction amongst you if there should be any

[1] We learn from Hutchinson, who, as well as Hubbard and Prince, appears to have had the leaf now torn out of the Colony Records, containing the proceedings of the courts held April 8 and 30, 1629, that, "of the four ministers provided, Ralph Smith was required to give under his hand, that he would not exercise his ministry within the limits of the patent without the express leave of the Governor upon the spot." He seems to have been a Separatist in England, which occasioned the caution used with him. He remained but a very short time at Salem, for in the end of June, says Gov. Bradford, "he goes with his family to some straggling people at Nantasket ; where some Plymouth people, putting in with a boat, find him in a poor house that would not keep him dry. He desires them to carry him to Plymouth ; and seeing him to be a grave man, and understanding he had been a minister, they bring him hither ; where we kindly entertain him, send for his goods and servants, and desire him to exercise his gifts among us ; afterwards choose him into the ministry, wherein he remains for sundry years." Hubbard speaks disparagingly of his abilities, saying that the Plymouth people, in calling him to

exercise the office of a pastor among them, "were more induced thereunto, possibly, by his approving the rigid way of Separation principles, than any fitness for the office he undertook ; being much overmatched by him that he was joined with in the presbytery, [Elder Brewster,] both in the point of discretion to rule and aptness to teach ; so as, through many infirmities, being found unable to discharge the trust committed to him with any competent satisfaction, he was forced soon after to lay it down." Gov. Winthrop says, that in Dec. 1635, Smith " gave over his place," that John Norton might have it. This, perhaps, was only temporarily ; for Morton says, that in Dec. 1638, Gorton was summoned to the court at Plymouth to answer a complaint made against him by Smith. He was residing there as late as 1641, and Sept. 27, 1642, sold his house and land to the Rev. John Reyner, his successor in the church. In Nov. 1645, he was called to preach at Manchester, on Cape Ann, and he died at Boston March 1, 1662. See Hutchinson's Mass. i. 10 ; Winthrop, i. 91, 175, ii. 253 ; Hubbard, pp. 97, 121 ; Prince, pp. 257, 261, 262 ; Morton's Mem. p. 202 ; Mass. Hist. Coll. iv. 110 ;. Felt's Salem, i. 80.

CHAP. siding, though we have a very good opinion of his
V.
~~~ honesty, yet we shall not, [we] hope, offend in charity
1629. to fear the worst that may grow from their different
April
17. judgments. We have therefore thought fit to give
you this order, that unless he will be conformable to
our government, you suffer him not to remain within
the limits of our grant.

We take notice that you desire to have Frenchmen
sent you that might be experienced in making of salt
and planting of vines.[1] We have inquired diligently
for such, but cannot meet with any of that nation.
Nevertheless, God hath not left us altogether unpro-
vided of a man able to undertake that work; for that
we have entertained Mr. Thomas Graves,[2] a man

---

[1] It appears somewhat singular
that they should have seriously
thought of planting vineyards in
this cold region. "Vine-planters"
are mentioned on page 42 among
what the Company were to "provide to send for New-England." In
1634, the yearly rent of Governor's
Island, in Boston harbour, was a
hogshead of wine. That island had
been granted to Gov. Winthrop
April 3, 1632, on condition that he
should plant a vineyard or orchard
there. See Col. Rec. i. 85, 141.

[2] Of Thomas Graves, the engineer, very little is known, except
what is contained in the preceding
Records of the Company and in this
letter. Very soon after his arrival
at Salem, at the end of June, he was
sent by Gov. Endicott, with the
Rev. Francis Bright, Abraham Palmer, and others, to take possession
of Massachusetts Bay, in conformity
with the instructions sent over by
the Company. He pitched on Mishawum, (now Charlestown,) where
he found Walford, the smith, and
perhaps the Spragues, (unless, as is
more probable, they were of the 100
who came with him.) The Charlestown records inform us that he mo-

delled and laid out the plan of that
town, with streets about the hill,
measured out two acre lots for the
inhabitants, and "built the great
house for such of the Company as
are shortly to come over, which
afterwards became the meeting-
house." At the end of the third
edition of Higginson's New-England's Plantation, printed in London
in 1630, is "a letter sent from New-
England by Master Graves, Engineer, now there resident." In
White Kennett's American Library,
or Catalogue of Books and Papers
which he gave in 1713 to the Society for the Propagation of the Gospel in Foreign Parts, page 237, is
the following entry : "A copy of a
Letter from an Engineer sent out to
New-England, written to a friend in
England, A. D. 1629, giving an account of his landing with a small
company at Salem, and thence going
and making a settlement at Massachusetts Bay, and laying the foundation of a town, to which the Governor gave the name of Charlestown ; with a pleasing description of
the exceeding pleasantness and fruit-
fulness of the country, and of the
civility of the natives. In one sheet

commended to us as well for his honesty, as skill in
many things very useful. First, he professeth great
skill in the making of salt, both in ponds and pans,
as also to find out salt springs or mines. Secondly,
he is well seen in mines and minerals, especially
about iron ore and iron works. Thirdly, he is able
to make any sort of fortifications. Fourthly, he is
well able to survey and set forth lands. He hath
been a traveller in divers foreign parts to gain his
experience. Therefore we pray you take his advice
touching the premises, and where you intend to sit
down in, to fortify and build a town, that it may be
qualified for good air and water, according to your
first instructions,[1] and may have as much natural
help as may be ; whereby it may with the less labor
and cost be made fit to resist an enemy. So soon as
you have made trial of his sufficiency, write us your
opinion how long you conceive it will be fit for us to
continue him in our service ; for that he is tied[2] to

MS. Ex dono Rev. Alexandri
Young, S. T. B." There can be
no doubt that the author of this letter was Graves. This circumstance,
to say nothing of the identity of the
donor's name with my own, prompt-
ed me to apply, four years ago, to
Gov. Everett, then our Minister at
the Court of Great Britain, to procure for me a copy of it. He very
obligingly applied in my behalf to
the Secretary of the Society, but no
document of the kind was to be
found in their archives. Search was
then made, at his instance, in the
Library at Lambeth, but with like
ill success. It is to be feared that
the manuscript is irrecoverably lost.
— Graves was admitted a freeman
May 18, 1631, and Prince, p. 321,
appends to his name this remark,
" after, a rear-admiral in England."
I think he confounds the engineer

with another Thomas Graves, who
was mate of the Talbot on her
first voyage, and who, according to
Winthrop, writing under June 3,
1635, " had come every year for
these seven years." Besides, the
rear-admiral of that name was born
in 1605, and in 1629 was only twenty-four years old, whilst the engineer
at this time had a family of five
children. It is probable that he soon
returned to England, as no notice of
him occurs in the subsequent history
of the Colony. See page 54 ; Winthrop's Hist. i. 161, and Frothingham's excellent History of Charlestown, p. 26.

[1] These first instructions to Endicott are not preserved. See Hutchinson's Mass. i. 9.

[2] Graves's contract is printed on
pp. 56–59.

CHAP.
V.

1629
April
17.

serve us one whole year absolutely, and two years more if we should give him order to stay there so long. So we hope to receive your advice time enough to give him order to stay out full three years, or to come home at the end of one year. His salary costs this Company a great sum of money ; besides which, if he remain with us, the transporting of his wife, and building him a house, will be very chargeable; which we pray you take into your consideration, that so we may continue or surcease this charge, as occasion shall require.

In our next we intend to send you a particular of such as are to have land allotted and set out unto them, that so you may appoint unto each man an equal proportion by lot, according to what is to be allowed in the first dividend ;[1] touching which we shall then give you more large instructions. Meanwhile, for such as have sent over servants and cattle in these ships,[2] and for such as have more to come in two other ships,[3] which we hope will be ready to set sail within ten days, our desire is, they should either be accommodated at Nahumkeeke, or in the Mattachusetts Bay, or in both places, if they desire it, with all the conveniency that may be ; and for such grounds as shall be allotted unto them, that the same be conveyed unto them, if they desire it, at any time within one year after their entering upon it, and to be accounted as part of their first dividend. But if they shall dislike it at any time before a general distribution be made by lot to all the adventurers,

---

[1] See pp. 69, 73-77.
[2] The George, the Talbot, and the Lion's Whelp.

[3] They despatched three others, the Mayflower, the Four Sisters, and the Pilgrim.

then they may have liberty to do it, and take in lieu CHAP.
thereof as by lot shall fall out amongst other private
adventurers.

1629.

We recommend unto you Sir Richard Saltonstall April 17.
and Mr. Isaac Johnson, who send over servants and
cattle in these ships, desiring you will take care for
their present accommodation, as aforesaid ; and as
for them, so we may not omit to pray you likewise
to give all good accommodation to our present Governor, Mr. Matthew Cradock, who, with some particular brethren of our Company, have deeply engaged
themselves in their private adventures in these ships,
and those to come ; and as we hold these men that thus
deeply adventure in their private, to be, under God,
special instruments for the advancing and strengthening of our Plantation, which is done by them without any charge to the Company's general stock,
wherein notwithstanding they are as deep or deeper
engaged than any other, so being contented to be
debarred from all private trading in furs for three
years, we do hold it very requisite in all other their
desires to give them all accommodation and furtherance that reasonably may be propounded by them,
or any for them ; their good beginnings in the infancy of our Plantation worthily deserving of us all
favor and furtherance.

We have caused a common seal[1] to be made, which
we send you by Mr. Sharpe.

[1] This seal, mentioned on page 42, is stamped on the back of this volume. In the centre stands an Indian, raising the Macedonian cry, (Acts, xvi. 9,) " Come over and help us ;" in allusion to the main end of the Plantation, the conversion of the natives to Christianity. The appropriateness of this device is lost in the present seal of the Commonwealth, where the Indian is retained, but an arm brandishing a sword is placed over his head, and for the old motto is substituted Algernon Sidney's well-known line, " Ense petit placidam sub libertate quietem."

If you want any swine, we have agreed with those of New Plymouth that they deliver you six sows with pig, for which they are to be allowed £9 in account of what they owe unto Mr. Goffe, our Deputy. And for goats, we have bought forty-two for the general and particular men's accounts, which shall be sent you by these and the next ships, or at leastwise so many of them as they can conveniently carry.

We have followed your advice, and sent most of our guns snaphance,[1] bastard musket bore ; and we have also sent store of powder and shot, grain for seed, both wheat, barley, and rye, in the chaff, &c.[2] As for fruit-stones and kernels, the time of the year fits not to send them now ; so we purpose to do it per our next. Tame turkeys shall be now sent you, if may be ; if not, per other ships. We are disappointed of the provisions ordered to have been sent you for yourself and Mrs. Endicott ; but, God willing, they shall come by the next.

We have made our servants' apparel of cloth and leather ; which leather is not of oil skins,[3] for we found them over dear. Yet if this prove not profitable, upon your second advice we will send you oil skins.

For such of our nation as sell munition, guns, or other furniture, to arm the Indians against us, or teach them the use of arms, we would have you to apprehend them and send them prisoners for England,[4] where they will not escape severe punishment,

---

[1] See note [3] on page 44.
[2] See page 42.
[3] See pages 40 and 42.
[4] It was on this ground that, before Endicott's arrival, Standish had already arrested Morton, at Mount Wollaston, and sent him home. See note [1] on page 48, and Mass. Hist. Coll. iii. 62 ; Morton's Memorial, 136–141 ; Prince's Annals, pp. 250 to 252.

being expressly against the Proclamation.[1]  You CHAP.<br>V.
have had former caution given you to take heed of
being too secure in trusting the Indians,[2] which we 1629.
again commend to your care ; and that you may be April<br>17.
the better able to resist both foreign enemies and
the natives, if either should assail you, we pray you
let all such as live under our government, both our
servants and other planters and their servants, be
exercised in the use of arms, and certain times
appointed to muster them ; in which business Mr.
Sharpe[3] and Mr. Graves will be assistant to you.
Mr. Sharpe is by us entertained[4] to be master-gunner
of our ordnance ; in which service he is to employ
so much of his time as the charge of that office doth
require, and in the rest he is to follow other employments of our Governor's and others, for whose employment he is particularly sent over.

Enclosed you shall receive a factory[5] of such provision of victual and other necessaries as we have
sent for the general account, to which we refer you,
nothing doubting but you will be a provident steward to husband our provisions to the best advantage.
We also send you the particular names of such as
are entertained for the Company's service ; amongst
which we hope you will find many religious, discreet, and well-ordered persons, which you must set

---

[1] See pages 83 and 84.
[2] In Cradock's letter. See page 136.
[3] Samuel Sharpe was chosen an Assistant of the Company in England April 30, 1629, and again Oct. 20, 1629.  But being out of the country, and not able to take the oath, he was superseded in his place, Feb. 10, 1630, by Roger Lud-

low.  He was Cradock's agent in the Colony.  He remained at Salem, where he was chosen a ruling elder of the church.  He was never afterwards a magistrate ; and died in 1658. See pages 50, 59 and 124; Prince, p. 271.
[4] See the agreement with Sharpe on page 50.
[5] Inventory.

over the rest, dividing them into families, placing some with the ministers, and others under such as being honest men, and of their own calling, as near as may be, may have care to see them well educated in their general callings as Christians, and particular according to their several trades, or fitness in disposition to learn a trade. And whereas, amongst such a number, notwithstanding our care to purge them, there may still remain some libertines, we desire you to be careful that such, if any be, may be forced, by inflicting such punishment as their offences shall deserve, (which is to be, as near as may be, according to the laws of this kingdom,) to conform themselves to good order; with whom, after admonition given, if they amend not, we pray you proceed without partiality to punish them, as the nature of their fault shall deserve; and the like course you are to hold both with planters and their servants; for all must live under government and a like law. And to the end you may not do anything contrary to law, nor the power granted us by his Majesty's letters patents, we have, as aforesaid, sent you the duplicate of the letters patents under the great seal of England, ordering and requiring you and the rest of the Council there, not to do anything, either in inflicting punishment on malefactors, or otherwise, contrary to or in derogation of the said letters patents; but, if occasion require, we authorize you and them to proceed according to the power you have. Nevertheless, we desire, if it may be, that errors may be reformed with lenity, or mild correction; and if any prove incorrigible, and will not be reclaimed by gentle correction, ship such persons home by the

Lion's Whelp,[1] rather than keep them there to infect or to be an occasion of scandal unto others; we be- ing fully persuaded that if one or two be so reship- ped back, and certificate sent home of their misde- meanour, it will be a terror to the rest, and a means to reduce them to good conformity. And, above all, we pray you be careful that there be none in our precincts permitted to do any injury, in the least kind, to the heathen people ; and if any offend in that way, let them receive due correction. And we hold it fitting you publish a proclamation to that effect, by leaving it fixed under the Company's seal in some eminent place, for all to take notice at such time as both the heathen themselves, as well as our people, may take notice of it. And for the avoiding of the hurt that may follow through our much famil- iarity with the Indians, we conceive it fit that they be not permitted to come to your Plantation but at certain times and places, to be appointed them. If any of the salvages pretend right of inheritance to all or any part of the lands granted in our patent, we pray you endeavour to purchase their title, that we may avoid the least scruple of intrusion.[2]

---

[1] This was Endicott's authority and apology for sending home the Brownes.

[2] These instructions were literally and scrupulously observed by the first settlers of Massachusetts as well as of Plymouth. They made conscience of paying the natives to their satisfaction for all parts of the territory which were not depopula- ted, or deserted, and left without a claimant. The government of the Province, writing home to Lord Shelburne, the Secretary for the Colonies, in 1767, say, " We are satisfied there are no complaints against this Province by his Majes- ty's agents for Indian affairs; and that no settlement has been made or attempted by us without proper au- thority. It is with much pleasure we remind your Excellency and in- form the world, that greater care was taken of the Indians by our pious ancestors during the old char- ter, and by this government under the new, even to this day, than was ever required of us by the British government. Nothing has been omitted by the province since 1633

CHAP.
V.

1629.
April
17.

We have, in the former part of our letter, certified you of the good hopes we have of the love and unanimous agreement of our ministers, they having declared themselves to us to be of one judgment, and to be fully agreed on the manner how to exercise their ministry; which we hope will be by them accordingly performed.[1] Yet, because it is often found that some busy persons, led more by their will than any good warrant out of God's word, take opportunities by moving needless questions to stir up strife, and by that means to beget a question, and bring men to declare some difference in judgment, most commonly in things indifferent, from which small beginnings great mischiefs have followed, we pray you and the rest of the Council, that if any such disputes shall happen amongst you, that you suppress them, and be careful to maintain peace and unity.[2]

We desire you to take notice of one Lawrence Leech,[3] whom we have found a careful and painful

---

to this day, which justice or humanity required, within this jurisdiction. We glory in the conduct of our government, we make our boast of it as unexampled; and we have been free and spontaneous on our part. We assure you, that being animated by the same principles with our ancestors, we shall do everything which duty to the King, and the maxims of good policy, of justice and equity to the Indians can require." The first President Adams being asked his opinion concerning the treatment of the Indians in New-England, replied, that he believed it to have been just. "In all my practice at the bar," said he, "I never knew a contested title to lands, but what was traced up to the Indian title." See Chronicles of Plymouth, p. 259; Hutchinson's Mass. ii. 266;

Holmes's Annals, i. 217, ii. 150; Colony Laws, p. 132.

[1] "By this," says Prince, p. 258, "it appears Mr. Bright was a Puritan; and Mr. Hubbard seems mistaken in supposing him a Conformist; unless he means in the same sense as were many Puritans in those days, who by particular favor omitted the more offensive ceremonies and parts in the Common Prayer, while, for the unity and peace of the Church, and in hopes of a farther reformation, they used the other." See Hubbard, pp. 112, 113, and Johnson, Hist. N. E., ch. 9.

[2] This would serve to justify Endicott in his summary proceedings to suppress the schismatical and anarchical conduct of the Brownes.

[3] Lawrence Leach was admitted a freeman May 18, 1631. He was

man, and we doubt not but he will continue his diligence ; let him have deserving respect.   The like
we say of Richard Waterman,[1] whose chief employment will be to get you good venison.

We have sent six shipwrights, of whom Robert
Molton[2] is chief.  These men's entertainment is
very chargeable to us ; and by agreement it is to be
borne two-thirds at the charge of the general Company, and the other third is to be borne by Mr. Cradock, our Governor, and his associates, interested
in a private stock.  We hope you will be careful to
see them so employed as may countervail the charge,
desiring you to agree with Mr. Sharpe that their
labor may be employed two thirds for the general

one of the thirteen men (selectmen) of Salem ; and that town, in 1636, made him a grant of 100 acres of land.  He died in 1662, aged 83, having been a useful and respectable citizen.  See Felt's Annals of Salem, pp. 215, 536, (1st ed. 1827.)

[1] Richard Waterman lived at Salem till he was required by the General Court, March 12, 1638, with other familists or antinomians, to quit the Colony.  He joined Roger Williams at Providence, in October, and became one of the founders of that city and of the Baptist church there, the first of the name in America.  In Jan. 1643, with Randall Holden and Samuel Gorton, he purchased of the Indians the tract of land called Shawomet, (now Warwick,) and in September was arrested there, with the rest of Gorton's company, by order of the General Court of Massachusetts, and brought to Boston.  After his discharge, he returned to Providence.  He was one of the commissioners for that town in the General Assembly of Rhode Island in 1650, and one of the town magistrates in 1655.  He was living as late as 1658.  See Col. Rec. i. 218 ; Winthrop, ii. 120, 137,

148 ; Callender's Hist. Disc. 89, 97 ; Backus, Hist. of the Baptists in N. E., i. 92 ; Hague, Hist. Disc. p. 32 ; Staples, Annals of Providence, pp. 30, 33, 35, 76, 112, 121 ; Mass. Hist. Col. xix. 170, 182.

[2] Robert Moulton was admitted a freeman May 18, 1631.  He was chosen constable of Charlestown April 1, 1634, and the same year was a deputy from that town in the General Court.  " May 14, 1634, Mr. Beecher, Mr. Pierce, and Robert Moulton are desired to treat with Mr. Stevens and Mr. Mayhew for the building of the sea-fort by the great."  After this he removed to Salem ; for in 1637 he was one of the thirteen men, and represented that town the same year in the General Court, and was one of those that were ordered to be disarmed for signing the petition or remonstrance in favor of Wheelwright.  Morton's Point, in Charlestown, (or Molten's, as it was formerly called, according to Winthrop, i. 154,) was probably named after him.  He died in 1655.  See page 94 ; Col. Rec. MS. i. 111, 117 ; Felt's Salem, 105, 527, (ed. 1827) ; Savage's Winthrop, i. 129, 215, 248.

Company, and one third for Mr. Cradock and his
associates ; praying you to accommodate the said
Mr. Cradock's people in all fitting manner, as he
doth well deserve.

Such cattle, both horses, mares, cows, bulls and
goats, as are shipped by Mr. Cradock, are to be
divided in equal halves 'twixt him and the Company;
which was omitted to be done here, for avoiding
partiality ; so you must do it equally there.

We pray you to be careful to make us what
returns you possibly may, the better to enable us
to send out a fresh supply. We hope you have
converted the commodities you carried with you
for truck, into beaver, otter, or other furs, which
we pray you send us by the Talbot ; as also any
other commodities you have provided in readiness
against the ship's coming thither. But pray do
not detain her any long time to cut timber, or any
other gross lading ; for she is at £150 a month
charges, which will soon eat out more than the
goods she should stay for is worth. Wherefore,
pray make what expedition you can to unlade her
goods, and to put such things aboard her as you
have ready, and send her hitherward again as soon
as you may.

We have sent five weight of salt in the Whelp,
and ten weight in the Talbot. If there be any
shallops to be had to fish withal, and the season of
the year fit, pray let the fishermen, (of which we
send six from Dorchester,) together with some of
the ships' company, endeavour to take fish, and let
it be well saved with the said salt, and packed up in
hogsheads, or otherwise, as shall be thought fittest,

and send it home by the Talbot or Lion's Whelp.
Now, forasmuch as the Lion's Whelp belongeth to
the Company, you may, if there be hope to do good
by it, keep her there some time after the Talbot;
but unless it be to very good purpose, do not detain
her, but let her come home in company of the Talbot.  The George Bonaventure is to land her passengers, and other things belonging to the general
Company or to particular men, and so set sail for
Newfoundland ; and we pray you let it be your care
to despatch her as soon as may be.

William Ryall and Thomas Brude, coopers and
cleavers of timber, are entertained by us in halves
with Mr. Cradock, our Governor.  Pray join others
that can assist them unto them, and let them provide us some staves, and other timber of all sorts, to
be sent us by the Talbot, Whelp, or the other two
ships that come after.  But we pray you consider
the charge of these ships, and detain them not for
small matters.  Rather use all diligence to send
them away.

If, at the arrival of this ship, Mr. Endicott should
be departed this life, (which God forbid,) or should
happen to die before the other ships arrive, we authorize you, Mr. Skelton, and Mr. Samuel Sharpe,
to take care of our affairs, and to govern the people
according to order, until further order.  And to the
end the Sabbath may be celebrated in a religious
manner, we appoint that all that inhabit the Plantation, both for the general and particular employments, may surcease their labor every Saturday
throughout the year at three of the clock in the
afternoon ; and that they spend the rest of that day

CHAP.  in catechising and preparation for the Sabbath, as the
V.
ministers shall direct.[1]

1629.    If it shall please God to take away by death any
April    of the thirteen that shall be chosen and appointed
17.
for the Council, (of which yourself or your successor
is to be one,) in such case the then being Governor and the surviving Council shall from time to
time make choice of one or more to supply the place
of such as shall be wanting ; and that there may no
difference arise about the appointing of one to be
minister with those you send to inhabit at Mattachusetts Bay, we will have you, in case the ministers
cannot agree amongst themselves who shall undertake that place, to make choice of one of the three
by lot ; and on whom the lot shall fall, he to go with
his family to perform that work.[2]

We have advised you of the sending of William
Ryall and Thomas Brude, cleavers of timber.[3]    But

[1] This serves to show that the
custom, once universal throughout
New-England, of "keeping" Saturday afternoon and evening, was
not of home origin or invention, but
was early enjoined and introduced
from abroad.  The practice no doubt
originated from the injunction in Le-
viticus, xxiii. 32, " From even unto
even shall ye celebrate your sabbath."  The Jewish sabbath (Saturday,) began at six o'clock of our
Friday evening, and the preparation
for it at three in the afternoon.
There is an allusion to this in
Matthew xxvii. 62, and John xix.
42, where " the day of the preparation," and " the Jews' preparation
day," are spoken of.  Mather says
that John Cotton " began the sabbath the evening before ; for which
keeping of the sabbath from evening
to evening he wrote arguments before his coming to New-England ;
and I suppose 'twas from his reason

and practise that the Christians of
New-England have generally done
so."  Hutchinson says it was some
time before this custom was settled.
Mr. Hooker, in a letter written
about the year 1640, says, " The
question touching the beginning of
the sabbath is now on foot among
us, hath once been spoken to, and
we are to give in our arguments,
each to the other, so that we may
ripen our thoughts concerning that
truth, and if the Lord will, it may
more fully appear ;" and in another
letter, March, 1640, " Mr. Huit
hath not answered our arguments
against the beginning the sabbath
at morning."  See Mather's Magnalia, i. 253, and Hutchinson's
Mass. i. 428.

[2] Bright went, as appears from
the Charlestown records.  He had
a wife and two children.

[3] See page 150.

indeed the said Thomas his name is Brand, and not CHAP.<br>V.
Norton;[1] but there is one Norton,[2] a carpenter,
whom we pray you respect as he shall deserve. 1629.
There is one Richard Ewstead, a wheelwright, April 17.
who was commended to us by Mr. Davenport for a
very able man, though not without his imperfections.
We pray you take notice of him, and regard him as he
shall well deserve. The benefit of his labor is to be
two-thirds for the general Company and one-third for
Mr. Cradock, our Governor, being his charges is to
be borne according to that proportion; and withal
we pray you take care that their charges who are for
partable employments, whether in halves or thirds,
may be equally defrayed by such as are to have
benefit of their labors, according to each party's proportion. Their several agreements, or the copies
thereof, shall be (if God permit) sent you by the
next ships.

We have entertained Lambert Wilson, chirurgeon,
to remain with you in the service of the Plantation;
with whom we are agreed that he shall serve this
Company and the other planters that live in the
Plantation, for three years, and in that time apply
himself to cure not only of such as came from hence
for the general and particular accounts, but also for
the Indians, as from time to time he shall be directed
by yourself or your successor and the rest of the
Council. And moreover he is to educate and instruct in his art one or more youths,[3] such as you

---

[1] Probably an error of the pen for Brude.

[2] Probably the Mr. Norton with whom the congregation at Salem agreed to build a suitable meeting-house in 1634. See Felt's Salem, p. 72, (ed. 1827.)

[3] We have here the embryo of a Medical School, undoubtedly the first contemplated on the continent of America. Whether it ever went into operation, or how it succeeded, we are not informed.

CHAP.
V.

1629.
April
17.

and the said Council shall appoint, that may be helpful to him, and, if occasion serve, succeed him in the Plantation ; which youth or youths, fit to learn that profession, let be placed with him ; of which Mr. Hugesson's son,[1] if his father approve thereof, may be one, the rather because he hath been trained up in literature ; but if not he, then such other as you shall judge most fittest, &c.

*The 21st of April, in Gravesend.*[2]

21. The afore-written is, for the most part, the copy[3] of our General Letter, sent you together with our patent under the broad seal, and the Company's seal in silver, by Mr. Samuel Sharpe, passenger in the George, who, we think, is yet riding in the Hope ;[4] but, by means of stormy weather, the Talbot and Lion's Whelp are yet at Blackwall.[5] By these ships that are to follow we intend (God willing,) to supply both in our advice and in our provisions what is

---

[1] This was John, the eldest son, at this time nearly thirteen years old, having been born Aug. 6, 1616. He had been educated at the grammar school in Leicester, England. After his father's death in August, 1630, he accompanied his mother to Charlestown, and afterwards to New Haven. For a while he taught a school at Hartford, and having studied divinity, became a preacher in 1637, and officiated three or four years as a chaplain at Saybrook fort. His mother died in 1640, and in 1641 he removed to Guildford, and in 1660 succeeded his father in the church at Salem, being its sixth minister. He died there Dec. 9, 1708, aged 92, having been a preacher more than seventy years. See Mather's Magnalia, i. 10, 330 ; Hutchinson's Mass. i.

425, ii. 176 ; Trumbull's Connecticut, i. 279, 280, 296 ; Kingsley's Hist. Disc. p. 102.

[2] Gravesend is on the right bank of the Thames, 22 miles below London, in Kent. All vessels sailing from the port of London were, till recently, obliged to clear out at Gravesend. Gov. Cradock had probably gone down there to take leave and put his letters on board.

[3] This identical copy, in the handwriting of Burgess, the Secretary of the Company, is preserved in excellent order at the end of the first volume of Deeds in the Registry of Suffolk ; and it is from that we print.

[4] A reach in the Thames, just below Gravesend.

[5] Blackwall is only four miles from St. Paul's, down the Thames.

wanting now.   In the mean-while we pray you accommodate business with your true endeavours for
the general good in the best and discreetest manner
that you may.

For the better accommodation of businesses, we
have divided the servants belonging to the Company
into several families, as we desire and intend they
should live together ; a copy whereof we send you
here enclosed, that you may accordingly appoint
each man his charge and duty.   Yet it is not our intent to tie you so strictly to this direction, but that
in your discretion, as you shall see cause from time
to time, you may alter or displace any as you shall
think fit.

Our earnest desire is that you take special care,
in settling these families, that the chief in the family,
at least some of them, be grounded in religion ;
whereby morning and evening family duties may be
duly performed, and a watchful eye held over all in
each family, by one or more in each family to be
appointed thereto, that so disorders may be prevented, and ill weeds nipped before they take too great
a head.   It will be a business worthy your best endeavours to look unto this in the beginning, and, if
need be, to make some exemplary to all the rest ;
otherwise your government will be esteemed as a
scarecrow.   Our desire is to use lenity, all that may
be ; but, in case of necessity, not to neglect the
other, knowing that correction is ordained for the
fool's back.   And as we intend not to be wanting on
our parts to provide all things needful for the maintenance and sustenance of our servants, so may we
justly, by the laws of God and man, require obe-

dience and honest carriage from them, with fitting labor in their several employments ; wherein if they shall be wanting, and much more if refractory, care must be taken to punish the obstinate and disobedient,[1] being as necessary as food and raiment. And we heartily pray you, that all be kept to labor, as the only means to reduce them to civil, yea a godly life, and to keep youth from falling into many enormities, which by nature we are all too much inclined unto. God, who alone is able and powerful, enable you to this great work, and grant that our chiefest aim may be his honor and glory. And thus wishing you all happy and prosperous success, we end and rest

Your assured loving friends,

The Governor and Deputy

Of the New-England Company

For a Plantation in Mattachusetts Bay.

Through many businesses we had almost forgotten to recommend unto you two brethren of our Company, Mr. John and Mr. Samuel Browne, who, though they be no adventurers in the general stock, yet are they men we do much respect, being fully persuaded of their sincere affections to the good of our Plantation. The one, Mr. John Browne, is sworn an Assistant here, and by us chosen one of the Council there ; a man experienced in the laws of our kingdom, and such an one as we are persuaded will worthily deserve your favor and furtherance ; which we desire he may have, and that in the first division of lands there may be allotted to either of them two hundred acres.

---

[1] Some word, such as order or discipline, is here accidentally omitted.

I find Mr. Oldham's[1] grant from Mr. Gorge is to CHAP.
him and John Dorrell, for all the lands within Mat- V.
tachusetts Bay, between Charles river and Abousett[2] 16 29.
river, containing in length, by a straight line, five April
miles up the said Charles river, into the main land 21.
northwest from the border of the said Bay, including
all creeks and points by the way, and three miles in
length from the mouth of the foresaid river of Abousett, up into the main land, upon a straight line south-
west, including all creeks and points, and all the land
in breadth and length between the foresaid rivers,
with all prerogatives, royal mines excepted. The
rent reserved is twelve pence on every hundred acres
of land that shall be used ; William Blaxton,[3] clerk,

---

[1] We hear nothing more of Oldham, after his unsuccessful attempt
to negotiate with the Massachusetts
Company and to get his claim to
territory within their patent allowed,
till May 18, 1631, when he was admitted a freeman of the Colony. Of
course, before this was done, he
must have abandoned his pretensions
and made terms with the colonial
government. When he came over,
for the last time, is uncertain,
whether in the vessel he was at this
time providing, or in one of the
Company's three ships that sailed
in June, after Higginson's departure,
or in one of Winthrop's fleet. He
was one of the early settlers of Watertown, and was evidently trusted
and respected in the Colony. We
find him in May, 1632, one of the
two deputies sent from Watertown
to advise with the Governor and Assistants about raising a public stock;
and he was also one of the three representatives of that town in the first
General Court of Delegates, held
May 14, 1634. He was a fearless
and enterprising trader with the natives, and his murder by the Indians
of Block Island in July, 1636, was

the immediate cause of the Pequot
War. See Winthrop's Hist. i. 76,
80, 129, 189–192, ii. 362.
[2] Saugus river, in Lynn. See
Lewis's History of Lynn, p. 21.
[3] William Blackstone, (or Blaxton, as it was spelt by his son, and
by Ed. Johnson, in his History of
New-England,) the first European
occupant of the peninsula on which
Boston is built, was a clergyman, a
Puritan and Nonconformist, and was
educated at Emanuel College, Cambridge, where he took the degree of
A. B. in 1617, and of A. M. in 1621.
He was one of the first settlers in
Massachusetts Bay, having been assessed in June, 1628, for the campaign against Morton of Mount Wollaston. Lechford, who was here in
1637, says that Blackstone lived at
Boston nine or ten years. Now, as
he left Boston in the spring of 1635,
this would determine his residence
here as early as 1625 or 1626. He
may have been one of the company
whom Robert Gorges brought over
in Sept. 1623, and one of " the undertakers " to whose charge and
custody he left his plantation at
Wessagusset, when he returned to

CHAP.
V.
1629.

April
21.

and William Jeffryes,[1] gentleman, authorized to put John Oldham in possession. Having a sight of his

England in 1624. It certainly appears from this letter, that he was at this time acting as an agent of John Gorges, (who, after his brother Robert's death, had succeeded to his patent,) and was empowered by him, in conjunction with Jeffries, to put Oldham in possession of the territory which he had leased him. According to the united testimony of the Charlestown Records, Edward Johnson, and Roger Clap, Blackstone, at the time of Winthrop's arrival, "was dwelling alone at a place called by the Indians Shawmut, where he only had a cottage,—that plain neck called Blackstone's neck, —on a point of land called Blackstone's Point." This was the place afterwards called Barton's Point, near Craigie's bridge, and opposite the State's Prison. He was admitted a freeman May 18, 1631. Mather, i. 221, and after him, Hutchinson, i. 21, says, that Blackstone claimed the whole peninsula, on the ground that he was the first person that had slept upon it. Such a claim could not be allowed by the government of Massachusetts, since by their charter the whole territory within the Bay vested in them. Still they seem to have treated him generously; for at a Court held April 1, 1633, it was "agreed that Mr. Wm. Blackstone shall have fifty acres of ground set out for him near to his house in Boston, to enjoy forever;" which must have been at least a fourteenth part of the whole peninsula. The next year, 1634, he sold this land to the other inhabitants of the town for £30, reserving for himself only about six acres on the Point where he had built his house. To pay this sum, a rate of six shillings to each householder was assessed Nov. 10, 1634 ; and Blackstone probably removed the next spring, 1635, with a stock of cows which he had purchased with the money he had received. Lech-

ford says that Blackstone "went from Boston because he would not join with the church;" and Cotton Mather says, that "this man was, indeed, of a particular humour, he would never join himself to any of our churches, giving this reason for it, 'I came from England because I did not like the lord-bishops; but I can't join with you, because I would not be under the lord-brethren.'" There is no ground, however, for the intimation thrown out by certain writers, that he was driven away by intolerance or harsh usage. He seems to have been a contemplative, recluse sort of person, and, amidst the growing population of the peninsula, he doubtless pined for the seclusion and quiet which he had enjoyed when he was its solitary, undisturbed possessor. These he found in his new residence, in the southern part of the present town of Cumberland, in Rhode Island, about thirty-five miles to the southward of Boston, and three miles above the village of Pawtucket, on the eastern bank of the beautiful river that now bears his name. The spot he selected was then within the jurisdiction of New-Plymouth, the government of which, in 1671, granted him the land on which he had settled, being about 200 acres. In the Records of that Colony, under 1661, his place is mentioned as that "where one Blackstone now sojourneth." The antiquarian pilgrim may identify it by inquiring for the Whipple farm, within a few rods of Whipple's bridge, a mile and a half above Valley Falls, on the west side of the stage road from Pawtucket to Worcester. Here Blackstone lived a retired and quiet life, cultivating his garden and orchard, and studying his books, of which he had 186 volumes, among them three bibles and eleven Latin folios and quartos, which he probably brought with him

grant, this I found. Though I hold it void in law, CHAP. V. yet his claim being to this, you may, in your discretion, prevent him by causing some to take possession 1629. April 21. of the chief part thereof.[2]

from Emanuel College. These books were all destroyed with his house, in Philip's War, which broke out only a few weeks after his death. On July 4th, 1659, he was married at Boston, by Gov. Endicott, to Sarah Stevenson, widow of John Stevenson, by whom he had one son, John, who survived him, and was a minor at the time of his father's death. The old man died in May, 1675, and was buried on his own farm on the 28th of the month. He could not have been far from eighty years of age, as he was probably about 21 when he graduated at Cambridge in 1617. His well, with the stoning almost entire, is still to be seen, and also the cellar of his house, and his lonely grave by the side of Study Hill. A few years since it was marked by a large round white stone. But this has disappeared, and two rude stones now stand at the head and foot of the grave. How long will it be before some one of the princely merchants of the renowned peninsula which he first tenanted, will erect a worthy monument over his grave, or build a cenotaph to his memory in the metropolis of New-England? See Savage's Winthrop, i. 44, ii. 362; Mass. Hist. Coll. iii. 63, xii. 70, 86, xix. 174, xx. 170, xxiii. 97, 399, xxviii. 247; Hazard, i. 391; Holmes's Annals, i. 377; Prince's Annals, pp. 221–224; Snow's Boston, pp. 31, 50; Frothingham's Charlestown, p. 45; Daggett's Attleborough, pp. 24–34; Bliss's Rehoboth, pp. 2–14.

[1] William Jeffrey, or Jeffries, was an old planter in New-England before the arrival of Endicott; for we find his name among those who, in June, 1628, were assessed for the expenses of arresting Morton and sending him home. He was at this time probably residing at Cape Ann or Ipswich. It is not known when or how he came over. He was among the first admitted to be freemen, May 18, 1631. Jeffrey's Creek, now Manchester, and Jeffrey's Neck, in Ipswich, were undoubtedly called after him. In 1638, with Nicholas Easton, he removed to the vicinity of the Rhode Island Plantations; and in 1642 his name appears among the proprietors of Weymouth. He appears to have claimed the neck of land in Ipswich, called by his name, on the ground of a purchase from the natives; for we find by an act of the General Court, passed in 1666, that 500 acres of land were granted to him " on the south side of our patent, [probably at Weymouth,] to be a final issue of all claims by virtue of any grant heretofore made by any Indians whatsoever." By a letter which Morton, of Merry Mount, wrote to him in May, 1634, it would seem that Jeffrey was formerly one of his friends, for he addresses him with the familiar title, " My very good gossip." See Winthrop's Hist. i. 44, 138, ii. 361; Hutchinson's Mass i. 31; Mass. Hist. Coll. iii. 63; Felt's Hist. of Ipswich, p. 9; Leach's Hist. of Manchester, MS. p. 4, in the Archives of the Mass. Hist. Society.

[2] This last paragraph, in the singular number, was probably written by Gov. Cradock.

# CHAPTER VI.

*London, 28th May,* 1629.

CHAP.
VI.

1629.
May
28.

AFTER our hearty commendations—our last unto you was of the 17th and 21st April, sent by the last ships, viz. the George Bonaventure, Thomas Cox, master, who set sail from the Isle of Wight the 4th of this month, and seconded[1] by the Talbot, Thomas Beecher, master, and the Lion's Whelp, John Gibbs, master, who set sail also from the Isle of Wight about the 11th of this month ; which letter being large, and consisting of many particulars, hath been confirmed here ; and herewith you shall receive a copy[2] thereof, desiring you to take especial care of the performance and putting in execution of all things material therein mentioned, and particularly, amongst others, that point concerning publication to be made that no wrong or injury be offered by any of our peo-

---

[1] The duplicate of their first letter was sent by the Talbot. See page 166.

[2] It is this second copy, probably, that is preserved in the first book of the Suffolk Registry of Deeds, and from which we have printed the letter. See page 166.

ple to the natives there.[1] To which purpose we desire you, the Governor, to advise with the Council in penning of an effectual edict, upon penalty to be inflicted upon such as shall transgress the same ; which being done, our desire is, the same may be published, to the end that all men may take notice thereof, as also that you send a copy thereof unto us by the next return of the ships.

We have, sithence our last, and according as we then advised, at a full and ample Court[2] assembled, elected and established you, Captain John Endicott, to the place of present Governor in our Plantation there, as also some others to be of the Council with you, as more particularly you will perceive by an Act of Court[3] herewith sent, confirmed by us at a General Court,[4] and sealed with our common seal ; to which Act we refer you, desiring you all punctually to observe the same, and that the Oaths[5] we herewith send you, (which have been here penned by learned counsel, to be administered to each of you in your several places,) may be administered in such manner and form as in and by our said Order is particularly expressed ; and that yourselves do frame such other Oaths, as in your wisdoms you shall think fit to be administered to your Secretary or other officers, according to their several places respectively.

---

[1] See page 159.
[2] This Court was held April 30, 1629. See page 66.
[3] This Act of Court, establishing the government in New-England, is preserved, and is printed at the end of this letter. See also pp. 68, 78.
[4] The four quarterly meetings, or general assemblies of the Company,

authorized by the Charter, were called Great and General Courts. Hence the origin of the title by which the Legislature of Massachusetts is still designated.
[5] These oaths are preserved, and are printed in a subsequent part of this volume. See also page 69.

We have further taken into our consideration the
fitness and conveniency, or rather a necessity, of
making a dividend of land, and allotting a proportion
to each adventurer, and otherwise ; and to this purpose have made and confirmed an Act,[1] and sealed
the same with our common seal, to the particulars
whereof we refer you, desiring you with all convenient expedition to put the same in execution ; and
for your better direction in the allotment, we have
herewith sent you (as by our last we promised) a
list of all the several adventurers, and of the sum by
each of them adventured,[2] desiring that upon the
dividend each adventurer may have his allotment of
land ; as also such others as are no adventurers,
coming in person at their own charge,[3] and the servants of adventurers sent over to reside upon the
Plantation, may have such a proportion of land allotted unto and for them as by our said Order is appointed.  And whereas divers of the Company are
desirous to have the lands lie together,[4] we holding
it fit herein to give them all accommodation, as tend-

---

[1] This Act will also be found at
the end of this letter.  See also pp.
74–78.

[2] The following is a list of the
names of the adventurers in May,
1628.  The first two subscribed
£100 each, and the rest £50 each :
— Sir Richard Saltonstall, Knt.,
Isaac Johnson, Esq., Mr. Samuel
Aldersey, John Venn, Hugh Peter,
John Humfrey, Thomas Stevens,
George Harwood, John Glover,
Matthew Cradock, Simon Whet-
combe, Francis Webb, Increase
Nowell, Mr. A. C., Richard Tuff-
neale, Richard Perry, Joseph Of-
field, John White, Joseph Caron,
Thomas Adams, Richard Davis,
Abraham Palmer, William Darby,

John Endicott, Daniel Hodsen, Edward Ford, Daniel Ballard, Thomas
Hewson, Andrew Arnold, Richard
Bushord, Richard Young, George
Way, Richard Bellingham, Job
Bradshaw, Joseph Bradshaw, Henry
Durley, Thomas Hutchins, Charles
Whichcoyt, George Foxcroft, William Crowther, Nathaniel Mans-
trey.  Several of these names have
not occurred in the Company's Records, and of these two we know
came over, Richard Bellingham and
Abraham Palmer.  See Felt's Salem, i. 509.

[3] The Brownes were of this class.
See pages 61 and 168.

[4] See page 69.

ing to the furtherance of the Plantation, do pray you CHAP.
to give way thereunto for such as shall desire the
same, whether it be before a dividend be made ac- 1629.
cording to our direction, or at the time of the allot- May 28.
ment to observe the same course.

You shall also receive herewith the copies of all
the several agreements made with the servants and
others sent over in the three last ships for account
of the Company, together with their several names,
for your better direction in employing them in their
several places according to those agreements ; as
also the names of the servants of such particular
members of the Company as went over in the said
ships ; desiring you that a due register be taken and
kept, from time to time, of all the persons formerly
sent over, or that shall hereafter come to the Plantation, both of the names, and quality, and age of each
particular person, and for or by whom they are sent
over.[1]

We send you also herewith a particular of all the
goods and cattle sent in those forenamed ships, as
also of what goods, cattle, or other provisions we
now send upon[2] these three ships, viz. the Mayflower,[3] of Yarmouth, William Peirse master, the
Four Sisters, of London, Roger Harman master, the
Pilgrim, of London, William Wollridge master ;
amongst which we have remembered you, the Governor there, with certain necessaries promised by
our last ;[4] and if in aught we have been now wanting,

---

[1] The agreements, lists of names and registers, mentioned in this paragraph, are not preserved.
[2] Upon used for in, as on p. 176.
[3] The Mayflower is the renowned vessel that brought the Pilgrim Fathers to Plymouth in 1620. See Chronicles of Plymouth, pp. 99, 108, and Savage's Winthrop, i. 1.
[4] See page 156.

CHAP.
VI.

1629.
May
28.

we shall, upon notice from you, see the same supplied by our next.[1]

Whereas in our last we advised you to make composition with such of the salvages as did pretend any title or lay claim to any of the land within the territories granted to us by his Majesty's charter, we pray you now be careful to discover and find out all such pretenders, and by advice of the Council there to make such reasonable composition with them as may free us and yourselves from any scruple of intrusion ;[2] and to this purpose, if it might be conveniently done, to compound and conclude with them all, or as many as you can, at one time, not doubting but by your discreet ordering of this business, the natives will be willing to treat and compound with you upon very easy conditions.

We pray you, as soon as these ships are discharged, to cause a particular to be taken and sent us at their return for England, of the names of all such persons as come upon them to remain in the country ; as also a note of the cattle and all manner of goods, of what kind soever, landed out of them, with the several marks, and names of the owners thereof. The like whereof we desire to receive from you of the former three ships, viz. the George, Talbot, and Lion's Whelp ; to the end we may compare the same with the invoices here, and receive freight, if any be omitted.

The charge we are at in sending over servants for the Company is very great, the recompense whereof

---

[1] We have no other General Letter from the Company ; and probably none was written. The transfer of the Charter and Government to the Colony the next spring rendered further instructions unnecessary.

[2] See page 159.

(under God) depends upon their labor and endeavours ; and therefore our desire is that you appoint a
careful and diligent overseer to each family, who is
to see each person employed in the business he or
they are appointed for.  And to the end both yourselves there and we here may from time to time have
notice how they employ their time, we have sent you
divers paper books, which we pray you to distribute
to the said overseers, who are to keep a perfect register of the daily work done by each person in each
family ; a copy whereof we pray you send unto us
once every half year, or as often as conveniently you
may.  But if you conceive that the said register may
be too much to write particularly every day, we desire that a summary may be taken thereof, at the
least every week, registered in the book kept for
that family, and at each week's end the same to be
examined and subscribed by two, three, or four such
discreet persons as you shall think fit to appoint for
that purpose.

And for the better governing and ordering of our
people, especially such as shall be negligent and
remiss in performance of their duties, or otherwise
exorbitant, our desire is that a house of correction[1]
be erected and set up, both for the punishment of
such offenders, and to deter others by their example
from such irregular courses.

Richard Claydon,[2] a wheelwright, recommended
unto us by Dr. Wells to be both a good and painful
workman, and of an orderly life and conversation,

---

[1] Thus early was this useful and necessary institution contemplated, if not established, in the Colony.

[2] In his contract, on page 61, he is called a carpenter, and is to instruct in the trade of a ploughwright.

CHAP.
VI.

1629.
May
28.

our desire is, that upon all occasions he may have your furtherance and good accommodation, as you shall find him by his endeavours to deserve ; to whom, as to all others of fitness and judgment, let some of our servants be committed, to be instructed by him or them in their several arts, &c.

There is also one Richard Haward and Richard Inkersall,[1] both Bedfordshire men, hired for the Company with their families, who we pray you may be well accommodated, not doubting but they will well and orderly demean themselves.

Our Governor, Mr. Cradock, hath entertained two gardeners, one of which he is content the Company shall have use of, if need be ; and we desire that Barnaby Claydon,[2] a wheelwright, may serve Mr. Sharpe for our said Governor here, or

---

[1] Richard Ingersoll remained at Salem, where he received from the town, April 6, 1635, two acres for a house lot, in 1636 eighty acres more, and Dec. 23, 1639, twenty acres of meadow in the great meadow. — "The 16th of 11th mo. 1636, it is agreed that Richard Inkersell shall henceforward have one penny a time for every person he doth ferry over the north ferry, during the town's pleasure." He died in 1644, leaving a widow, Ann, and three sons, George, John, and Nathaniel, and four daughters. It appears from his will, which was witnessed and probably written by Gov. Endicott, and from the inventory of his estate attached to it, that, at the time of his death, he was a substantial farmer, owning two houses, 203 acres of land, and a large number of cattle. His son Nathaniel was chosen deacon of the church at Salem Village, (Danvers,) Nov. 24, 1689, and at the same time was lieutenant, and inn-holder, and took an active part in the witchcraft delusion in 1692. His great grandson, Nathaniel, married Bethiah Gardner in 1737, and had nine children, one of whom, Mary, married Habakkuk Bowditch, and was the mother of the late Dr. Bowditch, the eminent mathematician, the author of the Practical Navigator, and the world-renowned commentator on La Place. What a contrast between the sphere and the influence of the two extreme links in this long genealogical chain — between the humble ferryman who transported the first settlers of Naumkeak over North River, and the great pilot who by means of his invaluable book steers the ships of a nation round the globe ! — Numerous descendants of Richard Ingersoll are living in Salem, and also in Gloucester, and all the children of Dr. Bowditch bear the honorable surname of the ancient ferryman. Records of the Bowditch family, MS.

[2] Brother of Richard. See p. 61.

some other person in lieu of him that may give him content.

Some things we are desired by Mr. Whyte,[1] the minister, to recommend unto your care, viz. that you would show all lawful favor and respect unto the planters that came over in the Lion's Whelp out of the counties of Dorset and Somerset ; that you would appoint unto William Dodge,[2] a skilful and painful husbandman, the charge of a team of horses ; to appoint Hugh Tilly and William Edes for servants to Sir Richard Saltonstall ; to give approbation and furtherance to Francis Webb[3] in setting up his sawmill ; and to take notice that all other persons sent over by Mr. Whyte are servants to the Company, whatsoever he hath written to the contrary, this being now his own desire.

The charge of these three ships now sent, though every man that hath any private adventure in them is to pay for his particular, yet the hazard of profit and loss by the freighting of them all, and men's wages and victual, with victual for the passengers, is to be borne one half by the Company's general stock, and one half by the Governor and his partners their private stock ; so is also the fishing to be returned by them, as the salt sent in them is.

---

[1] See notes on pages 16 and 26.

[2] William Dodge lived at Salem, on Bass river, or Cape Ann side ; and when that part of the territory was incorporated as Beverly, he was chosen, Nov. 23, 1668, one of the first selectmen of the new town, and was one of the founders of the church there in 1667. It was probably his son, William Dodge, jr., who was out in King Philip's War, and Jan. 21, 1676, saved the life of his friend and killed two Indians. See Hubbard's Indian Wars, p. 59 ; Stone's Hist. of Beverly, p. 15 ; and Farmer's Gen. Register.

[3] Francis Webb was one of the adventurers, and a member of the Company. He subscribed £50 to the joint stock in May, 1628, and his name occurs at six of the courts in the preceding Records. Felt, i. 171, errs in putting his name among the colonists. See pp. 69 and 174.

Wherefore we pray you, when your ships are dis-
chaged, if any surplus shall be in victuals that they
can spare, as also of other provisions, that was provided for the passengers' accommodation, let the same
be equally divided, one half to the Governor there
for the Company, the other half to Mr. Samuel
Sharpe for the use of Mr. Cradock, our Governor,
and his partners. All provisions for the fishing at
sea is here equally borne in halves. So are all the
provisions for shipping of all the cattle in these three
ships ; and accordingly we desire the deals and cask
may be divided there.

The provisions for building of ships, as pitch, tar,
rosin, oakum, old ropes for oakum, cordage and sail-
cloth, in all these ships, with nine firkins and five
half-barrels of nails in the Four Sisters, are two-
thirds for the Company in general, and one-third for
the Governor, Mr. Cradock, and his partners ; as is
also the charge of one George Farr,[1] now sent over
to the six shipwrights, formerly sent. Our desire is,
a storehouse may be made, apt for the provisions of
the shipwrights and their tools, whereof Robert
Moulton[2] to have the chief charge, and an inventory
to be sent us of all the tools, the new by themselves
and old by themselves, that are sent over for the use
of the said shipwrights, or any of them, in these and
the former ships ; in like manner of all provisions
any way concerning shipping ; to the end we may
here examine and find that the Company may be
duly charged with their two-thirds parts of the

[1] George Farr was a farmer at
Lynn in 1630, was admitted a freeman May 6, 1635, and died in 1661,
leaving eight children, and a widow,    Elizabeth, who was buried March
11, 1687. See Lewis's History of
Lynn, p. 27.
[2] See pages 94 and 161.

charge, and no more, and the Governor likewise and
his partners with one-third part, and no more ; and
our desire is, that these men be kept at work
together, adding to their help such of the Company's
servants as you shall find needful, and proportionably
one half as many of Mr. Cradock's, which course we
hold most equal ; and that accordingly as any vessels be built, first that both parties may be accommodated for the present occasion ; but so soon as
three shallops shall be finished, two of them to be
set out for the Company, by lot, or as you shall agree
there to make an equal division, and one for our
Governor and his partners ; with whose agent, Mr.
Sharpe, if you shall think fit to agree upon equal
terms, either in thirds or halves, to fish together,
when you shall have vessels fitting, or for setting any
other design forward that may conduce to the good
of all parties, the charge to be borne indifferently by
each party proportionably, we leave to your care
and good discretions, desiring and heartily praying
that love and unity may be continued without any
heart-burning.   And as our Governor[1] hath engaged
himself beyond all expectation in this business, not
only in his particular, but by great sums disbursed
for the general, to supply the wants thereof, so our
desire is, that you endeavour to give all furtherance
and friendly accommodation to his agents and servants there, not doubting but you shall find them
likewise ready to accommodate the Company in what
they may, the Company standing in need of their
help.

[1] Matthew Cradock.  See note [2] on page 137.

The cattle[1] now and formerly sent have been all provided by the Governor, excepting three mares that came out of Leicestershire ; but as well those, as all the rest, are agreed upon to be shipped, the one half at the charge and upon the adventure of the general Company, the other half for the Governor and his partners. And because all occasions shall be avoided of just exceptions in their division, it is agreed the division shall be made after the arrival there; that so whatsoever it shall please God to send thither in safety, a division may be then made thereof by lot, or in such equal manner as you, the Governor there, and Mr. Sharpe, shall hold to be indifferent. And in case Mr. Samuel Sharpe should be sick or absent, the Governor's desire is, that Henry Haughton[2] supply his place herein, and in other his occasions there.

And as in our former,[3] so now again we especially desire you to take care that no tobacco be planted by any of the new planters under your government, unless it be some small quantity for mere necessity, and for physic, for preservation of their healths ; and that the same be taken privately by ancient men, and none other ; and to make a general restraint thereof, as much as in you is, by persuading the old planters to employ themselves in other business, according to our example, and not to permit that any tobacco be laden there upon our ships.[4]

[1] The George had on board, when she sailed, thirty cows, twelve mares and some goats ; and thirty cows and ten mares were expected by the ships that were now sent.

[2] Henry Houghton was the first ruling elder of the church in Salem, and died in the winter of 1629–30, leaving one child. See Prince's Annals, pp. 263, 271 ; Hutchinson's Coll. p. 51.

[3] See page 146.

[4] See pages 136 and 146. Tobacco derives its name not from the

Since the above written, we have, upon further CHAP. consideration, resolved that the charge of the six VI. fishermen sent over in the Lion's Whelp, and three[1] 1629. more now sent by our Governor, should be borne, May 28. two-thirds by the general Company and one-third by Mr. Cradock and partners; the like for salt and other necessaries for fishing. In consideration whereof, and for that they will have a like interest in the shallops, our desire is, that the benefit of their labor,

island of Tobago, nor from Tabaco, a province of Yucatan, but from the forked tube through which the natives of Hayti inhaled its fumes into their nostrils. It was sent from America into Spain and Portugal by Hernandez de Toledo in the year 1559. Jean Nicot, ambassador from France to the court of Lisbon, in 1660, transmitted the seeds of the plant to his sovereign, Catharine de Medici; and hence it derived the popular title of the *Queen's Herb*, and the *Ambassador's Herb*, and its botanical name of *Nicotiana*. On its first introduction into Europe, numerous and extraordinary medicinal virtues were ascribed to it, as may be seen in Monardes and Frampton. It appears to have been brought into England by Ralph Lane and his companions on their return from Virginia in 1586, and to have become fashionable there among the young gallants, and even the ladies of the court, by the example of its use set by Sir Walter Raleigh. King James, however, on his accession to the throne, blew his "Counterblast to Tobacco," and in 1604 issued a commission to restrain the consumption of it, by laying a duty on it of 8*s*. 8*d*. a pound, and prohibiting its use by "persons of mean and base condition," and confining it to "the better sort." In 1620 he issued another Proclamation, in which, after declaring his "dislike of the use of tobacco, being a weed of no necessary use," he forbade

the planting of it in England, and the importation of it, except by persons licensed for the purpose, and then only from Virginia and the Sommer Islands,—a Proclamation which was renewed by Charles I. in 1625, and followed by another in 1634, in which he assumed the sole preëmption of it, and appointed a commission to manage the monopoly. The planting of tobacco in England is still prohibited by law, and the import duty is about 1200 per cent. — In 1638, it was ordered by the General Court of Massachusetts, that "no man shall take any tobacco within ten poles of any house, or near any barn, corn, or hay-cock, as may occasion the firing thereof, nor shall take any tobacco in any inn, except in a private room there, so as neither the master of the said house, nor any other guest there, shall take offence thereat." See Oviedo, Sommario della Naturale et Generale Historia dell' Indie Occidentali, lib. v. cap. 2, in Ramusio, iii. 113; Frampton, Ioyfull Newes out of the New-found Worlde, fol. 34–45; Bigelow's Medical Botany, ii. 171–199; Raleigh's Works, i. 73–77, (Oxford, 1829); Rymer's Fœdera, xvi. 601, xvii. 190, 233, 621, 633, 668, xviii. 19; Mass. Colony Laws, p. 146, (ed. 1672,) p. 194, (ed. 1814.)

[1] Two of these were subsequently dismissed by the Governor, and did not come over; as will be seen hereafter.

both in fishing and otherwise, (the trade of beaver
excepted, in which, if you use any of these fishermen
as seamen, you must recompense their labors by
other men to supply their place,) be equally divided,
two-thirds for the use of the general Company, and
one-third for our Governor, Mr. Cradock, and partners, proportionably. And for such others as are to
be assisting to these men in their fishing, you are to
appoint two-thirds of them to be of the general Company's servants, and one-third of the servants of Mr.
Cradock and his partners accordingly.

The charge of the freight of these three ships,
their men, victuals, &c., will stand us in about
£2400 ; and their freight outward will nothing near
countervail that charge. Wherefore we pray you
to ease it what you may by sending us returns in fish
or other lading ; and we desire you to give them all
expedition, for otherwise their monthly pay, being
about £400 per month for these three ships, will
soon swallow up the gains we shall make of anything
they may bring home from thence.

We have now sent by these three ships twenty-
nine weight of salt, viz. eleven weight in the Mayflower, fifteen in the Four Sisters, and three weight
in the Pilgrim, together with lines, hooks, knives,
boots, and barrels, necessary for fishing ; desiring
our men may be employed either in harbour or upon
the Bank[1] to make use thereof for lading our ships ;
wherein we desire you to confer and advise with Mr.
Peirce, who hath formerly fished there. And if you

---

[1] Of Newfoundland, which, very
early after the discovery of the coast
of North America, became a favorite place of resort for the fishermen
of Europe.

send the ships to fish at the Bank, and expect them CHAP.
VI.
not to return again to the Plantation, that then you
send our bark,[1] that is already built in the country, 1629.
to bring back our fishermen, and such provisions as May 28.
they had for fishing, viz. of salt, if any remainder be,
as also of hooks, lines, knives, boots, and barrels,
which to them will be of no use, their fishing being
ended, but may be of use to you upon all occasions.
And as we have hereby desired that a store-house
be built for the shipwrights and their provisions, and
an inventory kept thereof, so we desire likewise that
the same course be observed for the fishermen, and
an inventory be duly kept of all the provisions and
implements for fishing, and a copy thereof to be sent
unto us ; and that such a careful person be appointed to take care and charge thereof, to preserve the

[1] This was probably the first vessel built in the Colony, and preceded,
by at least two years, the building
of Winthrop's bark at Mistick, called the Blessing of the Bay, of 30
tons, which was launched July 4,
1631. Cradock, as we have seen,
page 137, carried on ship-building
at his plantation on Mistick river,
and in 1633 had a vessel on the
stocks of 100 tons, and the next year
was to build another of twice the
burden. In 1636, a ship of 120
tons, called the Desire, was built at
Marblehead. In 1640 Hugh Peters
" procured some to join for building
a ship at Salem of 300 tons, and the
inhabitants of Boston, stirred up by
his example, set upon building another at Boston of 150 tons." Her
name was the Trial. In the summer of 1642 five ships more were
built, three at Boston, one at Dorchester, and one at Salem. In 1644,
a ship of 250 tons was built at Cambridge, and another of 200 at Boston. Oct. 17, 1646, a ship of 300
tons was launched at Boston. The
author of New-England's First
Fruits, writing from Boston, Sept.
26, 1642, says, " Besides many
boats, shallops, hoys, lighters, pinnaces, we are in a way of building
ships of an 100, 200, 300, 400 tons.
Five of them are already at sea,
many more in hand at this present,
we being much encouraged herein
by reason of the plenty and excellency of our timber for that purpose,
and seeing all the materials will be
had there in short time." Such
was the origin and early progress
of ship-building in Massachusetts,
a branch of her industry which,
in the year ending April 1, 1845,
employed 1017 men, and produced
112 vessels, whose burthen was
26,312 tons, and whose value was
$ 1,172,147. See Savage's Win-
throp, i. 57, 60, 193, ii. 24, 65,
173, 278 ; Mass. Hist. Coll. i. 248 ;
Statistics of the Condition and Pro-
ducts of certain Branches of Industry in Massachusetts, p. 362.

same from loss and spoil, as you in your discretions shall think fit; which we pray you take into your especial care and consideration; and so to order this and other business, by distributing the care thereof to several persons, that the burthen be not too heavy to any particular, and so the business itself suffer. And this care we desire may be taken, for that we know not how soon we may resolve of some other division.

Thomas Beard,[1] a shoemaker, and Isaac Rickman, being both recommended to us by Mr. Simon Whetcombe,[2] to receive their diet and house-room at the charge of the Company, we have agreed they shall be with you, the Governor, or placed elsewhere, as you shall think good, and receive from you, or by your appointment, their diet and lodging; for which they are to pay, each of them, after the rate of £10 per annum. And we desire to receive a certificate under the hand of whomsoever they shall be so dieted and lodged with, how long time they have remained with them, in case they shall otherwise dispose of themselves, before the year be expired, or at leastwise at the end of each year, to the end we may here receive payment according to the said agreement. The said Thomas Beard hath in the ship the Mayflower divers hides, both for soles and upper leathers, which he intends to make up in boots and shoes there in the country. We pray you let Mr. Peirce, the master of the said ship, view the said leather, and estimate what tonnage the same may import; that so

---

[1] Thomas Beard was admitted a freeman May 10, 1643.

[2] Whetcombe was one of the patentees named in the Charter, and, as appears from the preceding Records, was a very active member of the Company, and a constant attendant at its meetings.

the said Beard may either pay unto you there after CHAP.<br>VI.
the rate of £4 per ton for freight of the same; the
like for his diet, if there be occasion to use any of his 1629.
commodities; or otherwise, upon your advice, we May<br>28.
may receive it of Mr. Whetcombe, who hath promised to see the same discharged. We desire also
the said Thomas Beard may have fifty acres of land
allotted to him, as one that transports himself at his
own charge. But as well for him as all others that
shall have land allotted to them in that kind, and are
no adventurers in the common stock, which is to
support the charge of fortifications, as also for the
ministry[1] and divers other affairs, we hold it fit that
these kind of men, as also such as shall come to inherit lands by their service, should, by way of acknowledgment to such from whom they receive these
lands, become liable to the performance of some service, certain days in the year, and by that service
they and their posterity after them to hold and inherit
these lands;[2] which will be a good means to enjoy
their lands from being held *in capite*, and to support
the Plantation in general and particular.

We may not omit, out of our zeal for the general
good, once more to put you in mind to be very cir-
cumspect in the infancy of the Plantation to settle
some good orders, whereby all persons resident upon
our Plantation may apply themselves to one calling,

---

[1] See pages 96 and 148. Hutchinson, i. 14, says that no notice was
taken in the Colony of the provision
that one half of the charge of the
fortifications and support of the ministers should be paid out of the joint
stock.

[2] This feudal tenure was never
established. Land was too plentiful
and cheap to authorize it, or render
it practicable; and accordingly it
was all held in fee simple. One of
the early settlers, writing home from
New-Plymouth in 1621, says, " We
are all freeholders; the rent-day
doth not trouble us." See Chronicles of Plymouth, p. 250.

or other, and no idle drone be permitted to live amongst us ;[1] which if you take care now at the first to establish, will be an undoubted means, through God's assistance, to prevent a world of disorders, and many grievous sins and sinners.

The course we have prescribed for keeping a daily register in each family, of what is done by all and every person in the family, will be a great help and remembrance to you, and to future posterity[2] for the upholding and continuance of this good act, if once well begun and settled ; which we heartily wish and desire, as aforesaid.

And as we desire all should live in some honest calling and profession, so we pray you to be unpartial in the administration of justice, and endeavour that no man whatsoever, freeman or servant to any, may have just cause of complaint herein. And for that it cannot be avoided but offences will be given, we heartily pray you to admit of all complaints that shall be made to you, or any of you that are of the Council, be the complaint never so mean, and pass it not slightly over, but seriously examine the truth of the business ; and if you find there was just cause for the complaint, endeavour to right the oppressed in the best manner you can. But, howsoever, take some strict course to prevent the like ; and such as are by us put in authority, as subordinate governors of families, if they shall abuse any under their government, and after a gentle admonition do not reform

---

[1] This is noteworthy.

[2] Posterity would have liked to see these family registers, and regrets that none of them have been preserved. They might have thrown light on the history of families, and the character and struggles of the first planters.

it, fail not speedily to remove them, as men more fit CHAP.
to be governed than to govern others, and place
more fit and sufficient men in their stead. But if 1629.
you find any complaint to be made without just cause 28.
given, let not such a fault escape without severe
punishment, and that forthwith, and in public,
whereby to terrify all others from daring to complain
against any that shall be set over them without a just
cause. We pray you take this earnestly to heart,
and neglect not the due execution thereof upon
plaintiff or defendant, according to the nature of the
offence. It will be a means, through God's mercy,
of preventing many inconveniences and disorders,
that otherwise will undoubtedly befall you and the
whole government there.

And amongst other sins we pray you make some
good laws for the punishing of swearers, whereunto
it is to be feared too many are addicted that are servants sent over formerly and now. These and other
abuses we pray you who are in authority to endeavour seriously to reform, if ever you expect comfort
or a blessing from God upon our Plantation.

We have discharged divers servants here that we
had entertained and been at great charges with some
of them. Yet fearing their ill life might be prejudicial to the Plantation, we rather thought fit to dis-
miss them and lose our charges, than to burthen the
Plantation with them.[1] Amongst others, in like

---

[1] The Company seem to have taken all possible precautions to prevent immoral persons from going over to their Plantation. They intended to colonize only "the best." As was said by William Stoughton, afterwards Lieutenant-Governor, in the Election Sermon which he preached in 1668, "God sifted a whole nation, that he might send choice grain over into this wilderness."

CHAP.
VI. manner dismissed by the Governor, two of the three
fishermen of his formerly mentioned are gone.   We
1629. doubt not but God will in due time provide us suffi-
May
28. ciently with honest and able servants, and we hope
these sent will be conformable to good government ;
which if they do willingly and cheerfully, will be the
greater comfort to you and us ; if otherwise, we
doubt not but you in your good discretions will know
how to proceed with such.   Wherein, and in all
things else you go about, we beseech the Almighty
so to direct you, as that God alone may have the
glory, and you and we comfort here temporally, and
hereafter perpetually.

We pray you to take notice that in these and the
former ships there is shipped in cattle and other provisions, according to particular invoices here enclosed ; but whether all things be inserted in the same
invoices we make doubt, and therefore pray you to
be careful a due register be kept of all put ashore.

We pray you endeavour, though there be much
strong waters sent for sale, yet so to order it as that
the salvages may not, for our lucre sake, be induced
to the excessive use, or rather abuse of it ;[1] and at
any hand take care our people give no ill example ;
and if any shall exceed in that inordinate kind of
drinking as to become drunk, we hope you will take
care his punishment be made exemplary for all
others.   Let the laws be first published to forbid
these disorders, and all others you fear may grow
up ; whereby they may not pretend ignorance of the

---

[1] In conformity with this direction, several orders were made, at
different times, forbidding any person in the Colony selling strong
liquors to the Indians.   See Mass.
Colony Laws, p. 76, (ed. 1672,) p.
134, (ed. 1814.)

one nor privilege to offend ; and then fear not to put CHAP.
good laws, made upon good ground and warrant, in
due execution. 1629.

And so recommending you and all your affairs to May 28.
the protection of the Almighty, we conclude, and
rest, Yours, &c.

*Gravesend*, **3** *June*, 1629.

To the worshipful our very loving friends, CAPT. JOHN ENDECOTT,
ESQ., Governor, FRANCIS HIGGENSON, SAMUEL SKELTON,
FRANCIS BRIGHT, JOHN and SAMUEL BROWNE, SAMUEL
SHARPE, THOMAS GRAVES, and the rest of the Council for
London's Plantation in the Mattachusetts Bay, in New-
England.[1]

---

[1] These two General Letters of Instructions to Gov. Endicott and his Council, are bound up at the end of the first book of Deeds in the Registry of Suffolk. How they came there, is not known. They are in the hand-writing of Burgess, the second Secretary of the Company, as will be manifest to any one who will inspect and compare them with his entries in the first volume of the Court Records at the State House. The manuscript is either the duplicate mentioned on page 166, or part of the Company's Letter Book, mentioned on page 99.

# CHAPTER VII.

## THE FORM OF GOVERNMENT FOR THE COLONY.

CHAP.
VII.

1629.
April
30.

A GENERAL Court holden at London the 30th day of April, 1629, by the Governor and Company of the Mattachusetts Bay, in New-England.[1]

Whereas the King's most excellent Majesty hath been graciously pleased to erect and establish us, by his letters patents under the great seal of England, to be a body corporate, entitled *The Governor and Company of the Mattachusetts Bay in New-England ;* and thereby hath endowed us with many large and ample privileges and immunities, with power to make good and wholesome laws, orders, and ordinances, for the better maintenance and support of the said privileges, and for the better and more orderly and regular government to be observed in the prosecution and propagation of our intended voyages and the Plantation there ; authorizing us to nominate and appoint and select fit persons amongst ourselves for the managing, ordering and governing of our affairs, both in England and in the places specified and

[1] See pages 66, 68, 73, and 144.

granted unto us by virtue of his Majesty's said char- CHAP.
ter : We have, in the prosecution of the said power VII.
and authority given us, and in conformity thereunto, 1629.
and to the purpose and intent thereof, and not other-April 30
wise, thought fit to settle and establish an absolute[1]
government at our Plantation in the said Mattachusetts Bay, in New-England ; which, by the vote and
consent of a full and ample Court now assembled, is
thought fit and ordered, as followeth, viz.

That thirteen of such as shall be reputed the most
wise, honest, expert, and discreet persons, resident
upon the said Plantation, shall, from time to time,
and at all time hereafter, have the sole managing and
ordering of the government and of our affairs there ;
who, to the best of their judgments, are to endeavour so to settle the same as may make most to the
glory of God, the furtherance and advancement of
this hopeful Plantation, the comfort, encouragement,
and future benefit of us and others, the beginners
and prosecutors of this so laudable a work ; the said
thirteen persons so appointed to be entitled by the
name of *The Governor and Council of London's Plantation in the Mattachusetts Bay in New-England.*

And having taken into due consideration the
merit, worth, and good desert of Captain John
Endecott, and others lately gone over from hence
with purpose to reside and continue there, we have,
with full consent and authority of this Court, and by
erection of hands, chosen and elected the said Captain John Endecott to the place of present Governor
in our said Plantation.

[1] This is noteworthy.

CHAP. VII.
1629.
April 30.

Also, by the same power, and with the like full and free consent, we have chosen and elected Mr. Francis Higgesson, Mr. Samuel Skelton, Mr. Francis Bright, Mr. John Browne, Mr. Samuel Browne, Mr. Thomas Graves, and Mr. Samuel Sharpe, these seven, to be of the said Council; and do hereby give power and authority to the said Governor and those seven to make choice of three others, such as they, or the greater number of them, in their discretions shall esteem and conceive most fit thereunto, to be also of the said Council.

And to the end that the former planters[1] there may have no just occasion of exception, as being excluded out of the privileges of the Company, this Court are content, and do order, by erection of hands, that such of the said former planters as are willing to live within the limits of our Plantation, shall be enabled and are hereby authorized, to make choice of two, such as they shall think fit, to supply and make up the number of twelve of the said Council; one of which twelve is by the Governor and Council, or the major part of them, to be chosen Deputy to the Governor for the time being.

And further, the Court doth authorize and give power to the said Governor and Council, or the major part of them, (whereof the Governor or Deputy to be always one,) to make choice of a Secretary and such other subordinate officers, to attend them at their courts, meetings, or otherwise, as in their discretions shall seem meet and needful. And to the end that every one of the forenamed officers, as well Governor, Deputy, and Council, as others whom

[1] Conant and his associates, employed by the Dorchester adventurers. See page 145.

they shall think fit to nominate and choose, may be CHAP.
the more careful in performance of the charge committed unto them, it is by this Court thought fit and 1629.
ordered, that each of them shall take an oath, proper April 30.
to that place he shall be elected and chosen to, which
is to be administered unto him or them at the time
of his or their election or admittance into the said
several place or places.

And we do hereby authorize [blank] to administer
unto the Governor the oath to his place appertaining ; and that the Governor, having taken his oath,
as aforesaid, shall administer the oath to the Deputy
appertaining to his place.  And we do further hereby
authorize the Governor, or Deputy, or either of them,
to administer the oath to the rest of the Council, and
unto all others the several officers respectively ;
which said oaths are to be administered in a public
Court, and not elsewhere.

It is further concluded on, and ordered by this
Court, that the said Governor, Deputy, and Council,
before named, so chosen and established in their
several places, shall continue and be confirmed
therein for the space of one whole year, from and
after the taking the oath, or until such time as this
Court shall think fit to make choice of any others to
succeed in the place or places of them, or any of
them.  And if it shall please God that any of them,
or any others to be hereafter chosen to any office
there, shall depart this life before the expiration
of the time they were so chosen, or for any misdemeanour or unfitness shall be held unmeet for the
place he was formerly chosen unto, that then the
Governor, or Deputy, and Council, or the greater
number of them, at an ample Court assembled, shall

have power, and hereby are authorized, not only to remove and displace such unfit person or persons,[1] but also to nominate and choose a fit person or persons to succeed him or them so deceased, removed, or displaced, as aforesaid, into the said place or places, for the residue of the time unexpired.

And it is further agreed on and ordered, that the Governor for the time being, shall have power, and is hereby authorized, to call courts and meetings in places and at times convenient, as to his discretion shall seem meet ; which power is hereby also conferred upon the Deputy, in the absence of the said Governor. And the said Governor or Deputy, together with the said Council, being chosen and assembled as aforesaid, and having taken their oaths respectively to their several places, they, or the greater number of them, whereof the Governor or Deputy to be always one, are authorized by this Act, grounded on the power derived from his Majesty's charter, to make, ordain, and establish all manner of wholesome and reasonable laws, orders, ordinances, and constitutions,[2] (so as the same be no way repugnant or contrary to the laws of the realm of England,) for the administering of justice upon malefactors, and inflicting condign punishment upon all other offenders, and for the furtherance and propagating of the said Plantation, and the more decent and orderly government of the inhabitants resident there.[3]

---

[1] This justified Endicott in displacing the Brownes from the Council. They had been guilty, to say the least, of a misdemeanour.

[2] Instructions, in the Charter and in the Company's Records. See p. 67.

[3] This Act for establishing the government in New-England, is printed from the copy transcribed into the Company's Records, by Secretary Burgess, fol. 11–14.

# CHAPTER VIII.

## THE ALLOTMENT OF THE LANDS.

AT a Court of Assistants on Thursday, the 21st of May, 1629.[1]

This Court taking into due and mature consideration how necessary it will be that a dividend be forthwith made of some competent quantity of land in the London Plantation in New-England, both for the present accommodation of the people lately gone thither, as well to build them houses, as to enclose and manure, and to feed their cattle on, have thought fit and ordered, that the Governor, Deputy, and Council there shall make a dividend accordingly, and allot the same unto the several adventurers and others, as followeth, viz.

That two hundred acres of land be by them allotted to each adventurer for £50 adventure in the common stock, and so after that rate, and according to that proportion, for more or less, as the adventure is, to the intent they may build their houses and improve their labors thereon.

[1] See pages 74–77.

CHAP.
VIII.
———
1629.
May
21.

That every adventurer in the common stock, or his servant for him or on his behalf, shall make request or demand to the Governor or Deputy and Council, to have a proportion of land allotted unto him accordingly ; and if, within ten days after such request or demand made, the same be not set out and allotted unto him, then such person or persons are, by virtue of this Act, permitted and authorized to seat him or themselves, and build his or their house or houses, and enclose and manure ground in any convenient place or places not formerly built upon or manured ; provided that the land so made choice of by any such person or persons do not exceed in quantity the one half of the land which is to be allotted unto him or them by dividend, according to this order above written ; with liberty also, when the first dividend shall be made, to take his or their allotment of land as others do, in lieu of this, if in the mean time the first choice shall be disliked by them, or any of them.

And for further explanation of this Act, it is thought fit, that if the plot of ground whereon the town is to be built be set out, and that it be publicly known to be intended for that purpose, that then no man shall presume to build his house in any other place, unless it be in the Mattachusetts Bay, and there according to such direction as shall be thought meet for that place. And in case his allotment for building his house within the plot of ground set out for building of the town be not appointed unto him within ten days after demand or request to the Governor or the Deputy and Council for the same, it shall be free for any, being an adventurer in the

common stock, or his servant for him or on his be- CHAP.
half, to build his house in any place within the said
plot set out for the town, and to impale to the quan- 1629.
tity of half an acre of ground for each £50 adventure May
in the common stock ; unless a greater or lesser 21.
proportion be formerly determined by the Governor
and Council, by which each builder is to be guided
and directed.

It is further thought fit and ordered, that all such
as go over in person, or send over others at their
own charge, and are adventurers in the common
stock, shall have lands allotted unto them for each
person they transport to inhabit the Plantation, as
well servants as all others ; which fifty acres of land,
so allotted to servants or others, is hereby ordered
to be to and for the use of his master or setter forth,
being an adventurer in the common stock, to dispose
of at his discretion, in regard the master, &c. is at
the charge of the said servant and others their transportation, wages, and otherwise. But for such as
being no adventurers in the common stock shall
transport themselves and their families, it is ordered
that fifty acres of land shall be allotted and set out
for the master of the family, and such a proportion
of land more, if there be cause, as, according to their
charge and quality, the Governor and Council of the
Plantation there shall think necessary for them,
whereby their charge may be fully and amply supported; unless it be to any with whom the Company
in London have or shall make any other particular
agreement, to which relation is to be had in such
case.

And to the end every adventurer may the more

CHAP.
VIII.

1629.
May
21.

safely and peaceably enjoy their said lands allotted unto them or chosen by them, and the houses they build thereupon, as abovesaid, it is thought fit and ordered by this Court, that conveyances shall be made thereof unto each particular man for the land he possesseth, in the Company's name, and the common seal of the Company to be thereunto affixed by the Governor and Council there, at the charge of the Company ; which common seal is by this Court thought fit and ordered to be committed to the charge and keeping of the Governor for the time being, and in his absence, to his Deputy there.

All which premises before mentioned the Company do by general consent ratify, establish and confirm ; and do also order, that copies of these Acts shall be sent over to the Governor and Council there resident, subscribed by the Governor, Deputy, and six of the Assistants here, and sealed with the common seal of the Company.[1]

[1] See page 78. This Act for the allotment of the lands is also taken from the Company's Records, in the handwriting of Secretary Burgess, fol. 11–16.

# CHAPTER IX.

OATHS OF OFFICE FOR THE GOVERNOR AND COUNCIL.[1]

*The Oath of the Governor in New-England.*[2]

YOU shall be faithful and loyal unto our Sovereign Lord, the King's Majesty, and to his heirs and successors. You shall support and maintain, to your power, the government and Company of the Mattachusetts Bay, in New-England, in America, and the privileges of the same, having no singular regard to yourself in derogation or hindrance of the common wealth of this Company ; and to every person under your authority you shall administer indifferent and equal justice. Statutes and ordinances shall you none make without the advice and consent of the Council for the government of the Mattachusetts Bay in New-England. You shall admit none into the freedom of this Company but such as may claim the same by virtue of the privileges thereof. You shall not bind yourself to enter into any business or process for or in the name of this Company, without

[1] See page 69.
[2] " This oath is also to be admin- istered to the Deputy." Marginal note in the MS.

the consent and agreement of the Council aforesaid, but shall endeavour faithfully and carefully to carry yourself in this place and office of Governor, as long as you shall continue in it. And likewise you shall do your best endeavour to draw on the natives of this country, called New-England, to the knowledge of the True God, and to conserve the planters, and others coming hither, in the same knowledge and fear of God. And you shall endeavour, by all good means, to advance the good of the Plantations of this Company, and you shall endeavour the raising of such commodities for the benefit and encouragement of the adventurers and planters as, through God's blessing on your endeavours, may be produced for the good and service of the kingdom of England, this Company, and their Plantations. All these premises you shall hold and keep to the uttermost of your power and skill, so long as you shall continue in the place of Governor of this fellowship. So help you God!

*The Oath of the Council in New-England.*

You swear to be faithful and loyal to our Sovereign Lord, the King's Majesty, and to his heirs and successors. You shall from time to time give your best advice and counsel for supporting and maintaining the common wealth and corporation of *The Governor and Company of the Mattachusetts Bay, in New-England* ; not sparing for love nor dread, for favor nor meed, but according to the statutes and ordinances made and to be made by virtue of the Charter of the said Company, shall effectually assist the Governor, or his Deputy and Council of the said Company, in executing the said statutes and ordinances; having no singular regard to yourself in derogation of the common wealth of the same. All these premises you shall hold and truly keep to your power, so long as you shall continue in the place or office of one of the said Council. So help you God![1]

CHAP.<br>IX.

1629.

May.

[1] These Oaths of Office for the Governor and Council, are copied from the first volume of the Records of the General Court of Massachusetts, pages 75 and 76, having been inserted there out of place, by some mistake. They are in the hand-writing of Secretary Burgess.

# THE COMPANY'S AGREEMENT

# WITH THE MINISTERS.

# CHAPTER X.

AGREEMENT OF THE NEW-ENGLAND COMPANY WITH
THE MINISTERS.[1]

*The Agreement with Mr. Bright.*

I, FRANCIS BRIGHT, of Roily,[2] in Essex, clerk, have this present 2d February, 1628, agreed with the Company of Adventurers for New-England, in America, to be ready with my wife, two children, and one maid-servant, by the beginning of March next, to take our passage to the Plantation at or near Massachusetts Bay, in New-England, as aforesaid ; where I do promise, God sparing me life and health, to serve the said Company in the work of the ministry, by my true and faithful endeavours, for the space of three years. For and in consideration whereof, these several particulars are this day agreed upon by the said Company, and by me accepted, namely :

1. That £20 shall be forthwith paid me by the Company's treasurer towards charges of fitting

---

[1] See page 143.
[2] The name of this town is now spelt Rayleigh. It is 26 miles from London. See Newcourt's Repertorium, ii. 482.

CHAP.
X.

1629.
Feb.
2.

myself with apparel and other necessaries for the voyage.

2. That £10 more shall be paid me by him towards providing of books ; which said books, upon my death or removal from the charge now intended to be transferred upon me, are to be and remain to such minister as shall succeed in my place for the said Company ; and before my departure out of England, I am to deliver a particular of the said books.

3. That £20 yearly shall be paid me for three years, to begin from the time of my first arrival in New-England, and so to be accounted and paid at the end of each year.

4. That during the said time, the Company shall provide for me and my family aforementioned, necessaries of diet, housing, firewood, and shall be at the charge of the transportation of us into New-England ; and at the end of the said three years, if I shall not like to continue longer there, to be at charges of transporting us back for England.

5. That in convenient time a house shall be built, and certain lands allotted thereunto ; which, during my stay in the country and continuing in the ministry, shall be for my use, and after my death or removal, the same to be for succeeding ministers.

6. That at the expiration of the said three years, one hundred acres of land shall be assigned unto me, for me and my heirs forever.

7. That in case I shall depart this life in that country, the said Company shall take care for my widow, during her widowhood and abode in that country and Plantation ; the like for my children whilst they remain on the said Plantation.

8. That the milk of two kine shall be appointed CHAP.<br>X.
me toward the charge of diet for me and my family,
as aforesaid, and half their increase during the said 1629.
three years, to be likewise mine ; but the said two Feb.<br>2.
kine and the other half of the increase to return to
the Company at the end of the said three years.

9. That I shall have liberty to carry bedding,
linen, brass, iron, pewter, of my own, for my necessary use during the said time.

10. That if I continue seven years upon the said
Plantation, that then one hundred acres of land more
shall be allotted to me for me and my heirs forever.[1]

---

*The Agreement with Mr. Higginson.*

A true note of the allowance that the New-England April<br>8.
  Company have, by common consent and order of
  their Court and Council, granted unto Mr. Francis
  Higginson,[2] minister, for his maintenance in New-
  England, April 8, 1629.

1. Imprimis, that £30 in money shall be forthwith paid him by the Company's treasurer towards
the charges of fitting himself with apparel and other
necessaries for his voyage.

2. Item, that £10 more shall be paid over by the
said treasurer towards the providing of books for
present use.

3. Item, that he shall have £30 yearly paid him
for three years, to begin from the time of his first

---

[1] See Felt's Annals of Salem, i. 510.     [2] See page 65.

14

CHAP.
X.
arrival in New-England, and so to be accounted and
paid him at the end of every year.

1629.
April
8.
4. Item, that during the said time, the Company
shall provide for him and his family necessaries of
diet, housing and firewood, and shall be at charges
of transporting him into New-England; and at the
end of the said three years, if he shall not like to
continue there any longer, to be at the charge of
transporting him back for England.

5. Item, that in convenient time a house shall be
built, and certain lands allotted thereunto; which,
during his stay in the country, and continuance in
the ministry, shall be for his use; and after his
death or removal, the same to be for succeeding
ministers.

6. Item, at the expiration of the said three years,
a hundred acres of land shall be assigned to him and
his heirs forever.

7. Item, that in case he shall depart this life in
that country, the said Company shall take care for
his widow during her widowhood and abode in that
country and Plantation; and the like for his children whilst they remain upon the said Plantation.

8. Item, that the milk of two kine shall be appointed towards the charges of diet for him and his
family as aforesaid, and half the increase of calves
during the said three years; but the said two kine,
and the other half of the increase, to return to the
Company at the end of the said three years.

9. Item, that he shall have liberty of carrying over
bedding, linen, brass, iron, pewter, of his own, for
his necessary use during the said time.

10. Item, that if he continue seven years upon the

said Plantation, that then a hundred acres of land CHAP.
more shall be allotted him for him and his forever.[1]
X.

---

*The 8th of April*, 1629. Mr. Francis Higgeson
and Mr. Samuel Skelton, intended ministers for this
Plantation, and it being thought meet to consider of
their entertainment, who expressing their willingness, together also with Mr. Francis Bright, being
now present, to do their endeavour in their places of
the ministry, as well in preaching, catechising, as
also in teaching or causing to be taught the Company's servants and their children, as also the salvages
and their children, whereby to their uttermost to
further the main end of this Plantation, being, by the
assistance of Almighty God, the conversion of the
salvages — the propositions and agreements concluded on with Mr. Francis Bright the 2d of February
last were reciprocally accepted of by Mr. Francis
Higgeson and Mr. Samuel Skelton;[2] who are in every
respect to have the like conditions as Mr. Bright
hath. Only, whereas Mr. Higgeson hath eight[3]

---

[1] This Agreement is printed from
an early MS.
[2] In Felt's Annals of Salem, i.
511–513, is an account of moneys
due to him from the Company in
1629 and 1630, including his charges
for provisions and clothing.
[3] Their names, and their ages at
this time, so far as I have been able
to determine them from the data I
have, were as follows : — 1. John,
thirteen, concerning whom see note [1]
on p. 166. 2. Francis, twelve, who
after studying at Leyden and other
universities on the continent, returned to England, and was settled in
the ministry at Kirkby-Stephen,
in Westmoreland, where he died in
1672, aged 55. 3. Timothy, ten.
4. Theophilus, nine. 5. Samuel,
eight, who at his mother's death in
1640, was bound as a servant to
Gov. Eaton, of New Haven, for two
years. 6. Ann, six. 7. Mary, four,
who died on the passage, May 19.
8. Charles, one, who. in 1640, was
bound apprentice to Thomas Fugill
for nine years. There was a 9th
child, born in Salem, called Neo-
phytus, who had been placed with
Atherton Hough, at Boston, to be
brought up. See Kingsley's Hist.
Disc. p. 103 ; Mather's Magnalia,
i. 330.

CHAP.
X.

1629.
April
8.

children, it is intended that £10 more yearly shall be allowed him towards their charges. And it is agreed that the increase to be improved of all their grounds, during the first three years, shall be at the Company's disposing, who are to find their diet during that time; and £10 more to Mr. Higgeson, towards his present fitting him and his for the voyage.

FRANCIS HIGGESON.
SAMUEL SKELTON.

Further, though it was not mentioned in the Agreement, but forgotten, Mr. Higgeson was promised a man-servant, to take care and look to his things, and to catch him fish and fowl, and provide other things needful, and also two maid-servants, to look to his family.

# HIGGINSON'S JOURNAL

OF

# HIS VOYAGE TO NEW-ENGLAND.

A TRUE Relation of the last Voyage to New-England, declaring all
circumstances, with the manner of the passage we had by sea,
and what manner of country and inhabitants we found when we
came to land; and what is the present state and condition of the
English people that are there already.
Faithfully recorded according to the very truth, for the satisfaction
of very many of my loving friends, who have earnestly requested
to be truly certified in these things.
Written from New-England, July 24, 1629.
If any curious critic that looks for exactness of phrases, or expert
seaman that regards propriety of sea terms, &c.

# CHAPTER XI.

A TRUE Relation of the last Voyage to New-England, made the last summer, begun the 25th of April, being Saturday, Anno Domini, 1629.

The Company of New-England, consisting of many worthy gentlemen in the city of London, Dorchester, and other places, aiming at the glory of God, the propagation of the Gospel of Christ, the conversion of the Indians, and the enlargement of the King's Majesty's dominions in America, and being authorized by his royal letters patents for that end, at their very great costs and charge furnished five ships to go to New-England, for the further settling of the English Plantation that they had already begun there.[1]

The names of the five ships were as followeth :

The first is called the Talbot,[2] a good and strong ship, of three hundred tons, and nineteen pieces of

---

[1] Under Endicott, in 1628, the year before. See pages 13 and 30.

[2] Francis Higginson, with his family, sailed in the Talbot. See page 143.

CHAP.
XI.

1629.
April.

ordnance, and served with thirty mariners. This ship carried above a hundred planters, six goats, five great pieces of ordnance, with meal, oatmeal, pease, and all manner of munition and provision for the Plantation for a twelvemonth.

The second the George,[1] another strong ship also, about three hundred tons, twenty pieces of ordnance, served with about thirty mariners. Her chief carriage were cattle, twelve mares, thirty kine, and some goats.[2] Also she had in her fifty-two planters, and other provision.

The third is called the Lion's Whelp,[3] a neat and nimble ship, of a hundred and twenty tons, eight pieces of ordnance, carrying in her many mariners and above forty planters, specially from Dorchester[4] and other places thereabouts, with provision, and four goats.

The fourth is called The Four Sisters, as I hear, of about three hundred tons ; which fair ship carried many cattle, with passengers and provision.

The fifth is called the Mayflower,[5] carrying passengers and provision.[6]

Now amongst these five ships, the George having some special and urgent cause of hastening her pas-

---

[1] Samuel Skelton, with his wife, went in the George. See page 143.

[2] The Colony of Massachusetts Bay was, in this particular, much earlier and better provided than the Colony of New Plymouth had been. The latter had no cattle till March, 1624, when Mr. Edward Winslow brought over a bull and three heifers ; whereas as early as 1626, twelve cows at least had been sent over to Cape Ann. See pages 9 and 12, and Prince's Annals, p. 225.

[3] Francis Bright, with his wife and two children, was in the Lion's Whelp. See page 143.

[4] See page 50.

[5] Thirty-five of the Leyden congregation, with their families, came over to Plymouth at this time in the Mayflower and Talbot. See Mass. Hist. Coll. iii. 66 ; Prince, pp. 261, 264 ; Chronicles of Plymouth, page 482.

[6] There was a sixth vessel sent, called the Pilgrim. See page 175.

sage,[1] set sail before the rest, about the midst of April. And the Four Sisters and the Mayflower, being not thoroughly furnished, intended, as we heard, to set forth about three weeks after us. But we that were in the Talbot and the Lion's Whelp, being ready for our voyage, by the good hand of God's providence, hoisted up sail from Gravesend on Saturday the 25th of April, about seven o'clock in the morning. Having but a faint wind we could not go far that day, but at night we anchored against Leigh,[2] which is twelve miles from Gravesend, and there we rested that night, and kept Sabbath the next day.

On Monday we set forward and came to the Flats,[3] a passage somewhat difficult by reason of the narrowness of the channel[4] and shallowness of the water; and going over this we were in some danger ; for our ship being heavy laden and drawing deep water, was sensibly felt of us all to strike three or four times on the ground. But the wind blowing somewhat strong, we were carried swiftly on, and at last, by God's blessing, came safe to anchor at Gorin[5] road.

Tuesday we went a little further, and anchored over against Margate town, staying for a wind for the Downs.

CHAP.
XI.

1629.
April.

25.

26.

27.

28.

---

[1] On account of the cattle she had on board — and also on account of the instructions she was carrying out to Endicott to anticipate Oldham in occupying Massachusetts Bay. See pages 68 and 150.

[2] Leigh is near the mouth of the Thames.

[3] These Flats, under different names, extend from the Nore and Sheerness to the North Foreland. See Norie's British Channel Pilot, pp. 13–17.

[4] The channel is called the Five Fathoms Channel.

[5] The Gore is one of the anchorages most commonly used, especially by large ships bound to the Downs, before coming to Margate and the North Foreland. See Norie, p. 17.

CHAP.
XI.

1629.
April
30.

May
1, 2.

3.

4.

Wednesday, we came safely, though with much turning and tacking, through the Gulls,[1] into the Downs,[2] and stayed that night.

Thursday, Friday, and Saturday, the wind blew hard from south-west, and caused our ship to dance; and divers of our passengers, and my wife specially, were sea-sick. Here the King's ship called the Assurance pressed two of our mariners. Here we saw many porpoises playing in the sea, which they say is a sign of foul weather.

Sabbath day, a windy day and cold. We kept Sabbath, staying still at the Downs.

Monday, God sent us a fair gale of wind, north north-east, whereby we came merrily from the Downs; and passing Dover we saw six or seven sail of Dunkirkers[3] wafting after us. But it seemed they saw our company was too strong for them, for then we had with us three or four ships that went for the Straits;[4] so they returned back from pursuing us any longer. But sailing with a good wind, we went speedily, and at night came near the Isle of Wight; but being dark, we durst not put into the channel,[5] but put back for sea-room four hours, and then other four hours sailed back again the same way.

---

[1] The common track for large ships to the Downs is through the Gull Stream. This is bounded on the eastern side by the Goodwin Sands, and on the western side by the Elbow, Gull, and Brake Sands. See Norie, p. 23.

[2] The Downs, or Dunes, properly signify sand-hills on the coast. But the word is now used to designate the well-known anchorage off Deal, inside of the Goodwin. See Chron-

icles of Plymouth, note [4] on page 123, and Norie, p. 28.

[3] Dunkirk was at this time part of the Spanish Netherlands, and there was war between England and Spain.

[4] Of Gibraltar, bound up the Mediterranean.

[5] The channel between the Isle of Wight and the coast of Hampshire, entering at St. Helen's, and coming out at the Needles.

Tuesday, early in the morning, we entered the CHAP.<br/>XI. channel, the wind being weak and calm, and passed by Portsmouth very slowly ; but in the afternoon 1629. the wind quickened, and we were forced to anchor a May 5. little on this side Cowcastle ;[1] but the wind growing more favorable, we weighed and came to anchor again right against Cowcastle, thinking to stay that night, the wind being very calm. Here I and my wife, and my daughter Mary, and two maids, and some others with us, obtained of the master of the ship to go ashore to refresh us and to wash our linens ; and so we lay at Cowes[2] that night. But the wind turning when we were absent, they hoisted sail and left us there, and anchored eight miles further, over against Yarmouth,[3] about eight of the clock at night.

Wednesday, betime in the morning, the shallop 6. was sent from the ship to fetch us to Yarmouth. But the water proved rough, and our women desired to be set on shore three miles short of Yarmouth ; and so went on foot by land, and lodged in Yarmouth that night.

On Thursday and Friday, there master Beecher,[4] 7, 8.

[1] A small castle, in the form of a crescent, was built at West Cowes, on each side of the river Medina, in the reign of Henry VIII. The part on the west side still remains. See Parl. Gaz. i. 517.

[2] See note [1] on page 127.

[3] Yarmouth is in the Isle of Wight.

[4] Thomas Beecher commanded the same vessel, the Talbot, in Winthrop's fleet, the next year. He was one of the early members of the church in Boston, and was admitted a freeman Nov. 6, 1632. He settled in Charlestown, and his name, with his wife's, Christian, stands second on the list of those who subscribed the covenant of the church in that place, Nov. 2, 1632, having been dismissed for that purpose from Boston church, Oct. 14. He was one of the first selectmen of Charlestown, and was one of its representatives at the first Court of Deputies held May 14, 1634, and again in 1635 and 1636. In May, 1635, he was appointed by the General Court captain of the fort at Castle Island. He died in 1637. See Col. Rec. i. 150 ; Savage's Winthrop, i. 2, ii. 363 ; Frothingham's

CHAP.
XI.  allowed by the Company,[1] gave me forty shillings to
make our provision of what things we would for the
1629. voyage.

May
9.    Saturday, we went to board again ; and this day
we had two other men pressed to serve the King's
ship ; but we got one again by entreaty.

10.   The Sabbath, next day, we kept the ship, where I
preached in the morning, and in the afternoon was
entreated to preach at Yarmouth ; where Mr. Meare
and Captain Borley[2] entertained us very kindly, and
earnestly desired to be certified of our safe arrival in
New-England, and of the state of the country.[3]

11.   Monday morning, blew a fair wind from east south-
east ; and the Lion's Whelp having taken in all her
provision for passengers, about three of the clock in
the afternoon we hoisted sail for the Needles,[4] and
by God's guidance safely passed that narrow passage
a little after four o'clock in the afternoon ; and being
entered into the sea, from the top of the mast we
discerned four sail of ships lying southward from us.
But night coming on, we took in our long-boat and

---

Hist. of Charlestown, p. 80 ; Budington's Hist. of First Church in
Charlestown, pp. 33, 184.

[1] The Company of Adventurers
for New-England, who had made
the Agreement with the ministers.
Skelton charged the Company £2
10s. for the expenses he incurred at
Tilbury, Cowes, and Yarmouth, being wind-bound. See Felt's Salem,
i. 511.

[2] " Captain Burleigh, captain of
Yarmouth castle, a grave, comely
gentleman, and of great age, came
aboard us, and stayed breakfast ;
and offering us much courtesy, he
departed, our captain giving him
four shot out of the forecastle for his
farewell. He was an old sea-cap-

tain in Queen Elizabeth's time, and
being taken prisoner at sea, was
kept prisoner in Spain three years.
Himself and three of his sons were
captains in Roe's voyage." Winthrop, i. 4. Burleigh was probably
a Puritan.

[3] It was partly, perhaps, to grat-
ify them, that Higginson wrote this
Journal of his Voyage and his New-
England's Plantation. See p. 214.

[4] The Needles' channel is so called from the sharp rocks, which, at
the western extremity of the Isle of
Wight, shoot up like needles. The
sharp-pointed granite peaks in the
neighbourhood of Mont Blanc are
called Aiguilles, or Needles.

shallop, and the next day we had a fair gale of east- CHAP.
erly wind, that brought us towards night as far as XI.
the Lizard.

1629.
May

Wednesday, the wind still holding easterly, we 13.
came as far as the Land's End, in the utmost part of
Cornwall, and so left our dear native soil of England
behind us ;[1] and sailing about ten leagues further,
we passed the isles of Scilly, and launched the same
day a great way into the main ocean. And now my
wife and other passengers began to feel the tossing
waves of the western sea, and so were very sea-sick.
And this is to be noted, that all this while our passage hath been upon the coast of England, and so
ought truly to be accounted the first day of our parting with Old England.

Thursday the same easterly wind blew all day and 14.
night, and the next day, so that some of the seamen 15.
thought we were come by this time two hundred
leagues from England ; but toward night the wind
was calm.

Saturday we were becalmed all day. This day 16.
met us a little ship of Bristol, that came from Christopher islands.[2]

---

[1] Cotton Mather says, that " when
they came to the Land's End, Mr.
Higginson, calling up his children
and other passengers unto the stern
of the ship, to take their last sight
of England, said, ' We will not say,
as the Separatists were wont to say
at their leaving of England, Farewell, Babylon ! Farewell, Rome !
But we will say, Farewell, dear
England ! Farewell, the Church of
God in England, and all the Christian friends there ! We do not go to
New-England as Separatists from
the Church of England ; though we
cannot but separate from the corruptions in it. But we go to practise the positive part of church reformation, and propagate the Gospel
in America.' And so he concluded
with a fervent prayer for the King,
and Church, and State, in England,
and for the presence and blessing of
God with themselves in their present
undertaking for New-England." —
See Mather's Magnalia, i. 328.

[2] " That every thing approaching
to an acknowledgment of the authority of the Pope, and his power of
canonization, might be avoided, they
never used the addition of Saint
when they spoke of the Apostles and

CHAP.
XI.
~~~~
1629.
May
17.

Sabbath, being the first Lord's day we held at sea, was very calm, especially in the morning. But we were disturbed in our morning service by the approach of a Biscayner's ship, a man-of-war, that made towards us, and manned out his boat to view us; but finding us too strong for him, he durst not venture to assault us, but made off.

This day my two children, Samuel and Mary, began to be sick of the small pox and purples together, which was brought into the ship by one Mr. Browne, which was sick of the same at Gravesend; whom it pleased God to make the first occasion of bringing that contagious sickness among us, wherewith many were after afflicted.

18.

Monday calm still, the wind being north-west, blowing a little towards evening, but contrary to our course.

19.

Tuesday wind south-west, as little helpful as the former, and blowing very weak. This day the master of our ship, myself and another, went aboard the Lion's Whelp, where Mr. Gibbs[1] made us welcome with bountiful entertainment. And this day, towards night, my daughter grew sicker, and many blue spots were seen upon her breast, which affrighted us. At the first we thought they had been the plague tokens; but we found afterwards that it was only a high measure of the infection of the pocks, which were struck again into the child; and so it was God's will the

the ancient Fathers of the Christian church; and even the usual names of places were made to conform. The island of St. Christopher's was always written Christopher's, and, by the same rule, all other places to which Saint had been prefixed." Hutchinson, Hist. of Mass. i. 429. See also note [3] on page 138; Winthrop, i. 60, ii. 33.

[1] John Gibbs was captain of the Lion's Whelp. See page 172.

child died about five of the clock at night, being the first in our ship that was buried in the bowels of the great Atlantic sea ; which, as it was a grief to us her parents, and a terror to all the rest, as being the beginning of a contagious disease and mortality, so in the same judgment it pleased God to remember mercy in the child, in freeing it from a world of misery, wherein otherwise she had lived all her days. For being about four years old, a year since, we know not by what means, swayed[1] in the back, so that it was broken, and grew crooked, and the joints of her hips were loosed, and her knees went crooked, pitiful to see. Since which time she hath had a most lamentable pain in her belly, and would ofttimes cry out in the day and in her sleep also, " My belly !" which declared some extraordinary distemper. So that in respect of her we had cause to take her death as a blessing from the Lord to shorten her misery.

Wednesday a wet morning. The wind was west south-west, and in the afternoon north-west and by west, both being contrary to our course, which was to sail west and by south. Thus it pleased God to lay his hand upon us by sickness and death and contrary winds ; and stirred up some of us to make the motion of humbling ourselves under the hand of God by keeping a solemn day of fasting and prayer unto God, to beseech him to remove the continuance and further increase of these evils from us ; which was willingly condescended unto, as a duty very fitting and needful for our present state and condition.

---

[1] Drawn to one side.

CHAP.
XI.
———
1629.
May
21.

Thursday, there being two ministers in the ship, Mr. Smith[1] and myself, we endeavoured, together with others, to consecrate the day as a solemn fasting and humiliation to Almighty God, as a furtherance of our present work. And it pleased God the ship was becalmed all day, so that we were freed from any incumbrance. And as soon as we had done prayers, (see and behold the goodness of God!) about seven o'clock at night the wind turned to north-east, and we had a fair gale that night as a manifest evidence of the Lord's hearing our prayers. I heard some of the mariners say, they thought this was the first sea-fast that ever was kept, and that they never heard of the like performed at sea before.

22. Friday the wind fair, and east northerly, and for our purpose for New-England. It did blow strongly, and carried us on amain with tossing waves, which did affright them that were not wonted to such sights.

23. Saturday the same wind blowing, but more gently. Now we were comforted with hope of my son Samuel's recovery of the pox.

24. The second Lord's day, a fair day, an orderly wind, and prosperous.

25. On Monday a fair, firm gale, the wind south southwest.

26. Tuesday, about ten of the clock in the morning, whilst we were at prayers, a strong and sudden blast came from the north, that hoisted up the waves, and tossed us more than ever before, and held us all the day till towards night, and then abated by little and

[1] Ralph Smith. See note [1] on page 151.

little till it was calm. This day Mr. Goffe's great CHAP. dog[1] fell overboard, and could not be recovered.

Wednesday the wind still north, and calm in the 1629. morning; but about noon there arose a south wind May 27. which increased more and more, so that it seemed to us, that are landmen, a sore and terrible storm; for the wind blew mightily, the rain fell vehemently, the sea roared, and the waves tossed us horribly; besides, it was fearful dark, and the mariners' mate was afraid, and noise on the other side, with their running here and there, loud crying one to another to pull at this and that rope. The waves poured themselves over the ship, that the two boats were filled with water, that they were fain to strike holes in the midst of them to let the water out. Yea, by the violence of the waves the long-boat's cord, which held it, was broken, and it had like to have been washed overboard, had not the mariners, with much pain and danger, recovered the same. But this lasted not many hours, after which it became a calmish day. All which while I lay close and warm in my cabin, but far from having list to sleep, with Jonah; Jonah, i. 5. my thoughts were otherwise employed, as the time and place required. Then I saw the truth of the Scriptures, Psalm cvii. from the 23d to the 32d; and my fear at this time was the less, when I remembered what a loving friend of mine, a minister, accustomed to sea-storms, said to me, that I might not be

---

[1] Why Mr. Goffe's great dog was sent over to the Colony, it is difficult to surmise, unless it was to defend the sheep from the wolves. There is a *naiveté* in relating this incident, which is quite noticeable. Mr. Goffe's great dog, buried in his watery grave, has thus become indissolubly connected with the history of the Colony, as much as the Deputy Governor himself, and they will go down to posterity together. See note [2] on page 70.

CHAP.
XI.

1629.
May
27.

dismayed at such storms, for they were ordinary at sea, and it seldom falls out that a ship perisheth at[1] them if it have sea-room ; which I the rather write, that others as well as myself, by the knowledge hereof, may be encouraged and prepared against these ordinary sea-storms.

28.      Thursday, south wind ; calm at night.

29.      On Friday a boisterous wind, blowing cross, but was allayed towards night with a shower of rain.

30.      Saturday, south-west wind, but fair and quiet.

31.      Sabbath day, being the third Lord's day, fair and calm. We saw abundance of grampus fishes,[2] two or three yards long, and a body as big as an ox.

June
1.

Monday, the wind westerly and calm. But besides our being stayed by contrary winds, we began to find the temperature of the air to alter and to become more sultry and subject to unwholesome fogs. For coming now to the height of the Western Islands, some of our men fell sick of the scurvy, and others of the small pox, which more and more increased ; yet, thanks be to God, none died of it but my own child mentioned. And therefore, according to our great need, we appointed another fast for the next day.

2.      Tuesday, we solemnly celebrate another fast. The Lord that day heard us before we prayed, and gave us answer before we called ; for early in the morning the wind turned full east, being as fit a wind as could blow ; and sitting at my study on the ship's poop, I saw many bonny fishes[3] and porpoises[4]

---

[1] *At* for *in* or *by*.
[2] See Chronicles of Plymouth, note [5] on page 152.
[3] Bonitos.

[4] The porpoise, (*delphinus phocæna*,) of the cetacean class of the Mammalia, *porcopesce*, Ital., *porc-poisson*, Fr., *hog-fish*, Eng. It is

pursuing one another, and leaping some of them a
yard above the water. Also, as we were at prayer
under the hatch, some that were above saw a whale
puffing up water not far from the ship. Now my
wife was pretty well recovered of her sea-sickness.

Wednesday a fair day, and fine gale of full east
wind. This day myself and others saw a large round
fish sailing by the ship's side, about a yard in length
and roundness every way. The mariners called it a
sun-fish.[1] It spreadeth out the fins like beams on
every side, four or five.

Thursday and Friday the wind full east. We
were carried with admiration on our journey. By
this we were more than half way to New-England.
This day I saw a fish very strange to me, (they call
it a carvel,) which came by the ship's side, wafting
along the top of the water. It appeared at the first
like a bubble above the water, as big as a man's
fist; but the fish itself is about the bigness of a man's
thumb ; so that the fish itself and the bubble resem-
bleth a ship with sails, which therefore is called a
carvel.[2]

Saturday wind direct east still.

The fourth Sabbath we kept at sea. The wind
full easterly till noon, and then it came full south-

---

so called from the supposed resem-
blance of its projecting snout to that
of the hog. See Griffith's Cuvier, iv.
453 ; Shaw's Zoölogy, ii. 504 ; Nat-
uralists' Library, Mammalia, vi. 222.

[1] A species of Acalephæ, *Medusa*
or *Cyanea*, familiarly known under
the names of *sea-jellies* and *sea-nettles*. The fins here mentioned are
its tentacles. See Griffith's Cuvier,
xii. 482, 562–569 ; Gould's Report
of the Invertebrata of Massachusetts,
p. 347.

[2] Carvel is a Spanish name for a
light vessel without decks. The
fish which resembled it, was probably the *Physalia*, called by sailors
the Portuguese man-of-war, a mo-
luscous animal, which has a large
air-bag to aid its swimming, and a
comb or crest, which answers as a
sail. See Griffith's Cuvier, xii. 490,
569–571 ; Chronicles of Plymouth,
note [2] on page 86.

CHAP.
XI.

1629.
June
9.

10.

11.

east, a strong gale that night and the next day till night.

Tuesday the same wind held till nine o'clock in the morning, and then a great shower, which lasted till about seven at night, and then it was a very calm. Here we sounded with a deep-lead[1] line above a hundred fathom, and found no bottom. This day we saw a fish called a turtle, a great and large shell-fish, swimming above the water near the ship.

Wednesday wind northerly, a fine gale, but calm-ish in the afternoon.

Thursday, the wind at north, an easy gale and fair morning. We saw a mountain of ice, shining as white as snow, like to a great rock or cliff on the shore. It stood still, and therefore we thought it to be on ground,[2] and to reach the bottom of the sea; for though there came a mighty stream from the north,[3] yet it moved not; which made us sound, and we found a bank[4] of forty fathom deep, where-upon we judged it to rest, and the height above was as much. We also saw six or seven pieces of ice float-ing on the sea, which was broken off from the former mountain. We also saw great store of water-fowl swimming by the ship within musket shot, of a pied

---

[1] The deep-sea-lead, spelt *dipled* in the manuscript, and commonly pronounced *dipsey*-lead, weighs from 14 to 18 or 20 pounds, and the deep-sea-line is from 90 to 110 fathoms. See Dana's Seaman's Friend, page 17.

[2] These icebergs are frequently grounded in 40 and 50 fathoms wa-ter, and in foggy weather their vi-cinity may be known by the intense coldness they diffuse, and by the roar of the waters breaking against them.

[3] This was the tide, or the strong current that runs counter to the Gulf Stream, from the Banks of New-foundland to Cape Florida.

[4] They were now on the eastern edge of the Grand Bank of New-foundland, which extends from about the latitude of 42° to 50°, or upwards. About the latitude of 45°, its breadth is nearly four degrees. To the northward and southward it narrows almost to a point, and seems insensibly to drop into fathomless water.

color, and about the bigness of a wild duck, about CHAP.
XI.
forty in a company; the mariners call them hag-birds.[1]
Toward night came a fog, that the Lion's Whelp was 1629.
June
lost till morning. And now we saw many bonitos,
porpoises, and grampuses, every day more and more.

Friday foggy and calmish, the wind northerly in the 12.
morning, but about noon it came south-east, a dainty
loom-gale,[2] which carried us six leagues a watch.

Saturday the same wind till night, and we saw 13.
great store of porpoises and grampuses.

The fifth Sabbath, the same wind. Towards noon 14.
it began to be foggy, and then it rained till night.
We went four or five leagues a watch.

Monday a fair day, but foggy; the same wind 15.
blowing, but with fresh gales, carried us seven
leagues a watch. In the afternoon it blew harder,
so the sea was rough, and we lost the sight of the
Lion's Whelp. It being foggy, we drummed for
them, and they shot off a great piece of ordnance;
but we heard not one another.

Tuesday wind south and by east; foggy till about 16.
10 o'clock. While we were at prayers, it cleared
up about an hour, and then we saw the Lion's Whelp
distant about two leagues southward. We presently
tacked about to meet her, and she did the same to
meet us; but before we could get together, a thick
fog came, that we were long in finding each other.
This day we sounded divers times, and found ourselves on another bank,[3] at first forty fathom, after

---

[1] Probably a species of the *Mer-
ganser*. The approach to the Banks
may be known by the appearance of
numerous sea-fowls, such as guille-
mots and divers.

[2] A gentle, easy gale of wind, in
which a ship can carry her topsails.
[3] "On the western side of the
Great Bank, and to the southward
of the island of Newfoundland and

CHAP.
XI.

1629.
June
16.

thirty-six, after thirty-three, after twenty-four. We thought it to have been the bank over against Cape Sable, but we were deceived ; for we knew not certainly where we were, because of the fog. After three or four hours' company we lost the Lion's Whelp again, and beat our drum and shot off a great piece of ordnance, and yet heard not of them. But perceiving the bank to grow still the shallower, we found it twenty-seven and twenty-four fathoms. Therefore, being a fog, and fearing we were too near land, we tacked about for sea-room for two or three watches, and steered south-east.

17. Wednesday very foggy still, and wind south and by west ; and sounding, found no bottom that we could reach.

18. Thursday wind full west, and contrary to us. This day a notorious wicked fellow, that was given to swearing and boasting of his former wickedness, bragged that he had got a wench with child before he came this voyage, and mocked at our days of fast, railing and jesting against Puritans ; this fellow fell sick of the pocks, and died. We sounded and found thirty-eight fathom, and stayed for a little to take some codfish, and feasted ourselves merrily.

19. Friday, wind west still, a very fair, clear day. About four o'clock in the afternoon some went up to the top of the mast, and affirmed, to our great comfort, they saw land to the north-eastward.

20. Saturday wind south-west, a fair gale. We sound-

---

Nova Scotia, a chain of banks extends almost two degrees from the land. These are called Green Bank, Banquereau, Sable Island Bank, &c. All these have soundings of various depths, from 20 to 70 fathoms, admirably situated, in dark weather, to warn the mariner of his approach towards the land." Blunt's American Coast Pilot, p. 12.

ed and found forty, thirty, twenty-two, and a little CHAP.<br>XI.
after no ground.

Sabbath, being the sixth Lord's day, wind west- 1629.
erly, but fair and calm. June<br>21.

Monday, wind easterly, a fair gale. This day we 22.
saw a great deal of froth not far from us. We feared
it might be some breach of water against some [   ].[1]
Therefore the master of our ship hoisted out the
shallop, and went with some of the men to see what
it was ; but found it only to be a froth carried by the
stream.

Tuesday the wind north-east, a fair gale. This 23
day we examined five beastly Sodomitical boys which
confessed their wickedness, not to be named. The
fact was so foul, we referred them to be punished by
the Governor, when we came to New-England,
who afterwards sent them back to the Company,
to be punished in Old England, as the crime deserved.[2]

Wednesday, wind north-east, a fair day and clear. 24.
About nine o'clock in the morning we espied a ship
about four leagues behind us, which proved the
Lion's Whelp, which had been a week separated
from us ; we stayed for her company. This day a
child of goodman Black's,[3] which had a consumption
before it came to ship, died. This day we had all a
clear and comfortable sight of America, and of the
Cape Sable, that was over against us seven or eight

---

[1] Here are two words which I
cannot decipher. They look like
*ned grales.* The copyist puts a star
over them, seeming to intimate that
he could not make them out. Hutchinson has it *rocks.* But no such word
is to be found in the MS.

[2] See pages 90 and 93.
[3] This man's name was probably
Blake. The name of that ancient
and respectable family, the Blakes
of Dorchester, is usually found written Black in old family papers and
records.

CHAP.
XI.

1629.
June
25.

26.

leagues northward.  Here we saw yellow gilliflowers on the sea.

Thursday wind still north-east, a full and fresh gale.  In the afternoon we had a clear sight of many islands and hills by the sea-shore.  Now we saw abundance of mackerel, a great store of great whales puffing up water as they go; some of them came near our ship.  Their greatness did astonish us that saw them not before ; their backs appeared like a little island.  At five o'clock at[1] night the wind turned south-east, a fair gale.  This day we caught mackerel.

Friday a foggy morning, but after clear, and wind calm.  We saw many schools of mackerel,[2] infinite multitudes on every side of our ship.  The sea was abundantly stored with rockweed and yellow flowers, like gilliflowers.  By noon we were within three leagues of Cape Ann ;[3] and as we sailed along the coasts, we saw every hill and dale and every island full of gay woods and high trees.  The nearer we came to the shore, the more flowers in abundance, sometimes scattered abroad, sometimes joined in sheets nine or ten yards long, which we supposed to be brought from the low meadows by the tide.  Now what with fine woods and green trees by land,

---

[1] Here the MS. ends ; and for the rest of the Journal I am obliged to rely upon Hutchinson, who used the MS. when it was entire.  See his Collection, p. 42.

[2] The spring mackerel appear on the coast of Massachusetts about the end of May, and towards the middle of June they become very plentiful. The numbers taken, however, vary exceedingly from year to year, and upon the whole the fishery seems to

be rapidly declining.  Thus in the year ending April 1, 1837, the number of barrels caught was 234,059, valued at $ 1,639,402, whilst in the year ending April 1, 1845, the number was only 86,628, valued at $637,052.  Compare the Statistical Tables of the Industry of Massachusetts for those years, and see Storer's Report on the Fishes of Massachusetts, p. 41.

[3] See page 22.

and these yellow flowers[1] painting the sea, made us CHAP.
all desirous to see our new paradise of New-England, whence we saw such forerunning signals of 1629.
fertility afar off.[2]   Coming near the harbour towards 26.
night, we tacked about for sea-room.

Saturday a foggy morning ; but after eight o'clock 27.
in the morning very clear.   The wind being somewhat contrary at south and by west, we tacked to
and again with getting little, but with much ado.
About four o'clock in the afternoon, having with
much pain compassed the harbour, and being ready
to enter the same, (see how things may suddenly
change !) there came a fearful gust of wind and rain
and thunder and lightning, whereby we were borne
with no little terror and trouble to our mariners,
having very much ado to loose down the sails when
the fury of the storm struck us.[3]   But, God be praised, it lasted but a while, and soon abated again.
And hereby the Lord showed us what he could have
done with us, if it had pleased him.   But, blessed be
God, he soon removed this storm, and it was a fair
and sweet evening.

We had a westerly wind, which brought us, between five and six o'clock, to a fine and sweet harbour, seven miles from the head point[4] of Cape Ann.
This harbour twenty ships may easily ride therein ;[5]

[1] These may have been butter-
cups, which had been washed from
the shore, and become mixed with
rock-weed, kelp, and tangle ;  or,
more probably, a species of animal
plants, *Actiniæ*, sea-anemones or
fixed sea-nettles.   See Griffith's
Cuvier, xii. 494, 572.

[2] How different was this scene
from that which met the eyes of the
Pilgrims, in November, 1620, when
they made the opposite headland of
Cape Cod !  See Chronicles of Plymouth, pp. 104–106.

[3] In Hutchinson, " held  up ;"
which is unquestionably an error.

[4] By the head-point I suppose he
means the part of the Cape near
Thacher's Island.

[5] The outer harbour will contain
400 ships, and the inner harbour 200
fishing-vessels.   It is an excellent
harbour, and well protected, except
from a south-west storm.

CHAP. where there was an island,[1] whither four of our men
XI.
~~~ with a boat went, and brought back again ripe straw-
1629. berries and gooseberries, and sweet single roses.[2]
June
27. Thus God was merciful to us in giving us a taste and
smell of the sweet fruit as an earnest of his bountiful
goodness to welcome us at our first arrival. This harbour was two leagues and something more from the
harbour at Naimkecke,[3] where our ships were to rest,
and the Plantation is already begun. But because
the passage is difficult, and night drew on, we put
into Cape Ann harbour.

28.     The Sabbath, being the first we kept in America,
and the seventh Lord's day after we parted with
England.

29.     Monday we came from Cape Ann to go to Naimkecke, the wind northerly. I should have told you
before, that, the planters spying our English colors,
the Governor[4] sent a shallop with two men on Saturday to pilot us. These rested the Sabbath with us
at Cape Ann; and this day, by God's blessing and
their directions, we passed the curious and difficult
entrance into the large, spacious harbour of Naimkecke. And as we passed along, it was wonderful
to behold so many islands,[5] replenished with thick
wood and high trees, and many fair, green pastures.
And being come into the harbour, we saw the

[1] Ten-pound Island, on which
there is now a light-house.
[2] The sweet briar. Gooseberries
are still found on the island, and before it was cleared up, wild strawberries were also obtained there.
[3] The distance from Gloucester to
Salem harbour is about nine miles.
[4] Endicott.
[5] Baker's Island, Great and Little
Miseries, Coney Island, and others,
a full topographical description of
which may be seen in Bentley's
History of Salem, in Mass. Hist.
Coll. vi. 219-222. See also Bowditch's Chart of the Harbours of
Salem, Beverly, Marblehead and
Manchester, and the accurate and
beautiful Map of Massachusetts,
made by order of the Legislature in
1844.

George to our great comfort, there being come on
Tuesday, which was seven days before us.     We
rested that night with glad and thankful hearts that
God had put an end to our long and tedious journey
through the greatest sea in the world.

The next morning the Governor came aboard to
our ship, and bade us kindly welcome, and invited
me and my wife to come on shore and take our lodging in his house ;[1] which we did accordingly.

Thus you have a faithful report, collected from
day to day, of all the particulars that were worth
noting in our passage.

Now in our passage divers things are remarkable.

First, through God's blessing, our passage was
short and speedy , for whereas we had a thousand
leagues, that is, three thousand miles English, to sail
from Old to New England, we performed the same
in six weeks and three days.

Secondly, our passage was comfortable and easy
for the most part, having ordinarily fair and moderate
wind, and being freed for the most part from stormy
and rough seas, saving one night only, which we that
were not used thought to be more terrible than indeed it was ; and this was Wednesday at night,
May 27th.

Thirdly, our passage was also healthful to our
passengers, being freed from the great contagion of
the scurvy and other maledictions,[2] which in other
passages to other places had taken away the lives of

---

[1] Higginson says, in another place, that it was "a fair house, newly
built for the Governor."

[2] Maladies, diseases.

CHAP.
XI.

1629.
June.

many. And yet we were, in all reason, in wonderful danger all the way, our ship being greatly crowded with passengers ; but, through God's great goodness, we had none that died of the pox but that wicked fellow that scorned at fasting and prayer. There were indeed two little children, one of my own, and another beside ; but I do not impute it merely to the passage, for they were both very sickly children, and not likely to have lived long, if they had not gone to sea. And take this for a rule, if children be healthful when they come to sea, the younger they are the better they will endure the sea, and are not troubled with sea-sickness as older people are, as we had experience in many children that went this voyage. My wife, indeed, in tossing weather, was something ill by vomiting ; but in calm weather she recovered again, and is now much better for the sea-sickness.[1] And for my own part, whereas I have for divers years past been very sickly, and ready to cast up whatsoever I have eaten, and was very sick at London and Gravesend, yet from the time I came on shipboard to this day I have been strangely healthful.[2] And now I can digest our ship diet very well, which I could not when I was at land. And indeed in this regard I have great cause to give God praise, that he hath made my coming to be a method to cure me of a wonderful weak stomach and continual pain of melancholy wind from the spleen. Also divers children were sick of the small pox, but are safely recovered again ; and two or three passengers, to-

[1] She lived till 1640, in which year she died, at New Haven, in Connecticut. See note [3] on page 211.

[2] Yet he died in August of the next year, — of a hectic fever, according to Cotton Mather. See the Magnalia, i. 329.

wards the latter end of the voyage, fell sick of the scurvy, but coming to land recovered in a short time.

Fourthly, our passage was both pleasurable and profitable. For we received instruction and delight in beholding the wonders of the Lord in the deep waters, and sometimes seeing the sea round us appearing with a terrible countenance, and, as it were, full of high hills and deep valleys ; and sometimes it appeared as a most plain and even meadow. And ever and anon we saw divers kinds of fishes sporting in the great waters, great grampuses and huge whales, going by companies, and puffing up water streams. Those that love their own chimney-corner, and dare not go far beyond their own town's end, shall never have the honor to see these wonderful works of Almighty God.

Fifthly, we had a pious and Christian-like passage ; for I suppose passengers shall seldom find a company of more religious, honest and kind seamen than we had. We constantly served God morning and evening by reading and expounding a chapter, singing, and prayer. And the Sabbath was solemnly kept, by adding to the former, preaching twice and catechising. And in our great need we kept two solemn fasts, and found a gracious effect. Let all that love and use fasting and praying, take notice that it is as prevailable by sea as by land, wheresoever it is faithfully performed. Besides, the shipmaster and his company used every night to set their eight and twelve o'clock watches with singing a psalm, and prayer that was not read out of a book.[1] This I write not

---

[1] That is, extempore, according to the mode of the early Christians.    Justin Martyr says, the officiating minister in the public worship of the

for boasting and flattery, but for the benefit of those that have a mind to come to New-England hereafter, that if they look for and desire to have as prosperous a voyage as we had, they may use the same means to attain the same.[1]

So letting pass our passage by sea, we will now bring our discourse to land, on the shore of New-England; and I shall, by God's assistance, endeavour to speak nothing but the naked truth, and both acquaint you with the commodities and discommodities of the country.[2]

primitive church, "offered prayers and thanksgivings according to his ability." See his Second Apology, towards the end, Opera, p. 98, (ed. Cologne, 1686.) Origen, too, contra Celsum, lib. viii. pp. 386, 402, says the same thing; and Tertullian in his Apol., cap. 30, says, "We pray without a prompter, because our prayers flow from our own minds : sine monitore, quia de pectore oramus." Opera, v. 80, (ed. Semler.)

[1] It appears from page 214, that this Journal was "written from New-England, July 24, 1629," and was undoubtedly sent home on the return of the Talbot and Lion's Whelp, which arrived in England before Sept. 19. See page 90.

[2] The principal part of the preceding Journal is printed from an old MS., which, though not the original, is unquestionably a very early copy. It was in the possession of Hutchinson, but not of Prince. It is now the property of the Massachusetts Historical Society. See page 232.

# FRANCIS HIGGINSON'S

# NEW-ENGLAND'S PLANTATION.

NEW-ENGLANDS PLANTATION. Or a Short and Trve Description
of the Commodities and Discommodities of that Countrey. Written by Mr. *Higgeson*,[1] a reuerend Diuine now there resident.
Whereunto is added a Letter, sent by Mr. *Graues*, an Enginere,
out of *New-England.* *The third Edition, enlarged.*
LONDON. Printed by *T.* and *R. Cotes* for *Michael Sparke*, dwelling at the Signe of the *Blew Bible* in *Greene Arbor.* 1630.
sm. 4to. pp. 25.

[1] Mr. Higginson's name does not
appear on the title-page of the first
edition, printed the same year; nor
is Graves's Letter printed in that
edition. I have both editions before
me, loaned me by Edward A. Crown-
inshield, Esq. of Boston. That they
were actually distinct editions, and
not merely different in their title-
pages, is demonstrated by the collation of the volumes, by which it appears that the typographical errors
of the first edition are not to be
found in the third. The appearance
of three editions of this pamphlet in
the course of a year, shows the interest with which the infant Plantation was regarded in England.

# TO THE READER.

Reader,

Do not disdain to read this Relation; and 1630. look not here to have a large gate, and no building within, a full-stuffed title, with no matter in the book. But here read the truth; and that thou shalt find without any frothy, bombasting words, or any quaint, new-devised additions, only as it was written (not intended for the press) by a reverend divine now there living, who only sent it to some friends[1] here which were desirous of his Relations; which is an epitome of their proceedings in the Plantation. And for thy part, if thou meanest to be no planter nor venturer, do but lend thy good prayers for the furtherance of it. And so I rest a well-wisher to all the good designs both of them which are gone, and of them that are to go.[2]

M. S.[3]

---

[1] Among them were Isaac Johnson and Increase Nowell, who was a relative, besides his parishioners at Leicester, and the persons who treated him so kindly at Yarmouth. See pages 65 and 220.

[2] This indicates that the first edition of the book was printed before the sailing of Winthrop's fleet, that is, before April.

[3] The initials of Michael Sparke, the publisher. See page 240.

# CHAPTER XII.

CHAP.
XII.

1629.
July
to
Sept.

LETTING pass our voyage by sea,[2] we will now begin our discourse on the shore of New-England. And because the life and welfare of every creature here below, and the commodiousness of the country whereas such creatures live, doth, by the most wise ordering of God's providence, depend, next unto himself, upon the temperature and disposition of the four elements, Earth, Water, Air, and Fire, (for as of the mixture of all these all sublunary things are composed, so by the more or less enjoyment of the wholesome temper and convenient use of these consisteth the only well being both of man and beast in a more or less comfortable measure in all countries under the heavens,) therefore I will endeavour

---

[1] This Relation was probably sent home on the return of the Four Sisters and Mayflower, which arrived in England before Nov. 20th. Of course it covers a space of only about three months, from the first of July to the middle or end of September. See pages 107 and 240.

[2] It is evident from page 238, that this Narrative was a continuation of the Journal of the Voyage. But the Journal, it seems, was not deemed of sufficient importance to be printed with it, and was accordingly omitted, and was never subsequently printed in England.

to show you what New-England is, by the consider- CHAP.<br>
ation of each of these apart, and truly endeavour, by<br>
God's help, to report nothing but the naked truth, 1629.<br>
and that both to tell you of the discommodities as July to<br>
well as of the commodities. Though, as the idle pro- Sept.<br>
verb is, " Travellers may lie by authority," and so
may take too much sinful liberty that way, yet I may
say of myself, as once Nehemiah did in another case,
" Shall such a man as I lie ?" No, verily. It be-
cometh not a preacher of truth to be a writer of
falsehood in any degree ;[1] and therefore I have been
careful to report nothing of New-England but what I
have partly seen with mine own eyes, and partly
heard and inquired from the mouths of very honest
and religious persons,[2] who by living in the country
a good space of time have had experience and knowledge of the state thereof, and whose testimonies I
do believe as myself.

*First therefore of the Earth of New-England, and all
the appurtenances thereof.*

It is a land of divers and sundry sorts all about
Masathulets[3] Bay, and at Charles river is as fat black
earth as can be seen anywhere ; and in other places

[1] And yet he was accused of ex-aggerating the advantages of the country. See Dudley's letter to the Countess of Lincoln, in a subsequent part of this volume.

[2] Conant and his associates ; per-haps, also, Gov. Bradford and others from the Colony of New-Plymouth, who came to Salem as messengers from the church to attend Higgin-son's installation on the 6th of Aug. and with whom he then had ample opportunity to confer. See Morton's Memorial, p. 146, and Prince's An-nals, p. 263.

[3] So spelt in the original ; possi-bly a typographical error, although it is spelt four times afterwards in the same manner.

CHAP.
XII.

1629.

July
to
Sept.

Psalm
lxxvi.
2.

you have a clay soil, in other gravel, in other sandy, as it is all about our Plantation at Salem, for so our town is now named.[1]

The form of the earth here, in the superficies of it, is neither too flat in the plainness, nor too high in hills, but partakes of both in a mediocrity, and fit for pasture or for plough or meadow ground, as men please to employ it. Though all the country be, as it were, a thick wood for the general, yet in divers places there is much ground cleared by the Indians,[2] and especially about the Plantation ; and I am told that about three miles from us a man may stand on a little hilly place and see divers thousands of acres of ground as good as need to be, and not a tree in the same. It is thought here is good clay to make brick and tiles and earthen pots, as need to be. At this instant we are setting a brick-kiln on work, to make bricks and tiles for the building of our houses. For stone, here is plenty of slates at the Isle of Slate[3] in Masathulets Bay, and limestone, freestone, and smooth-stone, and iron-stone, and marble-stone[3] also in such store, that we have great rocks of it, and a harbour hard by. Our Plantation is from thence called Marble-harbour.[4]

---

[1] See pages 12 and 31.

[2] See Chronicles of Plymouth, pp. 124, 167 and 206.

[3] This Isle of Slate and the marble-stone have never yet been found.

[4] A name nearly resembling this, now belongs to an adjoining town, which in 1649 was set off from Salem. Wood, who was here in 1633, says, in his New-England's Prospect, part i. ch. 10, " Marvilhead is a place which lieth four miles full south from Salem, and is a very convenient place for a plantation, especially for such as will set upon

the trade of fishing. There was made here a ship's loading of fish the last year, where still stand the stages and drying scaffolds." In Professor Sewall's oration, delivered in 1769 at the funeral of the Rev. Edward Holyoke, President of Harvard College, who had once been a minister in that town, it is thus graphically described : " *Marmaracria*, oppidum maritimum, saxis abundans, inde Nov-anglicè dictum *Marblehead;* asperrima vox, aures Latinas horridè perstringens." See Mass. Hist. Coll. viii. 51.

Of minerals there hath yet been but little trial made, yet we are not without great hope of being furnished in that soil.

The fertility of the soil is to be admired at, as appeareth in the abundance of grass that groweth every where, both very thick, very long, and very high in divers places. But it groweth very wildly, with a great stalk, and a broad and ranker blade,[1] because it never had been eaten with cattle, nor mowed with a scythe, and seldom trampled on by foot. It is scarce to be believed how our kine and goats,[2] horses and hogs do thrive and prosper here, and like well of this country.

In our Plantation we have already a quart of milk for a penny. But the abundant increase of corn proves this country to be a wonderment. Thirty, forty, fifty, sixty, are ordinary here. Yea, Joseph's increase in Egypt is outstripped here with us. Our planters hope to have more than a hundredfold this year. And all this while I am within compass; what will you say of two hundred fold, and upwards? It is almost incredible what great gain some of our English planters have had by our Indian corn. Credible persons have assured me, and the party himself avouched the truth of it to me, that of the setting of thirteen gallons of corn he hath had increase of it fifty-two hogsheads, every hogshead holding seven bushels of London measure, and every bushel was by him sold and trusted to the Indians for so much

---

[1] Probably the meadow spear grass (*poa nervata*), or the foul meadow grass. See Dewey's Report on the Herbaceous Plants of Massachusetts, p. 246, and Bigelow's Plants of Boston and Vicinity, p. 35.

[2] They had at this time in the Plantation about forty cows, and as many goats, as Higginson himself informs us in a letter at the end of this Relation.

beaver as was worth eighteen shillings ; and so of this thirteen gallons of corn, which was worth six shillings eight pence, he made about £327 of it the year following, as by reckoning will appear ; where you may see how God blesseth husbandry in this land. There is not such great and plentiful ears of corn I suppose any where else to be found but in this country, being also of variety of colors, as red, blue, and yellow, &c. ;[1] and of one corn there springeth four or five hundred. I have sent you many ears of divers colors, that you might see the truth of it.

Little children here, by setting of corn, may earn much more than their own maintenance.

They have tried our English corn at New Plymouth Plantation,[2] so that all our several grains will grow here very well, and have a fitting soil for their nature.

Our Governor hath store of green pease growing in his garden as good as ever I eat in England.

This country aboundeth naturally with store of roots of great variety and good to eat. Our turnips, parsnips and carrots are here both bigger and sweeter than is ordinarily to be found in England. Here are also store of pumpions, cowcumbers, and other things of that nature which I know not. Also, divers excellent pot-herbs grow abundantly among the grass, as strawberry leaves in all places of the country, and plenty of strawberries in their time, and penny-royal, winter-savory, sorrel, brooklime, liverwort, carvel,

---

[1] See Chronicles of Plymouth, note [1] on p. 131, and note [4] on p. 133; and Dewey's Report, p. 253.

[2] See Chronicles of Plymouth, pages 231 and 370.

and watercresses ; also leeks and onions are ordi- CHAP.
nary, and divers physical herbs.[1]  Here are also XII.
abundance of other sweet herbs, delightful to the 1629.
smell, whose names we know not, and plenty of July
single damask roses,[2] very sweet ; and two kinds of to
herbs that bear two kinds of flowers very sweet, Sept.
which they say are as good to make cordage or cloth
as any hemp or flax[3] we have.

Excellent vines are here up and down in the
woods.  Our Governor hath already planted a vineyard,[4] with great hope of increase.

Also, mulberries, plums, raspberries, currants,
chestnuts, filberts, walnuts, small-nuts, hurtleber-
ries, and haws of white-thorn, near as good as our
cherries in England, they grow in plenty here.

For wood, there is no better in the world, I think,
here being four sorts of oak, differing both in the
leaf, timber, and color, all excellent good.  There
is also good ash, elm, willow, birch, beech, sassafras, juniper, cypress, cedar, spruce, pines and fir,[5]
that will yield abundance of turpentine, pitch, tar,
masts, and other materials for building both of ships
and houses.  Also here are store of sumach[6] trees,
that are good for dyeing and tanning of leather ;
likewise such trees yield a precious gum, called
white benjamin, that they say is excellent for per-
fumes.  Also here be divers roots and berries,

---

[1] See Chronicles of Plymouth,
pp. 132, 165, and 234 ; Dewey's
Report, p. 209.

[2] The sweet briar (*rosa rubigi-
nosa*.)   See Chron. Plym. 234 ;
Dewey's Report, p. 55 ; and Bigelow's Plants, p. 209.

[3] See Chronicles of Plymouth,
note [2] on page 166 ; Dewey's Re-

port, p. 83 ; and Bigelow's Plants,
p. 130.

[4] See note [1] on page 152.

[5] See Chronicles of Plymouth,
pages 118, 124, 164, 165.

[6] See page 133 ; Dewey's Report, p. 200 ; and Bigelow's Plants,
page 125.

wherewith the Indians die excellent holding colors, that no rain nor washing can alter. Also we have materials to make soap ashes and saltpetre in abundance.

For beasts there are some bears, and they say some lions[1] also ; for they have been seen at Cape Anne. Also here are several sorts of deer, some whereof bring three or four young ones at once, which is not ordinary in England ; also wolves, foxes, beavers, otters, martens, great wild cats, and a great beast called a molke,[2] as big as an ox. I have seen the skins of all these beasts since I came to this Plantation, excepting lions. Also here are great store of squirrels, some greater, and some smaller and lesser ; there are some of the lesser sort, they tell me, that by a certain skin will fly from tree to tree, though they stand far distant.[3]

---

*Of the Waters of New-England, with the things belonging to the same.*

New-England hath water enough, both salt and fresh. The greatest sea in the world, the Atlantic Sea, runs all along the coast thereof. There are abundance of islands along the shore, some full of wood and mast to feed swine, and others clear of

[1] See Chronicles of Plymouth, note [1] on page 176.
[2] Probably an error of the press for *moose*. See Josselyn's New-England's Rarities, p. 19 ; Wood's New-England's Prospect, part i. ch. 6 ; and Emmons's Report on the Quadrupeds of Massachusetts, pp. 74–78.

[3] " The third kind is a flying squirrel, which is not very big, slender of body, with a great deal of loose skin, which she spreads square when she flies ; which the wind gets, and so wafts her bat-like body from place to place." Wood's New-England's Prospect, ch. 6.

wood, and fruitful to bear corn.  Also we have store
of excellent harbours for ships, as at Cape Anne,
and at Masathulets Bay, and at Salem, and at many
other places ; and they are the better, because for
strangers there is a very difficult and dangerous passage into them, but unto such as are well acquainted
with them they are easy and safe enough.

The abundance of sea-fish are almost beyond believing ; and sure I should scarce have believed it
except I had seen it with mine own eyes.  I saw great
store of whales, and grampuses, and such abundance of mackerels[1] that it would astonish one to behold ; likewise codfish, abundance on the coast, and
in their season are plentifully taken.  There is a fish
called a bass,[2] a most sweet and wholesome fish as
ever I did eat ; it is altogether as good as our fresh
salmon ; and the season of their coming was begun
when we came first to New-England in June, and so
continued about three months' space.[3]  Of this fish
our fishers take many hundreds together, which I
have seen lying on the shore, to my admiration.
Yea, their nets ordinarily take more than they are
able to haul to land, and for want of boats and men
they are constrained to let a many go after they have
taken them ; and yet sometimes they fill two boats
at a time with them.  And besides bass, we take
plenty of scate and thornback, and abundance of

---

[1] See note [2] on page 232.
[2] The striped bass, (*labrax linea-tus*.)  See Wood, ch. 9, and Sto-rer's Report on the Fishes of Massa-chusetts, page 7.
[3] This helps us to fix the date of this Relation.  It was not written till after the first of September, and

was probably sent home by the Mayflower or Four Sisters, both of which reached England before Nov. 20, and had brought a letter, dated the 5th of September, from Gov. Endicott and others.  See pages 107, 109 and 212.

CHAP.
XII.

1629.
July
to
Sept.

lobsters,[1] and the least boy in the Plantation may both catch and eat what he will of them. For my own part, I was soon cloyed with them, they were so great, and fat, and luscious. I have seen some myself that have weighed sixteen pound; but others have had divers times so great lobsters as have weighed twenty-five pound,[2] as they assured me.

Also, here is abundance of herring, turbot,[3] sturgeon, cusks, haddocks, mullets, eels, crabs, muscles, and oysters.[4] Besides, there is probability that the country is of an excellent temper for the making of salt; for, since our coming, our fishermen have brought home very good salt which they found candied by the standing of the sea-water and the heat of the sun upon a rock by the seashore; and in divers salt marshes that some have gone through, they have found some salt in some places crushing under their feet, and cleaving to their shoes.

And as for fresh water, the country is full of dainty springs,[5] and some great rivers, and some lesser brooks; and at Masathulets Bay[6] they digged wells and found water at three foot deep in most places; and near Salem they have as fine clear water as we

[1] The lobster, (*homarus Americanus*,) the largest of all crustaceous animals, is found about all the islands in Massachusetts Bay, and in every cove along the coast. Probably 200,000 are annually taken in our waters, one half of which are brought to Boston. See Gould's Report on the Invertebrate Animals of Massachusetts, pp. 330 and 360.

[2] Wood, ch. 9, mentions "very large ones, some being 20 pounds in weight." The largest that has been seen of late by the Boston fish-ermen, weighed 28 pounds. See Gould's Report, page 360.

[3] See Chronicles of Plymouth, note [3] on page 164.

[4] See Wood, ch. 9; Morton's New-English Canaan, book ii. ch. 7; and Gould's Report, pages 121, 135, 356, 360.

[5] See Chronicles of Plymouth, note [4] on page 129.

[6] At Charlestown, whither Graves had already gone. See note [2] on page 152.

can desire, and we may dig wells and find water
where we list.

Thus we see both land and sea abound with store of blessings for the comfortable sustenance of man's life in New-England.

*Of the Air of New-England, with the temper and creatures in it.*

The temper of the air[1] of New-England is one special thing that commends this place. Experience doth manifest that there is hardly a more healthful place to be found in the world that agreeth better with our English bodies. Many that have been weak and sickly in Old England, by coming hither have been thoroughly healed, and grown healthful and strong. For here is an extraordinary clear and dry air, that is of a most healing nature to all such as are of a cold, melancholy, phlegmatic, rheumatic temper of body. None can more truly speak hereof by their own experience than myself. My friends that knew me can well tell how very sickly I have been, and continually in physic, being much troubled with a tormenting pain through an extraordinary weakness of my stomach, and abundance of melancholic humors. But since I came hither on this voyage, I thank God I have had perfect health, and freed from pain and vomiting, having a stomach to digest the hardest and coarsest fare, who before could not eat finest meat ; and whereas my stomach could only digest and did require such drink as was both

---

[1] See Chronicles of Plymouth, pages 233, 369,

strong and stale, now I can and do oftentimes drink New-England water very well. And I that have not gone without a cap for many years together, neither durst leave off the same, have now cast away my cap, and do wear none at all in the day time; and whereas beforetime I clothed myself with double clothes and thick waistcoats to keep me warm, even in the summer time, I do now go as thin clad as any, only wearing a light stuff cassock upon my shirt, and stuff breeches of one thickness without linings. Besides, I have one of my children, that was formerly most lamentably handled with sore breaking out of both his hands and feet of the king's evil; but since he came hither he is very well ever he was, and there is hope of perfect recovery shortly, even by the very wholesomeness of the air, altering, digesting, and drying up the cold and crude humors of the body; and therefore I think it is a wise course for all cold complexions to come to take physic in New-England; for a sup of New-England's air is better than a whole draught of Old England's ale.

In the summer time, in the midst of July and August, it is a good deal hotter than in Old England, and in winter January and February are much colder, as they say; but the spring and autumn are of a middle temper.

Fowls of the air are plentiful here, and of all sorts as we have in England, as far as I can learn, and a great many of strange fowls which we know not. Whilst I was writing these things, one of our men brought home an eagle which he had killed in the wood; they say they are good meat. Also here are many kinds of excellent hawks, both sea hawks and land hawks; and myself walking in the woods with CHAP. XII. another in company, sprung a partridge[1] so big that through the heaviness of his body could fly but a 1629. July to Sept. little way; they that have killed them say they are as big as our hens. Here are likewise abundance of turkeys[2] often killed in the woods, far greater than our English turkeys, and exceeding fat, sweet, and fleshy; for here they have abundance of feeding all the year long, as strawberries (in summer all places are full of them) and all manner of berries and fruits. In the winter time I have seen flocks of pigeons,[3] and have eaten of them. They do fly from tree to tree, as other birds do, which our pigeons will not do in England. They are of all colors, as ours are, but their wings and tails are far longer; and therefore it is likely they fly swifter to escape the terrible hawks in this country. In winter time this country doth abound with wild geese, wild ducks,[4] and other sea-fowl, that a great part of winter the planters have eaten nothing but roast meat of divers fowls which they have killed.

---

Thus you have heard of the Earth, Water, and Air of New-England. Now it may be you expect something to be said of the Fire, proportionable to the rest of the elements.

[1] This, no doubt, was the partridge of New-England, the pheasant of the middle and western States, (*tretao umbellus.*) Wood and Morton both remark that they are bigger in body than the partridges of England. See Peabody's Report, page 354; Wilson's Amer. Ornithol. vi. 45; Audubon's Ornithol. Biog. i. 211; Nuttall, i. 657.

[2] See Josselyn's New-England's Rarities, p. 8; Bonaparte's Amer. Ornithol. i. 79; Audubon, i. 1; Nuttall, i. 639; Peabody, p. 352.

[3] See Wood, ch. 8; Wilson, v. 102; Audubon, i. 319; Nuttall, i. 629; Peabody's Report, p. 351.

[4] See Chronicles of Plymouth, note [6] on page 139, and note [1] on page 140.

CHAP.
XII.

1629.

July
to
Sept.

Indeed I think New-England may boast of this element more than of all the rest. For though it be here somewhat cold in the winter, yet here we have plenty of fire to warm us, and that a great deal cheaper than they sell billets and fagots in London; nay, all Europe is not able to afford to make so great fires as New-England. A poor servant here, that is to possess but fifty acres of land, may afford to give more wood for timber and fire as good as the world yields, than many noblemen in England can afford to do. Here is good living for those that love good fires. And although New-England have no tallow to make candles of, yet by the abundance of the fish thereof it can afford oil for lamps. Yea, our pine trees, that are the most plentiful of all wood, doth allow us plenty of candles, which are very useful in a house; and they are such candles as the Indians commonly use, having no other; and they are nothing else but the wood of the pine tree cloven in two little slices something thin, which are so full of the moisture of turpentine and pitch that they burn as clear as a torch.[1] I have sent you some of them, that you may see the experience of them.

----

Thus of New-England's commodities. Now I will tell you of some discommodities, that are here to be found.

First, in the summer season, for these three months, June, July, and August,[2] we are troubled

[1] Pine-knots. "Out of these pines is gotten the candle-wood, that is so much spoken of." Wood, ch. 5.
[2] See note [3] on page 249.

much with little flies called mosquitoes,[1] being the
same they are troubled with in Lincolnshire and the
fens; and they are nothing but gnats, which, except
they be smoked out of their houses, are troublesome
in the night season.

Secondly, in the winter season, for two months'
space, the earth is commonly covered with snow,
which is accompanied with sharp biting frosts, something more sharp than is in Old England, and therefore are forced to make great fires.

Thirdly, this country being very full of woods and
wildernesses, doth also much abound with snakes
and serpents, of strange colors and huge greatness.
Yea, there are some serpents, called rattlesnakes,[2]
that have rattles in their tails, that will not fly from
a man as others will, but will fly upon him and sting
him so mortally that he will die within a quarter of
an hour after, except the party stinged have about
him some of the root of an herb called snake-weed[3]
to bite on, and then he shall receive no harm. But
yet seldom falls it out that any hurt is done by these.
About three years since an Indian was stung to death
by one of them; but we heard of none since that time.

Fourthly and lastly, here wants as yet the good
company of honest Christians, to bring with them
horses, kine and sheep, to make use of this fruitful
land. Great pity it is to see so much good ground
for corn and for grass as any is under the heavens,
to lie altogether unoccupied, when so many honest
men and their families in Old England, through the

---

[1] See Wood, ch. 11; and Harris's
Report on the Insects of Massachu-
etts, page 401.

[2] See Josselyn, p. 38; Morton,
ch. 5; Wood, ch. 11.

[3] See Wood, ch. 11.

populousness thereof, do make very hard shift to live one by the other.

Now thus you know what New-England is, as also with the commodities and discommodities thereof. Now I will show you a little of the inhabitants[1] thereof, and their government.

For their governors they have kings, which they call saggamores, some greater and some lesser, according to the number of their subjects. The greater saggamores about us cannot make above three hundred men, and other less saggamores have not above fifteen subjects, and others near about us but two.

Their subjects, about twelve years since,[2] were swept away by a great and grievous plague that was amongst them, so that there are very few left to inhabit the country.

The Indians are not able to make use of the one fourth part of the land ; neither have they any settled places, as towns, to dwell in ; nor any ground as they challenge for their own possession, but change their habitation from place to place.

For their statures, they are a tall and strong-limbed people. Their colors are tawny. They go naked, save only they are in part covered with beasts' skins on one of their shoulders, and wear something before their privities. Their hair is generally black, and cut before, like our gentlewomen,

---

[1] For the Indians of New-England, see Edward Winslow, in Chronicles of Plymouth, pp. 354–367 ; Wood's New-England's Prospect, part ii. chaps. 1–20 ; Morton's New-English Canaan, book i. chaps. 1–20 ; and Daniel Gookin and Roger Williams in Mass. Hist. Coll. i. 141–226, and iii. 203–238.

[2] In 1617. See Chronicles of Plymouth, note [3] on page 183.

and one lock longer than the rest, much like to our CHAP.
XII.
gentlemen, which fashion I think came from hence
into England.                                          1629.

For their weapons, they have bows and arrows,         July
to
some of them headed with bone, and some with brass.  Sept.
I have sent you some of them for an example.

The men, for the most part, live idly; they do
nothing but hunt and fish. Their wives set their
corn, and do all their other work. They have little
household stuff, as a kettle, and some other vessels
like trays, spoons, dishes and baskets.

Their houses[1] are very little and homely, being
made with small poles pricked into the ground, and
so bended and fastened at the tops, and on the sides
they are matted with boughs and covered on the roof
with sedge and old mats; and for their beds that
they take their rest on, they have a mat.

They do generally profess to like well of our coming and planting here; partly because there is abundance of ground that they cannot possess nor make
use of, and partly because our being here will be
a means both of relief to them when they want,
and also a defence from their enemies,[2] wherewith
(I say) before this Plantation began, they were often
endangered.

For their religion, they do worship two Gods, a
good God and an evil God. The good God they
call Tantum, and their evil God, whom they fear
will do them hurt, they call Squantum.

For their dealing with us, we neither fear them

---

[1] See Chronicles of Plymouth, note [1] on page 144.

[2] These were the Tarrateens, or Eastern Indians, who lived on the borders of the Penobscot. See Chronicles of Plymouth, note [5] on page 225, and the Planters' Plea, page 27.

nor trust them ; for forty of our musketeers will drive five hundred of them out of the field. We use

them kindly.[1] They will come into our houses sometimes by half a dozen or half a score at a time when we are at victuals, but will ask or take nothing but what we give them.

We purpose to learn their language[2] as soon as we can, which will be a means to do them good.

---

*Of the present condition of the Plantation, and what it is.*

When we came first to Nehum-kek, we found about half a score houses, and a fair house newly built for the Governor.[3] We found also abundance

---

[1] As they were instructed to do. See pages 159 and 176.

[2] The first planters of Massachusetts have been reproached for not attending sooner to one of the professed designs of their Plantation, the conversion of the Indians to Christianity. The reproach is unmerited. They attended to it as soon as it was possible. For a while they had to struggle with disease and famine and the manifold hardships attendant upon a new settlement. They had also to set up a Church and a State in the wilderness. Then came the troubles of the Antinomian controversy, and immediately upon that, broke out the Pequot war. During all this period they had no fit opportunity to engage in this great work, and no suitable instruments to prosecute it. As soon as these were raised up by Providence, they entered upon the work, learned the Indian languages, and preached to the natives. In 1646 the General Court of Massachusetts passed an Act to encourage the carrying of the Gospel to the Indians, and it was recommended to the elders to consider how it might best be done. In the same year, John Eliot, the *Apostle to the In-*dians, as he has been called, preached to them in their own language, and subsequently undertook the Herculean task of translating the whole Bible into the language of the Massachusetts Indians, which was printed at Cambridge in 1663, and a second edition in 1685. A series of seven tracts, giving an account of the attempts to convert the natives of New-England to Christianity, from 1647 to 1655, may be seen in the Mass. Hist. Coll. xxiv. See also Daniel Gookin's Account in the same Coll. i. 169–224; Hutchinson's Mass. i. 161; and Francis's Life of Eliot in Sparks's American Biography, vol. 5.

[3] See page 240. According to the deposition of Richard Brackenbury, (who came over with Endicott in 1628,) taken in 1681, when he was eighty years old, the house here mentioned was built of the materials of another house erected at Cape Ann by Conant and his associates. It is said that some of its timbers are contained in a house now standing in Salem, at the corner of Court and Church streets. See note [2] on page 30, and Felt's Annals of Salem, i. 122.

of corn planted by them, very good and well liking. And we brought with us about two hundred passengers and planters more, which, by common consent of the old planters, were all combined together into one body politic, under the same Governor.

There are in all of us, both old and new planters, about three hundred, whereof two hundred of them are settled at Nehum-kek, now called Salem, and the rest have planted themselves at Masathulets Bay,[1] beginning to build a town[2] there, which we do call Cherton or Charles town.

We that are settled at Salem make what haste we can to build houses, so that within a short time we shall have a fair town.

We have great ordnance,[3] wherewith we doubt not but we shall fortify ourselves in a short time to keep out a potent adversary. But that which is our greatest comfort and means of defence above all others, is that we have here the true religion and holy ordinances of Almighty God taught amongst us.[4] Thanks be to God, we have here plenty of preaching, and diligent catechising, with strict and careful exercise, and good and commendable orders to bring our people into a Christian conversation with whom we have to do withal. And thus we doubt not but God will be with us ; and if God be with us, who can be against us ?

Here ends Master Higgeson's Relation of New-England.

---

[1] According to the Instructions of the Company. See page 150.

[2] It was laid out by Graves, the engineer. See note [2] on page 152. Winthrop, i. 29, 30, 39, 46, 127, calls it Charlton.

[3] See pages 45, 50, 157.

[4] The church of Salem was formed August 6th, and the pastor, and teacher, and ruling elder, were ordained the same day. See Morton's Memorial, p. 146, and Prince's Annals, p. 263.

CHAP.
XII.

1629.
Sept.

*Some brief Collections out of a Letter[1] that Mr. Higginson sent to his friends at Leicester.*

There are certainly expected here the next spring the coming of sixty families out of Dorsetshire,[2] who have by letters signified so much to the Governor, to desire him to appoint them places of habitations, they bringing their ministers with them. Also many families are expected out of Lincolnshire,[3] and a minister with them, and a great company of godly Christians out of London.

Such of you as come from Leicester,[4] I would counsel you to come quickly, and that for two reasons. First, if you linger too long, the passages of Jordan, through the malice of Sathan, may be stopped, that you cannot come if you would.[5] Secondly, those that come first speed best here, and have the

---

[1] "A letter then from New-England, and for a considerable time after, was venerated as a sacred script, or as the writing of some holy prophet; 'twas carried many miles, where divers came to hear it." Scottow's Narrative, p. 17.

[2] These were the west-country people, Warham and Maverick, Ludlow and Rossiter, of whom we shall hear more presently from Roger Clap, who came with them.

[3] These were the Boston people, with whom Cotton was expected to come. See note [3] on page 48.

[4] His former place of residence in England. See page 65.

[5] These obstructions to emigration were soon interposed. In 1633, Cotton, Hooker and Stone with great difficulty eluded the vigilance of the pursuivants, and escaped from the country. In 1635, Richard Mather was obliged to keep close till the vessel was fairly at sea; and Tho-

mas Shepard embarked under the assumed name of his elder brother John, a husbandman. In April, 1637, a Proclamation was issued "to restrain the disorderly transporting of his Majesty's subjects to the Colonies without leave." It commanded that "no license should be given them, without a certificate that they had taken the oaths of Supremacy and Allegiance, and had conformed to the discipline of the Church of England." And in May, 1638, a fresh Proclamation was published, " commanding owners and masters of vessels, that they do not fit out any with passengers and provisions to New-England, without license from the Commissioners of Plantations." See Chalmers's Annals, i. 161; Rushworth's Collections, ii. 409; Rymer's Fœdera, xx. 143, 223; Savage's Winthrop, i. 109; and Mass. Hist. Coll. xxviii. 268.

privilege of choosing choice places of habitations. CHAP.
XII.
Little children of five years old may, by setting corn
one month, be able to get their own maintenance 1629.
abundantly.  O what a good work might you that Sept.
are rich do for your poor brethren, to help them
with your purses only to convey them hither with
their children and families, where they may live as
well, both for soul and body, as any where in the
world.  Besides, they will recompense the cost by
helping to build houses and plant your ground for a
time ; which shall be difficult work at the first, except you have the help of many hands.  Mr. Johnson,[1] out of Lincolnshire, and many others, have
helped our godly Christians hither, to be employed in their work for a while, and then to live of
themselves.

We have here about forty goats that give milk,
and as many milch kine.  We have six or seven
mares and a horse, and do every day expect the
coming of half a score mares more, and thirty kine,[2]
by two ships[3] that are to follow us.  They that come
let them bring mares, kine and sheep, as many as
they can.  Ireland is the best place to provide sheep,
and lies in the way.  Bring none that are in lamb,
nor mares in foal, for they are in more danger to
perish at sea.  Of all trades, carpenters are most
needful ; therefore bring as many as you can.

It were a wise course for those that are of abilities
to join together and buy a ship for the voyage, and
other merchandise ; for the Governor would that

---

[1] Isaac Johnson, of whom more
hereafter.

[2] See note [2] on page 216.

[3] The Four Sisters and the Mayflower.  See page 216.

CHAP.
XII.

1629.
Sept.

any man may employ his stock in what merchandises he please, excepting only beaver skins, which the company of merchants reserve to themselves, and the managing of the public stock.[1]  If any be of the mind to buy a ship, my cousin Nowell's[2] counsel would be good. Also one Mr. [      ],[3] a very godly man and the master of the ship we went in, and likewise one Mr. Graves,[4] the master's mate, dwelling in Wapping, may herein stand you in stead. The payment of the transportation of things is wondrous dear, as £5 a man, and £10 a horse, and commonly £3 for every ton of goods; so that a little more than will pay for the passage will purchase the possession of a ship for all together.

No man hath or can have a house built for him here unless he comes himself, or else sends servants before to do it for him. It was an error that I now perceive both myself and others did conceive, by

---

[1] See pages 114 and 148.

[2] Increase Nowell, who was one of the patentees mentioned in the Charter, and whose name occurs so often in the Company's Records, was one of the Assistants from the beginning till his death, and a very active and efficient member of the Company. He came over with Gov. Winthrop, and settled at Charlestown, of which place he was the first town-clerk, and one of the selectmen for nineteen years. He was also chosen a ruling elder of Wilson's Church, but soon resigned that place on the ground of its being incompatible with the office of a civil magistrate. For six years, from 1644 to 1649, he was Secretary of the Colony, which he faithfully served. He died poor, Nov. 1, 1655, leaving a widow, Parnel, and five children, Samuel, Mehetable, Increase, Mary, and Alexander, of

whom the first and the last graduated at Harvard College in 1653 and 1664. See Savage's Winthrop, i. 31; Budington's Hist. of the First Church in Charlestown, pp. 31, 190; Prince's Annals, p. 334.

[3] This name, which the copyist could not decipher, was Beecher, Thomas. See note [4] on page 219.

[4] This Graves was, the next year, mate of the Arbella, the flag-ship of Winthrop's fleet, was afterwards commander of a vessel, and is mentioned by Winthrop, under date of June 3, 1635, as one "who had come every year for these seven years." He is probably the person who was made a rear-admiral by Cromwell for capturing a Dutch privateer, and is not to be confounded with Graves, the engineer, mentioned on pp. 56 and 152. See Savage's Winthrop, i. 8, 161.

not rightly understanding the merchants' meaning.
For we thought that all that put in their money into
the common stock should have a house built for them,
besides such a portion of land ; but it was not so.
They shall indeed have so much land allotted to
them when they come to take possession of it and
make use of it ; but if they will have houses, they
must build them. Indeed, we that are ministers, and
all the rest that were entertained and sent over and
maintained by the rest of the Company, as their servants, for such a time in such employments, all such
are to have houses built them of the Company's
charge,[1] and no others, nor otherwise. They that
put money into the stock, as they do a good work to
help forward so worthy a Plantation, so all the gain
they are like to have is according to the increase
of the stock at three[2] years' end by the trade of beaver, besides the lands, which they shall enjoy when
they will.

All that come must have victuals with them for a
twelvemonth. I mean they must have meal, oatmeal,
and such like sustenance of food, till they can get
increase of corn by their own labor. For otherwise,
so many may come without provision at the first, as
that our small beginnings may not be sufficient to
maintain them.

Before you come, be careful to be strongly instructed what things are fittest to bring with you for
your more comfortable passage at sea, as also for
your husbandry occasions when you come to the
land. For when you are once parted with England,

[1] See the Agreement with Bright and Higginson, on pp. 208 and 210.    [2] Probably an error for seven. See pp. 111, 114, 116 and 117.

CHAP.
XII.
——
1629.
Sept.

you shall meet neither with taverns, nor alehouse, nor butchers', nor grocers', nor apothecaries' shops to help what things you need, in the midst of the great ocean, nor when you are come to land ; here are yet neither markets nor fairs to buy what you want. Therefore be sure to furnish yourselves with things fitting to be had, before you come ; as meal for bread, malt for drink, woollen and linen cloth, and leather for shoes, and all manner of carpenters' tools, and a good deal of iron and steel to make nails, and locks for houses, and furniture for ploughs and carts, and glass for windows,[1] and many other things, which were better for you to think of them there than to want them here.

Whilst I was writing this letter,[2] my wife brought me word that the fishers had caught sixteen hundred bass at one draught ; which, if they were in England, were worth many a pound.

---

*A Letter[3] sent from New-England by Master Graves,[4] Engineer, now there resident.*

Thus much I can affirm in general, that I never came in a more goodly country in all my life, all

[1] See Chronicles of Plymouth, note [1] on page 237.

[2] The preceding letter was not a part of Higginson's New-England's Plantation. Yet it was written by him about the same time, and comes in more appropriately here than at the end of the Journal of his voyage, to which it was appended. I have taken the liberty to insert it in this place. Gov. Winthrop undoubtedly refers to it, when, in a letter to his son John, dated Oct. 9, 1629, he writes, "I have sent down all the late news from New-England. I would have some of you read it to your mother, and let Forth copy out the observations and all that follows from the ☞, and the Letter in the end, and show it Mr. Mott and others that intend this voyage." See Winthrop's Hist. i. 361.

[3] This Letter is not contained in the first edition, printed the same year. It may be a part of the letter mentioned in note [2] on page 152.

[4] See pages 53, 56, and note [2] on page 152.

things considered.  If it hath  not at any time been CHAP.<br>XII.
manured and husbanded,  yet it is very beautiful  in
open  lands,  mixed  with  goodly  woods,  and  again 1629.
open plains, in some places five hundred acres, some Sept.
places more, some less, not much troublesome for to
clear for the plough to go in ; no place  barren  but
on the tops of the hills.   The grass and weeds grow
up to a man's face in  the  lowlands,  and  by fresh
rivers abundance of grass and large meadows, without any tree or shrub to hinder the scythe.   I never
saw, except in Hungaria,[1] unto which I always parallel this country, in all or most respects ; for every
thing that is here either sown or planted prospereth
far better than in Old England.   The increase of
corn is here far beyond expectation, as I have seen
here by experience in  barley,  the which, because it
is so  much above your  conception, I will not mention.   And cattle do prosper very well, and those
that are bred here far greater than those with you in
England.  Vines do grow here plentifully, laden with
the biggest grapes that ever I saw ; some I have
seen four inches about.   So that I am bold to say of
this country, as it is commonly said in Germany of
Hungaria, that for cattle, corn, and wine, it excelleth.
We have many more hopeful commodities here in
this country, the which time will teach to make good
use of.   In the mean time, we  abound with  such
things which, next under God, do make us subsist ;
as fish, fowl, deer, and  sundry  sorts of fruits, as
musk-melons, water-melons, Indian pompions, Indian
pease, beans, and many other odd fruits that I cannot
name ; all which are made good and pleasant through

---

[1] " He hath been a traveller in divers foreign parts."  See p. 153.

this main blessing of God, the healthfulness of the country, which far exceedeth all parts that ever I have been in. It is observed that few or none do here fall sick, unless of the scurvy, that they bring from aboard the ship with them; whereof I have cured some of my company only by labor. Thus making an end of an imperfect description, and committing you to God, &c.

———

1630. A Catalogue of such needful things as every planter doth or ought to provide to go to New-England; as namely for one man; which, being doubled, may serve for as many as you please, viz.

*Victuals for a whole year for a man, and so after the rate for more.*

8 bushels of meal,
2 bushels of pease,
2 bushels of oatmeal,
1 gallon of aqua-vitæ,
1 gallon of oil,
2 gallons of vinegar,
1 firkin of butter.

*Apparel.*
1 Monmouth cap,[1]
3 falling bands,[2]
3 shirts,

1 waistcoat,
1 suit of canvass,
1 suit of frieze,[3]
1 suit of cloth,
3 pair of stockings,
4 pair of shoes,
2 pair of sheets,
7 ells of canvass, to make a bed and bolster,
1 pair of blankets,
1 coarse rug.

———

[1] See note 2 on page 41.
[2] See note 5 on page 40.

[3] A sort of coarse woollen cloth.

*Arms.*

1 armour, complete,
1 long piece,
1 sword,
1 belt,
1 bandoleer,[1]
20 pound of powder,
60 pound of lead,
1 pistol and goose shot.

*Tools.*

1 broad hoe,
1 narrow hoe,
1 broad axe,
1 felling axe,
1 steel handsaw,
1 whipsaw,
1 hammer,
1 shovel,
1 spade,
2 augers,
4 chisels,
2 piercers, stocked,
1 gimlet,
1 hatchet,

2 frowers,[2]
1 handbill,[3]
1 grindstone,
1 pickaxe,
  Nails, of all sorts.

*Household Implements.*

1 iron pot,
1 kettle,
1 frying-pan,
1 gridiron,
2 skillets,
1 spit,
  Wooden platters,
  Dishes,
  Spoons,
  Trenchers.

*Spices.*

Sugar,
Pepper,
Cloves,
Mace,
Cinnamon,
Nutmegs, Fruit.

Also, there are divers other things necessary to be taken over to this Plantation, as books, nets, hooks and lines, cheese, bacon, kine, goats, &c.[4]

---

[1] See note [5] on page 44.
[2] An edged tool, used in cleaving laths.
[3] An edged tool, with a hooked point, used to lop trees, hedges, &c.
[4] This list of articles is not contained in the first edition.

# GENERAL CONSIDERATIONS

# FOR PLANTING NEW-ENGLAND.

# CHAPTER XIII.

GENERAL CONSIDERATIONS FOR THE PLANTATION IN
NEW-ENGLAND; WITH AN ANSWER TO SEVERAL
OBJECTIONS.

FIRST, it will be a service to the Church of great
consequence, to carry the Gospel into those parts of
the world, and to raise a bulwark against the kingdom of Antichrist, which the Jesuits labor to rear up
in all places of the world.

Secondly, all other churches of Europe are brought
to desolation, and it may be justly feared that the like
judgment is coming upon us ; and who knows but
that God hath provided this place to be a refuge
for many whom he means to save out of the general
destruction ?

Thirdly, the land grows weary of her inhabitants,
so that man, which is the most precious of all creatures, is here more vile and base than the earth they
tread upon ; so as children, neighbours and friends,
especially of the poor, are counted the greatest
burdens, which, if things were right, would be the
chiefest earthly blessings.

Fourthly, we are grown to that excess and intemperance in all excess of riot, as no mean estate almost will suffice [a man][1] to keep sail with his equals ; and he that fails in it, must live in scorn and contempt. Hence it comes to pass, that all arts and trades are carried in that deceitful manner and unrighteous course, as it is almost impossible for a good, upright man to maintain his charge, and live comfortably in any of them.

Fifthly, the schools of learning and religion are so corrupted as, (besides the unsupportable charge of their education,) most children, even the best, wittiest, and of fairest hopes, are perverted, corrupted, and utterly overthrown by the multitude of evil examples and licentious governors of those seminaries.

Sixthly, the whole earth is the Lord's garden, and he hath given it to the sons of Adam to be tilled and improved by them. Why then should we stand starving here for places of habitation, (many men spending as much labor and cost to recover or keep sometimes an acre or two of lands as would procure him many hundreds of acres, as good or better, in another place,) and in the mean time suffer whole countries, as profitable for the use of man, to lie waste without any improvement ?

Seventhly, what can be a better work, and more noble, and worthy a Christian, than to help to raise and support a particular church while it is in its infancy, and to join our forces with such a company of faithful people as by a timely assistance may grow stronger and prosper, and for want of it may be put to great hazard, if not wholly ruined ?

---

[1] So in Mather, Magnalia, i. 65, who says he transcribes from a MS.

Eighthly, if any such as are known to be godly, and live in wealth and prosperity here, shall forsake all this to join themselves with this church, and run in hazard with them of a hard and mean condition, it will be an example of great use both for the removing of scandal and sinister and worldly respects, to give more life to the faith of God's people in their prayers for the Plantation, and also to encourage others to join the more willingly in it.

### OBJECTIONS.

OBJ. 1. It will be a great wrong to our own Church and country to take away the best people ; and we shall lay it more open to the judgments feared.

ANS. First, the number will be nothing in respect of those that are left. Secondly, many that live to no use here, more than for their own private families, may be employed to a more common good in another place. Thirdly, such as are of good use here may yet be so employed as the Church shall receive no loss ; and since Christ's coming, the Church is to be conceived as universal, without distinction of countries; so as he that doth good in any one place, serves the Church in all places, in regard of the unity. Fourthly, it is the revealed will of God that the Gospel should be preached to all nations ; and though we know not whether the Indians will receive it or not, yet it is a good work to observe God's will in offering it to them ; for God shall have glory by it, though they refuse it.

OBJ. 2. We have feared a judgment a long time ; but yet we are safe. Therefore it were better to stay till it come ; and either we may fly then, or if

CHAP. we be overtaken in it, we may well be content to
XIII.
~~~ suffer with such a Church as ours is.

1629. Ans. It is likely that this consideration made the Churches beyond the seas, as the Palatinate[1] and Rochelle,[2] &c. to sit still at home, and not look out for shelter while they might have found it. But the woful spectacle of their ruin may teach us more wisdom, to avoid the plague while it is foreseen, and not to tarry as they did, till it overtook them. If they were now at their former liberty, we may be sure they would take other courses for their safety. And though most of them had miscarried in their escape, yet it had not been half so miserable to themselves, or scandalous to religion, as this des-

[1] Frederic V., the Elector Palatine of the Rhine, married, in 1612, the princess Elizabeth, daughter of James I. of England, and in 1619 accepted the crown offered to him by the Protestants of Bohemia. This election gave great offence to Ferdinand, the Emperor of Germany, who claimed the kingdom as his own. He consequently invaded and reduced both the Palatinate and Bohemia, defeated the Palgrave near Prague in 1621, and put him under the ban of the Empire. A dreadful persecution of the Protestants now commenced through the Austrian territories, and the Catholic religion was forcibly introduced into the Palatinate. An edict was issued, that the Protestant ministers should be forever exiled, and their churches closed. See Mod. Univ. Hist. xxvii. 1–24; Coxe's Hist. of the House of Austria, i. 769–797, 815; Harte's Hist. of Gustavus Adolphus, i. 238–246.

[2] Rochelle, the principal seat and strong-hold of the Huguenots, was besieged by Cardinal Richelieu, and, after a long and desperate resistance, was reduced by famine in Oct. 1628. This disastrous event prostrated the Protestants in France, and broke their spirits and their strength. Their affairs became every day more afflictive and perilous. They saw and dreaded the approaching storm, but knew not how to evade it. Some of them fled to England, but found no peace there ; for Laud and other high churchmen drove them back. See Mosheim, Eccles. Hist. v. 351 ; and Dr. Holmes's Memoir of the French Protestants, in Mass. Hist. Coll. xxii. 18.

Prince, the Annalist, referring to the two events mentioned in the text, says, "In France and Navarre the King begins to persecute the Protestants, and turn them out of their churches. In Bohemia and Germany the Imperial and Spanish forces are ruining the Reformed interest ; and the King of England, extremely solicitous of matching his only son, Prince Charles, to the Spanish Infanta, refuses to support his own daughter, the excellent Queen of Bohemia, the darling of the British Puritans." Annals, p. 179.

perate backsliding and abjuring the truth, which
many of the ancient professors among them, and the
whole posterity that remain, are plunged into.

OBJ. 3. We have here a fruitful land, with peace,
and plenty of all things.

ANS. We are like to have as good conditions there
in time ; but yet we must leave all this abundance,
if it be not taken from us. When we are in our
graves, it will be all one whether we have lived in
plenty or in penury, whether we have died in a bed
of down or locks of straw. Only this is the advantage of the mean condition, that it is a more freedom
to die. And the less comfort any have in the things
of this world, the more liberty they have to lay up
treasure in heaven.

OBJ. 4. We may perish by the way, or when we
come there, having[1] hunger or the sword, &c. ; and
how uncomfortable will it be to see our wives and
children and friends come to such misery by our
occasion.

ANS. Such objections savor too much of the flesh.
Who can secure himself or his from the like calami-
ties here ? If this course be warrantable, we may
trust God's providence for these things. Either he
will keep those evils from us, or will dispose them
for our good, and enable us to bear them.

OBJ. 5. But what warrant have we to take that
land, which is and hath been of long time possessed
of others the sons of Adam ?

ANS. That which is common to all is proper to
none. This savage people ruleth over many lands

---

[1] Perhaps an error for *braving*.

CHAP.
XIII.
———
1629.

without title or property; for they enclose no ground, neither have they cattle to maintain it, but remove their dwellings as they have occasion, or as they can prevail against their neighbours. And why may not Christians have liberty to go and dwell amongst them in their waste lands and woods, (leaving them such places as they have manured for their corn,) as lawfully as Abraham did amongst the Sodomites?

Gen.
xiii.-xv.

For God hath given to the sons of men a twofold right to the earth; there is a natural right, and a civil right. The first right was natural, when men held the earth in common, every man sowing and feeding where he pleased. Then, as men and cattle increased, they appropriated some parcels of ground by enclosing and peculiar manurance; and this in time got them a civil right. Such was the right which Ephron the Hittite had in the field of Machpelah, wherein Abraham could not bury a dead corpse without leave, though for the outparts of the country, which lay common, he dwelt upon them and took the fruit of them at his pleasure. This appears also in Jacob and his sons, who fed their flocks as boldly in the Canaanites' land, for he is said to be lord of the country; and at Dothan and all other places men accounted nothing their own but that which they had appropriated by their own industry, as appears plainly by Abimelech's servants, who in their own country did often contend with Isaac's servants about wells which they had digged, but never about the lands which they occupied. So likewise between Jacob and Laban; he would not take a kid of Laban's without special contract, but he makes no bargain with him for the land where they fed. And it is

Gen.
xxiii.
9.

Gen.
xxxvii.
1, 17.

Gen.
xxvi.
20.

Gen.
xxx.

probable that if the country had not been as free for
Jacob as for Laban, that covetous wretch would have
made his advantage of him, and have upbraided Jacob
with it, as he did with the rest. Secondly, there
is more than enough for them and us. Thirdly, God
hath consumed the natives with a miraculous plague,[1]
whereby the greater part of the country is left void
of inhabitants. Fourthly, we shall come in with
good leave of the natives.

OBJ. 6. We should send our young ones, and
such as may best be spared, and not of the best of
our ministers and magistrates.

ANS. It is a great work, and requires more skilful
artisans to lay the foundation of a new building, than
to uphold and repair one that is already built. If
great things be attempted by weak instruments, the
effects will be answerable.

OBJ. 7. We see that those plantations that have
been formerly made, succeeded ill.

ANS. First, the fruit of any public design is not to
be discerned by the immediate success; it may appear in time, that they were all to good use. Secondly, there were great fundamental errors in
others, which are like to be avoided in this; for,
first, their main end and purpose was carnal, and not
religious; secondly, they aimed chiefly at profit, and
not at the propagation of religion; thirdly, they used
too unfit instruments, a multitude of rude, ungovern-
ed persons, the very scums of the land; fourthly,
they did not stablish a right form of government.[2]

---

[1] See page 256, and Chronicles of
Plymouth, note [3] on p. 183.
[2] This paper was drawn up before
August 21, 1629. For in a letter
of that date, written by John Winthrop, jr. to his father, he says,
"The CONCLUSIONS which you sent
down, I showed my uncle and aunt,

CHAP.
XIII.

1629.

who like them well. I think they are unanswerable ; and it cannot but be a prosperous action, which is so well allowed by the judgments of God's prophets, undertaken by so religious and wise worthies of Israel, and indented to God's glory in so special a service." Mr. Savage remarks on this, "The CONCLUSIONS spoken of by the son were, no doubt, a paper of Considerations for the Plantation, with an Answer to several Objections, probably drawn by our author (Gov. Winthrop.) I have had in my possession the larger part of the original;" which he since informs me was in the handwriting of Winthrop. Felt, in his Annals of Salem, i. 69, ascribes it to Higginson, but upon no other authority than the general title which Hutchinson prefixes to certain papers appended to the Journal of the Voyage. The MS. used by Hutchinson is now in my possession, and from that I print. It varies somewhat from Mather's copy in the Magnalia, i. 65. See Savage's Winthrop, i. 360.

# THE AGREEMENT AT CAMBRIDGE.

# CHAPTER XIV.

## THE TRUE COPY OF THE AGREEMENT AT CAMBRIDGE, AUGUST 26, 1629.

Upon due consideration of the state of the Plantation now in hand for New-England, wherein we,
whose names are hereunto subscribed, have engaged
ourselves, and having weighed the greatness of the
work in regard of the consequence, God's glory and
the Church's good ; as also in regard of the difficulties and discouragements which in all probabilities
must be forecast upon the prosecution of this business ; considering withal that this whole adventure
grows upon the joint confidence we have in each
other's fidelity and resolution herein, so as no man of
us would have adventured it without assurance of the
rest ; now, for the better encouragement of ourselves
and others that shall join with us in this action, and
to the end that every man may without scruple dispose of his estate and affairs as may best fit his preparation for this voyage ; it is fully and faithfully
AGREED amongst us, and every of us doth hereby
freely and sincerely promise and bind himself, in the

CHAP.
XIV.

1629.
Aug.
26.

word of a Christian, and in the presence of God, who is the searcher of all hearts, that we will so really endeavour the prosecution of this work, as by God's assistance, we will be ready in our persons, and with such of our several families as are to go with us, and such provision as we are able conveniently to furnish ourselves withal, to embark for the said Plantation by the first of March next, at such port or ports of this land as shall be agreed upon by the Company, to the end to pass the seas, (under God's protection,) to inhabit and continue in New-England : Provided always, that before the last of September next, the whole government, together with the patent for the said Plantation, be first, by an order of Court, legally transferred and established to remain with us and others which shall inhabit upon the said Plantation :[1] and provided also, that if any shall be hindered by such just and inevitable let or other cause, to be allowed by three parts of four of these whose names are hereunto subscribed, then such persons, for such times and during such lets, to be discharged of this bond. And we do further promise, every one for himself, that shall fail to be ready through his own default by the day appointed, to pay for every day's default the sum of £3, to the use of the rest of the company who shall be ready by the same day and time.

This was done by order of Court, the 29th of August, 1629.[2]

| | |
|---|---|
| RICHARD SALTONSTALL, | THOMAS SHARPE, |
| THOMAS DUDLEY, | INCREASE NOWELL, |
| WILLIAM VASSALL, | JOHN WINTHROP, |
| NICHOLAS WEST,[3] | WILLIAM PINCHON,[4] |
| ISAAC JOHNSON, | KELLAM BROWNE,[5] |
| JOHN HUMFREY, | WILLIAM COLBRON. |

<sup>1</sup> See pages 85–88, and 91.

<sup>2</sup> This seems to have been a note interpolated after the paper was signed. See page 88.

<sup>3</sup> West and Browne never came over to the Colony, and nothing is known concerning them.

<sup>4</sup> William Pynchon, whose name occurs so frequently in the Company's Records, was a gentleman of learning as well as religion. He was one of the Assistants named in the Charter, and came over with Gov. Winthrop. He laid the foundation of the town of Roxbury, and was the first member of the church in that place. Early in 1636 he removed to Connecticut river, with eight others, and was the father of the town of Springfield, which was so named after the town in England where he resided, near Chelmsford, in Essex. In 1650, there appeared in England a book entitled, " The Meritorious Price of our Redemption, Justification, &c., clearing it from some Errors, by William Pinchin, in New-England, gent." A copy of this book was brought over by a ship a few days before the meeting of the General Court, which was held Oct. 15, and which proceeded to pass the following order : " This Court having had a sight of a book lately printed, under the name of William Pinchon, in New-England, gent., and judging it meet, do therefore order ; first, that a Protest be drawn, fully and clearly to satisfy all men that this Court do utterly dislike it and detest it as erroneous and dangerous ; secondly, that it be sufficiently answered by one of the reverend elders ; thirdly, that the said William Pinchon, gent., be summoned to appear before the next General Court to answer for the same ; fourthly, that the said book, now brought over, be burnt by the executioner, and that in the market-place in Boston on the morrow, immediately after the Lecture." The Rev. John Norton, of Ipswich, was entreated to answer the book, which he did. The Protest of the Court

covers a page of their Records, and in it they condemn the book as " false, erroneous, and heretical," and declare their purpose " to proceed with the author according to his demerits, unless he retract the same, and give full satisfaction both here and by some second writing to be printed and dispersed in England." The grand error of the book consisted in regarding the sufferings of Christ as merely " trials of his obedience ;" and of course it was the first heretical work on the Atonement that was written in this country. At the next General Court, held May 7, 1651, Pynchon appeared, and explained or retracted the obnoxious opinions, after having conferred with the Rev. Messrs. Cotton, Norris, and Norton. He appeared before them again Oct. 14, 1651, but the judgment of the Court on his errors and heresies was suspended till the next session in May, 1652. Before that time, Mr. Pynchon, seeing the storm gathering, and doubtful what might be the result, prudently left the Colony and returned to England, accompanied by his son-in-law, Capt. Henry Smith, and the Rev. George Moxon, a graduate of Sydney College, Cambridge, in 1623, who had been the minister of Springfield since 1637. Is it not probable, that Moxon himself was infected with the same heresy, and perhaps had a hand in writing the book? From a letter of the Governor and Council, preserved in Mass. Hist. Coll. xxi. 35, it appears that Sir Henry Vane had written them a letter in behalf of Pynchon, April 15, 1652, previous to which he had probably arrived in England. They speak of him as " one whom we did all love and respect," and intimate that he had privately held this doctrine " above thirty years." He died at Wraysbury, on the Thames, in Buckinghamshire, in October, 1662, aged 72 or 74. His son, John, was a prominent man in the Colony, and a long line of descendants may be seen in Farmer's

CHAP.
XIV.

1629.
Aug.
26.

CHAP.
XIV.

1629.

Genealogical Register. No copy of Pynchon's book is known to exist in this country, but Mr. Savage found it in the British Museum, and two other tracts written by him. A series of papers, belonging to him and his family, is printed in the Mass. Hist. Coll. xviii. 228–249. See Col. Rec. ii. 280–3, 295, 328 ; Breck's Century Sermon at Springfield, pp. 15–17 ; Mass. Hist. Coll. xvi. 308, xxviii. 248, 288, 294.

# THE COMPANY'S LETTERS

TO

# HIGGINSON AND ENDICOTT.

# CHAPTER XV.

REVEREND FRIENDS,

THERE are lately arrived here,[2] being sent from the Governor, Mr. Endecott, as men factious and evil conditioned, John and Samuel Browne,[3] being

CHAP.
XV.

1629.
Oct.
16.

[1] See note on page 99.

[2] The Brownes arrived in London before Sept. 19, in the Talbot or Lion's Whelp. They probably left Salem soon after the installation of the ministers, which took place August 6. Of course they remained in New-England only five or six weeks, having landed at Salem June 30. See pages 89, 90, 235.

[3] The case of the Brownes has already been frequently mentioned and referred to. See pages 89, 91, 94, 123, 168. We are fortunate in having a statement of the affair from one who was a contemporary and probably an eye-witness. Gov. Bradford, who was at Salem on the day that Higginson and Skelton were ordained, Aug. 6, tells us, (for, as Prince says, p. xx. "Morton's History, down to 1646, is chiefly Gov. Bradford's manuscript abbreviated,") that "some of the passengers that came over at the same time, observing that the ministers did not at all use the Book of Common Prayer,

and that they did administer baptism and the Lord's supper without the ceremonies, and that they professed also to use discipline in the congregation against scandalous persons, by a personal application of the word of God, as the case might require, and that some that were scandalous were denied admission into the church, they began to raise some trouble. Of these, Mr. Samuel Browne and his brother were the chief, the one being a lawyer, the other a merchant, both of them amongst the number of the first patentees, men of estates, and men of parts and port in the place. These two brothers gathered a company together, in a place distinct from the public assembly, and there, sundry times, the Book of Common Prayer was read unto such as resorted thither. The Governor, Mr. Endicott, taking notice of the disturbance that began to grow amongst the people by this means, he convented the two brothers before him. They accused

CHAP.
XV.

1629.
Oct.
16.

brethren; who, since their arrival, have raised rumors (as we hear,) of divers scandalous and intemperate speeches passed from one or both of you in your public sermons or prayers in New-England, as also of some innovations attempted by you. We have reason to hope that their reports are but slanders; partly, for that your godly and quiet condi-

the ministers as departing from the orders of the Church of England, that they were Separatists, and would be Anabaptists, &c.; but for themselves, they would hold to the orders of the Church of England. The ministers answered for themselves, They were neither Separatists nor Anabaptists; they did not separate from the Church of England, nor from the ordinances of God there, but only from the corruptions and disorders there; and that they came away from the Common Prayer and ceremonies, and had suffered much for their non-conformity in their native land; and therefore being in a place where they might have their liberty, they neither could nor would use them, because they judged the imposition of these things to be sinful corruptions in the worship of God. The Governor and Council, and the generality of the people, did well approve of the ministers' answer; and therefore, finding those two brothers to be of high spirits, and their speeches and practices tending to mutiny and faction, the Governor told them that New-England was no place for such as they, and therefore he sent them both back for England at the return of the ships the same year; and though they breathed out threatenings both against the Governor and ministers there, yet the Lord so disposed of all, that there was no further inconvenience followed upon it." Morton's Memorial, p. 147.

It appears from page 89, that on their return to England, a committee of ten was appointed by the Compa-

ny, four of whom were nominated by the Brownes themselves, to investigate the affair. To what result that committee came, we are not informed; but the fact of the appointment of such a committee shows the disposition of the Company to do ample justice to the complainants, and disproves the charges of contempt and injustice alleged against them by Chalmers, (Annals, p. 146.) We find from page 94, that, at their request, the Brownes were furnished with a copy of Endicott's accusation against them, to enable them to prepare their defence, —and from page 123, that a statement of grievances, which they presented to the Company for loss and damage sustained in New-England, was referred to another committee, with full power to allow what indemnity they should think proper, and so end the matter. Endicott undoubtedly thought he was acting in conformity with his instructions, in sending them home. See pages 159, 160, 196. Grahame, in his History of the United States, i. 218, says, "Notwithstanding the censure with which some writers have commented on the banishment of these two individuals, the justice of the proceeding must commend itself to the sentiments of all impartial men." Bancroft, i. 350, remarks that "faction, deprived of its leaders, died away," and adds, that "the liberal Ebeling, i. 869, defends the measure." A mural tablet has been erected to the memory of the Brownes in the Episcopal church at Salem.

tions are well known to some of us ; as also, for that
these men, your accusers, seem to be embittered
against you and Captain Endecott for injuries which
they conceive they have received from some of you
there. Yet, for that we all know that the best advised may overshoot themselves, we have thought
good to inform you of what we hear, that if you be
innocent you may clear yourselves ; or if otherwise,
you may hereby be entreated to look back upon your
miscarriage with repentance ; or at least to take
notice that we utterly disallow any such passages,
and must and will take order for the redress thereof,
as shall become us. But hoping, as we said, of your
unblamableness herein, we desire only that this may
testify to you and others that we are tender of the
least aspersion which, either directly or obliquely,
may be cast upon the State here ;[1] to whom we owe
so much duty, and from whom we have received so
much favor in this Plantation where you now reside.

So with our love and due respect to your callings,
we rest,

Your loving friends,

| R. SALTONSTALL, | THO. ADAMS, |
|---|---|
| ISA. JOHNSON, | SYM. WHETCOMBE, |
| MATT. CRADOCK, *Governor*, | WILLIAM VASSALL, |
| THO. GOFF, *Deputy*, | WM. PINCHION, |
| GEO. HARWOOD, *Treasurer*, | JOHN REVELL, |
| JOHN WINTHROP, | FRANCIS WEBB.[2] |

*London*, 16 *October*, 1629.

[1] The Company seem to have been very solicitous that nothing should be done in their Plantation which might furnish a pretext for the Government to revoke their Charter. Such prudential considerations, however, weighed but little with Endicott, as we may infer from the daring and reckless spirit with which he afterwards cut the red cross out of the King's colors, not being able to brook what appeared to him a Popish and idolatrous emblem.

[2] See note [3] on page 179.

## THE COMPANY'S LETTER TO THE GOVERNOR.

SIR,

As we have written at this time to Mr. Skelton and Mr. Higgison touching the rumors of John and Samuel Browne, spread by them upon their arrival here, concerning some unadvised and scandalous speeches uttered by them in their public sermons or prayers, so have we thought meet to advertise you of what they have reported against you and them, concerning some rash innovations[1] begun and practised in the civil and ecclesiastical government. We do well consider that the Brownes are likely to make the worst of any thing they have observed in New-England, by reason of your sending them back, against their wills, for their offensive behaviour, expressed in a general letter from the Company there.[2] Yet, for that we likewise do consider that you are in a government newly founded, and want that assistance which the weight of such a business doth require, we may have leave to think that it is possible some undigested counsels have too suddenly been put in execution, which may have ill construction

---

[1] These innovations, I suppose, had reference principally to the formation of the church at Salem, the adoption of a confession of faith and covenant by the people, and their election and ordination of the ministers. Endicott, we know, sympathized fully with the Separatists of New-Plymouth. In a letter of his to Gov. Bradford, dated Naumkeak, May 11, 1629, he writes, "I rejoice much that I am by Mr. Fuller satisfied touching your judgment of the outward form of God's worship. It is, as far as I can yet gather, no other than is warranted by the evidence of truth, and the same which I have professed and maintained ever since the Lord in mercy revealed himself unto me, being far differing from the common report that hath been spread of you touching that particular." See Mass. Hist. Coll. iii. 66.

[2] It is to be regretted that this letter is not now in existence. See pages 89 and 94.

with the State here, and make us obnoxious to any CHAP.
adversary. Let it therefore seem good unto you to XV.
be very sparing in introducing any laws or commands 1629.
which may render yourself or us distasteful to the Oct.
State here, to which (as we ought) we must and will 16.
have an obsequious eye.[1] And as we make it our
main care to have the Plantation so ordered as may
be most for the honor of God and of our gracious
Sovereign, who hath bestowed many large privileges
and royal favors upon this Company, so we desire
that all such as shall by word or deed do any thing
to detract from God's glory or his Majesty's honor,
may be duly corrected, for their amendment and the
terror of others. And to that end, if you know any
thing which hath been spoken or done either by the
ministers, (whom the Brownes do seem tacitly· to
blame for some things uttered in their sermons or
prayers,) or any others, we require you, if any such
thing be, that you form due process against the offenders, and send it to us by the first, that we may, as
our duty binds us, use means to have them duly
punished.

So not doubting but we have said enough, we shall
repose ourselves upon your wisdom, and do rest
Your loving friends.
Dated and signed as the former letter to Mr.
Skelton and Mr. Higgison.

*To the Governor, Capt. Endecott.*[2]

---

[1] In dealing with such unscrupulous persons as Charles I. and Laud,
the Company had to exercise a good
deal of the wisdom of the serpent.
See note [1] on page 289.

[2] Nothing is known of the life
and history of JOHN ENDICOTT previous to his coming to New-England, except what is stated on page
143, that he had sat under Mr. Skelton's ministry, perhaps in Lincolnshire. He was of course superseded in his office of Governor of the
Colony by the arrival of Winthrop

CHAP. with the Charter, in 1630. He was,
XV. however, the same year chosen an
Assistant, which place he occupied
1629. nine years. In 1636, he was chosen
a colonel, and commanded the first
Oct. unsuccessful expedition in the Pe-
16. quot War. In 1641, he was elected
Deputy Governor, which office he
held four years. He was chosen
Governor in 1644, 1649, 1651–53,
and 1655–1665, sixteen years, a
longer period than any Governor of
the Colony was in office under the
old Charter, and exceeded one year
only, under the new, by Shirley
alone. In 1645 he was chosen Major General, which office he held for
four years. In 1644, he removed to
Boston, where he died, March 15,
1665, in his 77th year. His wife,
Anna Gover, a cousin of Gov. Cradock, died soon after his arrival at
Salem. See page 131. His house
stood on the lot now occupied by
the shops in Tremont-street, at the
head of Court-street, in front of Pemberton Square. His portrait hangs
in the Senate Chamber, at the State
House. See Savage's Winthrop,
i. 26, 156, 158, 192 ; Snow's Hist.
of Boston, p. 148; Mass. Hist. Coll.
xviii. 52.

Hutchinson says, i. 17, that " Endicott was among the most zealous
undertakers, and the most rigid in
principles. This disposition distinguished him, more than his other
mental accomplishments, or his outward condition in life. I have seen

a letter from the Secretary of State
in King Charles the Second's time,
in which is this expression, ' The
King would take it well if the people would leave out Mr. Endicott
from the place of Governor.' " Mr.
F. M. Hubbard, in his new edition
of Belknap's Amer. Biog. iii. 166,
remarks, " Gov. Endicott was undoubtedly the finest specimen to be
found among our Governors of the
genuine Puritan character. He was
of a quick temper, which the habit
of military command had not soften-
ed ; of strong religious feelings,
moulded on the sterner features of
Calvinism ; resolute to uphold with
the sword what he had received as
Gospel truth, and fearing no enemy
so much as a gainsaying spirit.
Cordially disliking the English
Church, he banished the Brownes
and the Prayer Book ; and, averse
to all ceremonies and symbols, the
cross in the King's colors was an
abomination he could not away with.
He cut down the Maypole at Merry
Mount, published his detestation of
long hair in a formal proclamation,
and set in the pillory and on the gal-
lows the returning Quakers. Inferior to Winthrop in learning, in com-
prehensiveness to Vane, in tolerance
even to Dudley, he excelled them all
in the eye keen to discern the fit
moment for action, in the quick resolve to profit by it, and in the hand
always ready to strike." See note [1]
on page 13.

# THE HUMBLE REQUEST.

THE HVMBLE REQVEST of His Majestie's loyall Subjects, the Governour and the Company late gone for NEVV-ENGLAND; To the rest of their Brethren, in and of the Church of England. For the obtaining of their Prayers, and the removall of suspitions, and misconstructions of their Intentions. LONDON. Printed for IOHN BELLAMIE. 1630. sm. 4to. pp. 12.

# CHAPTER XVI.

## THE COMPANY'S HUMBLE REQUEST.

REVEREND FATHERS AND BRETHREN,

THE general rumor of this solemn enterprise, wherein ourselves with others, through the providence of the Almighty, are engaged, as it may spare us the labor of imparting our occasion unto you, so it gives us the more encouragement to strengthen ourselves by the procurement of the prayers and blessings of the Lord's faithful servants. For which end we are bold to have recourse unto you, as those whom God hath placed nearest his throne of mercy; which, as it affords you the more opportunity, so it imposeth the greater bond upon you to intercede for his people in all their straits. We beseech you, therefore, by the mercies of the Lord Jesus, to consider us as your brethren, standing in very great need of your help, and earnestly imploring it. And howsoever your charity may have met with some occasion of discouragement through the misreport of our intentions, or through the disaffection or indiscretion of some of us, or rather amongst us,[1] (for we are not of those that dream of perfection in this world,) yet we desire you would be pleased to take notice of the principals and body of our Company, as those who esteem it our honor to call the Church of England, from whence we rise, our dear mother ; and cannot part from our native country, where she specially resideth, without much sadness of heart and many tears in our eyes,[2] ever acknowledging that such hope and part as we have obtained in the common salvation, we have received in her bosom and sucked it from her breasts.[3]  We leave it not therefore as loathing that milk wherewith we were nourished there ; but, blessing God for the parentage and education, as members of the same body, shall always rejoice in her good, and unfeignedly grieve for any sorrow that shall ever betide her, and while we have breath, sincerely desire and endeavour the continuance and abundance of her welfare, with the enlargement of her bounds in the kingdom of Christ Jesus.

Be pleased, therefore, reverend fathers and breth-

---

[1] There may be an allusion here to the case of the Brownes. See note [3] on page 287.

[2] This language, so full of sincere and tender affection, exposes the falsity of Chalmers's statement, where he speaks of "the savage fury with which they deserted their native land." And this too when he himself admits that they had been persecuted in England. See Chalmers's Pol. Annals, pages 152 and 165.

[3] John Cotton, in his Discourse entitled "God's Promise to his Plantation," p. 18, delivered just before the sailing of Winthrop's fleet, said, "Be not unmindful of our Jerusalem at home, whether you leave us or stay at home with us. *O pray for the peace of Jerusalem; they shall prosper that love her.* As God continueth his presence with us, (blessed be his name!) so be ye present in spirit with us, though absent in body. Forget not the womb that bare you, and the breasts that gave you suck. Even ducklings, hatched under a hen, though they take the water, yet will still have recourse to the wing that hatched them ; how much more should chickens of the same feather and yolk? In the amity and unity of brethren, the Lord hath not only promised but commanded a blessing, even life forevermore." See note [1] on page 126.

ren, to help forward this work now in hand; which
if it prosper, you shall be the more glorious, howsoever your judgment is with the Lord, and your re-
ward with your God. It is a usual and laudable exercise of your charity, to commend to the prayers of
your congregations the necessities and straits of your
private neighbours : do the like for a Church spring-
ing out of your own bowels. We conceive much
hope that this remembrance of us, if it be frequent
and fervent, will be a most prosperous gale in our
sails, and provide such a passage and welcome for us
from the God of the whole earth, as both we which
shall find it, and yourselves, with the rest of our
friends, who shall hear of it, shall be much enlarged
to bring in such daily returns of thanksgivings, as
the specialties of his providence and goodness may
justly challenge at all our hands. You are not ignorant that the spirit of God stirred up the apostle Paul
to make continual mention of the Church of Philippi,
which was a colony from Rome ; let the same spirit,
we beseech you, put you in mind, that are the Lord's
remembrancers, to pray for us without ceasing, who
are a weak colony from yourselves, making continual
request for us to God in all your prayers.

What we entreat of you, that are the ministers of
God, that we also crave at the hands of all the rest
of our brethren, that they would at no time forget us
in their private solicitations at the throne of grace.

If any there be who, through want of clear intelligence of our course, or tenderness of affection
towards us, cannot conceive so well of our way as
we could desire, we would entreat such not to de-
spise us, nor to desert us in their prayers and affec-

tions, but to consider rather that they are so much the more bound to express the bowels of their compassion towards us, remembering always that both nature and grace doth ever bind us to relieve and rescue, with our utmost and speediest power, such as are dear unto us, when we conceive them to be running uncomfortable hazards.

What goodness you shall extend to us in this or any other Christian kindness, we, your brethren in Christ Jesus, shall labor to repay in what duty we are or shall be able to perform, promising, so far as God shall enable us, to give him no rest on your behalfs,[1] wishing our heads and hearts may be as fountains of tears for your everlasting welfare when we shall be in our poor cottages in the wilderness, overshadowed with the spirit of supplication, through the manifold necessities and tribulations which may not altogether unexpectedly, nor, we hope, unprofitably, befall us. And so commending you to the grace of God in Christ, we shall ever rest

Your assured friends and brethren,

| JOHN WINTHROPE, *Gov.* | RICHARD SALTONSTALL, |
| CHARLES FINES,[2] | ISAAC JOHNSON, |
| | THOMAS DUDLEY, |
| GEORGE PHILLIPPS,[3] | WILLIAM CODDINGTON, |
| &c. | &c. |

*From Yarmouth, aboard the Arbella, April* 7,[4] 1630.[5]

---

[1] Edward Johnson, who was one of the company that came with Winthrop, says, "For England's sake they are going from England, to pray without ceasing for England. O England! thou shalt find New-England prayers prevailing with their God for thee." See his Hist. of New-England, ch. 12, in Mass. Hist. Coll. xii. 77.

[2] Fines never came over. He was probably a relative, perhaps a brother, of William Fiennes, Viscount Saye and Sele. In company with his noble kinsman, Sir Richard Saltonstall, John Pym, and the great John Hampden, he was one of the patentees named in the grant of Connecticut from the Earl of Warwick, in 1632, and is there styled

the honorable Charles Fiennes, Esq. See Hazard's State Papers, i. 318, and Trumbull's Connecticut, i. 495.

3 The Rev. George Phillips was educated at Gonville and Caius College, Cambridge, where he took the degree of A. B. in 1613, and of A. M. in 1617. He was settled in the ministry at Boxted, in Essex. He came over in the fleet with Gov. Winthrop, and united with Sir Richard Saltonstall and others in the settlement of Watertown, of which place he was chosen the minister, and remained there till his death, July 1, 1644. Winthrop calls him "a godly man, specially gifted, and very peaceful in his place, much lamented of his own people and others." Dr. Fuller, of New Plymouth, in a letter to Gov. Bradford, dated Charlestown, June 28, 1630, writes, "Here is come over, with these gentlemen, one Mr. Phillips, a Suffolk man, who hath told me in private, that if they will have him stand minister by that calling which he received from the prelates in England, he will leave them." Tradition says he lived in the Sawin house, now standing, opposite the old burial-ground in Watertown. His son, Samuel, was the minister of Rowley. Most of the families of the name of Phillips in New-England, are descended, it is believed, from the minister of Watertown. See Mather's Magnalia, i. 339 ; Savage's Winthrop, ii. 171; Francis's Hist. of Watertown, p. 33 ; Mass. Hist. Coll. iii. 74, xv. 186, xxviii. 248.

4 This was the day before they left England. See page 127, note 2.

5 Hubbard, in speaking of this beautiful and touching Address, remarks, "It is commonly said that the Declaration was drawn up by Mr. White, that famous minister of Dorchester, of whom there is oft mention made in this History ; if so, it had a reverend, learned and holy man for its author." It seems more probable, however, that it was written by Winthrop, or Johnson, or some other one of those who signed it. "This paper," says Hutchinson, i. 19, "has occasioned a dispute whether the first settlers of the Massachusetts were of the Church of England, or not." It has also exposed them to the imputation of inconsistency and insincerity. But there is no ground for such an imputation. When they wrote this letter, they belonged to the Church of England. They disliked her ceremonies, indeed, and abjured her errors, but had never renounced her fellowship. They were Puritans, Nonconformists, but not Separatists, differing in this respect from the Colonists of New Plymouth. It was not till they were in the wilderness, far away from the pursuivants and the bishops, that they set up churches of their own, independent of their mother Church. It should be recollected, too, that this Farewell Letter was addressed not to the persecuting prelates who had driven them into the wilderness, but to "their *brethren* of the Church of England." There were many in the Church at this time, both among the clergy and laity, who were sighing for purity and reform, as much so as those that emigrated, and were prevented from emigrating either by the lack of means or resolution, or perhaps preferred to remain at home and see what they could do there in the way of church reformation. With all such the departing colonists wished to hold spiritual communion, to retain their fellowship, and be benefited by their prayers.

The foregoing paper is printed from the original edition of 1630, a copy of which is preserved among the books in Prince's New-England Library. It was probably published immediately after the sailing of Winthrop's fleet, in April. See Mather's Magnalia, i. 69–71 ; Prince's Annals, 282–307 ; Mass. Hist. Coll. xv. 126 ; Chronicles of Plymouth, pp. 416, 435.

# DUDLEY'S LETTER

# TO THE COUNTESS OF LINCOLN.

# CHAPTER XVII.

## DEPUTY GOVERNOR DUDLEY'S LETTER.

*To the Right Honorable, my very good Lady,*
        *The Lady Bridget, Countess of Lincoln.*[1]

MADAM,

YOUR letters (which are not common nor cheap,) following me hither into New-England, and bringing with them renewed testimonies of the accustomed favors you honored me with in the Old, have drawn from me this narrative retribution, which, (in respect of your proper interest in some persons of great note amongst us,)[2] was the thankfullest present I had to send over the seas.    Therefore I humbly entreat

CHAP. XVII.

1631.
March 12.

---

[1] The wife of Theophilus, the fourth earl of Lincoln, and daughter of the Viscount Saye and Sele.— Dudley had been steward in the family.  See note [3] on page 75 in the Chronicles of Plymouth.

[2] The Lady Arbella, the wife of Isaac Johnson, who came over with Winthrop, was the sister of the Earl of Lincoln.  The Lady Susan, another sister, was married to John Humphrey, who had been chosen

Deputy Governor in England, Oct. 20, 1629, but did not come over till 1632.  See pp. 106 and 127.  This family had a more intimate connection with the New-England settlements, and must have felt a deeper interest in their success, than any other noble house in England.  Cotton Mather speaks of the family as "religious," and "the best family of any nobleman then in England." See Mather's Magnalia, i. 126.

your Honor this be accepted as payment from him
〜〜 who neither hath nor is any more than

Your Honor's

Old thankful servant,

T. D.[1]

*Boston, in New-England, March 12th, 1630.*[2]

---

FOR the satisfaction of your Honor and some
friends, and for the use of such as shall hereafter

[1] THOMAS DUDLEY, the author of this letter, and one of the leading planters of Massachusetts, was born at Northampton, in 1577, being the only son of Capt. Roger Dudley, who was killed in battle. Young Dudley was brought up in the family of the Earl of Northampton, and afterwards became a clerk to his maternal kinsman, Judge Nichols, and thus obtained some knowledge of the law, which proved of great service to him in his subsequent life. At the age of 20, he received a captain's commission from Queen Elizabeth, and commanded a company of volunteers, under Henry IV. of France, at the siege of Amiens, in 1597. On the conclusion of peace the next year, he returned to England, and settled near Northampton, where he was in the neighbourhood of Dod, Hildersham, and other eminent Puritan divines, and became himself a Nonconformist. After this, he was for nine or ten years steward to Theophilus, the young Earl of Lincoln, who succeeded to his father's title Jan. 15, 1619. But becoming desirous of a more retired life, he removed to Boston, in Lincolnshire, where he enjoyed the acquaintance and ministry of the Rev. John Cotton. He was afterwards prevailed upon by the Earl of Lincoln to resume his place in his family, where he continued till the storm of persecution led him to join the company that were meditating a removal to New-England. He was one of the signers of the Agreement at Cambridge, Aug. 29, 1629, and we find him present for the first time at the Company's courts, on the 16th of October. When Winthrop was chosen Governor, he was made an Assistant; and on Humphrey's declining to go over with the Charter, he was elected Deputy Governor in his place. He was continued in the magistracy from the time of his arrival in New-England till his death, having been chosen Governor in 1634 and three times afterwards, and Deputy Governor thirteen times. In 1644 he was appointed the first Major General of the Colony. He was the principal founder of Newtown, now Cambridge, and was very desirous to have it made the metropolis. On Mr. Hooker's removal to Hartford in 1636, he removed to Ipswich, and afterwards to Roxbury, where he died July 31, 1653, in his 77th year. His son Joseph was Governor, and his grandson Paul Chief Justice, of the Province of the Massachusetts Bay. His eldest son, Samuel, married Mary, daughter of Gov. Winthrop, and his daughter Ann, who was a poetess, was married to Gov. Bradstreet. See Mather's Magnalia, i. 120–123; Hutchinson's Mass. i. 14, 183; Savage's Winthrop, i. 50; Morton's Memorial, p. 255; and note [3] on page 125.

[2] That is, old style, the new year beginning on the 25th of March. See note [4] on page 138.

intend to increase our Plantation in New-England, I
have, in the throng of domestic, and not altogether
free from public business,[1] thought fit to commit to
memory our present condition, and what hath befal-
len us since our arrival here ; which I will do shortly, after my usual manner, and must do rudely, having yet no table, nor other room to write in than by
the fireside upon my knee, in this sharp winter ; to
which my family must have leave to resort, though
they break good manners, and make me many times
forget what I would say, and say what I would not.

* * *[2] sachim in New-England, whom I saw the
last summer. Upon the river of Naponset,[3] near to
the Mattachusetts fields,[4] dwelleth Chickatalbott,[5] who
hath between fifty and sixty subjects. This man
least favoreth the English of any sagamore (for so
are the kings with us called, as they are sachims
southwards,) we are acquainted with, by reason of
the old quarrel between him and those of Plymouth,
wherein he lost seven of his best men;[6] yet he lodged one night the last winter at my house in friendly

[1] Dudley, it will be recollected, was at this time Deputy Governor of the Colony. See page 127.

[2] A part of the MS. is here missing, probably, however, only a few lines, which may have contained a description of the bays and rivers, followed by a brief notice of the Indian tribes living on them.

[3] The Neponset river separates Dorchester from Quincy and Milton.

[4] "Three miles to the north of Wessaguscus, (Weymouth,) is Mount Wollaston, (in Quincy.) — This place is called Massachusetts Fields, where the greatest sagamore in the country lived, before the

plague, who caused it to be cleared for himself." Wood's New-England's Prospect, part i. ch. 10.

[5] This, no doubt, is the sagamore mentioned in the preceding note. His residence, according to Wood's map, made in 1633, was on the eastern bank of the Neponset, in Quincy, probably not far from Squantum. He died in November, 1633, with many of his people, of the small pox. See Savage's Winthrop, i. 48, 115 ; Drake's Book of the Indians, book ii. 43 ; and Chronicles of Plymouth, note [4] on page 226.

[6] See Chronicles of Plymouth, page 339.

CHAP.
XVII.
~~~~
1631.
March
12.

manner. About seventy or eighty miles westward from these are seated the Nipnett[1] men, whose sagamore we know not, but we hear their numbers exceed any but the Pecoates[2] and the Narragansets,[3] and they are the only people we yet hear of in the inland country. Upon the river of Mistick is seated sagamore John,[4] and upon the river of Saugus

[1] The Nipnets, or Nipmucks, dwelt chiefly about the great ponds in Webster, Massachusetts; but their territory extended southward into Connecticut more than twenty miles. They were partly tributary to the Narragansetts, and partly to the Massachusetts Indians. The Blackstone river was originally the Nipmuck river. See the map of New-England in Hubbard's Indian Wars, printed in 1677, which was copied and prefixed to Judge Davis's edition of Morton's Memorial; Trumbull's Connecticut, i. 43; Hutchinson's Massachusetts, i. 459; Mass. Hist. Coll. i. 147, 148, 185, 189–194.

[2] The Pequods, the most warlike and formidable tribe of Indians in New-England, dwelt between the Thames and Pawcatuck rivers, in Connecticut, their chief seats and forts being at New-London, Groton, and the head of Mystick river. In 1637, they were completely subdued and nearly exterminated by the Connecticut and Massachusetts forces under the command of Captains John Mason, John Underhill, and Israel Stoughton. There are four contemporaneous Narratives of the Pequot War, written by Mason, Underhill, Lion Gardiner, and P. Vincent, which are contained in the Mass. Hist. Coll. xviii. 120–153, xxiii. 131–161, xxvi. 1–13. But the best History of it, with an illustrative map, will be found in the Rev. George E. Ellis's Life of Capt. John Mason, in Sparks's Am. Biog. xiii. 340–405. See also Hubbard's

Indian Wars, p. 116; Trumbull's Connecticut, i. 41; Mass. Hist. Coll. i. 147.

[3] The Narragansetts, a numerous and powerful body of Indians, dwelt between Pawcatuck river, along the coast from Stonington round Point Judith, and on the bay in Rhode Island called by their name. On the north their territory was bounded by the Quinebaug and Nipmuck countries. See Hutchinson's Mass. i. 457; Potter's Early Hist. of Narragansett, pp. 1–11; Mass. Hist. Coll. v. 239, xviii. 122, xxi. 210.

[4] His Indian name was Wonohaquaham. He lived upon the neck of land in Malden, which lies between Malden river and the creek that separates the neck from Chelsea; but his territory also included Winesemett, afterwards called Rumney Marsh, and now Chelsea. He died Dec. 5, 1633, of the small pox, and almost all his people, more than thirty of whom were buried in one day by Mr. Maverick, who lived at Noddle's Island, now East Boston. The Charlestown Records speak of him as " of a gentle and good disposition," that he " loved the English, and gave them permission to settle here." He left one son, whom he commended to the care of the Rev. Mr. Wilson, of Boston. See Lewis's Lynn, pp. 16, 17; Felt's Salem, i. 13, 16; Hutchinson's Mass. i. 461; Savage's Winthrop, i. 49, 119, 120; New-England's First Fruits, p. 2; and the map in Wood's New-England's Prospect, made in 1633, which is

sagamore James,[1] his brother, both so named by the
English. The elder brother, John, is a handsome young man, [*one line missing*] conversant with us,
affecting English apparel and houses, and speaking well of our God. His brother James is of a far worse disposition, yet repaireth often to us. Both these brothers command not above thirty or forty men, for aught I can learn. Near to Salem dwelleth two or three families,[2] subject to the sagamore of Agawam, whose name[3] he told me, but I have forgotten it. This sagamore hath but few subjects, and them and himself tributary to sagamore James, having been before the last year (in James's minority) tributary to Chickatalbott. Upon the river Merrimack is seated sagamore Passaconaway,[4] having under his command four or five hundred men, being esteemed by his countrymen a false fellow, and by us a witch. For any more northerly, I know not, but leave it to after Relations.

Having thus briefly and disorderly, especially in my description of the bays and rivers, set down what is come to hand touching the [*one line missing.*]

Now concerning the English that are planted

---

copied and inserted in a subsequent part of this volume.

[1] His Indian name was Monto-wompate. His territory included the towns of Saugus, Lynn, and Marblehead. He also died in Dec. 1633, of the small pox, "and most of his folks." Consult the map and references in the preceding note.

[2] The Rev. John Higginson says, that when he came over with his father in 1629, "the Indian town of wigwams was on the north side of the North river, not far from Si-monds's, and then both the north and south side of that river was to-gether called Naumkeke." See Felt's Salem, i. 14.

[3] His name was Masconnomo, or Masconnomet. He came on board Winthrop's ship the day after his arrival at Salem ; and by a deed dated June 28, 1638, he sold to John Winthrop, jr. for £20, all the lands lying around the bay of Aga-wam, or Ipswich. See Savage's Winthrop, i. 27 ; and Felt's Histo-ry of Ipswich, pp. 3 and 8.

[4] See Chronicles of Plymouth, note [2] on page 366.

CHAP.
XVII.

1620.

here, I find that about the year 1620, certain English set out from Leyden, in Holland, intending their course for Hudson's river, the mouth whereof lieth south of the river[1] of the Pecoates, but ariseth, as I am informed, northwards in about 43°, and so a good part of it within the compass of our patent. These, being much weather-beaten and wearied with seeking the river,[2] after a most tedious voyage[3] arrived at length in a small bay lying north-east[4] from Cape Cod ;

Dec.
11.

where landing about the month of December, by the favor of a calm winter, such as was never seen here since, begun to build their dwellings in that place which now is called New Plymouth ; where, after much sickness, famine, poverty, and great mortality, (through all which God by an unwonted providence carried them,) they are now grown up to a people healthful, wealthy, politic and religious ; such things doth the Lord for those that wait for his mercies. These of Plymouth came with patents from King James,[5] and have since obtained others from our sovereign, King Charles,[6] having a governor and council of their own.

1622.

There was about the same time one Mr. Weston, an English merchant, who sent divers men to plant and trade, who sat down by the river of Wesaguscus.

[1] The Thames, in Connecticut, running from Norwich to New London, and emptying into Long Island Sound.

[2] From his silence on the point, it would seem that Dudley had never heard of the alleged treachery of the captain of the Mayflower in carrying the Pilgrims north of Hudson's river. See Chronicles of Plymouth, p. 101, note [2].

[3] The voyage was 64 days long. See Chronicles of Plymouth, p. 105.

[4] Plymouth harbour lies due west from Cape Cod.

[5] Not so. They had only a patent from the Virginia Company. See Chronicles of Plymouth, pages 74 and 383.

[6] Another mistake. This second patent was not from the King, but from the Council for New-England. See Prince's Annals, pp. 268–270 ; Chalmers's Political Annals of the United Colonies, p. 97.

But these coming not for so good ends as those of CHAP.
Plymouth, sped not so well ; for the most of them XVII.
dying and languishing away, they who survived were
rescued by those of Plymouth out of the hands of 1623.
Chickatalbott and his Indians, who oppressed these
weak English, and intended to have destroyed them,
and the Plymotheans also, as is set down in a tract
written by Mr. Winslow, of Plymouth.[1]

Also, since, one Captain Wollaston, with some 1625.
thirty with him, came near to the same place, and
built on a hill which he named Mount Wollaston.[2]
But being not supplied with renewed provisions,
they vanished away, as the former did.                1626.

Also, divers merchants of Bristow, and some other
places, have yearly for these eight years, or there- 1623–
abouts,[3] sent ships hither at the fishing times to trade 1631.
for beaver ; where their factors dishonestly, for their
gains, have furnished the Indians with guns, swords,
powder and shot.[4]

Touching the Plantation which we here have be- 1627.
gun, it fell out thus.  About the year 1627, some
friends being together in Lincolnshire,[5] fell into discourse about New-England, and the planting of the
Gospel there ; and after some deliberation we[6] imparted our reasons, by letters and messages, to some
in London[7] and the west country ;[8] where it was
likewise deliberately thought upon, and at length with
often negotiation so ripened, that in the year 1628[9] 1628.

[1] See Chronicles of Plymouth,
pp. 296–312, 327–345.
[2] In Quincy. See Hubbard, p. 102,
and Prince, pp. 231 and 240.
[3] See note [2] on page 5.
[4] See note [4] on page 84.
[5] See note [3] on page 48.

[6] Of course the writer, Dudley,
was one of them.
[7] See pages 12 and 29.
[8] See pages 5, 21, 22, 29.
[9] The Charter from the King is
dated March 4, 1628, that is, 1629,
new style.

CHAP.
XVII.

1628.

June
20.

1629.

April
and
May.

1630.

April
8.

we procured a patent from his Majesty for our planting between the Mattachusetts Bay and Charles river on the south, and the river of Merrimack on the north, and three miles on either side of those rivers and bay ; as also for the government of those who did or should inhabit within that compass. And the same year we sent Mr. John Endecott,[1] and some with him, to begin a Plantation, and to strengthen such as he should find there, which we sent thither from Dorchester[2] and some places adjoining. From whom the same year receiving hopeful news, the next year, 1629, we sent divers ships over, with about three hundred people,[3] and some cows, goats and horses,[4] many of which arrived safely.

These, by their too large commendations of the country and the commodities thereof,[5] invited us so strongly to go on, that Mr. Winthrop, of Suffolk, (who was well known in his own country, and well approved here for his piety, liberality, wisdom, and gravity,) coming in to us, we came to such resolution, that in April, 1630, we set sail from Old England with four good ships.[6] And in May following

[1] See pages 13, 30.
[2] See pages 23–29.
[3] Higginson's company. See pages 14, 215–238.
[4] Prince, page 257, quoting the Company's Records, says 140 head of cattle, and adds, that Dudley seems too short in his statement. See note [2] on page 66.
[5] He probably alludes to Higginson's and Graves's description of the country and its advantages. See pages 243 and 264.
[6] The Arbella, the Talbot, the Ambrose, and the Jewel. Winthrop, writing to his wife " from aboard the Arbella, riding at the

Cowes, March 28, 1630," says, " We have only four ships ready. The rest of our fleet, being seven ships, will not be ready this sen'-night. We are, in all our eleven ships, about seven hundred persons, passengers, and two hundred and forty cows, and about sixty horses. The ship which went from Plymouth [the Mary & John] carried about one hundred and forty persons, and the ship which goes from Bristowe [the Lion] carrieth about eighty persons." The whole number in these thirteen vessels then was 920 persons ; and as the Handmaid brought about sixty passen-

eight more followed; two having gone before in CHAP.
February and March,[1] and two more following in
June and August, besides another set out by a private merchant. These seventeen ships arrived all
safe in New-England,[2] for the increase of the Plantation here this year 1630, but made a long, a troublesome, and costly voyage, being all wind-bound long
in England,[3] and hindered with contrary winds after
they set sail, and so scattered with mists and tem-
pests that few of them arrived together. Our four
ships which set out in April arrived here in June
and July, where we found the Colony in a sad and
unexpected condition, above eighty of them being
dead the winter before; and many of those alive
weak and sick; all the corn and bread amongst them
all hardly sufficient to feed them a fortnight, inso-

*Margin notes:* CHAP. XVII. 1630. June and July.

gers, the emigrants amounted certainly to 980. See note [2] on page
127, and Savage's Winthrop, i. 37,
368.

[1] The Lion, Capt. William Peirce,
from Bristol, and the Mary & John,
Capt. Squeb, from Plymouth.

[2] We are indebted to Prince for the following table :

*A list of Ships which arrived in New-England this year.*

| No. | Names. | Whence set sail. | When set sail. | When arrived. | Where arrived. |
|---|---|---|---|---|---|
| | | *England.* | 1630. | 1630. | *New-England.* |
| 1 | Lion . . . . . . . . | Bristol, | Feb. | May, | Salem. |
| 2 | Mary & John . . . | Plymouth, | March 20, | May 30, | Nantasket. |
| 3 | Arbella . . . . . . | } Yarmouth, at the Isle of Wight, | April 8, | June 12, | } Salem. |
| 4 | Jewel . . . . . . . | | " | " 13, | |
| 5 | Ambrose . . . . . . | | " | " 18, | |
| 6 | Talbot . . . . . . . | | " | July 2, | |
| 7 | Mayflower . . . . . | Southampton, | May, | } " 1, | Charlestown. |
| 8 | Whale . . . . . . . | " | " | | |
| 9 | Hopewell . . . . . | " | " | } " 3, | [Salem.] |
| 10 | William & Francis. | " | " | | |
| 11 | Trial . . . . . . . . | " | " | } " 5, | { Charlestown. Salem. |
| 12 | Charles . . . . . . | " | " | | |
| 13 | Success . . . . . . | | " | " 6, | [Salem.] |
| 14 | Gift . . . . . . . . | | " | Aug. 20, | Charlestown. |
| 15 | Another . . . . . . | | June, | | |
| 16 | Handmaid . . . . . | | | Oct. 29, | Plymouth. |
| 17 | { Another set out by a private merchant | | | | |

[3] See pages 125–127, and Savage's Winthrop, i. 1–5.

CHAP.
XVII.
much that the remainder of a hundred and eighty servants we had the two years before sent over,
1630.
June.
coming to us for victuals to sustain them, we found ourselves wholly unable to feed them, by reason that the provisions shipped for them were taken out of the ship they were put in, and they who were trusted to ship them in another failed us and left them behind ; whereupon necessity enforced us, to our extreme loss, to give them all liberty, who had cost us about £16 or £20 a person, furnishing and sending over.

But bearing these things as we might, we began to consult of the place of our sitting down ; for Salem, where we landed, pleased us not.[1] And to that
17. purpose, some were sent to the Bay,[2] to search up the rivers for a convenient place ; who, upon their return, reported to have found a good place upon Mistick ;[3] but some other of us, seconding these, to approve or dislike of their judgment, we found a place [that] liked us better, three leagues up Charles river ;[4] and thereupon unshipped our goods into other vessels, and with much cost and labor brought
July. them in July to Charlestown. But there receiving

[1] "For the capital town," says Prince, p. 308.

[2] Massachusetts Bay, that is, Boston harbour, "made," as Wood says, "by a great company of islands, whose high cliffs shoulder out the boisterous seas." See note [1] on page 4, and N. E. Prospect, ch. 1.

[3] "We went up Mistick river about six miles," says Winthrop, i. 27.

[4] Probably at the place afterwards called Newtown and Cambridge, and not Watertown, as Prince, p. 308, suggests ; for Watertown is afterwards mentioned as a place distinct from this. The reckoning must have been from Conant's or Governor's island, and even then the distance up the river would hardly be three leagues. But distances at this time were computed, not measured, and of course could not be very exact. Dr. Fuller, of Plymouth, in a letter to Gov. Bradford, written from Charlestown, June 28, says, "The gentlemen here lately come over are resolved to sit down at the head of Charles river, and they of Matapan (Dorchester) purpose to go and plant with them. I have been at Matapan, at the request of Mr. Warham, and let some twenty of these people blood." See Mass. Hist. Coll. iii. 74.

advertisements, by some of the late arrived ships, from London and Amsterdam, of some French preparations against us, (many of our people brought with us being sick of fevers and the scurvy, and we thereby unable to carry up our ordnance and baggage so far,) we were forced to change counsel, and for our present shelter to plant dispersedly, some at Charlestown,[1] which standeth on the north side of the mouth of Charles river ; some[2] on the south side thereof, which place we named BOSTON,[3] (as we intended to have done the place we first resolved on;) some of us upon Mistick, which we named Medford;[4] some[5] of us westwards on Charles river, four miles from Charlestown, which place we named Watertown;[6] others of us two miles from Boston, in a place

---

[1] At the head of whom was Increase Nowell. See note [2] on page 262.

[2] Among whom were Winthrop, Johnson, Coddington, and Wilson.

[3] At "a Court of Assistants holden at Charlton, the 7th of September, 1630, it is ordered that Trimountain shall be called Boston, Mattapan Dorchester, and the town upon Charles river Waterton."— "Thus this remarkable Peninsula, about two miles in length and one in breadth, in those times appearing at high water in the form of two islands, whose Indian name was *Shawmut*, but I suppose on account of three contiguous hills appearing in a range to those at Charlestown, by the English called at first *Trimountain*, now receives the name of *Boston*." Prince's Annals, p. 315. See note [3] on p. 48 ; Wood's N. E. Prospect, part i. ch. 10 ; and Snow's Hist. of Boston, p. 32.

[4] This was where Cradock's men had commenced a plantation, on the north side of Mystick river, in the present town of Malden, and a different location from the present town of Medford. See Wood's N. E. Prospect, part i. ch. 10 ; Hutchinson's Mass. i. 22 ; and the very thorough note on pp. 89–93 of Frothingham's History of Charlestown.

[5] The chief of whom were Sir Richard Saltonstall and the Rev. George Phillips.

[6] Hubbard says, p. 135, "The reason of the name was not left upon record, nor is it easy to find ; most of the other Plantations being well watered, though none of them planted on so large a fresh stream as that was." Farmer says, "It seems highly probable that it was derived from Waterton, a small place in the West Riding of Yorkshire, and not far from Halifax, the residence of Gilbert Saltonstall, the ancestor of Sir Richard Saltonstall, who was one of the principal settlers of *our* Watertown, and who might, from some local attachment or other circumstance, have given this name to the tract ' westwards on Charles

we named Rocksbury ;[1] others upon the river of
Saugus,[2] between Salem and Charlestown ; and the
western men[3] four miles south from Boston, at a
place we named Dorchester.

This dispersion troubled some of us ; but help it
we could not, wanting ability to remove to any place
fit to build a town upon, and the time too short to
deliberate any longer, lest the winter should sur-
prise us before we had builded our houses. The
best counsel we could find out was to build a fort to
retire to, in some convenient place, if any enemy
pressed us thereunto, after we should have fortified
ourselves against the injuries of wet and cold. So
ceasing to consult further for that time, they who had
health to labor fell to building, wherein many were
interrupted with sickness, and many died weekly,
yea, almost daily.[4] Amongst whom were Mrs. Pynchon,[5] Mrs. Coddington,[6] Mrs. Phillips,[7] and Mrs.
Alcock,[8] a sister of Mr. Hooker's.[9] Insomuch that

river.' The early spelling of the
name, which is *Waterton* in the
earliest records, and throughout this
letter, except in the above single
instance, seems to give some support to this conjecture.'' But I
can find no such place as Waterton
on any map of England, or in any
Gazetteer. See Francis's Watertown, p. 11, and New Hampshire
Hist. Coll. iv. 231.

[1] At the head of whom was
William Pynchon, mentioned on
page 283.

[2] Afterwards called Lynn. See
note [2] on page 169.

[3] These were Ludlow, Rossiter,
Warham, Maverick, and their associates, who came in the Mary & John.

[4] Dr. Fuller, writing to Gov.
Bradford from Charlestown, August
2, says, " The sad news here is,
that many are sick, and many are

dead. The Lord in mercy look
upon them! I can do them no good,
for I want drugs, and things fitting
to work with. Mrs. Coddington is
dead." See Mass. Hist. Coll. iii.
76.

[5] The wife of William Pynchon,
one of the Assistants, an account of
whom is given on page 283, note [4].

[6] The wife of William Coddington, another of the Assistants.

[7] The wife of the Rev. George
Phillips. See note [3] on page 299.

[8] The wife of George Alcock,
deacon of the church in Dorchester,
and afterwards of the church in
Roxbury. He was a representative
from the latter town at the first General Court, May 14,1634, and died
December 30, 1640. See Prince's
Annals, p. 399.

[9] The Rev. Thomas Hooker, who
came over with John Cotton in Sept.

the ships being now upon their return, some for England, some for Ireland, there was, as I take it, not much less than a hundred, (some think many more,) partly out of dislike of our government, which restrained and punished their excesses, and partly through fear of famine, not seeing other means than by their labor to feed themselves, which returned back again;[1] and glad were we so to be rid of them. Others also, afterwards hearing of men of their own disposition, which were planted at Pascataway,[2] went from us to them ; whereby though our numbers were lessened, yet we accounted ourselves nothing weakened by their removal. Before the departure of the ships, we contracted with Mr. Peirce, master of the Lion, of Bristow, to return to us with all speed with fresh supplies of victuals, and gave him directions accordingly. With this ship returned Mr. Revell,[3] one of the five undertakers here for the joint

1633, and settled at Cambridge, but in 1636 removed to Hartford, on Connecticut river.

[1] How different was this from the conduct of the Pilgrims at Plymouth. Although of the hundred persons who came in the Mayflower, forty-four, nearly a half, had died before she returned to England, yet not one of the survivors embarked in her. See Chronicles of Plymouth, note [2] on page 199.

[2] In the spring of 1623, a settlement was commenced at two different places on the Piscataqua, by David Thompson, and Edward and William Hilton. Thompson planted himself on the southern shore of the river, at its mouth, which he called Little Harbour, and built a house on a peninsula, now called Odiorne's Point. The Hiltons seated themselves eight miles up the river, at Dover. Both parties had

been sent out by Gorges and Mason and certain merchants who styled themselves " The Company of Laconia." In 1628, Piscataqua was assessed £2 10s. for the campaign against Morton, of Mount Wollaston, a sum equal to that paid by Plymouth ; and yet, in 1631, there were but three houses on the river. In 1653, when the name of " Strawberry Bank" was exchanged for Portsmouth, there were but fifty or sixty families there. See Belknap's New Hampshire, (Farmer's edit.) pp. 4–9, 434 ; Adams's Annals of Portsmouth, pp. 10, 11 ; Mass. Hist. Coll. iii. 63 ; Prince's Annals, pp. 215, 239, 268 ; Hubbard, 214–219; Chronicles of Plymouth, pp. 251, 351.

[3] John Revell never returned to New-England. Mr. Savage suggests that " he was probably too rich to adventure life and fortune

CHAP. XVII.

1630. Aug.

stock of the Company,[1] and Mr. Vassall,[2] one of the Assistants, and his family, and also Mr. Bright,[3] a minister sent hither the year before.

The ships being gone, victuals wasting, and mortality increasing, we held divers fasts[4] in our several

with us." He had been chosen one of the Assistants Oct. 20, 1629, and he was one of the merchant adventurers interested in the Plymouth Colony. See pages 106 and 116 ; Savage's Winthrop, i. 20 ; and Mass. Hist. Coll. iii. 48.

[1] See page 116.

[2] William Vassall, as well as his brother Samuel, mentioned on page 89, were, according to Hutchinson, gentlemen of good circumstances in England. He came back in 1635, and settled at Scituate, in Plymouth Colony. In 1646 he returned to England, and in 1648 removed to Barbadoes, and there died in 1655. Winthrop speaks of him as "a man of a busy and factious spirit, and always opposite to the civil government of this country and the way of our churches." He left a son John in Scituate, who removed from that town in 1661. The Vassalls of Quincy and Cambridge were descendants of Samuel. See Savage's Winthrop, ii. 261, 321 ; Hutchinson's Mass. i. 17, 145 ; Deane's Hist. of Scituate, 60–89, 366–370 ; Mass. Hist. Coll. xiv. 244 ; Harris's Cambridge Epitaphs, p. 179.

[3] Francis Bright was the son of Edward Bright, of London, and was born in 1602. He was matriculated at New College, Oxford, Feb. 18, 1624, but probably left without taking a degree. In the Company's Instructions to Endicott, on page 143, he is said to have been " some time trained up under Mr. Davenport," and in his Agreement, on p. 207, he is called " of Rayleigh, in Essex," where he probably had a lectureship. Soon after his arrival at Salem, June 29, 1629, he went to Charlestown, in the records

of which place he is called " minister to the Company's servants." As the Lion sailed in August, he was in the country only about a year. Edward Johnson, who came in Winthrop's fleet, says, " All this while little likelihood there was building the temple for God's worship, there being only two that began to hew stones in the mountains, the one named Mr. Bright, and the other Mr. Blaxton ; and one of them began to build. But when they saw all sorts of stones would not fit in the building, as they supposed, the one betook him to the seas again, and the other to till the land, retaining no symbol of his former profession but a canonical coat." On the strength of this, Hubbard calls him a Conformist, and so does Morton. But the Company say in their Letter, that " the ministers have declared themselves to us to be of one judgment, and to be fully agreed on the manner· how to exercise their ministry." See note [1] on p. 160, and note [3] on p. 169 ; Morton's Memorial, p. 145 ; Mass. Hist. Coll. xv. 112, 113, xii. 70, xxviii. 250.

[4] Their first fast was kept Friday, July 30, when Winthrop, Dudley, Johnson, and Wilson entered into church covenant, and laid the foundation of the church of Charlestown, which is now the first church of Boston. The day was also observed by their brethren of Plymouth in their behalf. Another fast was kept Aug. 27, when John Wilson was ordained teacher, Increase Nowell ruling elder, and William Gager and William Aspinwall deacons. See Morton's Memorial, p. 159 ; Savage's Winthrop, i. 31 ; Mass. Hist. Coll. iii. 75.

congregations. But the Lord would not yet be de-
precated; for about the beginning of September died
Mr. Gager,[1] a right godly man, a skilful chirurgeon,
and one of the deacons of our congregation; and
Mr. Higginson,[2] one of the ministers of Salem, a zealous and a profitable preacher — this of a consumption,
that of a fever; and on the 30th of September died
Mr. JOHNSON,[3] another of the five undertakers, (the

[1] William Gager died Sept. 20. At the first Court of Assistants, held Aug. 23, it was "ordered that Mr. Gager should have a house builded him against the next spring, is to have a cow given him, and £20 in money for this year, to begin the 20th June, 1630, and after £30 per annum; and all this to be at the common charge." His son John went with the younger Winthrop to New London, and in 1660 was one of the founders of Norwich, where his descendants still remain. William Gager graduated at Yale College in 1721, and was ordained minister of the second church of Lebanon, May 27, 1725. See Hazard's State Papers, ii. 412; Trumbull's Connecticut, ii. 532; Caulkins's Hist. of Norwich, p. 103.

[2] FRANCIS HIGGINSON was born in 1588, and was educated at Jesus College, Cambridge, where he took the degree of A. B. in 1609, and received the degree of A. M. from St. John's College in 1613. He was a minister of one of the five parish churches of Leicester, but through his intimacy with Hildersham and Hooker, and his study of the Scriptures, he became a Nonconformist. He was accordingly excluded from his pulpit; but a lectureship was established for him, in which he was maintained by the voluntary contribution of the inhabitants. He was in this situation when invited by the New-England Company to go over to their Plantation. See p. 65. He was ordained at Salem Aug. 6, 1629, and lived

only a year afterwards. Mather says the last sermon he preached was to Winthrop's company on their arrival at Salem, from Matth. xi. 7, *What went ye out into the wilderness to see?* He left a wife and eight children, who after his death removed to Charlestown, and then to New-Haven. The portrait at the State House in Boston is not his, but his son John's. See note [3] on page 211, and note [1] on page 236; Mather's Magnalia, i. 322.

[3] ISAAC JOHNSON was of Clipsham, in the county of Rutland, son of Abraham Johnson, Esq. He was the largest subscriber to the joint stock of the Company, and in April, 1629, he valued his interest in the New-England adventure at £600. His landed estate lay in the counties of Rutland, Northampton, and Lincoln. He left no children. In his last will, dated March 8, 1630, a month before he sailed, of which will the great John Hampden was one of the executors, he left some part of his personal estate to the Governor and Company. In a previous will, dated April 28, 1629, he gave to the Rev. John Cotton, from whom he acknowledges to have received much help and comfort in his spiritual state, £30 and a gown-cloth, and to him and Mr. Dudley he gave the right of presentation to the parish church of Clipsham. Prince says, that Chief Justice Sewall informed him that Mr. Johnson was the principal cause of settling the town of Boston, and so of its becoming the metropolis; that he

CHAP.
XVII.

1630.
Sept.
30.

Oct.
23.

lady ARBELLA,[1] his wife, being dead a month before.)
This gentleman was a prime man amongst us, having
the best estate of any, zealous for religion, and the
greatest furtherer of this Plantation. He made a most
godly end, dying willingly, professing his life better
spent in promoting this Plantation than it could have
been any other way. He left to us a loss greater than
the most conceived. Within a month after, died Mr.
Rossiter,[2] another of our Assistants, a godly man,
and of a good estate ; which still weakened us more.

had removed hither, and had chosen
for his lot the great square, lying
between Tremont, Court, Washington and School streets. Tradition
places his house about the centre of
the north-east side, that is, near the
present site of the Court House.
He was buried, at his own request,
at the upper end of his lot, on Tremont-street, which was the origin
of the first burial ground in the town,
adjoining King's Chapel. Winthrop, i. 34, says " he was a holy
man, and wise, and died in sweet
peace, leaving some part of his substance to the Colony." Edward
Johnson, who came in the fleet with
him, says that " the Lord had in-
dued him with many precious gifts,
insomuch that he was had in high
esteem among all the people of God,
and as a chief pillar to support this
new-erected building. He very
much rejoiced, at his death, that the
Lord had been pleased to keep his
eyes open so long, as to see one
church of Christ gathered before his
death ; at whose departure there
was not only many weeping eyes,
but some fainting hearts, fearing the
fall of the present work." See
Hutchinson's Mass. i. 16 ; Prince's
Annals, pp. 316, 318, 333 ; Mass.
Hist. Coll. xii. 87, xxviii. 244 ;
Snow's Boston, p. 36.

[1] The Lady ARBELLA was a
daughter of Thomas, the third Earl

of Lincoln. Hubbard says that she
came " from a paradise of plenty
and pleasure, which she enjoyed in
the family of a noble Earldom, into
a wilderness of wants," and Mather
adds, that " she took New-England
in her way to heaven." Johnson
says that the name of the ship Eagle
had been changed to Arbella, in
honor of her, and that after the arrival of the fleet, she " and some
other godly women abode at Salem,
but their husbands continued at
Charlestown, both for settling the
civil government, and gathering another church of Christ." Dr. Holmes
says, Annals, i. 206, " Dr. Holyoke,
of Salem, aged 99, informs me that
she was buried about half a mile
distant from the body of the town,
near Bridge-street, leading to Beverly, about ten feet from the street."
The Johnson Grammar School, for
girls, in Boston, was so called as a
mark of respect to her name and
memory. See Mather's Magnalia,
i. 71, 340 ; Chronicles of Plymouth,
p. 75 ; Mass. Hist. Coll. xii. 79,
86, xv. 132.

[2] Edward Rossiter was of a good
family in the west of England, and
one of the founders of Dorchester.
His son lived afterwards at Combe,
in England, and his grandson, Edward, was deacon of the church in
Taunton in 1682. See Hutchinson's
Mass. i. 17.

So that now there were left of the five undertakers[1] CHAP.
but the Governor, Sir Richard Saltonstall, and myself, and seven other of the Assistants.[2]   And of the
people who came over with us, from the time of their
setting sail from England in April, 1630, until December following, there died by estimation about two
hundred at the least : so low hath the Lord brought
us !³

Well, yet they who survived were not discouraged,
but bearing God's corrections with humility, and
trusting in his mercies, and considering how, after a
lower ebb, he had raised up our neighbours at

XVII.

1630.
Oct.

---

[1] See page 116.
[2] Endicott, Ludlow, Nowell, Pynchon, Coddington, Bradstreet, and
Thomas Sharpe. See pp. 106, 127.
³ Gov. Winthrop, in his Journal
writes, " The poorer sort of people,
who lay long in tents, were much
afflicted with the scurvy, and many
died, especially at Boston and
Charlestown;" and writing to his
wife under date of Sept. 9 and Nov.
29, he says, "the lady Arbella is
dead, and good Mr. Higginson, my
servant, old Waters of Neyland,
and many others. — I have lost
twelve of my family, viz. Waters
and his wife, and two of his children, Mr. Gager and his man Smith
of Buxall, and his wife and two
children, the wife of Taylor of Haverhill and their child ; my son H.
makes the twelve. And, besides
many other of less note, as Jeff.
Ruggle of Sudbury, and divers
others of that town, (about twenty,)
and one of L. Kedby his sons, the
Lord hath stripped us of some principal persons, Mr. Johnson and his
lady, Mr. Rossiter, Mrs. Phillips,
and others unknown to thee. We
conceive that this disease grew from
ill diet at sea, and proved infectious." Winthrop's History, i. 44,
377, 379.

Henry Winthrop, the Governor's
second son, who had accidentally
been left behind at the Isle of
Wight, was unfortunately drowned
in a small creek at Salem, on the
2d of July, the very day he landed.
He was in his twenty-third year.
He left his wife, Elizabeth, behind
in England, and an only daughter,
Martha, who was baptized May 9,
1630. His father, in his first letter,
dated July 16, to his own wife, who
also was obliged to remain behind
in England, writes, " We have met
with many sad and discomfortable
things, as thou shalt hear after ;
and the Lord's hand hath been
heavy upon myself in some very
near to me. My son Henry! my
son Henry ! Ah, poor child ! Yet
it grieves me much more for my
dear daughter. The Lord strengthen
and comfort her heart to bear this
cross patiently. I know thou wilt
not be wanting to her in this distress. Yet, for all these things, (I
praise my God,) I am not discouraged ; nor do I see cause to repent
or despair of those good days here,
which will make amends for all."
See Savage's Winthrop, i. 7, 29,
372; Hubbard's Hist. p. 131 ; Mass.
Hist. Coll. xxviii. 296, 297.

Plymouth, we began again in December to consult about a fit place to build a town upon, leaving all thoughts of a fort, because upon any invasion we were necessarily to lose our houses, when we should retire thereinto. So after divers meetings at Boston, Roxbury, and Waterton, on the 28th of December we grew to this resolution, to bind all the Assistants (Mr. Endicott and Mr. Sharpe excepted, which last purposeth to return by the next ship into England,) to build houses at a place a mile east from Waterton, near Charles river,[1] the next spring, and to winter there the next year ; that so by our examples, and by removing the ordnance and munition thither, all who were able might be drawn thither, and such as shall come to us hereafter, to their advantage be compelled so to do ; and so, if God would, a fortified town might there grow up, the place fitting reasonably well thereto.

I should before have mentioned how both the English and Indian corn being at ten shillings a strike,[2] and beaver being valued at six shillings a pound, we made laws to restrain the selling of corn to the Indians, and to leave the price of beaver at liberty,[3] which was presently sold for ten and twenty shillings a pound. I should also have remembered, how the half of our cows and almost all our mares and goats, sent us out of England, died at sea in their passage hither, and that those intended to be sent us out of Ireland were not sent at all ; all which, together

---

[1] Winthrop, i. 39, says, "Dec. 21, we met again at Watertown, and there, upon a view of a place a mile beneath the town, all agreed it a fit place for a fortified town, and we took time to consider further about it." This was at Newtown, afterwards called Cambridge.

[2] Strike, a bushel.

[3] These orders were passed at the two Courts of Assistants held Sept. 28 and Nov. 9.

with the loss of our six months' building, occasioned CHAP.<br>XVII. by our intended removal to a town to be fortified, weakened our estates, especially the estates of the 1630. undertakers,[1] who were 3 or £4000 engaged in the joint stock, which was now not above so many hundreds. Yet many of us labored to bear it as comfortably as we could, remembering the end of our coming hither, and knowing the power of God, who can support and raise us again, and useth to bring his servants low that the meek may be made glorious Psalm<br>cxii. by deliverance.

In the end of this December departed from us the Dec. ship Handmaid, of London, by which we sent away one Thomas Morton,[2] a proud, insolent man, who has lived here divers years, and had been an attorney in the west countries while he lived in England. Multitude of complaints were received against him for injuries done by him both to the English and Indians;

[1] See page 116.

[2] Thomas Morton, if we may believe his own statement, first came to New-England in 1622 ; and if so, he was probably one of Weston's unfortunate colony, which arrived in June of that year, and settled at Wessaguscus, now Weymouth. In 1625 he was with Wollaston's company at Quincy ; and on Wollaston's departure for Virginia, Morton became such a troublesome and dangerous neighbour, by selling guns and ammunition to the natives, that in 1628 the scattered plantations in New-England combined, and employed Capt. Standish to apprehend him. He was sent prisoner to England in the custody of John Oldham, but returned in August, 1629, and took up his abode again at Merry Mount, as he called it. It was during his absence in England that Endicott visited the Mount, and cut down the Maypole. After being sent home a second time, by the Massachusetts government, he did all he could, in conjunction with Sir Christopher Gardiner and its other enemies, to injure the Colony, and in 1637 published a scurrilous book against it, entitled " New-English Canaan." He returned to New-England in Dec. 1643, when he was called to account for his malpractices. His book and an abusive letter which he had written, were produced against him, and he was imprisoned about a year, and in Sept. 1644, fined £100. Not being able to pay the fine, he was permitted to escape, and went to Agamenticus, in Maine, where he died, in 1645 or 1646. See Morton's Memorial, pp. 135–142 ; Savage's Winthrop, i. 34, 138, ii. 151, 189–92 ; Mass. Hist. Coll. iii. 61–64, Chronicles of Plymouth, pp. 296, 334 ; Morton's New-English Canaan, ch. 2.

CHAP.
XVII.
~~~

1630.
Dec.

and amongst others, for shooting hail-shot at a troop of Indians for not bringing a canoe unto him to cross a river withal; whereby he hurt one, and shot through the garments of another. For the satisfaction of the Indians wherein, and that it might appear to them and to the English that we meant to do justice impartially, we caused his hands to be bound behind him, and set his feet in the bilboes, and burned his house to the ground, all in the sight of the Indians, and so kept him prisoner till we sent him for England ; whither we sent him, for that my Lord Chief Justice there so required, that he might punish him capitally for fouler misdemeanours there perpetrated, as we were informed.

I have no leisure to review and insert things forgotten, but out of due time and order must set them down as they come to memory. About the end of

Oct.

October this year, 1630, I joined with the Governor and Mr. Maverecke[1] in sending out our pinnace to

---

[1] Samuel Maverick was found here by Gov. Winthrop, on his arrival in June, 1630, living at Nottle's Island, now East Boston. How long he had lived there, is unknown. As he was not assessed for the campaign against Morton, in 1628, it is to be presumed that he did not come over till the following year. Edward Johnson, one of Winthrop's company, says, that " on the north side of Charles river, they landed near a small island, called Noddle's island, where one Mr. Samuel Mavereck was then living, a man of a very loving and courteous behaviour, very ready to entertain strangers, yet an enemy to the reformation in hand, being strong for the lordly prelatical power. On this island he had built a small fort, with the help of one Mr. David Thompson, placing therein four murtherers to protect him from the Indians." Gov. Winthrop says, on his first visit to the Bay from Salem, " June 17, we lay at Mr. Maverick's." Josselyn, who was here in 1638, says, " July 10, I went ashore upon Noddle's island, to Mr. Samuel Maverick, the only hospitable man in all the country, giving entertainment to all comers gratis;" and Henry Gardner, in his New-England's Vindication, p. 9, (London, 1660,) speaks of him as " the most hospitable for entertainment of people of all sorts." Winthrop tells us in his Journal, under July, 1637, that " Mr. Vane went over to Nottle's island to dine with Mr. Maverick, and carried the Lord Ley with him." This characteristic hospitality of Mr. Maverick appears to have been at times somewhat troublesome, for at a General Court held

the Narragansetts, to trade for corn to supply our CHAP.
XVII.
wants ; but after the pinnace had doubled Cape Cod,
she put into the next harbour[1] she found, and there 1630.
Oct.
meeting with Indians, who showed their willingness
to truck, she made her voyage there, and brought us
a hundred bushels of corn, at about four shillings a
bushel, which helped us somewhat. From the coast
where they traded, they saw a very large island,[2]
four leagues to the east, which the Indians commended as a fruitful place, full of good vines, and free
from sharp frosts, having one only entrance into it,
by a navigable river, inhabited by a few Indians,
which for a trifle would leave the island, if the English would set them upon the main ; but the pinnace
having no direction for discovery, returned without
sailing to it, which in two hours they might have
done. Upon this coast they found store of vines full
of grapes dead ripe, the season being past ; whither
we purpose to send the next year sooner, to make
some small quantity of wine, if God enable us ; the
vines growing thin with us, and we not having yet
any leisure to plant vineyards.[3]

But now having some leisure to discourse of the
motives for other men's coming to this place, or their

March 4, 1635, it was "ordered, that Mr. Samuel Maverick shall, before the last of December next, remove his habitation for himself and his family to Boston, and in the mean time shall not give entertainment to any strangers for longer times than one night, without leave from some Assistant ; and all this to be done under the penalty of £100." This order, however, was repealed in the following September. The island on which he lived had been granted him April 1, 1633, and also Winnisimet ferry, both to Charlestown and Boston. He died March 10, 1664. See Winthrop, i. 27, 232, ii. 51 ; Mass. Hist. Coll. xii. 86, xxiii. 220.

[1] Probably the harbour of Chatham, called by the Indians Manamoyk. See Chronicles of Plymouth, pages 217 and 300.

[2] This was no doubt the island of Aquethneck, afterwards called Rhode Island. Prince, p. 323.

[3] See pages 152 and 247

CHAP.
XVII.

1631.

abstaining from it, after my brief manner I say this : that if any come hither to plant for worldly ends, that can live well at home, he commits an error, of which he will soon repent him ; but if for spiritual, and that no particular obstacle hinder his removal, he may find here what may well content him, viz. materials to build, fuel to burn, ground to plant, seas and rivers to fish in, a pure air to breathe in, good water to drink, till wine or beer can be made ; which, together with the cows, hogs and goats brought hither already, may suffice for food ; for as for fowl and venison, they are dainties here as well as in England. For clothes and bedding, they must bring them with them, till time and industry produce them here.   In a word, we yet enjoy little to be envied, but endure much to be pitied in the sickness and mortality of our people.   And I do the more willingly use this open and plain dealing, lest other men should fall short of their expectations when they come hither, as we to our great prejudice did, by means of letters[1] sent us from hence into England, wherein honest men, out of a desire to draw over others to them, wrote somewhat hyperbolically of many things here.   If any godly men, out of religious ends, will come over to help us in the good work we are about, I think they cannot dispose of themselves nor of their estates more to God's glory and the furtherance of their own reckoning.   But they must not be of the poorer sort yet, for divers years ; for we have found by experience that they have hindered, not furthered the work. And for profane and debauched persons, their over-

[1] These were probably the letters written by Higginson and Graves. See note [5] on page 310.

sight in coming hither is wondered at, where they shall find nothing to content them. If there be any endued with grace, and furnished with means to feed themselves and theirs for eighteen months, and to build and plant, let them come over into our Macedonia and help us,[1] and not spend themselves and their estates in a less profitable employment. For others, I conceive they are not yet fitted for this business.

Touching the discouragement which the sickness and mortality which every first year hath seized upon us and those of Plymouth, as appeareth before, may give to such who have cast any thoughts this way, (of which mortality it may be said of us almost as of the Egyptians, that there is not a house where there Exod. xii. 30. is not one dead, and in some houses many,) the natural causes seem to be in the want of warm lodging and good diet, to which Englishmen are habituated at home, and in the sudden increase of heat which they endure that are landed here in summer, the salt meats at sea having prepared their bodies thereto ; for those only these two last years died of fevers who landed in June and July ; as those of Plymouth, who landed in winter, died of the scurvy ;[2] as did our poorer sort, whose houses and bedding kept them not sufficiently warm, nor their diet sufficiently in heart. Other causes God may have, as our faithful minister, Mr. Wilson,[3] lately handling that point,

---

[1] This was the motto of the Colony Seal. See note [1] on page 155.
[2] See Chronicles of Plymouth, p. 198.
[3] John Wilson, the first minister of the first church in Charlestown and Boston, was born at Windsor in 1588  His father, Dr. William Wilson, was a prebendary of Roch-
ester, a canon of Windsor, and rector of Cliffe, in Kent ; and his mother was the niece of Dr. Edmund Grindall, archbishop of Canterbury, after whom he named his eldest son. After studying four years at Eton, Mather says he was admitted into King's College, Cambridge, in 1602, in which he afterwards obtained a

showed unto us ; which I forbear to mention, leaving this matter to the further dispute of physicians and divines.

---

fellowship. But Mr. Savage, who inspected the registers of the University in 1842, found that he took his degrees of A. B. and· A. M. at Christ's College in 1605 and 1609. Becoming a Puritan and Nonconformist, he was forced by the bishop of Lincoln to resign his fellowship and leave the University. Upon this his father sent him to London to study law at the Inns of Court, where he remained three years ; but finding him strongly bent on the ministry, he permitted him to return to Cambridge, and finish his studies, and take his Master's degree. After preaching at several places, he was settled in the ministry at Sudbury, in Suffolk, where he was a near neighbour to Winthrop, at Groton. After preaching here for a while, he was first suspended and then silenced by the bishop of Norwich ; but, through the interposition of the Earl of Warwick, he again obtained permission to exercise his ministry. Tired, however, of being thus harassed, he embarked, at the age of 42, with some of his neighbours, in Winthrop's fleet. At the first Court of Assistants, held at Charlestown, Aug. 23, 1630, it was ordered that a house should be built for Mr. Wilson, and that he should have £20 a year till his wife came over. She was a daughter of Lady Mansfield, widow of Sir John Mansfield, and a near relative of Sir William Bird. He returned from England without her, May 26, 1632 ; and it was not till his second visit that he could prevail upon her to accompany him to New-England, in 1635. She probably had been discouraged by the death of so many prominent females the first year. Gov. Winthrop's wife, who had been necessarily prevented from accompanying her husband, writes thus to her son in June, 1631, " Mr. Wilson is now

in London. He cannot yet persuade his wife to go, for all he hath taken this pains to come and fetch her. I marvel what mettle she is made of." Wilson was minister of the first church in Boston 37 years, 3 years before Mr. Cotton, 19 years with him, 7 years with Mr. Norton, and 4 years after him. Winthrop speaks of him as " a very sincere, holy man." He died Aug. 7, 1667, in his 79th year. His Life was written by Cotton Mather, and Hutchinson says he had it " in manuscript by another hand." His will is preserved in the Probate Records of Suffolk, lib. vi. fol. 1, and his portrait hangs in the hall of the Massachusetts Historical Society. His second son, John, who graduated in the first class at Harvard College, in 1641, was ordained colleague with Richard Mather at Dorchester, in 1649, and after two years removed to Medfield, where he was pastor forty years, and died Aug. 23, 1691, aged 70. He married Sarah, daughter of the Rev. Thomas Hooker, of Hartford, and his son John was baptized in his grandfather Wilson's church at Boston, July 8, 1649. It was Dr. Edmund Wilson, a physician, a brother of the minister of Boston, who gave £1000 to the Colony, with which they purchased artillery and ammunition. An inventory of these articles, sent over in the Griffin in 1634, may be found in Mass. Hist. Coll. xviii. 228. See also Winthrop, i. 50, 77, 81, 169, 172, 382 ; Morton's Memorial, p. 326 ; Mather, i. 275–292 ; Prince, 370 ; Hutchinson's Mass. i. 258 ; Emerson's Hist. of the First Church in Boston, pp. 1–106 ; Mass. Hist. Coll. xii. 59, xvii. 56, xxiii. 378, xxviii. 248, 316 ; Wood's Fasti Oxon. (edit. Bliss,) part i. 322, 360 ; Ashmole's Antiquities of Berkshire, iii. 157.

Wherefore to return, upon the 3d of January died
the daughter of Mr. Sharpe,[1] a godly virgin, making
a comfortable end, after a long sickness. The Plantation here received not the like loss of any woman
since we came hither, and therefore she well deserves to be remembered in this place.

And to add to our sorrows, upon the 5th day came
letters to us from Plymouth, advertising us of this
sad accident following.[2] About a fortnight before,
there went from us in a shallop to Plymouth six men
and a girl, who, in an hour or two before night, on
the same day they went forth, came near to the
mouth of Plymouth bay; but the wind then coming
strongly from the shore, kept them from entering,
and drove them to sea-wards; and they having no
better means to help themselves, let down their killock,[3] that so they might drive the more slowly, and
be nearer land when the storm should cease. But
the stone slipping out of the killock, and thereby they driving faster than they thought all the
night, in the morning, when they looked out, they
found themselves out of sight of land; which so as-
tonished them, (the frost being extreme and their
hands so benumbed with cold that they could not
handle their oars, neither had any compass to
steer by,) that they gave themselves for lost, and
lay down to die quietly. Only one man, who had
more natural heat and courage remaining than the
rest, continued so long looking for land, that, the
morning waxing clearer, he discovered land, and

---

[1] Thomas Sharpe.
[2] See Winthrop, i. 39, and
Wood's New-England's Prospect,
part i. ch. 2.

[3] A wooden frame enclosing a
stone, used for an anchor.

CHAP.
XVII.

1630.
Dec.
30.

16 31.
Jan.
2

with difficulty hoisted the sail ; and so the wind a little turning, two days after they were driven from Plymouth bay, they arrived at a shore unknown unto them.[1] The stronger helped the weaker out of the boat, and taking their sail on shore, made a shelter thereof, and made a fire. But the frost had so pierced their bodies, that one of them died about three days after their landing, and most of the others grew worse, both in body and courage, no hope of relief being within their view. Well, yet the Lord pitying them, and two of them, who only could use their legs, going abroad rather to seek than to hope to find help, they met first with two Indian women, who sent unto them an Indian man, who informed them that Plymouth was within fifty miles, and offered together to procure relief for them ; which they gladly accepting, he performed, and brought them three men from Plymouth, (the Governor and Council of Plymouth liberally rewarding the Indian, and took care for the safety of our people,) who brought them all alive in their boat thither, save one man, who, with a guide, chose rather to go over land ; but quickly fell lame by the way, and getting harbour at a trucking-house the Plymotheans had in those parts,[2] there he yet abides. At the others' landing at Plymouth, one of them died as he was taken out of the boat. Another, and he the worst in the company, rotted from the feet upwards, where the frost had gotten most hold, and so died within a few days. The other three,[3] after God had blessed

---

[1] On Cape Cod, according to Winthrop and Wood.

[2] At Scusset harbour, in Sand-

wich. See Chronicles of Plymouth, page 306.

[3] The name of one of them was

the chirurgeon's skill used towards them, returned CHAP. XVII. safe to us. I set down this the more largely, partly because the first man that died was a godly man of 1631. our congregation, one Richard Garrad,[1] who, at the Jan. time of his death, more feared he should dishonor God than cared for his own life ; as also because divers boats have been in manifest peril this year, yet the Lord preserved them all, this one excepted.

Amongst those who died about the end of this January, there was a girl of eleven years old, the daughter of one John Ruggles,[2] of whose family and kindred died so many,[3] that for some reason it was matter of observation amongst us ; who, in the time of her sickness, expressed to the minister, and to those about her, so much faith and assurance of salvation, as is rarely found in any of that age ; which I thought not unworthy here to commit to memory. And if any tax me for wasting paper with recording these small matters, such may consider that little mothers bring forth little children, small commonwealths matters of small moment, the reading whereof yet is not to be despised by the judicious, because small things in the beginning of natural or politic bodies are as remarkable as greater in bodies full grown.

Henry Harwood, " a godly man of the congregation of Boston." At a Court of Assistants, held the 16th of August following, it was ordered " that the executors of Richard Garrett shall pay unto Henry Harwood the sum of twenty nobles," probably for the danger and suffering to which he had involuntarily subjected him. See Savage's Winthrop, i. 40.

[1] Garrad, or Garrett, was a shoemaker, of Boston, and was the 55th member admitted to the church there.

[2] John Ruggles was admitted a freeman July 3, 1632.

[3] Winthrop mentions Jeffrey Ruggles, of Sudbury, among those who died. See note [3] on page 319.

Upon the 5th of February arrived here Mr. Peirce, with the ship Lion, of Bristow, with supplies of victuals from England ;[1] who had set forth from Bristow the 1st of December before.  He had a stormy passage hither, and lost one of his sailors[2] not far from our shore, who in a tempest having helped to take in the spritsail, lost his hold as he was coming down, and fell into the sea ; where, after long swimming, he was drowned, to the great dolor of those in the ship, who beheld so lamentable a spectacle without being able to minister help to him, the sea was so high and the ship drove so fast before the wind, though her sails were taken down.  By this ship we understood of the fight of three of our ships and two English men-of-war coming out of the Straits, with fourteen Dunkirkers,[3] upon the coast of England, as they returned from us in the end of the last summer; who, through God's goodness, with the loss of some thirteen or fourteen men out of our three ships, and I know not how many out of the two men-of-war, got at length clear of them ; the Charles, one of our three,[4] a stout ship of three hundred tons, being so torn, that she had not much of her left whole above water.  By this ship we also understood the death of many of those who went from us the last year to

---

[1] She arrived at Nantasket on the 5th, and anchored before Boston on the 9th.  The celebrated Roger Williams and his wife came in her.  Her cargo consisted of 34 hhds. wheat meal, 15 hhds. pease, 4 hhds. oatmeal, 4 hhds. beef and pork, 15 cwt. of cheese, butter, suet, seed barley and rye, &c.  They arrived in good order.  See Savage's Winthrop, i. 41, 43, 47.

[2] His name was Way, probably a son of Henry Way, one of the first settlers of Dorchester, who died in 1667, aged 84.  He had another son killed by the Eastern Indians in June, 1632.  See Savage's Winthrop, i. 43, 79 ; Blake's Annals of Dorchester, p. 24 ; Wood's New-England's Prospect, part ii. ch. 2.

[3] See note [3] on page 218.

[4] The other two were the Success and the Whale.  See Winthrop, i. 46.

Old England, as likewise of the mortality there; whereby we see there are graves in other places as well as with us.

Also, to increase the heap of our sorrows, we received advertisement by letters from our friends in England, and by the reports of those who came hither in this ship to abide with us, (who were about twenty-six,) that they who went discontentedly from us the last year, out of their evil affections towards us, have raised many false and scandalous reports against us, affirming us to be Brownists[1] in religion, and ill affected to our State at home, and that these vile reports have won credit with some who formerly wished us well. But we do desire, and cannot but hope, that wise and impartial men will at length consider that such malecontents have ever pursued this manner of casting dirt, to make others seem as foul as themselves, and that our godly friends, to whom we have been known, will not easily believe that we are so soon turned from the profession we so long have made in our native country. And for our further clearing, I truly affirm, that I know no one person, who came over with us the last year, to be altered in judgment and affection, either in ecclesiastical or civil respects, since our coming hither. But we do continue to pray daily for our sovereign lord the King, the Queen, the Prince, the royal blood, the Council and whole State, as duty binds us to do, and reason persuades others to believe. For how ungodly and unthankful should we be, if we should not thus do, who came hither by virtue of his Majesty's letters patent, and under his gracious pro-

---

[1] See Chronicles of Plymouth, pp. 416–444.

CHAP.
XVII.

1631.

tection ; under which shelter we hope to live safely, and from whose kingdom and subjects we now have received and hereafter expect relief. Let our friends therefore give no credit to such malicious aspersions, but be more ready to answer for us than we hear they have been. We are not like those which have dispensations to lie ; but as we were free enough in Old England to turn our insides outwards, sometimes to our disadvantage, very unlike is it that now, being *procul a fulmine*, we should be so unlike ourselves. Let therefore this be sufficient for us to say, and others to hear in this matter.

Amongst others who died about this time was Mr. Robert Welden,[1] whom, in the time of his sickness, we had chosen to be captain of a hundred foot ; but before he took possession of his place, he died, the

Feb.
16.

16th of this February, and was buried as a soldier, with three volleys of shot.

22.

Upon the 22d of February we held a general day of Thanksgiving throughout the whole Colony for the safe arrival of the ship which came last with our provisions.

About this time we apprehended one Robert Wright, who had been sometimes a linen draper in Newgate market, and after that a brewer on the Bank side and on Thames street. This man we lately understood had made an escape in London from those who came to his house to apprehend him for clipping the King's coin [*one or two words wanting*] had stolen after us. Upon his examination he con-

[1] Winthrop, i. 45, calls him "a hopeful young gentleman, and an experienced soldier," and says that he died at Charlestown of a con-

sumption on the 18th. Perhaps his military funeral took place on the 18th.

fessed the fact, and his escape, but affirmed he had the King's pardon for it under the broad seal; which he yet not being able to prove, and one to whom he was known charging him with untruth in some of his answers, we therefore committed him to prison, to be sent by the next ship into England.[1]

Likewise we were lately informed that one Mr. Gardiner, who arrived here a month before us, and who had passed here for a knight, by the name of Sir Christopher Gardiner, all this while was no knight, but instead thereof had two wives now living in a house at London, one of which came about September last from Paris in France (where her husband had left her years before) to London, where she had heard her husband had married a second wife, and whom, by inquiring, she found out. And they both condoling each other's estate, wrote both their letters to the Governor, (by Mr. Peirce, who had conference with both the women in the presence of Mr. Allerton,[2] of Plymouth,) his first wife desiring his return and conversion, his second his destruction for his foul abuse, and for robbing her of her estate, of a part whereof she sent an inventory hither, comprising therein many rich jewels, much plate, and costly linen. This man had in his family (and yet hath) a gentlewoman, whom he called his kinswoman, and whom one of his wives in her letter names Mary

[1] At a Court of Assistants held at Boston, March 1, it was " ordered that Mr. Wright shall be sent prisoner into England by the ship Lion, now returning thither."
[2] Isaac Allerton was at this time in London, as an agent of the Plymouth Colony, from which office,

however, he was discharged the same year for acting contrary to their instructions. See an account of him in the Chronicles of Plymouth, note [1] on page 195. See also Prince's Annals, pp. 358 and 361, and Winthrop, i. 57.

CHAP.
XVII.

1631.
April
21.
Grove, affirming her to be a known harlot, whose sending back into Old England she also desired, together with her husband. Shortly after this intelligence, we sent to the house of the said Gardiner, (which was seven miles from us,) to apprehend him and his woman, with a purpose to send them both to London to his wives there. But the man, who having heard some rumor from some who came in the ship, that letters were come to the Governor requiring justice against him, was readily prepared for flight, so soon as he should see any crossing the river, or likely to apprehend him; which he accordingly performed. For he dwelling alone, easily discerned such who were sent to take him, half a mile before they approached his house; and, with his piece on his neck, went his way, as most men think, northwards, hoping to find some English there like to himself. But likely enough it is, which way soever he went, he will lose himself in the woods, and be stopped with some rivers in his passing, notwithstanding his compass in his pocket, and so with hunger and cold will perish before he find the place he seeks.[1]  His woman was brought unto us, and

---

[1] Winthrop says that " he travelled up and down among the Indians about a month ; but, by means of the Governor of Plymouth, he was taken by the Indians about Namasket, (Middleborough,) and brought to Plymouth, and from thence he was brought, by Capt. Underhill and his lieutenant, Dudley, May 4, to Boston." There seems to be a mystery hanging over Gardiner, as well as Morton of Merry Mount, which it is difficult to clear up. They appear to have had no definite object in view in coming to New- England, but seem actuated by a spirit of adventure and an unaccountable love of frolic. Morton says, that Gardiner " came into those parts, intending discovery." It is not unlikely, however, that they were both in the employment of Sir Ferdinando Gorges, who claimed a great part of the Bay of Massachusetts, and had been sent over as his agents or spies. We know that Gorges corresponded with them both, and by his intercepted letters it appears that he had some secret design to recover his pretended

confessed her name, and that her mother dwells CHAP.<br>XVII.
eight miles from Boirdly, in Salopshire, and that
Gardiner's father dwells in or near Gloucester, and 1631.
was (as she said) brother to Stephen Gardiner, Bishop of Winchester,[1] and did disinherit his son for his twenty-six years' absence in his travels in France, Italy, Germany, and Turkey ; that he had (as he told her) married a wife in his travels, from whom he was divorced, and the woman long since dead ; that both herself and Gardiner were Catholics till of late, but were now Protestants ; that she takes him to be a knight, but never heard when he was knighted. The woman was impenitent and close, confessing no more than was wrested from her by her own contradictions. So we have taken order to send her to the two wives in Old England, to search her further.

Upon the 8th of March, from after it was fair day- March<br>8.
light until about eight of the clock in the forenoon, there flew over all the towns in our plantations so many flocks of doves, each flock containing many thousands, and some so many that they obscured the light, that it passeth credit, if but the truth should be written ;[2] and the thing was the more strange,

---

right, and that he reposed much trust in Gardiner. On his return to England Gardiner was very active in coöperating with Gorges and Morton in their endeavours to injure the colonists, and deprive them of their patent. These attempts, however, were defeated by the friends of the Colony in England, especially Sir Richard Saltonstall, Mr. Humphrey, Mr. Cradock, and Emanuel Downing. See Winthrop, i. 54, 57, 100, 102, 106 ; Morton's Mem. p. 163 ; Prince, p. 352 ; Morton's New-English Canaan, book iii. ch. 30 ; Mass. Hist. Coll. xxviii. 320, 323.

[1] This story, says Farmer, was probably invented by the pretended knight, to raise him in the estimation of his paramour. Gardiner, the bishop of Winchester, was born 147 years before this examination, and had been dead 75 years. See New Hampshire Hist. Coll. iv. 245, and Harington's Nugæ Antiquæ, ii. 64.

[2] Gov. Winthrop, writing in 1643, says, " The pigeons came in flocks, above 10,000 in one flock." See note [2] on page 253, and Winthrop, ii. 94, 331.

CHAP.  because I scarce remember to have seen ten doves
XVII.
~~~~  since I came into the country.  They were all tur-
1631. tles, as appeared by divers of them we killed flying,
somewhat bigger than those of Europe, and they flew
from the north-east to the south-west ; but what it
portends, I know not.

March.   The ship now waits but for wind ;[1] which when it
blows, there are ready to go aboard therein for England, Sir Richard Saltonstall,[2] Mr. Sharpe, Mr. Cod-

[1] The ship, the Lion, was at Salem, whence she sailed April 1.
See Winthrop, i. 49, 52.

[2] SIR RICHARD SALTONSTALL,
one of the principal founders of the
Colony, was the son of Samuel Saltonstall, and grandson of Gilbert
Saltonstall, of Halifax, in the West
Riding of Yorkshire.  His uncle,
Sir Richard, was Lord Mayor of
London in 1597.  He married Grace,
daughter of Robert Kaye, Esq.,
who probably died before her husband came over to this country, as
we find no mention of her, although
her daughters came with their father.  He was the founder of Watertown, and the first member of the
church there.   Edward Johnson
says, " This town began by occasion of Sir Richard Saltonstall, who
at his arrival, having some store of
cattle and servants, they wintered in
those parts."  He remained in the
country less than a year, taking
home with him his two daughters
and one of his younger sons, and
leaving behind his two oldest sons,
Richard, the elder, being at this
time 20 years of age.  He still continued, however, to take a deep interest in the welfare of the Colony,
and befriended it essentially at home
against the machinations of its enemies.  He was also largely interested in the joint stock of the Company, and in June, 1635, sent over
a bark of 40 tons, with twenty servants, to plant at Connecticut, of
which Colony he was one of the patentees.  By his will it appears he

was living in 1658.  There is a fine
portrait of him in the possession of
one of his descendants in New York.
His eldest son, Richard, was born at
Woodsome, in Yorkshire, in 1610.
He was admitted to Emanuel College, Cambridge, in 1627, but left
without taking a degree, in order to
accompany his father to New-England.  He went to England in Nov.
1631, and married Mariel, daughter
of Brampton Gurdon, Esq., of As-
sington, in Suffolk, whence his
grandson, the Governor of Connecticut, got the name of Gurdon Saltonstall.   Richard settled at Ipswich, and was chosen an Assistant
in 1637.  He went to England again
in 1672, and returned in 1680.  He
visited England a third time in
1683, having three daughters married there, and died at Holme,
April 29, 1694, aged 84.  A long
line of his descendants has illustrated the name of Saltonstall down to
the present day, among whom not
the least eminent and worthy was
the late lamented Leverett Saltonstall, of Salem, Mayor of that city,
President of the Senate of Massachusetts, and a Representative in
the Congress of the United States,
who died May 8, 1845, in his 62d
year.  See Winthrop, i. 49, 161 ;
Hutchinson's Mass. i. 15, 332 ;
Mass. Hist. Coll. xii. 94, xiv. 154–
168, xviii. 42, xxviii. 249, 314,
xxix. 117–125 ; Francis's Hist. of
Watertown, pp. 14–17 ; Thoresby's
Hist. of Leeds, (ed. Whitaker,) ii.
236.

dington,[1] and many others; the most whereof pur- CHAP.
pose to return to us again, if God will. In the mean XVII.
time, we are left a people poor and contemptible, 1631.
yet such as trust in God, and are contented with March.
our condition, being well assured that he will not
fail us nor forsake us.

I had almost forgotten to add this, that the wheat
we received by this last ship stands us in thirteen
or fourteen shillings a strike, and the pease about
eleven shillings a strike,[2] besides the adventure,
which is worth three or four shillings a strike; which
is a higher price than I ever tasted bread of before.

Thus, Madam, I have, as I can, told your Honor
all our matters, knowing your wisdom can make good
use thereof. If I live not to perform the like office
of my duty hereafter, likely it is some other will do
it better.

Before the departure of the ship, (which yet was
wind-bound,) there came unto us sagamore John,[3]

---

[1] William Coddington, the father
of Rhode Island, was of Boston, in
Lincolnshire, "a godly man and of
good estate," according to Winthrop. He was chosen an Assistant
at Southampton March 18, 1629,
just before the sailing of the fleet.
In a letter to John Cotton, written
after his return to England, and
dated June 4, 1632, he says, "I am,
I thank God, in bodily health; yet
not enjoying that freedom of spirit,
being withheld from that place
which my soul desireth, and my
heart earnestly worketh after; neither, I think, shall I see it till
towards the next spring." He returned to New-England in May,
1633, bringing his second wife,
Mary, with him. The next year
he was chosen treasurer of the Colony. He was one of the founders
and principal merchants of Boston,

where he built the first brick house.
In 1637, in the Wheelwright and
Hutchinsonian controversy, he sided
with Vane and Cotton against Winthrop and Dudley, and on this account the people left him out of the
magistracy. In April of the next
year he left his advantageous situation at Boston, and his large property and improvements at Braintree,
and removed to Rhode Island, of
which he was several times chosen
Governor, dying in that office, Nov.
1, 1678, in his 78th year. Callender dedicated his Historical Discourse on Rhode Island, in 1739, to
his grandson, the Hon. William
Coddington. See Winthrop, i. 50,
102, 132, 220, 224, 265, 382;
Hutchinson, i. 24; Callender, 49–
53, 84, 96 (ed. 1838.)

[2] See Winthrop, i. 46.

[3] See note [4] on page 306.

CHAP.
XVII.
⌣

1631.
March.

8.

17.

and one of his subjects, requiring satisfaction for the burning of two wigwams by some of the English ; which wigwams were not inhabited, but stood in a place convenient for their shelter, when upon occasion they should travel that way. By examination we found that some English fowlers, having retired into that which belonged to the subject, and leaving a fire therein carelessly, which they had kindled to warm them, were the cause of burning thereof. For that which was the sagamore's, we could find no certain proof how it was fired ; yet, lest he should think us not sedulous enough to find it out, and so should depart discontentedly from us, we gave both him and his subject satisfaction for them both.[1]

The like accident of fire also befell Mr. Sharpe[2] and Mr. Colborne[3] upon the 17th of this March ; both whose houses (which were as good and as well furnished as the most in the Plantation,) were in two hours' space burned to the ground, together with much of their household stuff, apparel, and other things ; as also some goods of others who sojourned with them in their houses ; God so pleasing to exercise us with corrections of this kind, as he hath

---

[1] "At a Court at Watertown, March 8, it was ordered that Sir Richard Saltonstall (as the fire had been occasioned by his servant, James Woodward,) satisfy the Indians for the wrong done to them ; which accordingly he did by giving them seven yards of cloth." See Col. Rec., and Prince, p. 345.

[2] Thomas Sharpe was chosen an Assistant Oct. 29, at the same time Winthrop was chosen Governor. His name stands the sixth on the list of the Boston church members. He may have been a brother of Samuel Sharpe, the master-gunner,

mentioned on page 157. The death of his daughter and the loss of his house probably induced him to return to England. He never came back. See pp. 106, 127, and 327.

[3] William Colburn was admitted a freeman May 18, 1631. He was a gentleman of great influence in Boston, and was representative of the town in 1635 and the two succeeding years. He was long a ruling-elder of the first church, after ceasing to be deacon, and died August 1, 1662. See Savage's Winthrop, i. 37, ii. 361 ; Prince, pp. 321, 322.

done with others. For the prevention whereof in our new town,[1] intended this summer to be builded, we have ordered that no man there shall build his chimney with wood, nor cover his house with thatch; which was readily assented unto, for that divers other houses have been burned since our arrival, (the fire always beginning in the wooden chimneys,) and some English wigwams, which have taken fire in the roofs covered with thatch or boughs.

And that this ship might return into Old England with heavy news, upon the 18th day of March came one from Salem, and told us that upon the 15th thereof there died Mrs. Skelton,[2] the wife of the other minister there ; who, about eighteen or twenty days before, handling cold things in a sharp morning, put herself into a most violent fit of the wind colic and vomiting ; which continuing, she at length fell into a fever, and so died, as before. She was a godly and a helpful woman, and indeed the main pillar of her family, having left behind her a husband and four children, weak and helpless, who can scarce tell how to live without her. She lived desired, and died lamented, and well deserves to be honorably remembered.

Upon the 25th of this March, one of Watertown having lost a calf, and about ten of the clock at night

CHAP.
XVII.

1631.
March.

18.

25.

---

[1] Called Cambridge in 1638. See Winthrop, i. 265. According to the agreement, mentioned on page 320, Dudley, Bradstreet, and the principal persons in the Colony, proceeded the next spring to build their houses at Newtown. Winthrop set up the frame of his house on the spot where he first pitched his tent; and Dudley finished his house and removed his family there before winter. Winthrop, however, to fulfil a promise which he had made to the people of Boston, took down his frame and removed it to the peninsula. This was a great disappointment to the rest of the company, and caused a temporary coolness between the Governor and Deputy. See Hubbard, p. 136 ; Winthrop, i. 82 ; Prince, p. 363.

[2] See note [4] on page 142.

CHAP.
XVII.

.1631.
March
25.

28.

hearing the howling of some wolves not far off, raised many of his neighbours out of their beds, that, by discharging their muskets near about the place where he heard the wolves, he might so put the wolves to flight, and save his calf. The wind serving fit to carry the report of the muskets to Rocksbury, three miles off, at such a time, the inhabitants there took an alarm, beat up their drum, armed themselves, and sent in post to us to Boston, to raise us also. So in the morning, the calf being found safe, the wolves affrighted, and our danger past, we went merrily to breakfast.[1]

I thought to have ended before; but the stay of the ship, and my desire to inform your Honor of all I can, hath caused this addition; and every one having warning to prepare for the ship's departure tomorrow, I am now, this 28th of March, 1631, sealing my letters.[2]

---

[1] See Winthrop, i. 49.

[2] This Letter was sent by the Lion, Capt. Peirce, which sailed from Salem April 1, and arrived at London April 29. Wilson probably carried it. See Winthrop, i. 52.

DUDLEY'S LETTER, the most interesting as well as authentic document in our early annals, first appeared in print at Boston, in 1696, in a 16mo. volume of 56 pages, entitled "MASSACHUSETTS, or the First Planters of New-England, the mode and manner of their coming thither, and abode there: in several Epistles." It contained also The Humble Request, Allin and Shepard's Preface to their Defence of the Answer to the Nine Questions, and John Cotton's Preface, in Latin, to Norton's Answer to the Questions of Apollonius. It is not unlikely that it was printed at the suggestion of Joshua Scottow, who seems to

have been the earliest person in the Colony who had an antiquarian turn of mind, and who had already, in 1691 and 1694, published two works of his own, entitled "Old Men's Tears for their own Declensions, mixed with fears of their and posterity's further falling off from New-England's primitive constitution. Published by some of Boston's old Planters and some other," and "A Narrative of the Planting of the Massachusetts Colony, anno 1628; with the Lord's signal presence the first thirty years." Where Dudley's Letter had lain all this time, from 1631 to 1696, sixty-five years, and why it had never been printed before, either in England or this country, it is difficult to explain. In 1834, that indefatigable antiquary, John Farmer, of Concord, N. H., printed an enlarged copy of it in the fourth volume of the Collections of the New Hampshire Historical Society. In his Preface to it he says, " The copy of Gov. Dudley's Letter to the Countess of Lincoln, from which the following is printed, has lately been discovered in a manuscript, of the chirography of the beginning of the seventeenth century, and bound up with Johnson's Wonder-working Providence, and Winslow's New-England's Salamander Discovered, works printed more than 180 years since. It is valuable on account of its containing much more than the printed copy which was used by the Annalist, Mr. Prince. It is to be regretted that the first part of the manuscript is missing; how much, cannot be ascertained, but probably only a small part. The description of the bays and rivers is wanting, and a few lines giving some account of the Indians. It has been copied and compared with scrupulous care. There is good reason to believe that the original printed copy was made from this manuscript, just so much of it being marked as was printed, and having the printer's mark (thus ] ) for the end of the signature." Farmer's copy has been followed in printing this Letter.— For an account of Scottow, see Mass. Hist. Coll. xiv. 100–104.

# ROGER CLAP'S MEMOIRS.

"MEMOIRS of Capt. ROGER CLAP. *Relating* some of GOD's Remarkable Providences to *Him*, in bringing him into *New-England;* and some of the Straits and Afflictions, the *Good People* met with here in their Beginnings. And Instructing, Counselling, Directing and Commanding his Children and Children's Children, and Household, to serve the LORD in their Generations to the latest Posterity.— Heb. xi. 4. *He being dead, yet speaketh.*

"BOSTON *in New-England :* Printed by *B. Green,* 1731." 18mo. pp. **34.**

# CHAPTER XVIII.

CAPTAIN ROGER CLAP'S MEMOIRS.

I THOUGHT good, my dear children, to leave with
you some account of God's remarkable providences to me, in bringing me into this land, and placing me here among his dear servants, and in his house, who am most unworthy of the least of his mercies. The Scripture requireth us to tell God's wondrous works to our children, that they may tell them to their children, that God may have glory throughout all ages. Amen.

I was born in England, in Sallcom,[1] in Devonshire,
in the year of our Lord 1609. My father was a man fearing God, and in good esteem among God's faithful servants. His outward estate was not great, I think not above £80 per annum. We were five brethren, (of which I was the youngest,) and two sisters. God was graciously pleased to breathe by his holy spirit (I hope) in all our hearts, if in mine ;

---

[1] Salcombe Regis is near the seacoast, about 12 miles east of Exeter. Population in 1831, 448. See   Prince's Annals, p. 368, and Parl. Gazetteer.

CHAP.
XVIII. which I am not altogether without hopes of. Four
of us brethren lived at home. I did desire my dear
father (my dear mother being dead,) that I might
live abroad ; which he consented to. So I first went
for trial to live with a worthy gentleman, Mr. William Southcot, who lived about three miles from the
city of Exon.[1] He was careful to keep a godly family. There being but a very mean preacher in that
place, we went every Lord's day into the city, where
were many famous preachers of the word of God. I
then took such a liking unto the Rev. Mr. John Warham, that I did desire to live near him. So I removed (with my father's consent,) into the city, and
lived with one Mr. Mossiour, as famous a family for
religion as ever I knew. He kept seven or eight
men, and divers maid-servants ; and he had a conference upon a question propounded once a week in
his own family. With him I covenanted.

1629.    I never so much as heard of New-England until I
heard of many godly persons that were going there,
and that Mr. Warham was to go also. My master
asked me whether I would go. I told him, were I
not engaged unto him, I would willingly go. He
answered me, that should be no hindrance ; I might
go for him, or for myself, which I would. I then
wrote to my father, who lived about twelve miles off,
to entreat his leave to go to New-England ; who was
so much displeased at first that he wrote me no answer, but told my brethren that I should not go.
Having no answer, I went and made my request to

---

[1] Exeter, the capital of Devonshire, and the emporium and orna-
ment of the west of England, is 173
miles west by south of London. Its
population in 1831 was 28,201.

him ; and God so inclined his heart, that he never CHAP.
XVIII.
said me nay. For now God sent the reverend Mr.
Maverick, who lived forty miles off, a man I never 1630.
saw before. He having heard of me, came to my
father's house ; and my father agreed that I should
be with him and come under his care ; which I did
accordingly. So God brought me out of Plymouth
the 20th of March, in the year 1629–30, and landed March
me in health at Nantasket on the 30th of May, 1630, 20.
I being then about the age of twenty-one years.
Blessed be God that brought me here !

There came many godly families in that ship. We
were of passengers many in number, (besides seamen,) of good rank. Two of our magistrates came
with us, viz. Mr. Rossiter and Mr. Ludlow.[1] These
godly people resolved to live together ; and therefore, as they had made choice of those two reverend
servants of God, Mr. John Warham and Mr. John
Maverick, to be their ministers, so they kept a solemn day of fasting in the New Hospital in Plymouth,
in England, spending it in preaching and praying ;
where that worthy man of God, Mr. John White,[2] of
Dorchester, in Dorset, was present, and preached unto
us the word of God in the fore part of the day ; and
in the latter part of the day, as the people did solemnly make choice of and call those godly ministers to
be their officers, so also the reverend Mr. Warham[3]

[1] See pages 310 and 123.
[2] See note [1] on page 26.
[3] John Warham remained in the ministry at Dorchester till September, 1636, when he removed, with the greater part of his church, to Windsor in Connecticut, and formed the first settlement in that place, where he died April 1, 1670. The only facts mentioned concerning him are, that he was the first minister in New-England who used a manuscript in the pulpit, and that he was subject to fits of religious melancholy, so much so, that at times, when he had administered the communion to his people, he shrunk from partaking of it himself. Ful-

CHAP.
XVIII.

1630.

May
30.

and Mr. Maverick[1] did accept thereof, and expressed the same. So we came, by the good hand of the Lord, through the deeps comfortably, having preaching or expounding of the word of God every day for ten weeks together by our ministers.

When we came to Nantasket, Capt. Squeb, who was captain of that great ship of four hundred tons,[2] would not bring us into Charles river, as he was bound to do, but put us ashore and our goods on Nantasket Point, and left us to shift for ourselves in a forlorn place in this wilderness. But, as it pleased God, we got a boat of some old planters, and laded her with goods ; and some able men, well armed, went in her unto Charlestown, where we found some

---

ler, the Plymouth physician, in his letter to Gov. Bradford, dated June 28, 1630, says, "I have been at Mattapan, at the request of Mr. Warham. I had conference with them till I was weary. Mr. Warham holds that the visible church may consist of a mixed people, godly and openly ungodly ; upon which point we had all our conference, to which, I trust, the Lord will give a blessing." He lost his wife in 1634. His daughter Eunice married Rev. Eleazer Mather, son of Richard Mather, of Dorchester, and first minister of the church at Northampton ; and her only daughter, Eunice, was the wife of Rev. John Williams, of Deerfield, and was killed by the Indians and French under Hertel de Rouville, when that town was burnt, and her husband and children carried into captivity, in March, 1704. See Mather, i. 399 ; Winthrop, i. 385 ; Trumbull's Conn. i. 65, 467 ; Mass. Hist. Coll. iii. 74 ; Hoyt's Indian Wars, p. 186 ; Williams's Redeemed Captive, printed in 1706.

[1] John Maverick intended to accompany his church to Windsor, but was prevented by his death,

which occurred Feb. 3, 1636, in his 60th year. Winthrop says that "he was a man of a very humble spirit, and faithful in furthering the work of the Lord here, both in the churches and civil state." The only fact that he mentions about him is, his narrow escape one day from the explosion of a small barrel of gunpowder, some of which he was drying in a fire-pan in the new meeting-house in Dorchester ! See Winthrop, i. 72, 181.

Prince says, that "Mr. Maverick was the elder person ; that they had both been ministers in the Church of England, and had therefore been ordained by some bishop or other ; as none other in those days were allowed to preach in that kingdom, nor any separate congregation allowed there till the Civil Wars began in 1642. Nor would Mr. Maverick and Warham have been allowed to form a Congregational church at Plymouth in England, were it not of those who had taken their passage for New-England, and were just ready to sail hither." See Prince's Annals, p. 369.

[2] The Mary & John. See page 311.

wigwams and one house ;[1] and in the house there was a man which had a boiled bass, but no bread, that we see. But we did eat of his bass, and then went up Charles river, until the river grew narrow and shallow, and there we landed our goods with much labor and toil, the bank being steep ;[2] and night coming on, we were informed that there were hard by us three hundred Indians. One English-man, that could speak the Indian language, (an old planter,) went to them, and advised them not to come near us in the night ; and they hearkened to his counsel, and came not. I myself was one of the sentinels that first night. Our captain was a Low Country soldier, one Mr. Southcot,[3] a brave soldier. In the morning, some of the Indians came and stood at a distance off, looking at us, but came not near us. But when they had been a while in view, some of them came and held out a great bass towards us ; so we sent a man with a biscuit, and changed the cake for the bass. Afterwards, they supplied us with bass, exchanging a bass for a biscuit cake, and were very friendly unto us.

Oh, dear children ! forget not what care God had

---

[1] Probably the " English palisa-doed and thatched house," which the Spragues found on their arrival at Charlestown, " wherein lived Thomas Walford, a smith." See the Charlestown Records, in the next chapter of this volume.

[2] The place where they landed is supposed to be near the spot where the United States' Arsenal now stands. This part of Watertown was, till quite a recent period, called *Dorchester Fields*, and it is so called in the town records. See Francis's Hist. of Watertown, pp. 9, 10, and Holmes's Annals, i. 203.

[3] Capt. Richard Southcot was one of the first settlers at Dorchester. At a Court held July 26, 1631, " Capt. Southcot hath liberty to go for England, promising to return with all convenient speed." He probably never came back, as his name does not afterwards occur in our annals. Had he been here, this " brave Low Country soldier" would undoubtedly have been en-gaged in the Pequot War. See Winthrop, i. 57, ii. 361 ; Prince, p. 358 ; Blake's Annals of Dorches-ter, p. 10 ; Harris's Memorials of the First Church in Dorchester, p.64.

over his dear servants, to watch over us and protect
us in our weak beginnings. Capt. Squeb turned
ashore us and our goods, like a merciless man;[1] but
God, even our merciful God, took pity on us, so that
we were supplied first with a boat, and then caused
many Indians (some hundreds) to be ruled by the
advice of one man, not to come near us. Alas,
had they come upon us, how soon might they have
destroyed us! I think we were not above ten in
number. But God caused the Indians to help us
with fish at very cheap rates. We had not been
there many days, (although by our diligence we had
got up a kind of shelter to save our goods in,) but
we had order to come away from that place, which
was about Watertown, unto a place called Mattapan,
now Dorchester, because there was a neck[2] of land
fit to keep our cattle on. So we removed, and came
to Mattapan. The Indians there also were kind
unto us.

12.     Not long after came our renowned and blessed
Governor, and divers of his Assistants with him.
Their ships came into Charles river, and many passengers landed at Charlestown, many of whom died
the winter following. Governor Winthrop purposed
to set down his station about Cambridge, or some-

---

[1] Winthrop, in his Journal, under
June 17, says, "As we came home,
(from Charlestown to Salem,) we
came by Nantasket, and sent for
Capt. Squib ashore, and ended a
difference between him and the passengers," undoubtedly growing out
of his recent ill treatment of them ;
and Trumbull says that " Capt.
Squeb was afterwards obliged to
pay damages for this conduct."
This information he may have derived from some early document left
by the first settlers of Windsor, who
came in the ship. See Winthrop's
Hist. i. 28, and Trumbull's Connecticut, i. 23.

[2] This neck was called Dorchester Neck till it was annexed to the
metropolis in 1804, since which time
it has been called South Boston.
See Harris's History of Dorchester
in Mass. Hist. Coll. ix. 162, and
Snow's Hist. of Boston, p. 319.

where on the river; but viewing the place, liked CHAP.<br>XVIII. that plain neck, that was called then Blackstone's Neck, now Boston.[1] But in the mean time, before 1630. they could build at Boston, they lived many of them in tents and wigwams at Charlestown, their meeting-place being abroad under a tree, where I have heard Mr. Wilson and Mr. Phillips preach many a good sermon.

Now coming into this country, I found it a vacant wilderness, in respect of English. There were indeed some English at Plymouth and Salem, and some few at Charlestown,[2] who were very destitute when we came ashore; and planting time being past, shortly after provision was not to be had for money. I wrote to my friends, namely to my dear father, to send me some provision; which accordingly he did, and also gave order to one of his neighbours to supply me with what I needed, (he being a seaman;) who coming hither, supplied me with divers things. But before this supply came, yea, and after too, (that being spent, and the then unsubdued wilderness yielding little food,) many a time if I could have filled my belly, though with mean victuals, it would have been sweet unto me. Fish was a good help unto me and others. Bread was so very scarce, that sometimes I thought the very crusts of my father's table would have been very sweet unto me. And when I could have meal and water and salt boiled together, it was so good, who could wish better ?

In our beginning many were in great straits for

[1] See note [3] on page 169.

[2] These were probably the Spragues and their companions, who came from Salem to Charlestown the year previous.

CHAP. XVIII.

1630.

want of provision for themselves and their little ones. Oh the hunger that many suffered, and saw no hope in an eye of reason to be supplied, only by clams, and muscles, and fish. We did quickly build boats, and some went a fishing. But bread was with many a very scarce thing, and flesh of all kind as scarce. And in those days, in our straits, though I cannot say God sent a raven to feed us, as he did the prophet Elijah, yet this I can say, to the praise of God's glory, that he sent not only poor ravenous Indians, which came with their baskets of corn on their backs to trade with us, (which was a good supply unto many,) but also sent ships from Holland and from Ireland with provisions, and Indian corn from Virginia, to supply the wants[1] of his dear servants in this wilderness, both for food and raiment. And when people's wants were great, not only in one town but in divers towns, such was the godly wisdom, care, and prudence, (not selfishness, but

[1] Edward Johnson, an eye-witness, gives a graphic description of the scarcity of provisions among the first colonists. " In the absence of bread, they feasted themselves with fish. The women once a day, as the tide gave way, resorted to the muscle and clam banks, (which are a fish as big as horse-muscles,) where they daily gathered their families food. Quoth one, ' My husband hath travelled as far as Plymouth, (which is near forty miles,) and hath with great toil brought a little corn home with him ; and before that is spent, the Lord will assuredly provide.' Quoth the other, ' Our last peck of meal is now in the oven at home a baking, and many of our godly neighbours have quite spent all, and we owe one loaf of that little we have.' Then spake a third, ' My husband hath ventured himself among the Indians for corn, and can get none ; as also our honored Governor hath distributed his so far, that a day or two more will put an end to his store, and all the rest. And yet, methinks, our children are as cheerful, fat, and lusty, with feeding upon those muscles, clams, and other fish, as they were in England with their fill of bread ; which makes me cheerful in the Lord's providing for us ; being further confirmed by the exhortation of our pastor to trust the Lord with providing for us, whose is the earth and the fulness thereof.' And as they were encouraging one another, they lift up their eyes, and saw two ships coming in ; and presently this news came to their ears, that they were come from Ireland, full of victuals." See Mass. Hist. Coll. xiii. 125.

self-denial,) of our Governor Winthrop and his As- CHAP.<br>XVIII.
sistants, that when a ship came laden with provisions,
they did order that the whole cargo should be bought 1630.
for a general stock ; and so accordingly it was, and
distribution was made to every town, and to every
person in each town, as every man had need.[1]  Thus
God was pleased to care for his people in times of
straits, and to fill his servants with food and glad-
ness.  Then did all the servants of God bless his
holy name, and love one another with pure hearts
fervently.

In those days God did cause his people to trust in
him, and to be contented with mean things.  It was
not accounted a strange thing in those days to drink
water, and to eat samp or hominy without butter or
milk.  Indeed, it would have been a strange thing
to see a piece of roast beef, mutton, or veal ; though
it was not long before there was roast goat.  After
the first winter, we were very healthy, though some 1631.
of us had no great store of corn.  The Indians did
sometimes bring corn, and truck with us for clothing
and knives; and once I had a peck of corn, or thereabouts, for a little puppy-dog.  Frost-fish, muscles,
and clams were a relief to many.  If our provision
be better now than it was then, let us not, and do
you, dear children, take heed that you do not, forget
the Lord our God.  You have better food and raiment than was in former times ; but have you better
hearts than your forefathers had ?  If so, rejoice in

[1] Winthrop mentions the same
circumstance under April 12, 1636.
" The Charity, of Dartmouth, of 120
tons, arrived here laden with provisions.  Mr. Peter bought all the
provisions at fifty in the hundred,
(which saved the country £200,)
and distributed them to all the towns,
as each town needed."  See Winthrop, i. 185, 388.

that mercy, and let New-England then shout for joy.
Sure, all the people of God in other parts of the
world, that shall hear that the children and grand-
children of the first planters of New-England have
better hearts and are more heavenly than their predecessors, they will doubtless greatly rejoice, and
will say, "This is the generation whom the Lord
hath blessed."

I took notice of it as a great favor of God unto me,
not only to preserve my life, but to give me content-
edness in all these straits; insomuch that I do not
remember that ever I did wish in my heart that I had
not come into this country, or wish myself back again
to my father's house.  Yea, I was so far from that,
that I wished and advised some of my dear brethren
to come hither also; and accordingly one of my
brothers,[1] and those two that married my two sisters,
1633. sold their means and came hither.[2]  The Lord Jesus
Christ was so plainly held out in the preaching of
the Gospel unto poor lost sinners, and the absolute
necessity of the new birth, and God's holy spirit in
those days was pleased to accompany the word with
such efficacy upon the hearts of many, that our hearts
were taken off from Old England and set upon heaven.
The discourse not only of the aged, but of the youth
also, was not, "How shall we go to England?"
(though some few did not only so discourse, but also

---

[1] This was Edward, an elder brother, who came over in 1633, and
settled in Dorchester, where he
died, Jan. 8, 1664.
[2] There were three cousins of
Roger Clap, the sons of his uncle
Richard, who came to Dorchester.
Their names were Thomas, Nicholas, and John.  Nicholas married

for his first wife a sister of Roger
Clap, whose name was Sarah.
George Weeks married the other
sister.  Of the 35 voters of the name
of Clap now living in Dorchester,
all but one are descended from Nicholas.  See the Collections of the
Dorchester Antiquarian and Historical Society, No. 1, pp. vi.–xi. 62.

went back again,) but "How shall we go to heaven?
Have I true grace wrought in my heart? Have I
Christ or no?" O how did men and women, young
and old, pray for grace, beg for Christ in those days.
And it ,was not in vain.   Many were converted, and
others established in believing.   Many joined unto
the several churches where they lived, confessing
their faith publicly, and showing before all the assembly their experiences of the workings of God's
spirit in their hearts to bring them to Christ ; which
many hearers found very much good by, to help them
to try their own hearts, and to consider how it was
with them, whether any work of God's spirit were
wrought in their own hearts or no.   O the many
tears that have been shed in Dorchester meeting-
house at such times, both by those that have declared God's work on their souls, and also by those that
heard them.   In those days God, even our own God,
did bless New-England!

After God had brought me into this country, he
was pleased to give me room in the hearts of his servants ; so that I was admitted into the church fellowship at our first beginning in Dorchester, in the year
1630.

I now return to declare unto you some of the
wonderful works of God in bringing so many of his
faithful servants hither into this wilderness, and pre-
serving us and ours unto this day, notwithstanding
our great unworthiness, and notwithstanding the
many assaults and stratagems of Satan and his instruments against God's people here.   I say, *wondrous*
works.   For was it not a wondrous work of God, to
put it into the hearts of so many worthies to agree

together, when times were so bad in England that
they could not worship God after the due manner
prescribed in his most holy word, but they must be
imprisoned, excommunicated, &c., I say that so
many should agree to make humble suit unto our
sovereign lord the King to grant them and such as
they should approve of, a Patent of a tract of land in
this remote wilderness, a place not inhabited but by
very barbarous nations ? And was it not a wondrous
good hand of God to incline the heart of our King so
freely to grant it, with all the privileges which the
Patent expresseth ? And what a wondrous work of
God was it, to stir up such worthies to undertake such
a difficult work, as to remove themselves, and their
wives and children, from their native country, and to
leave their gallant situations there, to come into this
wilderness to set up the pure worship of God here ;
men fit for government in the magistracy and in
families, and sound, godly, learned men for the ministry, and others that were very precious men and
women, who came in the year 1630.

Those that came then were magistrates ; men of
renown were Mr. Winthrop, Governor, Mr. Dudley,
Deputy Governor, Sir Richard Saltonstall, Mr. Johnson, Mr. Rossiter, Mr. Ludlow, Mr. Nowel, and
Mr. Bradstreet. Mr. Endicott came before, and
others came then, besides those named. And there
came famous ministers in that year, and afterwards ;
as, to name some, Mr. Wilson, Mr. Warham, Mr.
Maverick, and Mr. Phillips. In our low estate God
did cheer our hearts in sending good and holy men
and women, and also famous preachers of the word
of God ; as Mr. Eliot, Mr. Weld, Mr. Cotton, Mr.

Hooker, Mr. Bulkley, Mr. Stone,[1] Mr, Nathaniel CHAP.<br>XVIII. Rogers, and Mr. Ezekiel Rogers, Mr. Shepard, Mr. Mather, Mr. Peters, Mr. Davenport, Mr. Whiting, 1630. Mr. Cobbet, Mr. Hubbard, Mr. Brown, Mr. Flint, Mr. Thomson, Mr. Newman, Mr. Prudden, Mr. Norris, Mr. Huit, Mr. Street, and many others.[2] Thus did God work wonderfully for his poor people here. Before I proceed any further, I will inform you that God stirred up his poor servants to use means in their beginning for their preservation ; though a low and weak people, yet a willing people to lay out their estates for the defence of themselves and others. They having friends in divers places who thought it best for our safety to build a fort upon the island now called Castle Island, at first they built a castle 1634.

---

[1] Stoughton in the first edition of 1731, and all subsequent ones ; but in the copy which I have, which belonged to Prince, the Annalist, and contains his notes and corrections, he has written *Stone* in the margin. There was no minister by the name of Stoughton among the colonists.

[2] John Wilson * was the minister of Boston ; John Warham, of Dorchester, and afterwards of Windsor, Conn. ; John Maverick, of Dorchester ; George Phillips,* of Watertown ; John Eliot* and Thomas Weld,* of Roxbury ; John Cotton,* of Boston ; Thomas Hooker* and Samuel Stone,* of Hartford, Conn.; Peter Bulkley,* of Concord ; Nathaniel Rogers,* of Ipswich ; Ezekiel Rogers,* of Rowley ; Thomas Shepard,* of Cambridge ; Richard Mather,† of Dorchester ; Hugh Peters,* of Salem ; John Davenport,† of New-Haven, Conn., and afterwards of Boston ; Samuel Whiting,* of Lynn ; Thomas Cobbett, of Lynn, and afterwards of Ipswich ; Peter Hobart,* of Hingham : Edmund Brown, of Sudbury ; Henry Flint and William Tomson,† of

Braintree ; Samuel Newman,† of Rehoboth ; Peter Prudden, of Milford, Conn. ; Edward Norris, of Salem ; Ephraim Huet, of Windsor, Conn. ; Nicholas Street, of Taunton, and afterwards of New-Haven, Conn. Of these ministers, twenty-seven in number, fourteen, (marked thus *,) had been educated and taken their degrees at the University of Cambridge, in England ; and four (marked thus †,) had studied at Oxford. Most of the ministers who came to New-England, besides those contained in this list, had been educated at one of the Universities. Of some of the above, an account has already been given, and of others due notice will be taken. The limits of these Notes, however, will not permit us to do justice to them all ; and the reader is therefore referred to Mather's third book of the Magnalia, i. 213, to Eliot's New-England, and Allen's American Biographical Dictionaries. See also Wood's Athenæ et Fasti Oxon. and Mass. Hist. Coll. xxviii. 247-250.

CHAP.
XVIII.

1634.

1645.

1665.
July
15.

Aug.
10.

with mud walls, which stood divers years. First, Capt. Simpkins was commander thereof; and after him Lieut. Monish for a little space. When the mud walls failed, it was built again with pine trees and earth; and Capt. Davenport was commander. When that decayed, which was within a little time, there was a small castle built with brick walls, and had three rooms in it, a dwelling room below, a lodging room over it, the gun room over that, wherein stood six very good saker guns, and over it, upon the top, three lesser guns. All the time of our weakness, God was pleased to give us peace, until the wars with the Dutch in Charles the Second's time. At that time our works were very weak, and intelligence came to us that De Ruyter, a Dutch commander of a squadron of ships, was in the West Indies, and did intend to visit us; whereupon our battery also was repaired, wherein are seven good guns. But in the very time of this report, in July, 1665, God was pleased to send a grievous storm of thunder and lightning, which did some hurt at Boston, and struck dead here at the Castle Island that worthy, renowned Captain, Richard Davenport.[1] Upon which the General Court, in August 10th following, appointed another Captain[2] in the room of him that was slain. But, behold! God wrought for us; for although De Ruyter intended to come here,

---

[1] Being fatigued with labor, he had lain down upon his bed to rest, the window of the castle being open against him. Three or four of the people were hurt, and a dog was killed at the gate. There was only a wainscot partition between the room where the captain was killed, and the powder magazine. No injury was done to the building. See Hubbard, p. 642, and Hutchinson's Mass. i. 253.

[2] This was Capt. Clap himself, as we learn from the following record: "At a General Court, begun August 1, 1665, this Court having considered of the want of a captain for the Castle, do nominate and appoint Capt. Roger Clap to be captain thereof." Col. Rec. iv. 551.

yet God by contrary winds kept him out; so he CHAP.<br>XVIII. went to Newfoundland, and did great spoil there. And again, when danger grew on us by reason 1673. of the late wars with Holland, God permitted our castle at that very time to be burnt down, which was on the 21st day of March, 1672–3.[1] But still March God was pleased to keep this place in safety. The 21. Lord enlarge our hearts unto thankfulness! I will now return unto what I began to hint unto you before ; namely, that Satan and his instruments did malign us, and oppose our godly preachers, say-

[1] The history of "THE CASTLE," from its commencement to the present time, deserves to be recorded, and there are abundant materials for it in the Court Records, at the State House. The limits of a Note, however, will not permit us to use them; and the topic, too, belongs more properly to the history of the metropolis. The first notice of it we find in Winthrop's Journal, under July 29, 1634 ; "The Governor and Council, and divers of the ministers, and others, met at Castle Island, and there agreed upon erecting two platforms, and one small fortification to secure them both ; and, for the present furtherance of it, they agreed to lay out £5 a man, till a rate might be made at the next General Court. The Deputy, Roger Ludlow, was chosen overseer." At the General Court, Sept. 3, it was " ordered, that there should be a platform made on the north-east side of Castle Island, and a house built on the top of the hill, to defend the said platform." Edward Johnson informs us, that " there was a castle on an island, upon the passage into the Mattachusetts Bay, wholly built at first by the country in general. But, by reason the country affords no lime but what is burnt of oyster shells, it fell to decay in a few years after. Hereupon (in 1644) the next six towns take upon them to rebuild it. The castle is built on the north-

east of the island, upon a rising hill. The commander of it is one Captain Davenport, a man approved for his faithfulness, courage, and skill. Although this castle hath cost about £4000, yet are not this poor pilgrim people weary of maintaining it in good repair." Edward Randolph, in his Narrative of the state of New-England in 1676, writes, " Three miles from Boston, upon a small island, there is a castle of stone lately built, and in good repair, with four bastions, and mounted with 38 guns, 16 whole culverin, commodiously seated upon a rising ground sixty paces from the water-side, under which, at high-water-mark, is a small stone battery of six guns. The present commander is one Capt. Clap, an old man ; his salary £50 per annum. There belong to it six gunners, each £10 per annum." In 1705, its name was changed to Castle William, and in 1799, the island having been previously ceded to the United States, it received the name of Fort Independence. When the substantial fortress now building on the site is completed, it is hoped that the ancient name, " THE CASTLE," will be restored. See Col. Rec. i. 122 ; Winthrop, i. 137, ii. 155, 243 ; Hutchinson's Massachusetts, i. 284 ; Hutchinson's State Papers, p. 486 ; Holmes's Annals, i. 493, ii. 412 ; Mass. Hist. Coll. xvii. 56.

ing they were legal preachers, but themselves were for free grace and for the teachings of the Spirit ; and they prevailed so by their flatteries and fair speeches, that they led away not only "silly women, laden with their lusts," but many men also, and some of strong parts too, who were not ashamed to give out that our ministers were but legal preachers, and so endeavoured to bring up an evil report upon our faithful preachers, that they themselves might be in high esteem ; and many of them would presume to preach in private houses, both men and women, much like the Quakers. They would talk of the Spirit, and of revelations by the Spirit without the Word, as the Quakers do talk of the Light within them, rejecting the holy Scriptures. But God, by his servants assembled in a Synod at Cambridge in 1637, did discover his truth most plainly, to the establishment of his people, and the changing of some, and to the recovery of not a few, which had been drawn away with their dissimulations. Thus God delivered his people out of the snare of the Devil at that time. Let us, and do you in your generations, bless the holy name of the Lord. " The snare is broken, and we and ours are delivered." There were some that not only stood out obstinate against the truth, but continually reviled both our godly ministers and magistrates, and greatly troubled our Israel. But, by order of the General Court, they were banished out of this jurisdiction ; and then had the churches rest, and were multiplied.[1]

---

[1] The best account of this whole affair will be found in the Rev. George E. Ellis's " Life of Anne Hutchinson, with a Sketch of the Antinomian Controversy in Massachusetts," in Sparks's Am. Biog. xvi. 167–376. The original authorities are there all enumerated.

Many years after this, Satan made another assault CHAP.<br>XVIII.
upon God's poor people here, by stirring up the
Quakers to come amongst us, both men and women; 1656.
who pretended holiness and perfection, saying they July.
spake and acted by the Spirit and Light within, which
(as they say) is their guide ; and most blasphemously
said that the Light within is the Christ, the Saviour,
and deceived many to their persuasion.  But, blessed
be God, the Government and Churches both did bear
witness against them, and their loathsome and perni-
cious doctrine ; for which they were banished out of
this jurisdiction, not to return without license, upon
pain of death.  The reason of that law was, because
God's people here could not worship the true and
living God, as He hath appointed us in our public
assemblies, without being disturbed by them ; and
other weighty reasons, as the dangerousness of their
opinions, &c.  Some of them presumed to return, to
the loss of their lives for breaking that law, which
was made for our peace and safety.[1]

Now as Satan has been a lying spirit to deceive
and ensnare the mind, to draw us from God by error,
so hath he stirred up evil men to seek the hurt of this
country.  But God hath delivered his poor people
here from time to time ; sometimes by putting courage into our magistrates to punish those that did re-
bel, and sometimes God hath wrought for us by his
providence other ways.  Here was one Ratcliff[2]

[1] For an account of the treatment
of the Quakers in Massachusetts,
see Hutchinson's Hist. of Massachusetts, i. 196–205 ; Grahame's
Hist. of the United States, i. 303–
312 ; Mather's Magnalia, ii. 451–
463 ; Norton's Heart of New-England Rent ; Bishop's New-England
Judged ; Sewell's History of the
Quakers, pp. 160, 171, 193–200.
[2] Philip Ratcliff was a servant of
Governor Cradock.  On his return to
England, he became, with Morton
and Gardiner, a violent enemy to

spake boldly and wickedly against the Government
and Governors here, using such words as some judged deserved death. He was for his wickedness
whipped, and had both his ears cut off in Boston,
A. D. 1631. I saw it done. There was one Morton,[1] that was a pestilent fellow, a troubler of the
country, who did not only seek our hurt here, but
went to England, and did his utmost there, by false
reports against our Governor ; but God wrought for
us, and saved us, and caused all his designs to be of
none effect. There arose up against us one Bull,[2] who
went to the eastward a trading, and turned pirate,
and took a vessel or two, and plundered some planters thereabouts, and intended to return into the Bay,
and do mischief to our magistrates here in Dorchester and other places. But, as they were weighing
anchor, one of Mr. Short's[3] men shot from the shore,
and struck the principal actor dead, and the rest
were filled with fear and horror. They having taken
one Anthony Dicks,[4] a master of a vessel, did endeavour to persuade him to pilot them unto Virginia ;
but he would not. They told him that they were
filled with such fear and horror, that they were afraid
of the very rattling of the ropes ; this Mr. Dicks told

the Colony. See Col. Rec. i. 86 ;
Savage's Winthrop, i. 56 ; Morton's
New-English Canaan, book iii. ch.
25 ; Mass. Hist. Coll. xxix. 244.

[1] See note [2] on page 321.

[2] See Winthrop, i. 79, 96, 104 ;
Hubbard, p. 160 ; Williamson's
Maine, i. 252.

[3] Abraham Shurte, or Shurd, or
Short, came over to the shores of
Maine as early as 1625, as the agent
of Gyles Elbridge and Robert Aldworth, in which year he purchased
the island of Monhegan for them,

and afterwards resided at their plan-
tation at Pemaquid. See Savage's
Winthrop, i. 61, 79, ii. 177 ; Wil-
liamson's History of Maine, i. 694 ;
Hazard's State Papers, i. 315 ;
Hutchinson's Coll. p. 114.

[4] Anthony Dix arrived at Plymouth in the Anne, in the summer
of 1623. In Dec. 1638, he was cast
away, in a bark of thirty tons, upon
the head of Cape Cod. See Chronicles of Plymouth, p. 352, and Winthrop, i. 287.

me with his own mouth.    These men fled eastward,
and Bull himself got into England; but God destroyed this wretched man.    There was also one Capt.
Stone,[1] about the year 1633 or 1634, who carried
himself very proudly, and spake contemptuously of
our magistrates, and carried it lewdly in his conversation.    For his misdemeanour, his ship was stayed;
but he fled, and would not obey authority ; and there
came warrants to Dorchester to take him dead or
alive.    So all our soldiers were in arms, and sentinels were set in divers places ; and at length he was
found in a great cornfield, where we took him and
carried him to Boston ; but for want of one witness,
when he came to his trial, he escaped with his life.
He was said to be a man of great relation, and had
great favor in England ; and he gave out threatening
speeches.    Though he escaped with his life, not being hanged for adultery, there being but one witness,
yet for other crimes he was fined, and payed it ;
and being dismissed, he went towards Virginia.
But by the way putting into the Pequot country, to
trade with them, the Pequots cut off both him and
his men, took his goods, and burnt his ship.    Some
of the Indians reported that they roasted him alive.
Thus did God destroy him that so proudly threatened to ruin us, by complaining against us when he
came to England.    Thus God destroyed him, and
delivered us at that time also.

About that time, or not long after, God permitted
Satan to stir up the Pequot Indians to kill divers

---

[1] The murder of this man, Capt.
John Stone, in 1633, by the Indians,
was one of the principal causes of
the Pequot War.    See Winthrop,
i. 104, 111, 122, 148.

CHAP.
XVIII.

1636.

Englishmen, as Mr. Oldham,[1] Mr. Tilly,[2] and others; and when the murderers were demanded, instead of delivering them, they proceeded to destroy more of our English about Connecticut ; which put us upon sending out soldiers, once and again, whom God prospered in their enterprises until the Pequot people were destroyed.[3] See Mr. Increase Mather's *Relation of the Troubles which have happened in New-England by reason of the Indians, from* 1634 *to* 1675. I say nothing to you of the late war,[4] but refer you to the histories in print. Thus was the Lord pleased to deliver us at that time also, and to put a fear and dread of us into the hearts of the Indians round about us ; and many of them did voluntarily put themselves under the government of the English.

1646.

It also pleased God to put it into the hearts of some of our worthies, to consider that one end of our coming hither was to preach the Gospel of our Lord Jesus Christ to the Indians,[5] for the saving of God's elect, and for the bringing into Christ's kingdom those that were as in highways and hedges. Some did therefore set themselves to learn the Indian language, and so taught them to know God and the Lord Jesus Christ, whom they never knew or heard of before, nor their fathers before them, and to know themselves, namely, their misery by nature and by reason of sin. Among others, the principal was that

---

[1] John Oldham. See note [1] on page 169.
[2] John Tilley. See Winthrop, i. 200.
[3] See note [2] on page 306.
[4] Philip's War, which broke out in June, 1675. See Hubbard's In-

dian Wars ; Increase Mather's Brief History ; Church's History of King Philip's War ; Mather's Magnalia, ii. 485–499 ; Callender's Hist. Disc. pp. 126–136 ; Grahame, i. 346–351.
[5] See note [2] on page 258.

reverend man of God, Mr. John Eliot,[1] teacher of the CHAP.<br>XVIII.
church of Christ at Roxbury ; whose great labor and
pains in catechising, preaching the word, and trans- 1646.
lating the Bible into the Indian language, God has
blessed, I doubt not, to the converting of many
among them. " He that converteth souls shall shine
as the sun in the firmament." O how glorious will
the shining of that star be in heaven ! I rejoice to
think of it.

Furthermore, know ye, that God wrought wonderfully for our preservation, when men abroad (and
doubtless some at home) endeavoured to overthrow
our government, and prevailed so far that Commissioners were sent from England hither with such 1665.

---

[1] John Eliot was born in 1604, about November, as Prince supposes. His birth-place is unknown. Cotton Mather says, " it was a town in England, the name whereof I cannot presently recover." He was educated at Jesus College, Cambridge, where he took the degree of A. B. in 1622. After leaving the University, he was for some time an assistant in a school kept by the Rev. Thomas Hooker, (afterwards of Hartford, Conn.) at Little Baddow, near Chelmsford, in Essex. But the tyranny of Laud, which drove Hooker into Holland, led Eliot to flee to America ; and he landed at Boston, Nov. 3, 1631. Wilson, the minister of the Boston church, being at this time absent in England, Eliot was invited to officiate in his place, which he did for a year, till Nov. 5, 1632, when he was established teacher of the church in Roxbury, where he continued till his death, May 20, 1690, at the advanced age of 86. Eliot is chiefly known for his indefatigable labors in preaching the Gospel to the natives, which obtained for him the deserved title of *The Apostle to the Indians*, and for his arduous work of translating the whole Bible into the language of the Massachusetts Indians. "Since the death of the Apostle Paul," says President Everett, " a nobler, truer and warmer spirit, than John Eliot, never lived ; and taking the state of the country, the narrowness of the means, the rudeness of the age, into consideration, the History of the Christian Church does not contain an example of resolute, untiring, successful labor, superior to that of translating the entire Scriptures into the language of the native tribes of Massachusetts ; a labor performed not in the flush of youth, nor within the luxurious abodes of academic ease, but under the constant burden of his duties as a minister and a preacher, and at a time of life when the spirits begin to flag." His wife's name was Anna, and his sons, John and Joseph, were ministers of Newtown, Mass., and Guildford, Conn. See note [2] on page 258 ; Winthrop, i. 64, 93, ii. 303–5 ; Mather, i. 474– 532 ; Prince, pp. 378, 408 ; Hutchinson, i. 162, 211 ; Grahame, i. 281– 88 ; Mass. Hist. Coll. viii. 5–35, xxviii. 248 ; Francis's Life of Eliot, in Sparks's Am. Biog. vol. 5.

CHAP.
XVIII.

1665.

power and authority that doubtless put themselves (and too many among us) in hopes that they had attained their ends. They proceeded so far that they set up a Court, appointed the time and place, and gave out their summons, yea, for our then honored Governor and Company personally to appear before them. But the Lord our God was for us, though troubles were very near. He stirred up a mighty spirit of prayer in the hearts of his people. This poor country cried, and the Lord heard, and delivered them from all their fears. And the Lord put wisdom and courage into the hearts of his servants, then sitting in the General Court, to give such Answers and to make such a Declaration, published by a man appointed, on horseback, with the trumpet sounding[1] before the Proclamation, to give the people notice that something was to be published, — which was done in three several places in Boston, — that it put an end to their Court, and (through God's goodness) to our troubles at that time about that matter.[2] And as our Court did assert our privileges granted unto us by Patent, and did adhere thereto, so our God hath hitherto continued the same unto us : Blessed be his glorious name ! I humbly beg of God that he will in mercy continue those privileges unto you and yours in your generations, for Jesus Christ's sake. *Amen.*[3]

[1] See Hutchinson's Mass. i. 246.
[2] See Hutchinson's Mass. i. 230–256, 535 ; Hutchinson's Coll. 390, 407–425 ; Chalmers's Annals, pp. 386–389 ; Grahame's Hist. United States, i. 331–342.
[3] Roger Clap was a prominent citizen of Dorchester, both in civil and military affairs, and was captain of Boston Castle from 1665 to 1686, in which year he removed to Boston. In the Records of the General Court, Oct 19, 1664, I find the following order . " The Court judgeth it meet to grant Capt. Roger Clap £4, to be paid him by the Treasurer for his service in laying out the southern line of our Patent." He

was married, Nov. 6, 1633, to Joanna Ford, of Dorchester, England, who, with her parents, came over in the same ship with himself. He died Feb. 2, 1691, in his 82d year, and was buried in King's Chapel grave-yard, where his grave-stone may still be seen. A full account of his children and descendants may be seen in the first number of the Collections of the Dorchester Hist. and Antiq. Society. The family of Clap is still among the most numerous and respectable families in that ancient town, and one of the name at least (Ebenezer Clapp, jr.) cherishes the memory of the fathers, and is imbued with the true antiquarian spirit.

In Prince's list of the manuscripts which he used in compiling his Annals, he mentions " Capt. Roger Clap's Account of the ancient affairs of the Massachusetts Colony." This he obtained from James Blake, jr., of Dorchester, and caused it to be printed in 1731. I happen to possess Prince's own copy of that edition, which contains his marginal corrections and annotations, and in which he has, by marks and numbers, reärranged the whole composition, so as to make the parts succeed each other in chronological order, which was not the case in the manuscript. This he seems to have done with reference to a new edition of the work. This arrangement I have adopted, it being a manifest and decided improvement. I have also omitted whatever is not of a historical character; since Clap's exhortations to his children, and his account of his religious experiences, though excellent in their way, do not fall within the plan of this work, and would swell the volume beyond its assigned limits. The Memoirs were probably written not long after 1676, for on page 364 the author speaks of "the late war," by which he means Philip's War, which broke out in 1675, and lasted about a year.

# THE CHARLESTOWN RECORDS.

# CHAPTER XIX.

## THE EARLY RECORDS OF CHARLESTOWN.

CAPTAIN JOHN SMITH, having (in the reign of our CHAP. XIX. sovereign lord, James, by the grace of God King of England, Scotland, France, and Ireland, Defender of 1614. the Faith,) made a discovery of some parts of America, lighted, amongst other places, upon the opening betwixt Cape Cod and Cape Ann, situate and lying in 315 degrees of longitude, and 42 degrees 20 minutes of north latitude ; where, by sounding and making up, he fell in amongst the islands, and advanced up into the Massachusetts Bay, till he came up into the river between *Mishawum*, (afterwards called Charlestown,) and *Shawmutt*, (afterwards called Boston ;) and having made discovery of the land, rivers, coves, and creeks in the said Bay, and also taken some observations of the natures, dispositions, and sundry customs of the numerous Indians, or natives, inhabiting the same, he returned to England ;[1]

[1] Captain Smith, in the summer of 1614, ranged along the coast of New-England, in a small boat, with eight or nine men, from the Penobscot to Cape Cod, and in 1616 published his Description of New-England, which is reprinted in Mass. Hist Coll. xxvi. 95–140. The map is prefixed to vol. xxiii. of the same Collections. See note [1] on page 19.

CHAP. where it was reported, that upon his arrival, he pre-
XIX.
~~~~ sented a map of the Massachusetts Bay to the King,
1614. and that the Prince, (afterwards King Charles the
First,) upon inquiry and perusal of the foresaid river,
and the situation thereof upon the map, appointed it
to be called Charles river.

Now upon the fame that then went abroad of the
place, both in England and Holland, several persons
of quality sent over some at their own cost, who
planted this country in several parts; but for want
of judgment, care, and orderly living, divers died.
Others, meeting with many hazards, hardships, and
wants, at length being reduced to great penury and
extremity, were so tired out, that they took all
opportunities of returning to England; upon which
several places were altogether deserted, and left.
Only some few that, upon a better principle, transported themselves from England and Holland, came
1620. and settled their Plantation a little within Cape Cod,
and called the same Plymouth, notwithstanding all
their wants, hazards, and sufferings, continued several years in a manner alone; at which time this
country was generally called by the name of New-
England.

At length, divers gentlemen and merchants of
London obtained a patent and charter for the Massachusetts Bay, from our sovereign lord King Charles
the First, gave invitation to [such] as would transport themselves from Old England to New-England,
to go and possess the same; and for their encouragement, the said patentees, at their own cost, sent
over a company of servants under the government of
Mr. John Endicott; who, arriving within this Bay,

settled the first Plantation of this jurisdiction, called CHAP.
Salem; under whose wing there were a few also that
[did] settle and plant up and down, scattering in 1628.
several places of the Bay; where, though they met
with the dangers, difficulties, and [wants] attending
new plantations in a solitary wilderness, and so far
remote from their native country, yet were they not
long without company ; for in the year of our Lord
one thousand six hundred twenty-eight, came over
from England several people at their own charge,
and arrived at Salem. After which, people came
over yearly in great numbers; in [*torn off*] years
many hundreds arrived, and settled not only in the
Massachusetts Bay, but did suddenly spread themselves into other colonies also.

Amongst others that arrived at Salem at their own
cost, were Ralph Sprague,[1] with his brethren, Richard[2] and William,[3] who, with three or four more, by
joint consent and approbation of Mr. John Endicott,

[1] Ralph Sprague was the eldest
of the three brothers, and by occupation a farmer. Their father, Edward Sprague, is said to have been
a fuller, of Upway, in Dorsetshire,
England. Ralph is supposed to
have been about 25 years old when
he came to this country. He was a
prominent and useful man in Charlestown, one of the founders of the
church there in 1632, one of the selectmen several years, in 1630 the
first constable, in 1639 lieutenant,
and a representative in 1637, and
eight times afterwards. He died in
1650, leaving a widow, Joanna, four
sons, and a daughter. In 1639, the
General Court granted him 100 acres
of land, " he having borne difficulties in the beginning." See Frothingham's Charlestown, p. 21 ; Budington, pp. 33, 184.

[2] Richard Sprague was a merchant. He was one of the founders
of the church in Charlestown in
1632, a selectman several years,
and a representative of the town
from 1659 to 1666. He died Nov.
25, 1668, leaving a widow, Mary,
but no children. See Frothingham,
p. 22 ; Budington, pp. 33, 184.
[3] William Sprague was the youngest of the three brothers. In 1636
he removed to Hingham, where he
died Oct. 26, 1675, leaving a widow,
Millesaint, and eleven children. The
Spragues of Bridgewater are descended from him. See Frothingham, p. 22 ; Lincoln's History of
Hingham, p. 45 ; Mitchell's History
of Bridgewater, p. 306 ; Hosea
Sprague's Genealogy of the Sprague
family.

CHAP.
XIX.
1628.

Governor, did, the same summer of anno 1628, undertake a journey from Salem, and travelled the woods above twelve miles to the westward, and lighted of a place situate and lying on the north side of Charles river, full of Indians, called Aberginians.[1] Their old sachem being dead, his eldest son, by the English called John Sagamore,[2] was their chief, and a man naturally of a gentle and good disposition ; by whose free consent they settled about the hill of the same place, by the said natives called *Mishawum ;* where they found but one English palisadoed and thatched house,[3] wherein lived Thomas Walford,[4] a smith, situate on the south end of the westernmost hill of the East Field, a little way up from Charles river's side ;[5] and upon surveying, they found it was a neck of land, generally full of stately timber, as was the main, and the land lying on the east side of the river called Mistick river, (from the farm Mr. Craddock's[6] servants had planted, called Mistick, which this river led up unto ;) and indeed generally

---

[1] "The Abarginny men," says Edward Johnson, "consisted of the Massachusetts, Wippanaps, and Tarratines." See Mass. Hist. Coll. xii. 66.

[2] See note [4] on page 306.

[3] See page 349.

[4] How or when Walford came to Mishawum, is unknown. He probably remained there but a few years ; for, at a General Court held April 12, 1631, "Thomas Walford, of Charlton, is fined 40s., and is enjoined, he and his wife, to depart out of the limits of this Patent before the 20th day of October next, under pain of confiscation of his goods, for his contempt of authority and confronting officers, &c." A month afterwards, he was fined £2, which

"he paid by killing a wolf." He removed to Piscataqua ; but still seems to have been an object of distrust, for, Sept. 3, 1633, " it is ordered that the goods of Thomas Walford shall be sequestered and remain in the hands of Ancient Gennison, to satisfy the debts he owes in the Bay to several persons." He died in 1657. See Col. Rec. i. 71 ; Savage's Winthrop, i. 53 ; Belknap's New-Hampshire, pp. 28, 57, (Farmer's ed.) ; Adams's Annals of Portsmouth, pp. 18, 394 ; Frothingham, pp. 23, 84.

[5] Probably on the south side of Breed's Hill, a short distance from the water. See Frothingham, p. 24.

[6] See note [2] on page 137.

all the country round about was an uncouth wilder-  CHAP.
ness, full of timber.

The inhabitants that first settled in this place, and
brought it into the denomination of an English town,
were in anno 1628 as follows, viz., Ralph Sprague ;
Richard Sprague ; William Sprague ; John Meech ;[1]
Simon Hoyte ;[1] Abraham Palmer ;[2] Walter Palmer ;
Nicholas Stowers ;[3] John Stickline ;[1] Thomas Walford, smith, that lived here alone before ; Mr. [blank]
Graves,[4] who had charge of some of the servants of
the Company of Patentees, with whom he built the
great house[5] this year, for such of the said Company

---

[1] Of John Meech, Simon Hoyt, and John Stickline, or Stickland, nothing is known except that the two last were admitted freemen May 18, 1631. See Winthrop, ii. 361, 362.

[2] Abraham Palmer was a merchant, and a member of the Company in England. He was one of the fourteen who signed the instructions to Endicott, May 30, 1628, and in the same month he adventured £50 in the joint stock. He probably embarked with Higginson, and came to Charlestown with Graves, in 1629. He was an active and influential citizen, and filled the offices of town clerk and selectman. He was one of the two deputies from Charlestown at the first General Court held in 1634, and five times afterwards. He was a sergeant in the Pequot War, and did good service in the swamp fight. He removed to Barbadoes, where he died about 1653, leaving a widow, named Grace. See note [2] on page 174 ; Hutchinson's Mass. i. 9 ; Mass. Hist. Coll. xv. 122, xviii. 146 ; Frothingham's Charlestown, p. 22.

[3] Nicholas Stowers was herdsman in 1633. His duties were "to drive the herd forth to their food in the main every morning, and to

bring them into town every evening, and to have fifty bushels of Indian corn for keeping the milch cows till Indian harvest be taken in." He died May 17, 1646, leaving a widow, Amy, and five children. See Frothingham, p. 23.

[4] See note [2] on page 152.

[5] "April, 1633. Agreed and concluded by the inhabitants, that the sum of £10 be collected of the said inhabitants, and be paid to John Winthrop, Esq., Governor, and the rest of the gentlemen interested in the great house built in anno 1628, by Mr. Graves and the Company's servants ; which is for the purchase of the said house, now the public meeting-house in this town ; all which was accordingly done." It continued to be used as a place of public worship till 1636, when a new church was built " between the town and the neck." The great house was afterwards used as a tavern, or ordinary, and in 1711 was called " The Great Tavern." It was probably destroyed when the town was burnt by the British, June 17, 1775. It stood wholly in the Square, opposite the lane by the " Mansion House." See Frothingham, p. 96 ; Budington, pp. 35, 195.

CHAP.
XIX.
1629.
as are shortly to come over,[1] which afterwards became the meeting-house ; and Mr. [blank] Bright,[2] minister to the Company's servants.

By whom it was jointly agreed and concluded, that this place on the north side of Charles river, by the natives called *Mishawum*, shall henceforth, from the name of the river, be called Charlestown; which was also confirmed by Mr. John Endicott, Governor.

It is jointly agreed and concluded by the inhabitants of this town, that Mr. [blank] Graves do model and lay out the form of the town, with streets about the Hill ; which was accordingly done, and approved of by the Governor.

It is jointly agreed and concluded, that each inhabitant have a two acre lot to plant upon, and all to fence in common ; which was accordingly by Mr. [blank] Graves measured out unto them.

Upon which, Ralph Sprague and others began to build their houses, and to prepare fencing for their lots, which was afterwards set up almost in a semicircular[3] form on the south and south-east side of that field laid out to them, which lies situate on the north-west side of the Town Hill.[4]

---

[1] " The Charlestown Records here mistake in placing this in 1628; for Mr. Graves comes not over till 1629. And as by Deputy Governor Dudley's Letter (p. 319,) there was a great mortality among the English at the Massachusetts Colony, in the winter of 1629–30, so by Capt. Clap's account, (p. 349,) there was but one house and some few English at Charlestown in June succeeding." Prince, p. 261.

[2] Francis Bright. See note [3] on page 316.

[3] Hence the street on which these houses were built is called Bow-street.

[4] The Town Hill has been much reduced in height since the first settlement. In 1646 it was ordered that it " should lie common to the town forever," and in 1648, that " no more gravel should be digged or fetched from it." Yet in 1782 large quantities of gravel were taken from it. See Frothingham, p. 94, and Mass. Hist. Coll. xii. 168.

Walter Palmer[1] and one or two more shortly after began to build in a straight line upon their two acre lots on the east side of the Town Hill,[2] and set up a slight fence in common, that ran up to Thomas Walford's fence ; and this was the beginning of the East Field.

About the months of April and May, in the year of our Lord 1629, there was a great design of the Indians, from the Narragansetts, and all round about us to the eastward in all parts, to cut off the English ; which John Sagamore, who always loved the English, revealed to the inhabitants of this town. But their design was chiefly laid against Plymouth, (not regarding our paucity in the Bay,) to be effected under pretence of having some sport and pastime at Plymouth ; where, after some discourse with the Governor there, they told him, if they might not come with leave, they would without. Upon which the said Governor sent their flat-bottomed boat (which was all they had,) to Salem, for some powder and shot. At which time it was unanimously concluded by the inhabitants of this town, that a small fort should be made on the top of this Town Hill, with palisadoes and flankers made out ; which was performed at the direction of Mr. [blank] Graves, by all hands of men, women and children, who wrought at digging and building till the work was done. But that design of the Indians was suddenly broke up, by

---

[1] Walter Palmer, probably a brother of Abraham, removed soon after 1642 to Rehoboth, of which town he was one of the first settlers, and there died, about 1662, leaving eleven children. One of them, John, probably the eldest, remained in Charlestown. See Frothingham, p. 23, and Bliss's Rehoboth, p. 70.

[2] On the east side of Main-street.

the report of the great guns at Salem, only shot off
to clear them ; by which means they were so fright-
ed, that all their companies scattered and ran away ;
and though they came flattering afterwards, and called themselves our good friends, yet were we constrained by their conspiracies yearly to be in arms.[1]

In the months of June and July, 1629, arrived at
this town, John Winthrop, Esq. Governor, Sir Richard Saltonstall, knight, Mr. Johnson, Mr. Dudley,
Mr. Ludlow, Mr. Nowell, Mr. Pincheon, Mr. Broadstreet ; who brought along with them the charter or
patent for this jurisdiction of the Massachusetts Bay ;
with whom also arrived Mr. John Wilson and Mr.
[blank] Phillips, ministers, and a multitude of people,
amounting to about fifteen hundred, brought over
from England in twelve ships.[2]  The Governor and
several of the Patentees dwelt in the great house,
which was last year built in this town by Mr. Graves
and the rest of their servants.

The multitude set up cottages, booths and tents
about the Town Hill.  They had long passage ; some
of the ships were seventeen, some eighteen weeks
a coming.  Many people arrived sick of the scurvy,
which also increased much after their arrival, for
want of houses, and by reason of wet lodging in their
cottages, &c.  Other distempers also prevailed ; and
although [the] people were generally very loving
and pitiful, yet the sickness did so prevail, that the
whole were not able to tend the sick, as they should

[1] There is no account of this Indian conspiracy in Morton's Memorial, or anywhere else.  As Graves
did not come over till June, 1629, it
must have occurred, if it occurred at
all, in the next year, 1630.  See
Prince, p. 277.
[2] See note [2] on page 311.

be tended ; upon which many perished and died,[1] CHAP·
and were buried about the Town Hill.  By which XIX.
means [the] provisions were exceedingly wasted, 1630.
and no supplies could now be expected by planting. July.
Besides, there was miserable damage and spoil of
provisions by sea, and divers came not so well provided as they would, upon a report, whilst they were
in England, that now there was enough in New-England.  And unto all this there [*some few words missing*]
[and yet some imprudently selling much of the remainder[2]] to the Indians for beaver.  All which
being taken into consideration by the Governor and
gentlemen, they hired and despatched away Mr.
William Pearce, with his ship, of about two hundred
tons, for Ireland, to buy more ;[3] and in the mean
time went on with their work for settling.  In order
to which they, with Mr. John Wilson, one of the
ministers, did gather a church, and chose the said 30.
Mr. Wilson pastor ;  the greatest number all this
time intending nothing more than settling in this
town ; for which the Governor ordered his house to
be cut and framed here.  But the weather being hot,
many sick, and others faint after their long voyage,
people grew discontented for want of water, who
generally notioned no water good for a town but
running springs.[4]  And though this neck do abound
with good water, yet, for want of experience and

---

[1] See pages 314, 319, and 325.
[2] The words enclosed in [  ] are
obliterated in the MS., being at the
bottom of a page ; but restored from
Prince, p. 313, who copied from the
original.
[3] See pages 315 and 340.
[4] This same prejudice about running water was one of the reasons
offered Dec. 14, 1630, which decided the question in the negative
about building a fortified town on
the neck between Boston and Roxbury. See Savage's Winthrop, i.
38, and Chronicles of Plymouth,
note [4] on page 129.

CHAP.
XIX.

1630.
July.

industry, none could then be found to suit the humor of that time, but a brackish spring in the sands, by the water side,[1] on the west side of the North-west Field,[2] which could not supply half the necessities of the multitude; at which time the death of so many was concluded to be much the more occasioned by this want of good water.[3]

This caused several to go abroad upon discovery. Some went without the neck of this town, who travelled up into the main till they came to a place well watered; whither Sir Richard Saltonstall, knight, and Mr. [blank] Phillips, minister, went with several others, and settled a plantation, and called it Watertown. Others went on the other side of Charles river, and there travelled up into the country, and likewise finding good waters, settled there with Mr. Ludlow, and called the plantation Dorchester; whither went Mr. [blank] Maverick and Mr. [blank] Warham, who were their ministers.

In the mean time Mr. [blank] Blackstone,[4] dwelling on the other side Charles river alone, at a place

[1] This spring is supposed to have been not far from the site of the Winthrop Church, on the shore, to the south of the State's Prison. See Mass. Hist. Coll. xii. 165, and Frothingham's Charlestown, p. 31.

[2] The north-west field was in the vicinity of Washington-street.

[3] Edward Johnson, one of the sufferers, tells us, "The grief of this people was further increased by the sore sickness which befell among them, so that almost in every family lamentation, mourning, and wo was heard; and no fresh food to be had to cherish them. It would assuredly have moved the most locked-up affections to tears, no doubt, had they passed from one hut to another, and

beheld the piteous case these people were in. And that which added to their present distress, was the want of fresh water. For although the place did afford plenty, yet, for the present, they could find but one spring, and that not to be come at but when the tide was down; which caused many to pass over to the south side of the river, where they afterwards erected some other towns, and in October the Governor, Deputy, and Assistants, held their second Court, on the south side of the river, where they began to build, holding correspondency with Charlestown, as one and the same." See Mass. Hist. Coll. xii. 87.

[4] See note [3] on page 169.

by the Indians called *Shawmutt*, where he only had CHAP.
a cottage, at or not far off the place called Black- XIX.
stone's Point, he came and acquainted the Governor 1630.
of an excellent spring there ; withal inviting him
and soliciting him thither. Whereupon, after the
death of Mr. Johnson[1] and divers others, the Gov- Sept.
ernor, with Mr. Wilson and the greatest part of the 30.
church, removed thither ; whither also the frame of
the Governor's house, in preparation at this town,
was also (to the discontent of some,) carried ;[2] where
people began to build their houses against winter ;
and this place was called Boston.

After these things Mr. [blank] Pincheon and several others planted betwixt Boston and Dorchester ;
which place was called Roxbury.

Now after all this, the Indians' treachery being
feared, it was judged meet the English should place
their towns as near together as could be. For which
end Mr. Dudley and Mr. Broadstreet, with some
others, went and built and planted between Charlestown and Waterton ; who called it Newtown, which
was afterwards called Cambridge.[3]

Others issued out to a place between Charlestown
and Salem, called Saugust, since ordered to be called Linn.[4]

And thus, by reason of discouragements and difficulties, that strangers in a wilderness at first meet

---

[1] Isaac Johnson died Sept. 30. See note [3] on page 317.

[2] A similar dissatisfaction was felt when Winthrop removed the frame of his house from Newtown (Cambridge) to Boston, in 1632. See page 339, and Winthrop, i. 82.

[3] In 1638, out of regard to the place where so many of their minis-

ters and magistrates had been educated. See note [2] on page 357, and Winthrop, i. 265.

[4] So called in 1636, out of compliment, no doubt, to the Rev. Samuel Whiting, the minister of the place, who had been a preacher at Lynn Regis, in Norfolk, England. See Winthrop, i. 204.

CHAP.
XIX.
———
1630.

withal, though as to some things but supposed, as in this case people might have found water abundant in this town, and needed not to have perished for want, or wandered to other places for relief, would they but have looked after it. But this, attended with other circumstances, the wisdom of God made use of as a means for spreading his Gospel and peopling of this great and then terrible wilderness ; and this sudden spreading into several townships came to be of far better use for the entertainment of so many hundreds of people, that came for several years following hither in such multitudes from most parts of Old England, than if they had now remained all together in this town.

But after their departure from this town to the peopling and planting of the towns aforesaid, and in particular of the removal of the Governor, and the greatest part of our new gathered church, with the pastor, to Boston, the few inhabitants of this town remaining were constrained, for three[1] years after, generally to go to Boston on the Lord's day to hear the word and enjoy the sacraments, before they could be otherwise supplied.

A list of the names of such as stayed and became inhabitants of this town in this year 1629, as follows :

Increase Nowell, Esq.;[2] Mr. William Aspinwall ;[3]

---

[1] It was only *two* years ; for the Charlestown church was gathered and the covenant entered into, Nov. 2, 1632. See Budington's Hist. of First Church in Charlestown, pages 21 and 183 ; and Frothingham's Hist. of Charlestown, p. 70.

[2] See note [2] on page 262.

[3] William Aspinwall afterwards removed to Boston. Taking an active part in the Antinomian controversy, and having written the petition to the General Court in favor of Wheelwright, in 1637, he was disfranchised, disarmed, and banished. Whereupon he retired, with Coddington and others, to Rhode Island, and was the first Secretary of that

Mr. Richard Palsgrave;[1] Edward Convers;[2] William Penn;[3] William Hudson;[4] Mr. John Glover;[5] William Brackenburry;[6] Rice Cole;[7] Hugh Garrett; Ezekiel Richeson;[8] John Baker;[9] John Sales;[10] Capt. [blank] Norton;[11] Mr. Edward Gibbons;[12] Mr. William Jennings; John Wignall; these four went and built in the main, on the north-east side of the north-west creek of this town.

Colony. In 1642 he returned to Boston, tendered his submission, and was reconciled to the Church and State. He afterwards went to England, where he died. See Savage's Winthrop, i. 33, 245, 248, ii. 62; Callender's Rhode Island, p. 84.

[1] Richard Palsgrave was the first physician in Charlestown. He came from Stepney, in the county of Middlesex, in England, and died about 1656, leaving a widow, Anne, who removed to Roxbury. See Frothingham, p. 78.

[2] Edward Converse was the first ferryman between Boston and Charlestown, and one of the first settlers of Woburn, whither he removed as early as 1643, and which town he represented in 1660. He died Aug. 6, 1663, leaving a widow, Sarah, and three sons and two daughters. See Winthrop, ii. 349, and Frothingham, p. 78.

[3] I find no such name as William Penn among the colonists. It is probably an error for James Penn, who was chosen Aug. 23, 1630, "as a beadle, to attend upon the Governor, and always to be ready to execute his commands in public business." He was a ruling elder, a representative in 1648, and a leading man in the church and commonwealth. He died Sept. 30, 1671. See Col. Rec.; Winthrop, ii. 213, 216, 348; Prince, p. 404; Hutchinson's Mass. i. 269.

[4] William Hudson removed to Boston about 1640, and in 1643 returned to England, and engaged in

military service on the Parliament's side. See Snow's Boston, p. 108; Frothingham, p. 78.

[5] John Glover removed to Dorchester, where he became a prominent man, was a selectman, a captain, a representative in 1637, and an Assistant in 1652. Edward Johnson calls him "a man strong for the truth, a plain, sincere, godly man, and of good abilities." He died in Jan. 1654. See Winthrop, i. 46, 212; Mass. Hist. Coll. xiv. 24.

[6] William Brackenbury was a baker, and one of the principal men of Malden, and died in Aug. 1668, aged 66.

[7] Rise Coles was admitted a freeman April 1, 1633, and died May 15, 1646.

[8] Ezekiel Richardson was one of the first settlers of Woburn, and there died Oct. 28, 1647.

[9] John Baker was a tailor, and removed from Charlestown in 1637.

[10] John Sales enjoys the unenviable reputation of having been "the first known thief that was notoriously observed in the country." See page 385.

[11] He was killed by the Pequots in 1633. See Winthrop, i. 123.

[12] Edward Gibbons, according to Scottow, "being the younger brother of the house, of an honorable extract, and his ambition exceeding what he could expect at home, he rambled hither." He was originally one of Wollaston's plantation, and a young gentleman "of a jocund

CHAP.
XIX.

1630.

Agreed and concluded by the inhabitants of this town, that the great corn-field shall be on the east side of the Town Hill; the fence to range along even with those dwellings[1] where Walter Palmer's house stands, and so along towards the neck of land; and that to every inhabitant dwelling within the neck, be given two acres of land for a house-plot, and two acres for every male that is able to plant. But in consideration of the greatness of the charge in fencing down to the neck of land, it is concluded, that that be suspended at present, and that only a cross fence be drawn at the neck of land from Misticke river to the water on the west of the neck; which, being computed, ariseth to one pole and two foot an acre for so many acres as are at present allotted; and that the cattle be kept without upon the main.

But now, as the winter came on, provisions began

temper;" but being at Salem in August, 1629, when the church was gathered and the ministers ordained, he was so much affected by the solemnities, that he requested to be admitted to their fellowship. This request, however, was prudently declined on the ground of his being a stranger. He was soon afterwards admitted to the Boston church. Winthrop mentions Gibbons's " farm at Pullen Point;" and Edward Johnson, describing the country as it appeared in 1630, says, " about one mile distant, (from Noddle's island,) upon the river, (Charles,) ran a small creek, taking its name from major general Edward Gibbons, who dwelt there for some time after." He represented Charlestown in the General Court in 1635 and 1636; soon after which he removed to Boston, and became largely engaged in trade and navigation. He lost £2500 when La Tour's fort at St. John's was taken by D'Aulney in 1645, by which loss, says Winthrop, he was quite undone. He was chosen an Assistant in 1650, and was major general of all the forces from 1649 to 1651. Johnson, who knew him, and was himself a soldier, speaks of him as " a man of a resolute spirit, bold as a lion, being wholly tutored up in New-England discipline, very generous, and forward to promote all military matters." He died Dec. 9, 1654, leaving two sons, Jotham and John, who were born in Boston in 1633 and 1641. See Savage's Winthrop, i. 192, ii. 60, 238; Mather, i. 329; Scottow's Narrative, p. 10; Hutchinson's Mass. i. 135, 160; Mass. Hist. Coll. xii. 86, xvii. 54.

[1] This was the beginning of Main-street. Frothingham, p. 59.

to be very scarce, upon the grounds aforesaid, and CHAP.
XIX.
people were necessitated to live upon clams, and
muscles, and ground-nuts, and acorns, and these got 1630.
with much difficulty in the winter time.  Upon
which, people were very much tired and discouraged, especially when they heard that the Governor
himself had the last batch of bread in the oven ;[1] and
many were the fears of people that Mr. Pearce, who
was sent to Ireland to fetch provisions, was cast
away, or taken by pirates.  But God, who delights
to appear in greatest straits, did work marvellously
at this time ; for before the very day appointed to
seek the Lord by fasting and prayer, about the
month of February or March, in comes Mr. Pearce, 1631.
laden with provisions.  Upon which occasion the Feb.
5.
day of Fast was changed, and ordered to be kept as
a day of Thanksgiving ;[2] which provisions were by 22.
the Governor distributed unto the people proportionable to their necessities.


The summer this year proving short and wet, our 1632.
crops of Indian corn, (for all this while we had no
other,) was very small ; and great want threatened
us.  At which time here happened in this town the
first known thief that was notoriously observed in
the country.  His name was John Sales ; who, having stolen corn from many people in this scarce time,
was convicted thereof before the Court, and openly

---

[1] See pages 351 and 379. Mather says, that "on Feb. 5, 1631,
when he [Winthrop] was distributing the last handful of meal in the
barrel unto a poor man distressed
by the wolf at the door, at that instant they spied a ship arrived at
the harbour's mouth laden with provisions for them all." See Mather's
Magnalia, i. 111 ; Savage's note on
Winthrop, i. 46.
[2] See pages 330 and 332.

punished, and all he had by law condemned and sold, to make restitution.

1633. This winter also proved very sharp and long, and people were generally exceedingly pinched for want of provisions ; for there came very little over this year from England. But it pleased God to send an unexpected and early supply ; for one Mr. Stratton arrived here with his vessel in the beginning of March. March, laden with Indian corn, from Virginia, which he sold for ten shillings per bushel.

At this time began a most grievous and terrible sickness amongst the Indians, who were exceeding numerous about us, (called the Aberginians.) Their disease was generally the small pox, which raged not only amongst these, but amongst the Eastern Indians also, and in a few months swept away multitudes of them, young and old. They could not bury their dead ; the English were constrained to help ;[1] and that which is very remarkable is, that though the English did frequently visit them in their sickness, notwithstanding the infection, it was observed that not one Englishman was touched with the disease. But it was extremely infectious among themselves, and mortal where it took any of them ; insomuch as there was scarce any of them left. By

---

[1] " It wrought much with them," says Winthrop, " that when their own people forsook them, yet the English came daily and ministered to them ; and yet few, only two families, took any infection by it. Among others, Mr. Maverick, of Winesemett, is worthy of a perpetual remembrance. Himself, his wife, and servants, went daily to them, ministered to their necessities, and buried their dead, and took home many of their children. So did other of the neighbours." Edward Johnson, a contemporary, records the same general facts in his History of New-England, printed in 1654. See note 4 on page 306, and Winthrop, i. 119, 120 ; Morton's Memorial, p. 175 ; Hutchinson's Mass. i. 34 ; Mass. Hist. Coll. xiii. 127.

which awful and admirable dispensation it pleased CHAP.
God to make room for his people of the English na- 
tion ; who, after this, in the immediate years follow- 1634.
ing, came from England by many hundreds every
year to us, who, without this remarkable and terrible
stroke of God upon the natives, would with much
more difficulty have found room, and at far greater
charge have obtained and purchased land.[1]

---

[1] Prince enumerates among the manuscripts which he used in compiling his Annals of New-England, " the ancient records of the town of Charlestown ; in the first volume whereof is a particular history of the first coming and settling of the English there and in the neighbouring places." And afterwards, in quoting them, he says that they were " written by Mr. Increase Nowell, afterwards town-clerk of Charlestown, and Secretary of the Massachusetts Colony." But this is a mistake. Increase Nowell was town-clerk in 1636 and 1637, and assisted Abraham Palmer in the same office in 1639. But the records which he made are not now in existence. The earliest records now extant, from which the preceding Chapter is taken, were copied in 1664, nine years after Nowell's death, as appears by the following order. " At a meeting of the Selectmen, April 18, 1664, John Greene is appointed by us to transcribe the records of this town ; and having begun the same in a book as far as to folio eight, most whereof is gathered by information of known gentlemen that lived and were actors in those times, we do approve of the same, and consent that what is written on those seven pages remain as it is." Of course this record is not a contemporaneous document, but a digest from early papers and tradition. It contains, indeed, many interesting statements, and some few facts not to be found elsewhere. Yet, as an authority, it is not to be put upon a level with Dudley's touching Letter, or even with Roger Clap's homely Narrative. Its chronology, too, is all wrong, anticipating a whole year, in a most extraordinary manner, making Graves and Bright arrive in 1628, and Governor Winthrop and his company in 1629. It may be that this error extends also to the arrival of the Spragues, and that they did not come to Charlestown till 1629. See Prince's Annals, pp. xvii. 250 ; and Frothingham's History of Charlestown, pp. 2, 14, 61.

# WILLIAM WOOD'S

# DESCRIPTION OF MASSACHUSETTS.

NEW-ENGLANDS PROSPECT. A true, lively, and experimentall description of that part of *America*, commonly called NEVV ENGLAND: discovering the state of that Countrie, both as it stands to our new-come *English* Planters; and to the old Native Inhabitants.

Laying downe that which may both enrich the knowledge of the mind-travelling Reader, or benefit the future Voyager. By WILLIAM WOOD.

Printed at *London* by *Tho. Cotes*, for *Iohn Bellamie*, and are to be sold at his shop, at the three Golden Lyons in *Corne-hill*, neere the *Royall Exchange*. 1634. sm. 4to. pp. 112.

# CHAPTER XX.

## OF THE BAYS, HAVENS, INLETS, AND SEVERAL PLANT-ATIONS OF NEW-ENGLAND.

FORASMUCH as the King's most excellent Majesty <sub>CHAP. XX.</sub> hath been graciously pleased, by the grant of his letters patents, at first to give life to the Plantations 1633. of New-England, and hath daily, likewise, by his favors and royal protection, cherished their growing hopes ; whereby many of his Majesty's faithful subjects have been emboldened to venture persons, states, and endeavours, to the enlargement of his dominions in that western continent ; wherefore I thought fit, for the further encouragement of those that hereafter, either by purse or person, shall help forward the Plantation, to set forth these few observations, out of my personal and experimental knowledge.

The place whereon the English have built their Colonies, is judged by those who have best skill in discovery, either to be an island,[1] surrounded on the

[1] The first settlers of New-England generally considered it an island. See Chronicles of Plymouth, pp. 256, 368.

north side with the spacious river Cannada, and on the south with Hudson's river ; or else a peninsula, these two rivers overlapping one another, having their rise from the great lakes, which are not far off one another, as the Indians do certainly inform us. But it is not my intent to wander far from our Patent ; wherefore I refer you to the thrice memorable discoverer of those parts, Capt. Smith, who hath likewise fully described the southern and north-east parts of New-England, with the noted headlands, capes, harbours, rivers, ponds, and lakes, with the nature of the soil, and commodities both by sea and land, &c. within the degrees of forty-one and forty-five.[1]

The Bay of Massachusetts lieth under the degree of forty-two and forty-three, bearing south-west from the Land's End of England ; at the bottom whereof are situated most of the English plantations. This Bay is both safe, spacious, and deep, free from such cockling seas as run upon the coast of Ireland and in the channels of England. There be no stiff running currents, or rocks, shelves, bars, quicksands. The mariners having sailed two or three leagues towards the bottom, may behold the two Capes embracing their welcome ships in their arms, which thrust themselves out into the sea in form of a half-moon, the surrounding shore being high, and showing many white cliffs,[2] in a most pleasant prospect, with divers places of low land, out of which divers rivers vent themselves into the ocean, with many openings, where is good harbouring for ships of any

[1] See pages 19 and 371.
[2] The sand hills, at the extremity of Cape Cod, are of a dazzling white.

burthen. So that if an unexpected storm or cross CHAP.
XX.
wind should bar the mariner from recovering his desired port, he may reach other harbours, as Plim- 1633.
mouth, Cape Ann, Salem, Marvill Head ; all which
afford good ground for anchorage, being likewise
land-locked from wind and seas.

The chief and usual harbour is the still Bay of
Massachusetts,[1] which is close aboard the Plantations ; in which most of our ships come to anchor,
being the nearest their mart, and usual place of landing of passengers. It is a safe and pleasant harbour
within, having but one common and safe entrance,[2]
and that not very broad, there scarce being room for
three ships to come in, board and board, at a time ;
but being once within, there is room for the anchorage of five hundred ships. This harbour is made by a
great company of islands,[3] whose high cliffs shoulder
out the boisterous seas ; yet may easily deceive any
unskilful pilot, presenting many fair openings and
broad sounds,[4] which afford too shallow waters for
any ships, though navigable for boats and small pinnaces.

The entrance into the great haven is called Nantascot ;[5] which is two leagues from Boston. This
place of itself is a very good haven ; where ships

---

[1] Boston harbour, included between Nahant and Point Alderton.
Twice afterwards he calls it "the
still bay," to distinguish it from
the outer bay, included between
Cape Ann and Cape Cod.

[2] The ship channel, or main entrance into Boston harbour, commonly called the Light House Channel, lies between Boston Light on
the north side and Point Alderton
on the south, and then passes be-

tween George's and Lovell's islands.

[3] See a list of these islands, some
forty or more, in Mass. Hist. Coll.
iii. 295, and in Snow's History of
Boston, p. 114.

[4] The northern entrance to Boston harbour is called Broad Sound.
It is not considered a proper channel
for large vessels, though they sometimes pass through it.

[5] See note [3] on page 19.

commonly cast anchor, until wind and tide serve
them for other places.[1]  From hence they may sail
1633. to the river of Wessaguscus, Naponset, Charles river,
and Misticke river ; on which rivers be seated many
towns.  In any of these forenamed harbours, the seamen, having spent their old store of wood and water,
may have fresh supplies from the adjacent islands,
with good timber[2] td repair their weather-beaten
ships.  Here, likewise, may be had masts or yards,
being store of such trees as are useful for the same
purpose.

Having described the situation of the country in
general, with all his commodities arising from land
and sea, it may add to your content and satisfaction,
to be informed of the situation of every several plantation, with his conveniences, commodities, and discommodities, &c.

Where, first, I will begin with the outmost plantation in the Patent, to the southward ;[3] which is
called *Wessaguscus*,[4] an Indian name.  This as yet is

[1] Nantasket Road is still a favorite anchorage.  It lies between
George's island and Hull.
[2] This shows that the islands
were at this time well wooded ; although the settlers of New Plymouth, on their first visit to the
harbour in Sept. 1621, found some
of them " cleared from end to end."
See Chronicles of Plymouth, p. 229.
[3] Bordering on the Old Colony of
Plymouth.  The dividing line between the Colonies is marked on the
splendid topographical Map of Massachusetts, made by order of the
Legislature in 1844.
[4] Wessaguscus, afterwards called
Weymouth, was first planted by
fifty or sixty men sent over by Tho-

mas Weston in the summer of 1622.
The plantation, however, was broken up and abandoned the next
spring.  A few months afterwards,
the ground was reöccupied by Capt.
Robert Gorges, son of Sir Ferdinando, with William Morell, an
episcopal clergyman, " and sundry
passengers and families."  Losing
much of their goods and provisions
by a fire at Plymouth in November,
some of them returned to England,
out of discontent and dislike of the
country.  Morell remained a year,
and wrote a Latin poem descriptive
of the country and its productions,
which is printed in Mass. Hist. Coll.
i. 125-139.  "At his going away,"
says Gov. Bradford, " he told some

but a small village ; yet it is very pleasant, and CHAP.<br>XX.
healthful, very good ground, and is well timbered,
and hath good store of hay-ground.  It hath a very 1633.
spacious harbour for shipping before the town, the
salt water being navigable for boats and pinnaces
two leagues.  Here the inhabitants have good store
of fish of all sorts, and swine, having acorns and
clams at the time of year.  Here is likewise an alewife river.

Three miles to the north of this, is *Mount Walles-
ton*,[1] a very fertile soil, and a place very convenient
for farmers' houses, there being great store of plain
ground, without trees.  This place is called *Massachusetts Fields*, where the greatest sagamore[2] in the
country lived, before the plague, who caused it to be
cleared for himself.  The greatest inconvenience is,
that there is not very many springs, as in other
places of the country ; yet water may be had for
digging.  A second inconvenience is, that boats cannot come in at a low water, nor ships ride near the
shore.

Six miles further to the north lieth *Dorchester*,
which is the greatest town in New-England,[3] well

of our people he had a power of
superintendency over the churches
here, but never showed it.  And
thus the second plantation at the
Massachusetts ended."  But " some
few remain," he adds ; and these
may have been the nucleus of the
subsequent permanent settlement.
See p. 309 ; Savage's Winthrop, i.
43 ; Prince's Annals, pp. 204, 214,
221, 224 ; Chronicles of Plymouth,
pp. 297, 342.

  [1] This hill in Quincy, near the
shore, and not far from President
Adams's seat, still bears the name
of Mount Wollaston.

  [2] Chickatabot.  See page 305.
  [3] Dorchester originally included
in its territory the towns of Milton,
Stoughton, Sharon, Canton, and
Foxborough.  It was then about 35
miles in length, and in some places
from six to eight in width.  Some
idea of its comparative wealth at
that time may be obtained from the
fact, that in this year, 1633, when a
rate of £400 was assessed upon the
Colony, Dorchester was called upon
to pay £80, one-fifth of the whole,
whilst Boston, Roxbury, Charlestown, and Watertown were each
taxed only £48, and Salem £28.

CHAP. wooded and watered, very good arable grounds, and
XX.
hay-ground, fair corn-fields and pleasant gardens,
1633. with kitchen gardens. In this plantation is a great
many cattle, as kine, goats, and swine. This plantation hath a reasonable harbour for ships. Here is
no alewife river, which is a great inconvenience.
The inhabitants of this town were the first that set
upon the trade of fishing in the Bay ; who received
so much fruit of their labors, that they encouraged
others to the same undertakings.

A mile from this town lieth *Roxberry*, which is a
fair and handsome country-town, the inhabitants of it
being all very rich. This town lieth upon the main,
so that it is well wooded and watered, having a clear
and fresh brook running through the town ; up
which, although there come no alewives, yet there is
great store of smelts, and therefore it is called Smelt
Brook.[1] A quarter of a mile to the north side of the
town is another river, called Stony river, upon which
is built a water-mill.[2] Here is good ground for corn,
and meadow for cattle. Up westward from the town
it is something rocky ; whence it hath the name of
Roxberry. The inhabitants have fair houses, store
of cattle, impaled corn-fields, and fruitful gardens.

Twenty years later, viz. in 1652, Edward Johnson thus describes the town. " Dorchester, a frontier town, is situated very pleasantly both for facing the sea, and also its large extent into the main land, well watered with two small rivers. Her houses for dwelling are about 140 ; orchards and gardens full of fruit trees ; plenty of corn-land ; although much of it hath been long in tillage, yet hath it ordinarily good crops. The number of trees are near upon 1500 ; cows, and other cattle of that kind, about 450. Thus hath the Lord been pleased to increase his poor dispersed people, whose number in this flock are near about 150." See Savage's Winthrop, i. 112, and Mass. Hist. Coll. ix. 159, xii. 90.

[1] This is probably the brook that divides Roxbury from Dorchester.

[2] It is still called Stony Brook, and the water-mill, now called White's Mill, is yet at work near where the road to Brookline crosses the Providence rail-road.

Here is no harbour for ships, because the town is
seated in the bottom of a shallow bay, which is made
by the neck of land on which Boston is built ; so
that they can transport all their goods from the ships
in boats from Boston, which is the nearest harbour.[1]

BOSTON is two miles north-east from Roxberry.
His situation is very pleasant, being a peninsula,
hemmed in on the south side with the bay of Roxberry, on the north side with Charles river, the
marshes[2] on the back side being not half a quarter
of a mile over ; so that a little fencing will secure
their cattle from the wolves. Their greatest wants
be wood and meadow-ground, which never were in
that place,[3] being constrained to fetch their building

---

[1] Compare with this Edward Johnson's description of the place in 1652. " Roxbury, situated between Boston and Dorchester, is well watered with cool and pleasant springs, issuing forth the rocky hills, and with small freshets, watering the valleys of this fertile town ; whose form is somewhat like a wedge double pointed, entering between the two forenamed towns, filled with a very laborious people, whose labors the Lord hath so blest, that in the room of dismal swamps and tearing bushes, they have very goodly fruit trees, fruitful fields and gardens. Their herd of cows, oxen and other young cattle of that kind, about 350, and dwelling-houses near upon 120. Their streets are large, and some fair houses ; yet have they built their house for church assembly destitute and unbeautified with other buildings. The church of Christ here is increased to about 120 persons. Their first teaching elder called to office is Mr. Eliot, a young man at his coming thither, of a cheerful spirit, walking unblamable, of a godly conversation, apt to teach, as by his indefatigable pains

both with his own flock and the poor Indians doth appear, whose language he learned purposely to help them to the knowledge of God in Christ, frequently preaching in their wigwams, and catechising their children." Johnson's History of New-England, ch. 21.

[2] The marshes were on the isthmus or neck which connects Boston with Roxbury.

[3] " Mr. Wood was wrong in asserting that ' wood was never in this place.' It had doubtless been the favorite residence of the natives for many years, and a considerable portion had been cleared by burning, as was their custom, for the culture of corn. Hence it was sometimes called the *plain neck ;* and compared with the surrounding country, covered with interminable forests, it might with propriety be called *plain.* There were, however, many large clumps left, sufficient for fuel and timber. The growth was probably similar to that of the islands. Had the peninsula been wholly denuded of trees, even the temptation of Mr. Blackstone's spring of fresh water could not have induced the first

CHAP.
XX.

1633.

timber and firewood from the islands in boats[1] and their hay in lighters. It being a neck, and bare of wood, they are not troubled with three great annoyances, of wolves, rattlesnakes, and mosquitoes. These that live here upon their cattle, must be constrained to take farms in the country, or else they cannot subsist ; the place being too small to contain many, and fittest for such as can trade into England for such commodities as the country wants, being the chief place for shipping and merchandise.

This neck of land is not above four miles in compass ;[2] in form almost square, having on the south side, at one corner, a great broad hill,[3] whereon is planted a fort, which can command any ship as she sails into any harbour within the still bay. On the north side is another hill,[4] equal in bigness, whereon stands a windmill. To the north-west, is a high

planters to settle at Shawmut at the approach of a rigorous winter.'' Shaw's History of Boston, p. 77.

[1] At a Court held Nov. 7, 1632, '' it is ordered that the inhabitants of Boston shall have liberty to fetch wood from Dorchester neck of land for twenty years, the propriety of the land to remain to Dorchester.'' Col. Rec. i. 94.

[2] The peninsula on which Boston is built, contained originally about 700 acres. Its whole length, from Roxbury line to Winnisimet ferry is two miles and three-fourths and 238 yards. Its greatest breadth, from Foster's wharf to Barton's point, is one mile and 139 yards. See Mass. Hist. Coll. iii. 242.

[3] This hill was originally called Corn Hill ; but after the fort was built, it received the name of Fort Hill, which it still retains. It is situated at the eastern extremity of the city, directly opposite the har-

bour. The fortification was begun May 24, 1632, the people of Charlestown, Roxbury, and Dorchester working upon it in rotation ; and in May, 1634, '' it was in defence, and divers pieces of ordnance mounted in it.'' See Winthrop, i. 77, 99, 132.

[4] This hill at the north end of the city, opposite Charlestown, and which formerly rose to the height of 50 feet above the sea, was first called Windmill Hill, from the windmill on its summit, which was brought down from Watertown in August, 1632, '' because it would not grind but with a westerly wind.'' On the map of Boston, printed in 1722, it is called Snow Hill. About the time of the Revolution, in 1775, it bore the name, which it still retains, of Copp's Hill, after William Copp, the earliest proprietor of a portion of it. See Winthrop, i. 87 ; Snow's Boston, p. 105.

mountain,[1] with three little rising hills on the top of CHAP.
XX.
it ; wherefore it is called

1633.

THE TRAMOUNT.

From the top of this mountain a man may overlook
all the islands which lie before the bay, and descry
such ships as are upon the sea-coast. This town,
although it be neither the greatest nor the richest,
yet it is the most noted and frequented, being the
centre of the plantations, where the monthly Courts
are kept.[2] Here likewise dwells the Governor.
This place hath very good land, affording rich corn-
fields and fruitful gardens ; having likewise sweet
and pleasant springs.[3]

[1] The top of this beautiful hill, which was in the rear of the State House, was 138 feet above the level of the sea. With its two adjoining eminences it occupied about 100 acres of ground. The easternmost hill was where Pemberton Square now stands, and the westernmost occupied what is now called Mount Vernon, near Louisburgh Square. The central elevation received the name of Sentry and afterwards Beacon Hill, from the beacon which was placed on its summit to alarm the country in case of invasion, by setting fire to a tar-barrel fixed on the top of it. This beacon was blown down by the wind in Nov. 1789. The wood-cut represents the three hills as they appeared when seen from Charlestown. See p. 313 ; Snow's Boston, pp. 65, 112, 315 ; Mass. Hist. Coll. iii. 244.

[2] At a Court held Oct. 3, 1632, " it is thought, by general consent, that Boston is the fittest place for public meetings of any place in the Bay." It is still thought so, and probably always will be.

[3] " BOSTON," says Johnson, writing in 1652, " is the centre town and metropolis of this wilderness work. Environed it is with brinish floods, saving one small isthmus, which gives free access to the neighbour towns by land on the south side. On the north-west and north-east two constant ferries are kept for daily traffic thereunto. The form of this town is like a heart,

CHAP.
XX.
1633.

The inhabitants of this place, for their enlargement, have taken to themselves farm-houses in a place called *Muddy-river*,[1] two miles from their town ;[2] where is good ground, large timber, and store of marsh land and meadow. In this place they keep their swine and other cattle in the summer, whilst the corn is on the ground at Boston, and bring them to the town in winter. On the north side of Charles river is *Charles Towne*,[3]

naturally situated for fortifications, having two hills on the frontice-part thereof next the sea ; the one well fortified on the superficies thereof with store of great artillery, well mounted. The other hath a very strong battery, built of whole timber, and filled with earth, at the descent of the hill, in the extreme point thereof. Betwixt these two strong arms lies a large cove or bay, in which the chiefest part of this town is built, overtopped with a third hill. All three, like overtopping towers, keep a constant watch to foresee the approach of foreign dangers, being furnished wi h a beacon and loud-babbling guns, to give notice, by their redoubled echo, to all their sister towns. The chief edifices of this city-like town are crowded on the sea-banks, and wharfed out with great industry and cost ; the buildings beautiful and large, some fairly set forth with brick, tile, stone, and slate, and orderly placed, with comely streets, *whose continual enlargement presageth some sumptuous city.* The wonder of this modern age, that a few years should bring forth such great matters by so mean a handful ; and they so far from being enriched by the spoils of other nations, that the states of many of them have been spoiled by the lordly prelacy, whose lands must assuredly make restitution. At this people's landing, the hideous thickets in this place were such, that wolves and bears nursed

up their young from the eyes of all beholders, in those very places where the streets are full of girls and boys, sporting up and down, with a continued concourse of people. Good store of shipping is here yearly built, and some very fair ones. Both tar and masts the country affords from its own soil ; also store of victual both for their own and foreigners' ships, who resort hither for that end. This town is the very mart of the land. French, Portugals, and Dutch come hither for traffic." Johnson's Hist. N. E., ch. 20. See p. 313.

[1] This place continued to be called Muddy-river and Muddy-river Hamlet, till Nov. 24, 1705, when it was incorporated as a distinct town, by the name of Brookline. See Winthrop, i. 88, 290 ; Dr. Pierce's Hist. of Brookline, in Mass. Hist. Coll. xii. 145.

[2] That is, in a direct line across the water, over which they used to pass in boats when they went to their farms. The Rev. John Cotton, of Boston, had a farm here. It included the two estates now owned by John Kenrick and Moses Andem. See Dr. Pierce's Address at Brookline, Oct. 14, 1845, p. 17.

[3] "This town of Charles," says Johnson in 1652, "is situated on the north side of Charles river, from whence it took its name, the river being about five or six fathoms deep ; over against the town many small islands lying to the seaward of it, and hills on either side. By which

which is another neck of land, on whose north side runs Misticke river. This town, for all things, may be well paralleled with her neighbour Boston, being in the same fashion with her bare neck, and constrained to borrow conveniences from the main, and to provide for themselves farms in the country for their better subsistence: At this town there is kept a ferry-boat[1] to convey passengers over Charles river ; which, between the two towns, is a quarter of a mile over, being a very deep channel. Here may ride forty ships at a time.

Up higher it is a broad bay,[2] being above two miles between the shores, into which runs Stony river and Muddy river.[3] Towards the south-west, in the middle of this bay,[2] is a great oyster bank.[4]

Towards the north-west of this bay is a great creek, upon whose shore is situated the village of

---

means it proves a very good harbour for ships ; which hath caused many seamen and merchants to sit down there. The form of this town, in the frontice-piece thereof, is like the head, neck, and shoulders of a man. Only the pleasant and navigable river of Mistick runs through the right shoulder thereof, and by its near approach to Charles river in one place, makes a very narrow neck ; by which means the chief part of the town, whereon the most buildings stand, becomes a peninsula. It hath a large market-place, near the water side, built round with houses comely and fair ; forth of which there issue two streets, orderly built, with some very fair houses, beautified with pleasant gardens and orchards. The whole town consists, in its extent, of about 150 houses. Their meeting-house for Sabbath assembly stands in the market-place, very comely built and large. The number of souls, (church members) is about 160. Their corn land in tillage in this town is about 1200 acres ; their great cattle are about 400 head ; sheep near upon 400." Johnson's N. E., ch. 18.

[1] By an order of the Court of Assistants, June 14, 1631, Edward Converse was permitted " to set up a ferry between Charlton and Boston, for which he is to have 2d. for every single person, and 1d. apiece if there be two or more." See Col. Rec.; and Frothingham's Charlestown, p. 94.

[2] The Back Bay, as it is called, west of the Common, across which runs the Mill-dam road, or Western Avenue.

[3] Muddy river is the boundary between Roxbury and Brookline.

[4] "Aug. 6, 1633. Two men, servants to one Moody, of Roxbury, returning in a boat from the windmill, (on Copp's Hill,) struck upon the oyster bank." Winthrop, i. 106.

CHAP. *Medford,*[1] a very fertile and pleasant place, and fit
XX.
for more inhabitants than are yet in it.   This town
1633. is a mile and a half from Charlestown ; and at the
bottom of this bay the river begins to be narrower,
being but half a quarter of a mile broad.

By the side of this river is built *Newtown,* which is
three miles by land from Charlestown, and a league
and a half by water.   This place was first intended
for a city ;[2] but, upon more serious considerations, it
was not thought so fit, being too far from the sea,
being the greatest inconvenience it hath.   This is one
of the neatest and best compacted towns in New-England, having many fair structures, with many handsome contrived streets.   The inhabitants, most of
them, are very rich, and well stored with cattle of
all sorts, having many hundred acres of ground paled
in with one general fence, which is about a mile and
a half long, which secures all their weaker cattle
from the wild beasts.   On the other side of the river
lieth all their meadow and marsh ground for hay.[3]

---

[1] " Medford and Mistick were then distinct places, though not so at present.   Medford I take to have been a small village at the lower part of Mistick river, now called Neck of Land, where a creek also ran into Charles river."   Hutchinson's Mass. i. 22.   See Winthrop, i. 69.

[2] See pages 320 and 339.

[3] " At this time those who were in place of civil government, having some additional pillars to underprop the building, began to think of a place of more safety, in the eyes of man, than the two frontier towns of Charlestown and Boston were for the habitation of such as the Lord had prepared to govern this Pilgrim people.   Wherefore they rather made choice to enter farther among the Indians, than hazard the fury of malignant adversaries, who in a rage might pursue them ; and therefore chose a place, situate on Charles river, between Charlestown and Watertown, where they erected a town, called Newtown, now named Cambridge.   This town is compact closely within itself, till of late years some few straggling houses have been built.   The liberties of this town have been enlarged of late in length, reaching from the most northerly part of Charles river to the most southerly part of Mystick river.   It hath well-ordered streets, and comely, completed with the fair building of Harvard College.   Their first pastor was the faithful and laborious Mr. Hooker.   The people of this town are at this day in a

Half a mile westward of this plantation, is *Water-* CHAP.<br>
*towne*, a place nothing inferior for land, wood, mea- XX.<br>
dow, and water, to New-towne. Within half a mile 1633.
of this town is a great pond,[1] which is divided between those two towns, which divides their bounds
northward. A mile and a half from this town is a
fall of fresh waters,[2] which convey themselves into
the ocean through Charles river. A little below this
fall of waters, the inhabitants of Water-towne have
built a wear to catch fish, wherein they take great
store of shads and alewives. In two tides they have
gotten one hundred thousand of those fishes. This
is no small benefit to the plantation.[3] Ships of small

thriving condition in outward things;
also both corn and cattle, neat and
sheep, of which they have a good
flock, which the Lord hath caused
to thrive much more in these latter
days than formerly. This town was
appointed to be the seat of government; but it continued not long.
This year (1633) a small glean of
rye was brought to the Court as the
first fruits of English grain; at
which this poor people greatly rejoiced to see the land would bear it.
But now the Lord's blessing that
way hath exceeded all people's expectation, clothing the earth with
plenty of all kinds of grain." Johnson, chap. 28. An excellent history of Cambridge, written by the
Rev. Dr. Holmes, the accurate author of the Annals of America, is
contained in Mass. Hist. Coll. vii.
1–67. A more enlarged history of
the town, prepared with indefatigable labor and research, is soon expected from the pen of the Rev.
Lucius R. Paige, of Cambridge.

[1] Fresh Pond, from which most
of the ice is obtained that is export-
ed from Boston.

[2] From Wood's description, it
would appear that the original settlement at Watertown was in a very

different spot from the present village. Winthrop, too, says that "a
wear was erected by Watertown
men upon Charles river, *three miles
above the town*, where they took
great store of shads." Winthrop,
i. 73.

[3] "Watertown," says Johnson,
"is situate upon one of the branches
of Charles river, a fruitful plot, and
of large extent, watered with many
pleasant springs and small rivulets,
running like veins throughout her
body; which hath caused her inhabitants to scatter in such manner,
that their Sabbath assemblies prove
very thin, if the season favor not,
and hath made this great town, consisting of 160 families, to show nothing delightful to the eye in any
place. This town began by occasion of Sir Richard Saltonstall, who,
at his arrival, having some store of
cattle and servants, they wintered in
those parts. This town abounds in
several sorts of fish at their seasons,
bass, shad, alewives, frost-fish, and
smelts. Their herd of kine, and
cattle of that kind, are about 450,
with some store of sheep and goats.
Their land in tillage is near upon
1800 acres. This church is increased to near about 250 souls in church

CHAP.
XX. burthen may come up to these two towns ; but the
1633. oyster banks[1] do bar out the bigger ships.

The next town is *Misticke*,[2] which is three miles from Charles-towne by land, and a league and a half by water. It is seated by the water's side very pleasantly ; there be not many houses as yet. At the head of this river are great and spacious ponds,[3] whither the alewives press to spawn. This being a noted place for that kind of fish, the English resort thither to take them. On the west side of this river the Governor hath a farm,[4] where he keeps most of his cattle. On the east side is Master Cradock's plantation, where he hath impaled a park, where he keeps his cattle, till he can store it with deer. Here likewise he is at charges of building ships. The last year one was upon the stocks of a hundred ton.[5] That being finished, they are to build one twice her burthen. Ships, without either ballast or loading, may float down this river. Otherwise, the oyster bank would hinder them, which crosseth the channel.

The last town in the still bay is *Winnisimet*,[6] a very sweet place for situation, and stands very com-

fellowship. Their first pastor was Mr. Phillips, a man mighty in the Scriptures, and very diligent to search out the mind of Christ therein contained." Johnson's Hist. of New-England, ch. 23. An excellent History of Watertown, in 151 pages octavo, was published in 1830, written by the Rev. Convers Francis, formerly minister of the town, and now a professor in the Divinity School at Cambridge.

[1] See page 401.
[2] Mistick is now Medford. It was originally the name of Cradock's farm or plantation, containing about 2500 acres, on the north side of Mystick river. Medford continued a manor or plantation till Oct. 15, 1683, when it was made a separate town. See pages 313 and 374; Savage's Winthrop, ii. 161 ; Frothingham's Charlestown, pp. 89–93.
[3] Mystick, Horn, and Spy Ponds.
[4] Governor Winthrop's farm on the banks of the Mystick was called Tenhills, which name is still retained. See note [1] on page 104.
[5] See note [1] on page 185.
[6] Chelsea. A flourishing village in this town, connected with Boston by a steam-ferry, retains the ancient name of Winnisimet.

modiously, being fit to entertain more planters than CHAP.
are yet seated. It is within a mile of Charlestown,
the river¹ only parting them.

The chief islands which keep out the wind and
the sea from disturbing the harbours are, first, Deer
Island,² which lies within a flight-shot of Pullin-point.
This island is so called because of the deer, which
often swim thither from the main, when they are
chased by the wolves ; some have killed sixteen
deer in a day upon this island.  The opposite shore
is called Pullin-point, because that is the usual channel boats use to pass through into the bay ; and the
tide being very strong, they are constrained to go
ashore, and haul their boats by the seaside, or roads;
whereupon it was called Pullin-point.³

The next island of note is Long Island, so called
from his longitude.  Divers other islands be within
these, viz. Nodle's Isle, Round Isle, the Governor's
Garden, where is planted an orchard, and a vineyard,
with many other conveniences, and Slate Island,
Glass Island, Bird Island, &c.⁴  These isles abound
with woods, and water, and meadow ground, and
whatsoever the spacious fertile main affords.  The
inhabitants use to put their cattle in these for safety,
viz. their rams, goats, and swine, when their corn is
on the ground.  Those towns that lie without the

¹ Mystick.
² Deer island, lying between Point
Shirley and Lovell's Island, keeps
its original name.
³ It is now called Point Shirley.
See Winthrop, i. 90 ; Prince, p. 403 ;
Mass. Hist. Coll. iii. 299.
⁴ Long island still retains its ancient name.  Noddle's island is now
East Boston.  Round Isle is proba-

bly Apple Island.  The Governor's
Garden is the island on which Fort
Warren is built.  Slate Island is off
Crow Point, in Hingham.  Grass
Island (Glass probably an error,) is
off Weymouth.  Bird island was
between Noddle's and Governor's.
Its soil is washed away, but it is
dry at low water.

CHAP.
XX.
1633.

bay, are a great deal nearer the main, and reap a greater benefit from the sea, in regard of the plenty both of fish and fowl which they receive from thence; so that they live more comfortably, and at less charges, than those that are more remote from the sea, in the inland plantations.

The next plantation is *Saugus*, six miles north-east from Winnesimet. This town is pleasant for situation, seated at the bottom of a bay, which is made on the one side with the surrounding shore, and on the other side with a long sandy beach. This sandy beach is two miles long, at the end whereon is a neck of land, called *Nahant.*[1] It is six miles in circumference, well wooded with oaks, pines, and cedars. It is, besides, well watered, having, besides the fresh springs, a great pond[2] in the middle ; before which is a spacious marsh. In this neck is store of good ground, fit for the plough ; but for the present it is only used for to put young cattle in, and wether-goats, and swine, to secure them from the wolves. A few posts and rails from the low-water marks to the shore keeps out the wolves, and keeps in the cattle. One Black William,[3] an Indian duke, out of his generosity, gave this place in general to this plantation of Saugus ; so that no other can appropriate it to himself.

Upon the south[4] side of the sandy beach the sea beateth, which is a true prognostication to presage

[1] See Lewis's History of Lynn, (2d ed.) pp. 21–27.
[2] This is called Bear Pond. See Lewis's Lynn, p. 29.
[3] An Indian, called Black Will, was hung at Richmond's Isle in 1632, for being concerned in the

murder of Walter Bagnall. He was, probably, however, a different person from the Duke of Saugus. See Winthrop, i. 62, 99 ; Lewis's Lynn, p. 51.
[4] More properly on the *east* side.

storms and foul weather, and the breaking up of the
frost. For when a storm hath been, or is likely to
be, it will roar like thunder, being heard six miles;
and after storms, casts up great store of great clams,
which the Indians, taking out of their shells, carry
home in baskets.

On the north side of this bay is two great marshes,
which are made two by a pleasant river[1] which runs
between them. Northward, up this river, goes
great store of alewives, of which they make good red
herrings; insomuch that they have been at charges
to make a wear, and a herring-house to dry these
herrings in. The last year were dried some four or
five last,[2] for an experiment; which proved very
good. This is like to prove a great enrichment to
the land, (being a staple commodity in other countries,) for there be such innumerable companies in
every river, that I have seen ten thousand taken in
two hours by two men, without any wear at all, saving a few stones to stop their passage up the river.
There likewise come store of bass, which the Indians
and English catch with hook and line, some fifty or
threescore at a tide.

At the mouth of this river runs up a great creek[3]
into that great marsh, which is called *Rumny Marsh*;[4]
which is four miles long and two miles broad, half of
it being marsh ground, and half upland grass, without tree or bush. This marsh is crossed with divers
creeks, wherein lie great store of geese and ducks.

---

[1] Saugus or Abousett river. See
page 169.

[2] A last of white herrings is 12
barrels; of red herrings, 20 cades,
or 20,000. See Richardson's Dictionary.

[3] Now called Chelsea Creek.

[4] In Chelsea. There is said to
be a place of the same name in the
County of Kent, England. See
Am. Antiq. Soc. Trans. ii. 441.

CHAP. There be convenient ponds for the planting of duck-
XX.
oys. Here is likewise, belonging to this place,[1]
1633. divers fresh meadows, which afford good grass, and
four spacious ponds,[2] like little lakes, wherein is
store of fresh fish, within a mile of the town ; out of
which runs a curious fresh brook,[3] that is seldom
frozen, by reason of the warmness of the water.
Upon this stream is built a water-mill, and up this
river come smelts and frost-fish, much bigger than a
gudgeon. For wood, there is no want, there being
store of good oaks, walnut, cedar, asp, elm. The
ground is very good, in many places without trees,
fit for the plough. In this plantation is more English tillage than in all New-England and Virginia
besides ; which proved as well as could be expected, the corn being very good, especially the barley,
rye, and oats.

The land affordeth the inhabitants as many rarities
as any place else, and the sea more ; the bass continuing from the middle of April to Michaelmas,
which stays not above half that time in the bay.
Besides, here is a great deal of rock-cod and mackerel, insomuch that shoals of bass have driven up
shoals of mackerel from one end of the sandy beach
to the other, which the inhabitants have gathered up
in wheelbarrows. The bay that lieth before the
town, at a low spring tide, will be all flats for two
miles together ; upon which is great store of muscle-
banks and clam-banks, and lobsters amongst the
rocks and grassy holes. These flats make it unnavi-

[1] That is, Saugus, or Lynn.
[2] Their names are Flax, Tomline,
Cedar, and Spring. See Lewis's
Lynn, p. 29.

[3] The name of it is Strawberry
Brook. It conects the three first-
named ponds with Saugus river.
See Lewis's Lynn, pp. 20, 29, 84.

gable for ships. Yet, at high water, great boats, CHAP.<br>XX.
lighters, and pinnaces of twenty and thirty ton, may
sail up to the plantation; but they need have a skil- 1633.
ful pilot, because of many dangerous rocks and foam-
ing breakers, that lie at the mouth of that bay. The
very aspect of the place is fortification enough to
keep off an unknown enemy. Yet may it be fortified
at a little charge, being but few landing places thereabout, and those obscure.[1]

Four miles north-east from Saugus, lieth *Salem,*
which stands on the middle of a neck of land very
pleasantly, having a South river on the one side, and
a North river on the other side. Upon this neck,
where the most of the houses stand, is very bad and
sandy ground. Yet, for seven years together, it
hath brought forth exceeding good corn, by being
fished but every third year. In some places is very
good ground, and very good timber, and divers
springs, hard by the sea-side. Here, likewise, is
store of fish, as basses, eels, lobsters, clams, &c.
Although their land be none of the best, yet beyond
those rivers is a very good soil, where they have

[1] "Lynn," says Johnson, "is
between Salem and Charlestown.
Her situation is near to a river,
whose strong freshet, at breaking
up of winter, filleth all her banks,
and with a furious torrent vents itself into the sea. This town is furnished with minerals of divers kinds,
especially iron and lead. The form
of it is almost square; only it takes
too large a run into the land-ward,
as most towns do. It is filled with
about 100 houses for dwelling.
Here is also an iron mill in constant
use; but as for lead, they have tried
but little yet. Their meeting-house
is on a level land, undefended from
the cold north-west wind, and therefore made with steps descending
into the earth. Their streets are
straight and comely, yet but thin of
houses. The people mostly inclining to husbandry, have built many
farms remote there; cattle exceedingly multiplied; goats, which were
in great esteem at their first coming,
are now almost quite banished; and
now horse, kine, and sheep, are
most in request with them. The
first feeder of this flock of Christ
was Mr. Stephen Batchelor, gray
and aged." Johnson's Hist. N. E.,
ch. 22. There is a History of Lynn,
including Nahant, by Alonzo Lewis,
in octavo, 278 pages, 2d ed., 1844.

CHAP.
XX.

1633.

taken farms, and get their hay, and plant their corn. There they cross these rivers with small canoes, which are made of whole pine trees, being about two foot and a half over, and twenty foot long. In these likewise they go a fowling, sometimes two leagues to sea. There be more canoes in this town, than in all the whole Patent; every household having a water-house or two. This town wants an alewife river, which is a great inconvenience. It hath two good harbours, the one being called Winter, and the other Summer harbour,[1] which lieth within Derby's fort;[2] which place, if it were well fortified, might keep ships from landing of forces in any of those two places.

*Marvill Head*[3] is a place which lieth four miles full south from Salem, and is a very convenient place for a plantation, especially for such as will set upon the trade of fishing. There was made here a ship's loading of fish the last year, where still stand the stages and drying scaffolds. Here be good harbour for boats, and safe riding for ships.

*Agowamme*[4] is nine miles to the north from Salem,

[1] Winter harbour is now called Cat Cove; and Summer harbour is the principal harbour of Salem. See Felt, i. 231, 241.

[2] This fort was probably built on Naugus' Head, on Marblehead side. It may have got its name from William Darby, one of the Company in London, who in May, 1628, subscribed £50 to the joint stock. See p. 174, and Felt, i. 111, 205.

[3] See note [4] on page 244.

[4] By order of Court, Aug. 4, 1634, called Ipswich. "This town," says Johnson, "is situated on a fair and delightful river, whose first rise or spring begins about five and twenty miles farther up in the country, issuing forth a very pleasant pond. But soon after it betakes its course through a most hideous swamp of large extent, even for many miles, being a great harbour for bears. After its coming forth this place, it groweth larger by the income of many small rivers, and issues forth in the sea, due east over against the Island of Sholes, a great place of fishing for our English nation. The peopling of this town is by men of good rank and quality, many of them having the yearly revenue of large lands in England before they came to this wilderness.

which is one of the most spacious places for a plantation. Being near the sea, it aboundeth with fish,
and flesh of fowls and beasts, great meads and
marshes and plain ploughing grounds, many good
rivers and harbours, and no rattlesnakes.

In a word, it is the best place but one, which is
*Merrimacke,*[1] lying eight miles beyond it, where is a
river twenty leagues navigable. All along the river
side is fresh marshes, in some places three miles
broad. In this river is sturgeon, salmon, and bass,
and divers other kinds of fish. To conclude, the

---

This town lies in the sagamoreship or earldom of Agawam, now by our English nation called Essex. It is a very good haven town, yet a little barred up at the mouth of the river. Some merchants here are ; but Boston being the chiefest place of resort of shipping, carries away all the trade. They have very good land for husbandry, where rocks hinder not the course of the plough. The Lord hath been pleased to increase them in corn and cattle of late, insomuch that they have many hundred quarters to spare yearly, and feed, at the latter end of summer, the town of Boston with good beef. Their houses are many of them very fair built, with pleasant gardens and orchards, consisting of about 140 families. Their meeting-house is a very good prospect to a great part of the town, and beautifully built. The church of Christ here consists of about 160 souls." Johnson's N. E., ch. 30. See Winthrop, i. 101, 133, 137. A History of this town, written by the Rev. J. B. Felt, in 300 pages octavo, was printed in 1834.

[1] Merrimack I take to be Newbury, which Johnson thus describes. "This town is situate about twelve miles from Ipswich, near upon the wide venting streams of Merrimack river, whose strong current is such that it hath forced its passage through the mighty rocks ; which causeth some sudden falls, and hinders shipping from having any access far into the land. Her banks are in many places stored with oaken timber of all sorts ; of which that which they commonly call white oak is not inferior to our English timber. In this river lie some few islands of fertile land. This town is stored with meadow and upland ; which hath caused some gentlemen, (who brought over good estates, and finding then no better way to improve them,) to set upon husbandry; among whom that religious and sincere-hearted servant of Christ, Mr. Richard Dummer, some time a magistrate in this little commonwealth, hath holpen on this town. Their houses are built very scattering, which hath caused some contending about removal of their place for Sabbath assemblies. Their cattle are about 400 head, with store of cornland in tillage. It consists of about seventy families. The souls in church fellowship are about a hundred." Johnson's Hist. of. N. E., chap. 31. See Chronicles of Plymouth, pp. 402, 403. A History of Newbury, by Joshua Coffin, was published in 1845, in octavo, 416 pages.

CHAP.
XX.
1633.

Aug.
15.

country hath not that which this place cannot yield. So that these two places may contain twice as many people as are yet in New-England, there being as yet scarce any inhabitants in these two spacious places. Three miles beyond the river of Merrimack is the outside of our patent for the Massachusetts Bay.

These be all the towns that were begun when I came for England ; which was the 15th of August, 1633.

I have informed you of the country in general, and of every plantation in particular, with their commodities, and wherein one excelleth another. But some, peradventure, may say that they have heard that the people have been often driven to great wants and extremities. To which I answer; it is true that some have lived for a certain time with a little bread, others without any. Yet all this argues nothing against the country in itself, but condemns the folly and improvidence of such as would venture into so rude and unmanaged a country without so much provisions as should have comfortably maintained them in health and strength, till by their labors they had brought the land to yield his fruit. I have myself heard some say, that they heard it was a rich land, a brave country ; but when they came there, they could see nothing but a few canvass booths and old houses, supposing at the first to have found walled towns, fortifications, and corn-fields ; as if towns could have built themselves, or corn-fields have grown of themselves, without the husbandry of man. These men, missing of their expectations, returned home and railed against the country.

Others may object, that of late time there hath CHAP.
been great want. I deny it not. But look to the
original, and tell me from whence it came. The 1633.
root of their want sprung up in England. For many
hundreds, hearing of the plenty of the country, were
so much their own foes and country's hindrance,
as to come without provision ; which made things
both dear and scant. Wherefore, let none blame
the country, so much as condemn the indiscreetness
of such as will needs run themselves upon hardship.
And I dare further assure any, that will carry provision enough for a year and a half, shall not need to
fear want, if he either be industrious himself, or have
industrious agents to manage his estate and affairs.

And whereas many do disparage the land, saying
a man cannot live without labor ; in that they more
disparage and discredit themselves, in giving the
world occasion to take notice of their dronish disposition, that would live of the sweat of another
man's brows. Surely they were much deceived, or
else ill informed, that ventured thither in hope to
live in plenty and idleness, both at a time ; and it is
as much pity that he that can work and will not,
should eat, as it is pity that he that would work and
cannot, should fast. I condemn not such, therefore,
as are now there, and are not able to work. But I
advise, for the future, those men that are of weak
constitutions to keep at home, if their estates cannot
maintain servants. For all New-England must be
workers in some kind. And whereas it hath been
formerly reported, that boys of ten or twelve years
of age, might do much more than get their living,[1]

---

[1] See page 246.

CHAP.
XX.

1633.

that cannot be. For he must have more than a boy's head, and no less than a man's strength, that intends to live comfortably ; and he that hath understanding and industry, with a stock of £100, shall live better there than he shall do here of £20 per annum.

But many, I know, will say, If it be thus, how comes it to pass then that they are so poor ? To which I answer, that they are poor but in comparison. Compare them with the rich merchants or great landed men in England, and then I know they will seem poor. There is no probability they should be exceeding rich, because none of such great estate went over yet. Besides, a man of estate must first scatter before he gather. He must lay out moneys for transporting of servants and cattle and goods, for houses, and fences and gardens, &c. This may make his purse seem light, and to the eye of others seem a leaking in his estate. Whereas these disbursements are for his future enrichments ; for he being once well seated and quietly settled, his increase comes in double. And howsoever they are accounted poor, they are well contented, and look not so much at abundance as a competency. So little is the poverty of the country, that I am persuaded if many in England, which are constrained to beg their bread, were there, they would live better than many do here that have money to buy it.

Furthermore, when corn is scarce, yet may they have either fish or flesh for their labor. And surely that place is not miserably poor to them that are there, where four eggs may be had for a penny, and a quart of new milk at the same rate ; where butter is six pence a pound, and Cheshire cheese at five

pence. Sure Middlesex affords London no better CHAP.
pennyworths. What though there be no such plenty
as to cry these things in the streets? Yet every day 1633.
affords these pennyworths to those that need them
in most places, I dare not say in all. Can they be
very poor, where for four thousand souls there are
fifteen hundred head of cattle, besides four thousand
goats, and swine innumerable? In an ill sheep year
I have known mutton as dear in Old England, and
dearer than goat's flesh is in New-England; which
is altogether as good, if fancy be set aside.[1]

[1] Of WILLIAM WOOD, the author of the preceding very accurate topographical description of Massachusetts, I can obtain no information. He says in the Preface to his book, "I have laid down the nature of the country without any partial respect unto it, as being my dwelling-place, *where I have lived these four years*, and intend (God willing) to return shortly again." Of course, he must have come over in 1629, probably with Higginson. At the end of the 12th chapter of his first part he says that "the end of his travel was *observation*." He returned to England in the ship Elizabeth Bonadventure, Capt. Graves, and probably never came back. I presume he is the person referred to in the following order of the General Court. "Sept 3, 1634, it is ordered that there shall be letters of thankfulness signed by the Court, and sent to the Countess of Warwick, Mr. Paynter, Mr. *Wood*, and others, that have been benefactors to this Plantation." See Col. Rec. i. 127, and Winthrop, i. 104, 107.

# JOHN COTTON'S LIFE AND LETTERS.

# CHAPTER XXI.

## CONCERNING THE LIFE OF THE FAMOUS MR. COTTON, TEACHER TO THE CHURCH OF CHRIST AT BOSTON, IN NEW-ENGLAND.

WHAT I have to add concerning the life of this CHAP. XXI. blessed man of God, now triumphing in glory, to what hath been already set forth by the reverend Mr. Davenport,[1] the worthy pastor of the Church of Christ at New Haven, I shall hold forth in these particulars ; first, concerning the place of his birth and education, till he went to the University, and his abode in Cambridge ; secondly, concerning his removal from Cambridge to Boston, in Lincolnshire, and what he met with and did there ; thirdly, concerning his departure from thence into New-Eng-

---

[1] Davenport's account is also mentioned on page 51, and is quoted on page 32, of John Norton's Life of Cotton. Whether it was ever printed, I have not been able to ascertain. Dr. Bacon does not mention it in his list of Davenport's writings. Cotton Mather says, that " when the tidings of Mr. Cotton's decease reached New-Haven, Mr. Davenport, with many tears, bewailed it in a public discourse." Perhaps it was the manuscript of this discourse that Whiting and Norton saw and used. Richard Mather also preached a funeral sermon on his friend, which probably was never printed. See note [1] on p. 102 ; Mather's Magnalia, i. 249 ; Leonard Bacon's Historical Discourses, p. 389.

CHAP.
XXI.

1585.
Dec.
4.

1598.

land, and what service the Lord made him an instrument of in that remote country.

I. For the first, the place of his birth was the
town of Derby,[1] the most eminent place in that
country. His father[2] trained him up to such learning as the school afforded for the fitting him for
Cambridge ; whither he went when he was very
young, at thirteen years of age, and was admitted
into the famous society of Trinity College ; where
he fell so hard to his study, and so profited in the
knowledge of the tongues and arts, that he had undoubtedly been Fellow there, but that at that time
their great Hall was then in building,[3] which caused
such expenses to them that the election was put by,
or at least deferred, till some longer time. And
this providence I cannot pass by concerning him,
that his father, whose calling was to be employed in
the study and practice of the law, had not many
clients that made use of his advice in law matters
before. It pleased God, after he was gone to Cambridge, to put his father upon great practice, so that
he was very able to keep him there and allow him
liberal maintenance ; insomuch that the blessed man
said, " God kept me at the University."[4]

[1] Derby is a borough and market town, the capital of Derbyshire, 126 miles northwest of London. Population in 1841, 32,741.

[2] His father's Christian name was Roland, after whom he called one of his own sons. John's grandson, the minister of Sandwich, was baptized at Dorchester May 3, 1668, with the name Role-on-God. It was afterwards spelt Roland. See Mass. Hist. Coll. ix. 193.

[3] This must refer to the additions made in the mastership of Thomas Nevile, who died in 1615, and who

is said to have spent £3000 in enlarging and improving his College. To him it is indebted for the Great Court, as it is at present ; and he built two sides of the Court, which, after his name, has since been called Nevile's Court. See Le Keux's Memorials of Cambridge, vol. i. Trinity College, p. 29 ; Fuller's Hist. of the Univ. p. 174 ; Dyer's Hist. of the Univ. ii. 331.

[4] He was admitted to the degree of A. M. at Trinity College in 1606. See Mass. Hist. Coll. xxviii. 247.

From Trinity College he removed to Emmanuel CHAP.<br>XXI.
College,[1] the happy seminary of learning and piety,
where he was honored with a fellowship in that Society, after a diligent and strict examen, according
to the statutes of that House. Wherein this is worth
the taking notice of, that when the poser came to
examine him in the Hebrew tongue, the place where
he was to be examined was that in Isaiah iii., that
speaks against the bravery of women, which hath
more hard words together than any place in the Bible within so narrow a compass, and might have
posed a very good Hebrician; but he was very
ready at it, and all those difficult words were easy
to him. Afterwards he was head-lecturer, and dean,
and catechist in the College, and was a diligent tutor
to many pupils, and very much beloved of them.
His exercises that he performed in the College,
whether in the way of common-place or dispute,
wanted not sinews and strength, were highly commended and applauded of those that knew him.

The first time that he became famous throughout
the whole University, was from a funeral oration
which he made in Latin for Dr. Some,[2] who was 1608.
Master of Peter House; which was so elegantly and
oratoriously performed, that he was much admired

---

[1] The Puritan College, at which
more of our first ministers and magistrates were educated than at any
other. It was founded in 1585, by
Sir Walter Mildmay. Fuller says,
that " coming to Court after he had
founded his College, the Queen
(Elizabeth) told him, ' Sir Walter,
I hear you have erected a Puritan
foundation.' ' No, madam,' saith he,
' far be it from me to countenance
any thing contrary to your established laws ; but I have set an acorn,

which, when it becomes an oak,
God alone knows what will be the
fruit thereof.' " See note [2] on page
357; Fuller's Hist. of the University,
p. 205, (8vo. ed.); Dyer's Hist. of
the Univ. ii. 344–396 ; Le Keux's
Memorials of Cambridge, vol. 2;
Mass. Hist. Coll. xxviii. 247, 248.

[2] Robert Soame was elected Master of Peter House in 1589, and died
in 1608. See Fuller's History of
the University of Cambridge, p. 48.

CHAP.
XXI.

1608.

for it by the greatest wits in the University. After that, being called to preach at the University Church, called St. Mary's, he was yet more famous for that sermon, and very much applauded by all the gallant scholars for it. After that, being called to preach there again, God helped him not to flaunt, as before, but to make a plain, honest sermon, which was blessed of God to famous Dr. Preston's[1] soul's eternal good. His *Concio ad Clerum*, when he took his degree for Bachelor of Divinity, which was after he had been at Boston half a year or more, was very much admired, and applauded more than he desired. His text was out of Matthew, v. 13. *Vos estis sal terræ ; quòd si sal infatuatus fuerit, quo salietur ?* In handling of which, both the matter and the rhetorical strains, elegancy of phrase, and sweet and grave pronunciation, rendered him yet more famous in the University. And so did his answering of the Divinity Act in the Schools, though he had a very nimble opponent, Mr. William Chappel by name, who disputed with him.

II. Concerning his removal from Cambridge to Boston,[2] in Lincolnshire, this is to be said, that his call was good, for their desire was urgent, their need pressed, their assembly of people very great, himself very able, and his heart inclining to come to them. At his first coming, he found some obstruction from the Bishop of the Diocese, which was B. Barlow,[3] who told him he was a young man, and unfit to be

[1] Dr. John Preston, at this time fellow of Queen's, was afterwards Master of Emmanuel College. — Some account of him will be found on a subsequent page. See the Index.

[2] See note on page 49 ; Pishey Thompson's Hist. of Boston, p. 86 ; and Mass. Hist. Coll. xxviii. 343.

[3] Barlow was succeeded in the see of Lincoln by Dr. John Williams, in August, 1621.

over such a factious people.   Mr. Cotton, being in- CHAP.<br>XXI.
genuous, and undervaluing himself, thought so too,
and was purposing to return to the College again.
But some of Mr. Cotton's Boston friends, understanding that one Simon Biby[1] was to be spoken with,
which was near the Bishop, they presently charmed
him ; and so the business went on smooth, and Mr.
Cotton was a learned man with the Bishop, and he
was admitted into the place, after their manner in
those days.

Well, to Boston the good man came, and for three 1612.
years he preached and lived so amongst them, that
they accounted themselves happy, as they well
might, in the enjoyment of him, both the town and
country thereabout being much bettered by him.
But it pleased God, after three or four years being 1615.
there, that he could not digest the ceremonies, that
were so pressed, nor conformity to them ; which, in
some space of time after, bred him trouble in the
Court of Lincoln, from which he was advised to ap-
peal to a higher Court.   And employing Mr. Lev-
erit[2] (which was afterwards one of the ruling elders
of the Church at Boston in New-England,) to deal in

---

[1] " Which some call *Simony and
Bribery.*"   Marginal Note, by the
author, Samuel Whiting.—It was
by the influence of this same Simon
Biby, " a near alliance of the Bishop's visiter," that Richard Mather
was restored to his parish at Toxteth in Nov. 1633, having been suspended in the preceding August for
Nonconformity. See Mather's Magnalia, i. 405.

[2] Thomas Leverett was an alderman of the borough of Boston ;
which office he resigned July 22,
1633, in view of embarking with his
pastor for New-England, where he

arrived Sept. 4.   On the 10th Oct.
he was chosen a ruling elder of Boston church.   Winthrop speaks of
him as " an ancient, sincere professor, of Mr. Cotton's congregation in
England."   His wife, Ann, came
with him.   His son, John, knighted by Charles II. in 1676, was
Governor of the Colony from 1673
until his death, March 16, 1679, and
his great-grandson, John, was President of Harvard College from 1708
to his death, May 3, 1724.   See
Winthrop, i. 114, ii. 245 ; Hubbard,
p. 190 ; Hutchinson's Mass. i. 269,
323 ; Mass. Hist. Coll. xxviii. 343.

CHAP.
XXI.
that business, and he being a plain man, as Jacob was, yet subtile to get such a spiritual blessing, so far insinuated himself into one of the proctors of the High Court, that he sware *in animam Domini*, that Mr. Cotton was a conformable man, and so he was restored to Boston ; as likewise by the means that a gentleman of Boston, called Mr. Bennett, used to bring him in again.

After which, he was marvellous successful in his ministry, till he had been twenty years there. And 1632. in that twenty years' space he, on Lord's day, on afternoons, went over thrice the whole body of divinity in a catechistical way, and gave the heads of his discourse to those that were young scholars, and others in that town, to answer to his questions in public in that great congregation ; and after their answers, he opened those heads of divinity, and sweetly applied all to the edification of his people, and to such strangers as came to hear him. In the morning on the Lord's day, he preached over the first six chapters of the Gospel by John,[1] the whole Book of Ecclesiastes, the Prophecy of Zephaniah,[2] and many other Scriptures ; and when the Lord's Supper was administered, (which was usually every month,) he preached upon 1 Cor. xi. and the whole 30th chapter of the 2 Chronicles, and some other Scriptures about the Lord's Supper. On his lecture days, he preached through the whole 1st and 2d Epistles of John, the whole book of Solomon's Song, the Parables of our Saviour, set forth in Matthew's Gospel to the end of chapter 16th, comparing them with Mark and Luke. He took much pains in private,

---

[1] See note [3] on page 138, and note [2] on page 221.

[2] Norton, in his Life of Cotton, p. 17, says *Zechariah*.

and read to sundry young scholars that were in his CHAP.<br>XXI. house, and some that came out of Germany, and had his house full of auditors. Afterwards, seeing some inconveniences in the people's flocking to his house, besides his ordinary lecture on the fifth[1] day of the week, he preached thrice more on the week days, on the fourth and sixth days, early in the morning, and on the last day, at three of the clock in the afternoon. Only these three last lectures were performed by him but some few years, before he had another famous colleague[2] with him, and not many years before he left Boston. He always preached at the election of their mayors, and at that time when they took their oath, and were installed in their office, and always (if he were at home,) at the funerals of those of the abler sort that died. He was frequent in duties of humiliation and thanksgiving; in which I have known him in prayer and opening the word and applying it, five or six hours; so indefatigable he was in the Lord's work, and so ready to spend and be spent for his people's souls.

He was of admirable candor, of unparalleled meekness, of rare wisdom, very loving even to those that differed in judgment from him, yet one that held his own stoutly, *arctè tenens accuratèque defendens* what himself judged to be the truth. He answered many

---

[1] This fifth day or Thursday lecture he transferred to Boston in New-England, where it has been continued ever since by his successors, the pastors of the First Church. The first notice of it is found in Winthrop's Journal under March 4, 1634, by which it appears that it was already established. " By order of Court a mercate was erected at Boston, to be kept upon Thursday, the fifth day of the week, being the Lecture day." See Winthrop, i. 112, 124; Frothingham's Sermon at the close of the Second Century since the establishment of the Thursday Lecture; and Waterston's Discourse on its reöpening, Dec. 14, 1843, in the Christian Examiner, xxxvi. 24.

[2] Anthony Tuckney, who married his cousin, and succeeded him in the vicarage.

CHAP. letters that were sent far and near; wherein were
XXI.
handled many difficult cases of conscience, and many
doubts by him cleared to the greatest satisfaction.

He was exceedingly beloved of the best, and
admired and reverenced of the worst of his hearers.
Nothing was wanting to make him a complete minister, nothing lacking to make him a perfect Christian, but the perfection of grace which he hath now
attained to, and the glory he hath now arrived at.
He was a man that was in great favor with Dr. Williams,[1] the Bishop of Lincoln, who admired him for
his learning, and (as I have been told,) when he was
Lord Keeper of the great seal, he went to King
James, and speaking of Mr. Cotton's great learning
and worth before him, the King was willing, notwithstanding his Nonconformity, to give way that he
should have his liberty to go on without interruption
in his ministry ; which was very marvellous, considering how the King's spirit was carried out against
such men. The mystery of which Mr. Samuel Ward,[2]

[1] Dr. John Williams succeeded
Lord Bacon as Keeper of the Great
Seal, July 10, 1621. Within a
month afterwards he was made Bishop of Lincoln, and in 1641 Archbishop of York. He was mild and
tolerant towards the Puritans and
Nonconformists, and this probably
was the cause of the bitter hatred
and cruel persecution which he en-
countered from Laud. " This prosecution " says Bishop Warburton,
" must needs give every one a bad
idea of Laud's heart and temper.
You might resolve his high acts of
power in the State into reverence
and gratitude to his master ; his tyranny in the Church to his zeal for
and love of what he called religion ;
but the outrageous prosecution of
these two men (Dr. Williams and

the Rev. Mr. Osbaldiston,) can be
resolved into nothing but envy and
revenge." He died March 25,
1649. See Fuller's Worthies, ii.
585, and Ch. Hist. iii. 290, 388, 402,
484–490 ; Hallam's Const. Hist. i.
447 ; Aikin's Life of James I., ii.
132, 250, 254 ; Aikin's Life of
Charles I., i. 422–430, ii. 190 ;
Neal's Puritans, ii. 197, 308.
[2] Samuel Ward was the son of
the Rev. John Ward, of Haverhill,
and brother of our Nathaniel Ward,
mentioned on page 112. He seems
to have had the same vein of humor
with the author of " The Simple
Cobbler of Agawam." He was
educated at Sidney College, Cambridge, " of which he became fellow," 'says Fuller, " being an excellent artist, linguist, divine and

of Ipswich, being ignorant of, spake merrily among some of his friends, " Of all men in the world I envy Mr. Cotton, of Boston, most ; for he doth nothing in way of conformity, and yet hath his liberty, and I do everything that way, and cannot enjoy mine."

He had many enemies at Boston, as well as many friends, and some that rose up against him, and plotted secretly to undermine him, and others that practised more openly against him.  But they all of them were blasted, either in their names, or in their estates, or in their families, or in their devices, or else came to untimely deaths ; which shows how God both owned his servant in his holy labors, and that in the things wherein they dealt proudly against him, he would be above them.

One thing more, and I have done with him, as he was one of England's glories, and then come to him as over the Atlantic ocean, and in New-England ; and it is this, concerning his hospitality, wherein he did exceed most that ever I heard of.  And especially his heart and doors were open to receive, as all that feared God, so especially godly ministers, which he most courteously entertained, and many other strangers besides.  Only one minister, Mr. Hacket by name, which had got into the fellowship of famous Mr. Arthur Hildersham,[1] with many other

preacher. From Cambridge he was preferred minister of Ipswich, having a care over, and a love from, all the parishes in that populous place. Indeed he had a magnetic virtue (as if he had learned it from the loadstone, in whose qualities he was so knowing,) to attract people's affections. Yet found he foes as well as friends, who complained of him to the High Commission. He had three brethren ministers ; on the same token that some have said, that these four put together would not make up the abilities of their father. Nor were they themselves offended with this hyperbole, to have the branches lessened to greaten their root." See Fuller's Worthies, ii. 344 ; Brook's Lives of the Puritans, ii. 452.

[1] See note [1] on page 66.

428

THE LIFE OF JOHN COTTON.THE LIFE OF JOHN COTTON.

CHAP.CHAP.
XXI. godly ministers, and being acquainted with their
secrets, betrayed them into the prelates' hands, this
man, coming into Boston, and meeting with Mr.
Cotton, the good man had not the heart to speak to
him, nor invite him to his house ; which he said he
never did to any stranger that he knew before, much
less to any minister.

III. Concerning the last thing, viz. his departure
from Boston to New-England. The times growing
perilous, he was envied of some at home, and others
abroad ; and letters missive were come to convent
him before the High Commission Court ; and a pro-
fligate fellow and a filthy fornicator, Gowen Johnson
by name, who not long after died of the plague, was
to bring the letters to him, as he did to some others
near him. Which when Mr. Cotton understood, he
looked for nothing from the Court but scorns and
prison ; and therefore, with advice from many able
heads and gracious hearts, he kept close for a time,
and fitted himself to go to New-England.[1]

1633.    And God bringing him and his company over in
Sept.
4.   safety, through his mercy, after they had been there
a while, there grew some trouble between those that
were to settle matters in church and commonwealth.
But Mr. Cotton then preaching before the General

[1] " His forced flight " says John
Davenport, " from Boston to London for his safety from pursuivants
sent to apprehend him, I well remember ; and admire the special
providence of God towards myself
and some others in it, amongst
whom safe retirement and hiding-
places were provided for him in and
about London." Davenport was at
this time vicar of St. Stephen's, in
Coleman-street, London. — " They
got out of England with much difficulty," says Winthrop, " all places
being belaid to have taken Mr. Cotton and Mr. Hooker, who had been
long sought for to have been brought
into the High Commission. But
the master being bound to touch at
the Wight, the pursuivants attended
there, and in the mean time, the
ministers were taken in at the
Downs." See note [1] on page 102,
and note [5] on page 260 ; Norton's
Life of Cotton, pp. 21, 32 ; Winthrop, i. 109 ; Mather, i. 240, 241.

Court an excellent sermon out of Haggai, ii. "*Be strong, Zerubbabel, and be strong, Joshua, and be strong, ye people of the land,*" &c., it pleased God so to compose and calm and quiet spirits, that all apprehensions were laid aside, and they went about the work of the Lord very comfortably, and were much encouraged.[1] After which time, how useful he was to England, to New-England, to magistrates, ministers, people, in public, in private, by preachings, counsels, dissolving hard knots and answering difficult questions, all knew that knew the grace of God so evidently manifested in him. What Scriptures he went over on Lord's days, in expounding and preaching, I cannot certainly say, because I was of another church,[2] serving there according to the grace bestowed upon me. But surely he went through very many. For on his Lecture days he preached over the whole book of the Revelation, Ecclesiastes, and Canticles, the second and third Epistles of John, the two Epistles of Timothy, with divers others ; all which shows the unwearied pains which he took in the Lord's work, besides all the books[3] that were written by him, and other unknown labors that he went through.[4]

---

[1] Cotton preached the Election Sermon in May, 1634. See Winthrop, i. 132.

[2] Whiting was the pastor of the church at Lynn, where he was settled in Nov. 1636. See Winthrop, i. 204.

[3] A list of Cotton's writings may be seen in Emerson's History of the First Church in Boston, page 85.

[4] Cotton died on Thursday, Dec. 23, 1652, between the hours of 11 and 12, after the bell had called to the Lecture. Upon the 29th he was interred in a brick tomb in the old burying-ground, (adjoining the King's Chapel,) in the northern corner, near the Savings' Bank, and not far from Winthrop's tomb. In the same grave with Cotton's, repose the ashes of his friend, John Davenport. His daughter Maria married Increase Mather, and was the mother of Cotton Mather. His son Seaborn married Dorothy, the daughter of Gov. Bradstreet, and was settled in the ministry at Hampton, in New-Hampshire, where he was succeeded by his son John. Seaborn's younger brother, John, was the minister of Plymouth, and had two sons, John and Roland, who

CHAP.<br>XXI. I could speak much more ; but at this present want strength. But this I say ; he may be a pattern to us all, and happy they that come nearest him in those things wherein he most followed Christ. I am not like to live to see such another in New-England, though I know God is able to double the spirit of that Elias upon him that succeeds him, and upon many others in our native country and here. It is well for both the Bostons that they had such a light, if they walk in the light, and continue in that word of Christ and light of grace and truth that he held out to them. I end all with that of our Saviour concerning John Baptist, " he was a burning and a shining light ;" and God grant the after words be not verified of both Englands, and both Bostons. I speak my fears, but would be glad to entertain better hopes. My prayers shall be, that it may never be said as of old, *Fuimus Troes, fuit Ilium ; sed jam seges est ubi Troja fuit. Fuimus fideles, fuimus φιλόθεοι ; fuit Anglia, fuit Nov-Anglia, fuit Bostonia, Europæa, Americana. Deus, Pater miserationum, avertat omen per viscera Jesu Christi !* Amen.

SAMUEL WHITING.[1]<br>Pastor Linnensis Nov-Anglicanus.

were the ministers of Yarmouth and Sandwich. See Norton's Life of Cotton, p. 46 ; Mather's Magnalia, i. 300.

[1] SAMUEL WHITING, the author of the preceding biography, was of a reputable family in Boston, in Lincolnshire, where he was born Nov. 20, 1597. His father and brother were both mayors of that borough. He was educated at Emanuel College, Cambridge, where he took the degree of A. B. in 1616, and of A. M. in 1620. At the University he had for a chamber-mate his cousin, Anthony Tuckney, the colleague and successor of Cotton in Boston church. He was a minister three years at Lynn Regis in Norfolk, and afterwards at Skirbeck, less than a mile from Boston ; "where," says Mather, "he was refreshed with the delightful neighbourhood of his old friends, and especially those eminent persons, Mr. Cotton and Mr. Tuckney, to both of whom he had some affinity." Being harassed for his Nonconformity, he

embarked for New-England, and arrived at Boston May 26, 1636. After spending a month with his kinsman, Atherton Hough, he removed to Lynn, where he was ordained in November, and where he continued till his death, Dec. 11, 1679, in his 83d year. His second wife, Elizabeth, was the daughter of Oliver St. John, who was Chief Justice of England in Cromwell's reign, and whose second wife was a cousin of Cromwell's. One of Whiting's sons, Samuel, was the first minister of Billerica. His vicinity to Cotton, before their removal to America, afforded him the best opportunities to obtain information concerning his life and history; and we are under great obligations to him for his admirable biographical sketch. It forms the foundation of Norton's as well as of Mather's Life of this great man. Both of them appropriate Whiting's labors most unceremoniously, and add but little to his original sketch. See note [1] on page 419 ; Winthrop, i. 204 ; Mather, i. 249, 452–461 ; Hutchinson's Mass. i. 19 ; Carlyle's Cromwell, i. 94, 97, 556 ; Thompson's Hist. of Boston, pp. 100, 263, 264 ; Mass. Hist. Coll. xxviii. 248, 344.

CHAP.
XXI.

COTTON'S LETTER TO HIS WIFE.

DEAR WIFE, AND COMFORTABLE YOKE-FELLOW,

CHAP.
XXI.

1632.
Oct.
3.

IF our heavenly Father be pleased to make our yoke more heavy than we did so soon[1] expect, remember (I pray thee,) what we have heard, that our heavenly husband, the Lord Jesus, when he first called us to fellowship with himself, called us unto this condition, to deny ourselves and to take up our cross daily, to follow him. And truly, sweet heart, though this cup may be brackish at the first taste, yet a cup of God's mingling is doubtless sweet in the bottom to such as have learned to make it their greatest happiness to partake with Christ, as in his glory, so in the way that leadeth to it.

Where I am for the present,[2] I am very fitly and welcomely accommodated, I thank God ; so, as I see, here I might rest, (desired enough,) till my friends at home shall direct further. They desire also to see thee here; but that I think it not safe yet, till we see how God will deal with our neighbours at home. For if you should now travel this way, I fear you will be watched and dogged at the heels. But I hope shortly God will make way for thy safe coming.

Meanwhile, send me now by this bearer such linen as I am to use.

---

[1] May we not infer from this expression that they had been recently married ?

[2] Cotton was at this time in concealment in London. See note [1] on page 428.

If Margarett be fit to come with this bearer, whither I shall direct him, she may come behind him upon my mare, unless she desire to stay with some other, at Boston ; which if she do, help her therein.

I pray you go to my mother, Havered,[1] and commend my hearty respect and love to her ; and the rather because I had not time to see her at my coming out. To many other friends it will not be meet to speak of me now. The Lord watch over you all for good, and reveal himself in the guidance of all our affairs.

So with my love to thee, as myself, I rest, desirous of thy rest and peace in Him,

J. C.

*October* 3, 1632.

When you have read my letter to Margarett, seal it up and give it her. Once again, Farewell in the Lord. If she be not ready to come with him now, he may come for her the next week.

[*Addressed on the outside,*]
    To my dear wife, Mrs. SARAH COTTON,[2]
        deliver this with speed.

---

[1] Was this the mother of his first wife, whom Mather, i. 237, calls Horrocks, married again to a Mr. Havered ?

[2] This letter was written to his second wife, Sarah Story, who was a widow when he married her, probably in 1632. His first wife, Elizabeth Horrocks, with whom he lived eighteen years, but had no children, was living as late as Oct. 2, 1630, as appears from another letter of his printed in the Appendix to the Rev. Dr. Harris's Memorials of the First Church in Dorchester, p. 57. Cotton's widow married the Rev. Richard Mather, of Dorchester. — It appears from an endorsement on this letter, in the handwriting of Prince, the Annalist, that it was once in the possession of Increase Mather. Prince prints a part of it on page 419 of his Annals. It is printed now for the first time entire, from the original, preserved among Prince's manuscripts in the Archives of the Mass. Hist. Society. See Norton's Life of Cotton, p. 18 ; Mather's Magnalia, i. 237.

COTTON'S LETTER TO THE BISHOP OF LINCOLN.[1]

*To the Right Reverend and my very honorable good Lord, John,
Lord Bishop of Lincoln, at his palace in Buckden,[2] present these.*

MY VERY GOOD LORD,

CHAP.
XXI.

1633.
May
7.

It is now above twenty years ago, since, by
the goodness of God, and for a good part of this time
by your Lordship's lawful favor, I have enjoyed the
happiness to minister to the Church of God at Boston, a remote corner of your Lordship's diocese.
What I have done there, all this while, and how I
have spent my time and course, I must ere long give
account to the Great Shepherd of the sheep, the
Bishop of our souls. Meanwhile, give me leave to
make your Lordship this short account.

The bent of my course hath been, (according to
my weak measure,) to make and keep a threefold
Christian concord amongst the people; between God
and their conscience ; between true-hearted loyalty
and Christian liberty ; between the fear of God and
the love of one another. That wherein I have most
seemed to your Lordship to fail, to wit, in not discerning Christian liberty to practise some commands
of authority in some circumstances, I do humbly

[1] Dr. John Williams. See note [1]
on page 426.
[2] Buckden is in the county of
Huntingdon, on the western bank of
the Ouse, four miles southwest from
Huntingdon. The ancient palace of
the Bishop of Lincoln, situated here,
was pulled down by an order of
Council, April 3, 1838. Some of
the bishops of Lincoln have been
interred in the church at Buckden.

thank your Lordship, and freely acknowledge your
Lordship hath not been wanting freely and often to
admonish me thereof, and that with such wisdom and
gravity, and with such well-tempered authority and
mildness, that I profess unfeignedly no outward respect in the world could have detained me from re-
questing your Lordship's favor, with ready subjec-
tion to your Lordship's counsel, that I might have
prolonged mine own peace and your Lordship's favor
together.    But so it is, my good Lord, though I do
unfeignedly and deservedly honor your Lordship,
and highly esteem many hundreds of other reverend
divines, great lights of the Church, (in comparison of
whom, what am I, poor spark?) who doubt not of
their liberty in those matters, yet to this day, (I
speak in the simplicity of my heart,) I can only follow your Lordship with observance, and them with
reverence, but not with that plerophory of faith in
these things which in such cases the Apostle requireth.    Your Lordship well knoweth it is both the
Apostles' and Prophets' principle, (and it holdeth
in every righteous man, from the meanest to the
greatest,) *Justus ex fide suâ vivit, non alienâ;* and
therefore, howsoever I do highly prize and much
prefer other men's judgment and learning and wisdom and piety, yet in things pertaining to God and
his worship, still I must, as I ought, live by mine
own faith, not theirs.    Nevertheless, where I cannot
yield obedience of faith, I am willing to yield patience of hope.

And now, my good Lord, I see the Lord, who
began a year or two ago to suspend, after a sort, my
ministry from that place by a long and sore sickness,

CHAP.
XXI.

1633.
May
7.

the dregs whereof still hang about me, doth now put a further necessity upon me wholly to lay down my ministry there, and freely to resign my place into your Lordship's hands. For I see neither my bodily health, not the peace of the Church, will now stand with my continuance there. I do now therefore humbly crave this last favor at your Lordship's hand, to accept my place as void, and to admit thereto such a successor as your Lordship shall find fit, and the patron, which is the corporation of Boston, shall present to you therefor.[1] The congregation is great, and the church duties many, and those many times requiring close attendance ; and I would be very loth the service of God or the help of the people should be in any sort neglected by my long discontinuance.

What though this resignation of my place into your Lordship's hands may be defective in some form of law, yet I trust your Lordship will never forget the ancient moderation and equity of that honorable

[1] " At an assembly holden at the Guildhall of the Borough of Boston, in the county of Lincoln, this 22d day of July, 1633, before the Mayor, Aldermen, and Common Council :

" At this assembly, Mr. John Cotton, late vicar of Boston, yielded up his place of being vicar, by his letter dated in July, 1633, which this House have accepted.

" At this assembly there was an intimation delivered to the Mayor and Burgesses of this Borough, from the right honorable John, Lord Bishop of Lincoln, by the hands of Mr. Thomas Cony, [town-clerk] of this town, intimating that the 8th of July, 1633, Mr. John Cotton, late vicar of Boston, had resigned his said vicarage to the said Bishop, and that the said Lord Bishop did the same day, at his house in the College of Westminster, accept of the same resignation, and did then pronounce the same vicarage to be actually void of incumbent, and that he did then, by the said Thomas Cony, intimate to the Mayor and Burgesses of Boston the voidance of the same, to the end that the said Mayor and Burgesses may, when they please, present some able person thereunto."

Whereupon the Corporation proceeded forthwith, as the Record shows, and made choice of Mr. Anthony Tuckney to be their vicar, who continued in office till 1660, twenty-seven years. We are indebted to Mr. Savage for this transcript from the records of Boston. See his Gleanings for New-England History, in Mass. Hist. Coll. xxviii. 344 ; and Thompson's Hist. of Boston, pp. 86, 271.

and high Court of Chancery, whereunto your Lordship was advanced, to temper the rigor of legal justice to the relief of many distressed. Never, I think,
came there any cause before your Lordship more distressed, nor more justly craving Christian equity.

Now the Lord of heaven and earth so guide and
keep and bless your Lordship on earth, that he may
delight to crown your Lordship with honor in heaven, at the end of your days, through Jesus Christ.
Thus at once commending my humble suit, and late
vicarage, and the comfort of the whole congregation,
to your Lordship's honorable favor and integrity, I
humbly take leave, and rest

A bounden suppliant to your Lordship,

And for you,      J. C.

*May* 7, 1633.

COTTON'S REASONS FOR HIS REMOVAL TO
NEW-ENGLAND.

REVEREND AND BELOVED BROTHER IN OUR BLESSED SAVIOUR,[1]

CHAP.
XXI.

1634.
Dec.
3.

THAT which you observe touching the wonderful goodness of the Lord to my wife and child in the midst of deep dangers,[2] I desire never to forget it, but to walk, (as the Lord shall be pleased to help me,) according to that abundant faithfulness of his to one so undeserving, all my days. Help me with your faithful prayers so to do, that as by the prayers of yourself and other brethren I acknowledge the former mercy to have been granted me, so by the same a faithful and fruitful use of it may be granted to me likewise. Otherwise, (I may say it with shame,) I see a frame of spirit in myself ready to turn every grace of God into unprofitableness, yea, and forgetfulness of the most high God, the God of our salvation. Howsoever God dealt otherwise with my cousin Tuckney,[3] (which might give unto some whom

[1] This letter was addressed to one of the Puritan ministers in England, perhaps John Davenport, Richard Mather, or Thomas Shepard.

[2] This refers to the birth of his eldest son, born on the voyage in August, 1633, and whom he named *Seaborn*, "to keep alive (said he,) in me, and to teach him, if he live, a remembrance of sea-mercies from the hand of a gracious God." In the Triennial Catalogue of the Graduates of Harvard College, under 1651, he is called *Marigena*. He

was baptized at Boston Sept. 8, four days after his father's arrival. He was ordained the third minister of Hampton, in 1660, and died April 19, 1686, aged 52. See Winthrop, i. 110; Norton's Life of Cotton, page 18.

[3] The wife of Anthony Tuckney, his colleague and successor in the church at Boston. Tuckney was born in Sept. 1599, at Kirton, four miles from Boston, of which place his father was minister. He was educated at Emmanuel College,

it nearly concerned a seasonable advertisement,) yet CHAP.<br>XXI. I am persuaded it was in much faithfulness to her that God took her away, to prevent the disquietness and 1634. discouragement of her spirit; which the evils ensu- Dec.<br>3. ing, evils hastening upon the town,[1] would have brought upon her. The Lord is wise and gracious, and knoweth how to deliver his out of the hour of temptation; blessed forever be his name in Christ!

The questions you demand I had rather answer by word of mouth than by letter. Yet I will not refuse to give you account of my brother Hooker's removal and mine own, seeing you require a reason thereof from us both. We both of us concur in a threefold ground of our removal.

1. God having shut a door against both of us from ministering to him and his people in our wonted congregations, and calling us, by a remnant of our people, and by others of this country, to minister to them here, and opening a door to us this way, who are we that we should strive against God, and refuse to follow the concurrence of his ordinance and providence together, calling us forth to minister here? If we may and ought to follow God's calling three hundred miles, why not three thousand?

Cambridge, with his cousin, our Samuel Whiting, of Lynn. After graduating, he was chaplain to the Earl of Lincoln till he was chosen fellow of his College. In 1645, he was chosen Master of Emmanuel, and in 1653 Master of St. John's. He was also vice-chancellor of the University in 1648, and Regius Professor of Divinity. He was one of the Assembly of Divines that met at Westminster in 1643, and had a hand in drawing up the Assembly's Catechism, but voted against subscribing the Confession. After the Restoration he was one of the Commissioners at the Conference held at the Savoy in 1661. He was soon, however, compelled to resign all his places, on account of his Puritanism and Nonconformity, and died at London, in February, 1670, in his 71st year. See note on page 430; Calamy's Nonconformists' Memorial, i. 264; Neal's History of the Puritans, iii. 141; Dyer's Hist. of Univ. of Cambridge, i. 119, ii. 354.

[1] Boston, in Lincolnshire.

CHAP.
XXI.

1634.
Dec.
3.

Matth.
x. 23.

John,
xxi. 7.

2. Our Saviour's warrant is clear and strong (as we conceive,) in our case, that when we are distressed in our course in one country, (*ne quid dicam gravius*,) we should flee to another. To choose rather to bear witness to the truth by imprisonment than by banishment, is indeed sometimes God's way; but not in case men have ability of body and opportunity to remove, and no necessary engagement for to stay. Whilst Peter was young, he might gird himself and go whither he would; but when he was old and unfit for travel, then indeed God called him rather to suffer himself to be girt of others, and led along to prison and to death. Nevertheless, in this point I conferred with the chief of our people, and offered them to bear witness to the truth I had preached and practised amongst them, even unto bonds, if they conceived it might be any confirmation to their faith and patience. But they dissuaded me that course, as thinking it better for themselves, and for me, and for the church of God, to withdraw myself from the present storm, and to minister in this country to such of their town [1] as they had sent before hither, and such others as were willing to go along with me, or to follow after me ; the most of the [*obliterated*] choosing rather to dwell in the [*a line and a half obliterated*] there. What service myself or brother Hooker might do to our people or other brethren in prison, (especially in close prison, which was feared,) I suppose we both of us, by God's help, do the same, and much more, and with more freedom from hence, as occasion is offered ; besides all our other service to the people here, which yet is

---

[1] Boston, in Lincolnshire. See note [3] on page 48.

enough, and more than enough, to fill both our hands, CHAP.
XXI.
yea and the hands of many brethren more, such as
yourself, should God be pleased to make way for 1634.
Dec.
your comfortable passage to us.[1] To have tarried in 3.
England for the end you mention, to appear in defence of that cause for which we were questioned,
had been, as we conceive it in our case, to limit
witness-bearing to the cause (which may be done
more ways than one,) to one only way, and that such a
way as we did not see God calling us unto. Did not
Paul bear witness against the Levitical ceremonies,
and yet choose rather to depart quickly out of Hierusalem, because the most of the Jews would not Acts,
xxii. 18.
receive his testimony concerning Christ in that question, than to stay at Hierusalem to bear witness to
that cause unto prison and death ? Not that we came
hither to strive against ceremonies, or to fight against
shadows ; there is no need of our further labor in
that course. Our people here desire to worship
God in spirit and in truth ; and our people left in
England know as well the grounds and reasons of our
suffering against these things, as our sufferings themselves ; which we beseech the Lord to accept and
bless in our blessed Saviour. How far our testimony
there hath prevailed with any others to search more
seriously into the cause, we do rather observe in
thankfulness and silence, than speak of to the prejudice of our brethren.

3. It hath been no small inducement to us to
choose rather to remove hither than to stay there,
that we might enjoy the liberty, not of some ordinances of God, but of all, and all in purity. For

[1] See note 1 on page 438.

CHAP.
XXI.
—~—
1634.
Dec.
3.

though we bless the Lord with you for the gracious means of salvation which many of your congregations do enjoy, (whereof our own souls have found the blessing, and which we desire may be forever continued and enlarged to you,) yet seeing Christ hath instituted no ordinance in vain, (but all to the perfecting of the body of Christ,) and we know that our souls stand in need of all to the utmost, we durst not so far be wanting to the grace of Christ and to the necessity of our own souls, as to sit down somewhere else, under the shadow of some ordinances, when by two months' travel we might come to enjoy the liberty of all.

To your second question, How far ministers are bound to bear witness against corruptions cast upon the face of God's ordinances, it is too large a point for me to give answer to in the heel of a letter. But thus much briefly. Witness is to be borne against

Rev.
xvi. 15.

corruptions, 1. By keeping a man's own garments clean ; I mean his own outward practice. 2. By

Acts,
xx.
26, 27.

declaring the whole counsel of God to his people, not shunning any part of it, as reasonable occasion

1 Thes.
v. 22.

is offered, to prevent sin in them. 3. By avoiding appearances of evil, as well as evil itself. Eleazar durst not eat mutton, or bread, or any other clean

2 Mac.
vi.
21-25.

food, when it had an appearance of eating swine's flesh, but chose death rather than deliverance by such means ; whose story, though it be Apocryphal, yet the example is authentical, as being ratified by the Apostle's testimony among the rest of like na-

Heb.
xi. 35.

ture, where, by the *others* he speaketh of, he meaneth not other women, but other men; for the word is ἄλλοι, (masculine.) Howsoever, Peter's dissembling

is evidently blamed by Paul in a like case, when by
his example he countenanced the imposing of ceremonies upon the Gentiles, to whom God never gave
them. 4. By contending for the truth in a holy
manner, when others contend with us against it.
5. By giving account of our faith before magistrates,
if they call us to do it publicly, requiring to be informed of our doctrine and manner of life. Otherwise, if they call us to know our opinions in private,
(intending to bring us into trouble,) or publicly,
rather as captious questionists than judicial governors, in such a case I suppose we may conceal our
minds, and put our adversaries upon proof, as our
Saviour did.

But why do I spend time and words to you in
these things, who know them as well as I can tell
you ? I rather desire you may be kept in a peaceable way of bearing witness to the truth, (if the will
of God be such,) than exposed to hazards by such
confessions as might prejudice your liberty. My
poor requests are to Heaven for you, as I desire you
might not forget me and mine, and all us here.
Now the God of peace and power guide and support
your spirit in all your holy endeavours, bless and
prosper your labors, and keep you as a chosen vessel
in the shadow of his hand, through him that hath
loved us.

Present my humble service to my right honorable
Lord ;[1] as also my dear affection to Mr. Ball,[2] Mr.
Slater, and all the brethren with you, especially to

CHAP.
XXI.

1634.
Dec.
3.

Gal.
ii.
11-14.

Jude,
3, 4.

1 Peter,
iii. 15.

John,
xviii.
19-21.

---

[1] The Earl of Lincoln.
[2] There were two Puritan clergymen living in England at this
time by the name of Ball, John and

Thomas, the former of whom was a
graduate of Oxford, and the latter
of Cambridge. Thomas is probably
the one here mentioned. He was

CHAP.
XXI.

1634.
Dec.
3.

Mr. Dod,[1] Mr. Cleaver,[2] Mr. Winston, Mr. Cotton, with earnest desire of the continuance of all their prayers, with your own, in our behalf. So I rest

Your very loving brother

in our blessed Saviour,

J. C.

*Boston, Dec. 3, 1634.*[3]

educated at Queen's College, was a fellow of Emmanuel, and was settled in the ministry at Northampton, where he died June 21, 1659, aged 69. He wrote a Life of Dr. Preston, Master of Emmanuel. See Wood's Athenæ, ii. 670 (ed. Bliss); Fuller's Worthies, ii. 232 ; Neal's Puritans, ii. 365 ; Brook's Lives of the Puritans, ii. 440, iii. 534.

[1] John Dod was an eminent Puritan divine. He was born at Shotwick, in Cheshire, in 1550, and was educated at Jesus College, Cambridge, of which he was a fellow. Fuller classes him among the learned writers of that College, and says that " he was a passive Nonconformist, an excellent scholar, and an exquisite Hebrician ; by nature a witty, by industry a learned, and by grace a godly divine ; successively minister of Hanwell, in Oxford, Fenny-Compton in Warwick, Cannons-Ashby and Fawsley, in Northamptonshire, though for a time si-

lenced in each of them. He died in 1645, in his 96th year, and was buried at Fawsley ; with whom the Old Puritan may seem to expire, and in his grave to be interred ; humble, meek, patient, hospitable, charitable, as in his censures of, so in his alms to, others." See Fuller's Worthies, i. 191 ; Fuller's Ch. History, iii. 479 ; Fuller's Hist. of Cambridge, p. 129 ; Brook's Lives of the Puritans, iii. 1–6 ; Neal's Hist. of the Puritans, iii. 322.

[2] Perhaps Robert Cleaver, who was a Puritan minister at Drayton, in Northamptonshire, but silenced by archbishop Bancroft for Nonconformity. He and Dod were joint authors of several valuable religious works. See Brook's Lives of the Puritans, iii. 6, 516.

[3] The original of this Letter is preserved among the Hutchinson manuscripts in the library of the Mass. Hist. Society.

# RICHARD MATHER'S JOURNAL.

# CHAPTER XXII.

## RICHARD MATHER'S JOURNAL.

PRAISE the Lord, O my soul ; and all that is within me, praise his holy name ! Praise the Lord, O my soul, and forget not all his benefits ! Yea, let all that is within me, and all that is without me, praise his holy name ! And let every thing that hath breath praise the name of the Lord for ever and ever ! Who gave unto us, his poor servants, such a safe and comfortable voyage to New-England ; the particular passages whereof were as followeth.

We came from Warrington[1] on Thursday, April 16, and came to Bristol[2] on the Thursday following, viz. April 23 ; and had a very healthful, safe, and prosperous journey all the way, (blessed be the name of our God for the same,) taking but easy journeys, because of the children and footmen, despatching

---

[1] Warrington is a market town in Lancashire, on the river Mersey, 77 miles from Birmingham, and 20 miles equidistant from Manchester and Liverpool by railway. Population in 1841, 21,901.

[2] Bristol is 114 miles west from London, on the Avon, and in 1841 had a population of 140,158.

a hundred and nineteen or twenty miles in seven days.[1]

Coming to Bristol, we found divers of the company come before us ; but some came not till after us. Howbeit, the last was come by the first of May. Nevertheless, we went not aboard the ship until Saturday, the 23d of May ; so that the time of our staying in Bristol was a month and two days ; during all which time we found friendship and courtesy at the hands of divers godly Christians in Bristol. Yet our stay was grievous unto us, when we considered how most of this time the winds were steady, and served directly for us. But our ship was not ready; so ill did our owners deal with us.

Going aboard the ship in King Road the 23d of May, we found things very unready, and all on heaps, many goods being not stowed, but lying on disordered heaps here and there in the ship. This day there came aboard the ship two of the searchers, and viewed a list of all our names, ministered the oath of Allegiance[2] to all at full age, viewed our certificates from the ministers in the parishes from whence we came, approved well thereof, and gave us tickets, that is, licenses under their hands and

---

[1] Cotton Mather says that his grandfather, on his journey "to Bristol, to take ship there, was forced to change his apparel, that he might escape the pursuivants, who were endeavouring to apprehend him." See Mather's Magnalia, i. 406.

[2] Sir Ferdinando Gorges says, "In a short time, numbers of people of all sorts flocked thither (to New-England,) in heaps, that at last it was specially ordered by the King's command, that none should be suffered to go without license first had and obtained, and they to take the oaths of Supremacy and Allegiance." Certificates were to be given by the ministers and justices of the several parishes, that this regulation had been complied with. The principal object of it seems to have been to prevent the emigration of Puritan ministers to New-England. But the measure was wholly ineffectual. See note [5] on page 260; Chronicles of Plymouth, note [2] on page 64 ; Mass. Hist. Coll. xxvi. 80, xxviii. 252–276.

seals to pass the seas, and cleared the ship, and so CHAP. XXII. departed. When we came to King Road, which is a spacious harbour of five or six miles broad, and four 1635. May or five miles distant from Bristol,[1] we found near our 23. ship another ship of Bristol, called the Diligence, bound for Newfoundland, riding at anchor.

The 24th, being the Lord's day, the wind was 24. strong in the morning, and the ship danced, and many of our women and some children were not well, but seasick, and mazy or light in their heads, and could scarce stand or go without falling, unless they took hold of something to uphold them. This day Mr. Maud[2] was exercised[3] in the forenoon and I in the afternoon. The wind still easterly.

The 25th, we that were passengers would fain 25. have had anchor weighed and sail set, that we might have been gone. But the mariners would insist that they could not stir till the goods were stowed, and the hatches or deck above cleared, &c. ; so we were forced to sit still, and fall in hand with the goods. Which stay was a greater grief unto us, because the Diligence, that lay within two or three stones' cast of us, did this morning go out in our sight.

The [26th,] Tuesday morning, the wind being 26.

---

[1] Just below the junction of the Avon with the Severn.

[2] Daniel Maude was educated at Emmanuel College, Cambridge, where he took the degree of A. B. in 1606 and of A. M. in 1610. On the 12th of August, 1636, he was chosen " free-school master " of Boston. In 1642 he became minister of the church at Dover, N. H., where he continued till his death in 1655. Edward Johnson speaks of him as " godly and diligent in the work," and Hubbard says that he

was " a good man, and of a serious spirit, and of a peaceable and quiet disposition." See Savage's Winthrop, ii. 215 ; Snow's History of Boston, p. 348 ; Mass. Hist. Coll. xvi. 364, xvii. 33, xxviii. 248; New Hamp. Hist. Coll. iv. 7, 11.

[3] The same expression is used by Winthrop. " The Lord's day following, Mr. Cotton *exercised* in the afternoon." " Mr. Phillips *exercised* with us the whole day." See Winthrop's Hist. i. 110, 371.

CHAP.
XXII.
~~~
1635.
May
26.

easterly, and the deck somewhat cleared, the mariners began to address themselves for going. But
about nine of the clock, when they had taken up one
of their anchors, and were in a manner ready to set
forward, the wind turned directly against us, unto
the west ; so that we were forced to cast anchor
again, and sit still. This evening the Diligence,
that went out the day before, came in again, and
cast anchor about the place where she lay before,
and found us riding at anchor where she left us. And
another ship, also bound for New-England, came unto
us ; which other ship was called the Angel Gabriel.

27.    On Wednesday, the wind continuing still at the
west, we having sent some of our men ashore to
fetch more bread and victuals, and more water for
the cattle, our master, Captain Taylor, went aboard
the Angel Gabriel, Mr. Maud, Nathaniel Wales,[1]
Barnabas Fower,[2] Thomas Armitage,[3] and myself,
accompanying him. When we came there, we found
divers passengers, and among them some loving and
godly Christians, that were glad to see us there.
And soon after we were come aboard there, there
came three or four boats, with more passengers, and

---

[1] Nathaniel Wales was admitted
a freeman Nov. 2, 1637, at the same
time with John Harvard, the founder of the College. He settled in
Dorchester, but removed to Boston
as early as 1654, where he died
Dec. 4, 1661, at an advanced age.
His wife's name was Susan. He
had three sons, Nathaniel, jr., Timothy, and John. Nathaniel removed to Boston with his father, and
died there May 10, 1662. Timothy
and John settled in Dorchester.
Nathaniel, son of Nathaniel, jr.,
settled in Braintree, and had fifteen
children.

[2] Barnabas Fower settled at Dorchester with his minister. He subsequently removed to Boston, and
died there in 1654. His wife's
name was Dinah, who died Dec. 27,
1642 ; after which he married a second wife, whose name was Grace.
By his first wife he had a son Eleazar, born in 1636. See Blake's
Annals of Dorchester, p. 16.

[3] Thomas Armitage, according to
Lewis, was at Lynn in 1635, and in
1637 removed to Sandwich.

one wherein came Sir Ferdinando Gorge,[1] who came to see the ship and the people. When he was come, he inquired whether there were any people there that went to Massachusetts Bay. Whereupon Mr. Maud and Barnabas Fower were sent for to come before him.[2] Who being come, he asked Mr. Maud of his country, occupation, or calling of life, &c., and professed his good will to the people there in the Bay, and promised that, if he ever came there, he would be a true friend unto them.

On Thursday, the wind being still at west, the master of the Angel Gabriel and some of their passengers came aboard our ship, and desired to have our company, &c. This day their cattle came aboard, and our master and some of the sailors and passengers went ashore.

Friday morning, the wind was south-east; but our master and some of the mariners being away, we could not set sail. So being constrained to ride at anchor still, and fearing a want if our journey should prove long, some of our company were sent by boat to Bristol to provide some more oats for the cattle, and bread and other provisions for ourselves, which they performed, and so came aboard again at evening.

Saturday, at morning, the wind waxed strong at north-west, and against our going out ; and, besides, our master and some of the sailors were gone ashore and not come aboard again ; so that this day also we were constrained to sit still. In the afternoon the wind waxed louder, and our ship danced with wind

CHAP.
XXII.

1635.
May
27.

28.

29.

30.

---

[1] For an excellent account of Gorges see Belknap's Am. Biog. i. 346–393.

[2] Mather himself keeps in the background, probably from fear of being recognized and stopped. See note [1] on page 448.

CHAP.
XXII.

1635.
May
31.

June
1.

2.

3.

4.

and waves, and many passengers, especially women, and some children, were seasick.

The second Sabbath on shipboard. The wind easterly, and directly for us. But our master and many of the sailors being away, and it being also the Lord's day, there could be no going out that day. I was exercised in the forenoon, and Mr. Maud in the afternoon.

Monday, the wind was westerly, and against us. This day we sent some of our company ashore to wash linens, and some to buy more hay and provisions. Towards night the wind grew stronger, and our ship danced, and many of the passengers were ill through casting and seasickness.

Tuesday, the wind still westerly. This day we sent some of our people ashore to provide more water and hay for the cattle.

Wednesday morning, the wind was easterly, and good for our purpose. But our master and many of the sailors were away ; and those that were aboard with us told us it was no going out till the wind was settled, lest we should be forced to come in again, upon change of wind, as the Diligence was. This evening there came to anchor in King Road another ship of Bristol, of 240 tons, called the Bess, or Elizabeth, bound for Newfoundland, as there had done another two or three days before, called the Mary, which was also bound for Newfoundland.

Thursday morning, the wind serving for us, and our master and all the sailors being come aboard, we set sail, and began our sea voyage, with glad hearts that God had loosed us from our long stay wherein we had been holden, and with hope and trust that

he would graciously guide us to the end of our journey. We were, that set sail together this morning,
five ships, three bound for Newfoundland, viz. the
Diligence, a ship of 150 tons, the Mary, a small ship
of 80 tons, and the Besse ; and two bound for New-
England, viz. the Angel Gabriel, of 240 tons, [and]
the James, of 220 tons. And even at our setting
out, we that were in the James had experience of
God's gracious providence over us, in that the Angel
Gabriel, hauling home one of her anchors, had like,
being carried by the force of the tide, to have fallen
foul upon the forepart of our ship ; which made all
the mariners as well as passengers greatly afraid.
Yet, by the guidance of God, and his care over us,
she passed by without touching so much as a cable
or cord ; and so we escaped that danger. This day
we went about ten or twelve leagues afore twelve of
the clock, and then the wind turned to the west, and
the tide also was against us, so that we were forced
to come to anchor again in the channel, between
Wales and Winnyard,[1] in Somersetshire, and there
we abode till about six or seven of the clock at night;
and then the tide turning for us, we tacked about
with the tide to and fro, as the wind would suffer,
and gained little, yet continued all night till about
two of the clock after midnight, and then (the tide
turning,) we came to anchor again.

Friday morning, the wind still strong at west, we    5.
tacked about again with the tide to and fro, till about
one of the clock after dinner ; about which time the
tide and wind being both against us, we came to an-

---

[1] There is no such place as Winnyard in Somersetshire. It may possibly be an error for *Minehead*.

CHAP.
XXII.  chor again within sight of Lundy, about two leagues

~~~  short thereof; which Lundy is an island about twenty
1635.
June  leagues short of the Land's End, and twenty-eight
5.  leagues from King Road.[1]  This day many passengers were very seasick, and ill at ease through
much vomiting.

This day, at night, when the tide turned, we set sail
6.  again, and so came, on Saturday morning, to anchor
again under Lundy, where abiding, because the wind
was strong against us, some of us were desirous to go
ashore into the island. And speaking thereof to our
master, he was very willing to satisfy us therein, and
went with us himself.  Mr. Maude, Mathew Michell,[2]

---

[1] This island lies off the entrance of the Bristol Channel. It is high, rising upwards of 450 feet above the level of the sea, the shores consisting of perpendicular granite cliffs. It is about two miles and three quarters in length, and half a mile in breadth. There is still but one farm-house on the island ; and live stock, vegetables, and good water may be obtained from the shore. Lundy Road is on the east side of the island. See Norie's British Channel Pilot, p. 99.

[2] The father of the Rev. Jonathan Mitchell, who at this time was only eleven years of age, and in 1650 succeeded Shepard as pastor of the church in Cambridge. Matthew Mitchell was from Halifax, in Yorkshire. " All his family," says Mather, " were visited with sickness the winter after their first arrival at Charlestown, and the scarcity then afflicting the country added to the afflictions of their sickness. Removing to the town of Concord, his beginnings were there consumed by fire, and some other losses befell him in the latter end of that winter. The next summer he removed unto Saybrook, and the next spring unto Weathersfield, upon Connecticut

river, by which he lost yet more of his possessions, and plunged himself into other troubles. Towards the close of that year he had a son-in-law slain by the Pequot Indians ; and many of his cattle were destroyed, and his estate, unto the value of some hundreds of pounds, was damnified. A shallop, which he sent unto the river's mouth, was taken and burned by the Pequots, and three men in the vessel slain, in all of whom he was nearly concerned ; so that indeed the Pequot scourge fell more on this family than on any other in the land. Afterwards there arose unhappy differences in the place where he lived, wherein he met with many injuries ; for which causes he transferred himself, with his interests, unto Stamford, in the Colony of New-Haven, where he died in 1645, about the 55th year of his age." Matthew Mitchell's name is recorded by Trumbull among the first settlers of Stamford ; and Lion Gardiner speaks of " old Mr. Mitchell " being with him at Saybrook in the fall of 1636, and says that the Indians " took the brother of Mr. Mitchell, who is the minister of Cambridge, and roasted him alive." See Mather's Magna-

George[1] Kenrick, myself, and some others, accompanying him. When we came into the island, we found
only one house therein ; and walking in it from side
to side and end to end, one of the house being with
us, we found thirty or forty head of cattle, about
sixteen or twenty horses and mares, goats, swine,
geese, &c., and fowl and rabbits innumerable. The
island is seventeen hundred acres of land, but yields
no corn. Here we got some milk, and fowl, and
cheese, which things my children were glad of, and
so came aboard again. But the wind being strong
against us, especially towards night, we rode there
all night and the next day ; and many of our passengers were this evening very sick.

The third Sabbath on shipboard. This day the
wind still at west, against us, we lay still under
Lundy. Mr. Maude was exercised in the forenoon,
and I in the afternoon.

Monday, the wind still strong at west. This day
we sent some of our people on shore to Lundy, to
fetch more water for the cattle.

Tuesday, the wind still strong against us. This
morning the five ships, being all weary of lying at
Lundy, because the harbour was not very good, and
seeing the wind still contrary, weighed anchor again
and set sail for Milford Haven,[2] which is fourteen

lia, ii. 66 ; Morton's Memorial, p. 335 ; Hubbard, p. 199 ; Scottow's Narrative, p. 14 ; Trumbull's Connecticut, i. 67, 68, 79, 121, 125 ; Mass. Hist. Coll. vii. 47, xxiii. 142, 143.

[1] I am not sure that I have deciphered this word aright. It may possibly be John, who was at Boston in 1639, admitted a freeman in 1640, removed to Muddy-river, (Brookline,) where his wife, Amy, died Nov. 15, 1656, and from thence to Newton, where he died Aug. 29, 1686, aged 82. See Farmer's Gen. Reg.

[2] Milford Haven is the only safe port for a large ship between the Land's End and Holyhead. It is the most secure and commodious harbour in England, and may be entered without a pilot, either by night

CHAP.
XXII. leagues from Lundy, and lies upon Pembrokeshire,
in Wales, and came thither that night. This day,
1635.
June as we came from Lundy to Milford Haven, the sea
9. wrought and was rough, and most of the passengers
were very sick, worse than ever before.

10. Wednesday, the wind still against us, we lay still
in Milford Haven, and most of our people were in
good health, and many went on shore into the country, and brought more fresh water for the cattle,
more fresh victuals, as eggs, loaf bread, fresh fish, &c.
which things our children were glad of.

11 Thursday, the wind still against us. Many went
this day also on shore, to take the air, view the
country, &c., and some of us upon business, to provide more hay and provisions.

12. Friday. A knight of the country, dwelling near
Hartford West,[1] being aboard the Diligence, sent for
me to come to speak with him. Much wondering we
had what should be the matter, seeing I never knew
him, nor he me. When I came to him, he used me
courteously, invited me to his house, wished us all
good success, lamented the loss of them that stayed
behind, when so many of the best people, for upholding religion, were removed and taken away.[2] The
knight's name is Sir James Parret.

13. Saturday, wind still against us.

14. The fourth Sabbath on shipboard. This day Mr.
Maud, Mathew Michel, and many of our passengers,

or day, even with contrary winds, only taking the tide. In it the shipping of the whole British empire might ride together in perfect safety.
[1] So in the MS.; but the name of the town is Haverford-West. It is the capital of the county of Pem- broke, and one of the principal towns of South Wales, situated at one of the inland extremities of the creek or bay called Milford Haven. It is seven miles from Milford.
[2] See note [2] on page 127.

and of the Angel Gabriel's, went to a church on
shore, called Nangle,[1] where they heard two good
and comfortable sermons, made by an ancient, grave
minister, living at Pembrooke, whose name is Mr.
Jessop. His text was Psalm xci. 11. " He will give
his angels charge," &c.; and his coming was purposely for the comfort and encouragement of us that went
to New-England. I was exercised on shipboard both
ends of the day, remaining there for the help of the
weaker and inferior sort, that could not go on shore.

Monday, I went on shore to Nangle, with my wife
and children, John Smith and his wife, and Mary,
Susan Michel,[2] and divers others. It was a fair day,
and we walked in the fields, and at a house got some
milk, &c., wherewith we were much refreshed, and
came aboard again at evening.

Tuesday, a rainy day ; the wind still against us.

Wednesday, the wind still against us.

Thursday, the wind still against us. This day, in
the morning, our master and the seamen sent away
and set on shore one of the seamen, called Jephrey
Cornish, who had fallen out and been in quarrelling
and fighting with some of the seamen. The main
matter alleged against him, was his drunkenness, and
blasphemy, and brawling and cursing in his drunkenness. In the afternoon there came to the Angel
Gabriel and to our ship, Mr. Jessop,[3] to see the
Christians bound for New-England. He was a grave
and godly old man, one that had lost a good living

---

[1] Angle, a village on the right of
the entrance to Milford Haven, so
called from being, as it were, *in an-
gulo*, in a nook.
[2] Probably the wife of Matthew
Mitchell.

[3] He was the father of Constan-
tine Jessop, also a Nonconformist
minister. See Wood's Athen. Oxon.
iii. 540, Fasti, i. 461, (ed. Bliss) ;
Brook's Lives of the Puritans, iii.
375.

CHAP.
XXII.
~~~~
1635.
June

because of his Nonconformity, and wished us all well ; and we were much refreshed with his godly company and conference.

19.     Friday, a foggy morning ; wind still westerly.

20.     Saturday, the wind still hovering to and fro.

21.     The fifth Sabbath on shipboard ; a fair, cheerful summer day. This day I was exercised both ends of the day, and had much comfort therein, because the fairness of the day freed us from distraction, and fitted us the better for attendance. Besides, the day was more comfortable to us all, in regard of the company of many godly Christians from the Angel Gabriel, and from other vessels lying in the harbour with us ; who, wanting means at home, were glad to come to us, and we were also glad of their company, and had all of us a very comfortable day, and were much refreshed in the Lord.

22.     Monday morning, the wind serving, with a strong gale at east, we set sail from Milford Haven, where we had waited for wind twelve days, and were carried forth with speedy course, and about noon lost all sight of land. The wind being strong, the sea was rough this day, and most of our passengers were very sick and ill through much casting.

23.     Tuesday, the wind still easterly, and a very rainy day. We were carried forward apace, and launched forth a great way into the deep. But our people were still very sick. This day, at evening, we lost sight of the three ships bound for Newfoundland, which had been in company with us from King Road ; and our master thought it best for us to stay for the Angel Gabriel, being bound for New-England, as we were, rather than to leave her and go with the other

three. The Angel Gabriel is a strong ship, and well
furnished with fourteen or sixteen pieces of ordnance,
and therefore our seamen rather desired her company ; but yet she is slow in sailing, and therefore we
went sometimes with three sails less than we might
have done, that so we might not overgo her.

Wednesday, the wind still at east, but not so
strong as the other two days before. This morning
we saw abundance of porpoises[1] leaping and playing
about our ship ; and spent a great deal of time, till
two or three o'clock in the afternoon, in pursuing
(with the Angel Gabriel,) another ship, which we supposed to have been a Turkish pirate, and to have taken the Mary. The ground of which supposal was,
because yesternight the Mary was in our sight, behind
her fellows, and a little ship, like to the Mary, had
been with the other ship this morning when we first
espied them. But the little ship parted from the
other, and we doubted she had been the Mary, taken
and sent away as a prize by the Turk; and this made
us more willing to pursue them. But not being able
to overtake them, we left pursuing, and turned our
course again our own way.

Thursday, the wind still easterly ; in the morning
wet and rainy ; but about noon a fair, sunshiny day.
Many of our passengers, that had been sick before,
began to be far better, and came with delight to
walk above, upon the deck.

Friday, wind at north, and afterward more westward. This day we saw many porpoises leaping and
running like about our ship.

[1] See note [4] on page 226.

Saturday, wind still north-west ; but a fair, cool day.

The first Sabbath from Milford Haven, and the sixth on shipboard ; a fair, cool day ; wind northerly, good for our purpose. I was exercised in the forenoon, and Mr. Maud in the afternoon. This evening we saw porpoises about the ship, and some would fain have been striking ; but others dissuaded because of the Sabbath ; and so it was let alone.

Monday morning, wind still northerly ; a fair, cool day. This morning, about seven of the clock, our seamen struck a great porpoise, and hauled it with ropes into the ship ; for bigness, not much less than a hog of twenty or twenty-five shillings apiece, and not much unlike for shape, with flesh fat and lean, like in color to the fat and lean of a hog ; and being opened upon the deck, had within his entrails, as liver, lights, heart, guts, &c., for all the world like a swine. The seeing of him hauled into the ship, like a swine from the sty to the trestle,[1] and opened upon the deck in view of all our company, was wonderful to us all, and marvellous merry sport, and delightful to our women and children. So good was our God unto us, in affording us the day before spiritual refreshing to our souls, and this day morning also delightful recreation to our bodies, at the taking and opening of this huge and strange fish. In the afternoon the Angel Gabriel sent their boat to our ship, to see how we did ; and our master, Captain Taylor, went aboard the Angel, and took Mathew Michel and me along with him. When

---

[1] Trestle, a frame or support for a table, made triangular, or with three legs.

we came thither, we found their passengers that had been seasick now well recovered, the most of them, and two children that had had the small pox well recovered again. We were entreated to stay supper there with their master, &c., and had good cheer, mutton boiled and roasted, roasted turkey, good sack, &c. After which loving and courteous entertainment, we took leave, and came aboard the James again at night.

Tuesday, a fair, hot summer day, but small wind. This day we saw with wonder and delight abundance of porpoises, and likewise some grampusses, as big as an ox, puffing and spewing up water as they went by the ship.

Wednesday, a fair, hot summer day ; but the wind westerly, so that we gained little that day.

Thursday, rainy in the morning, but in the afternoon fair and clear ; but little wind all day.

Friday, wind strong at southward. We were carried on apace, after eight or nine leagues a watch, as the seamen conceived ; (a watch is four hours, a league is three miles.) This day some few of the weakest passengers had some small remembrance again of sea-qualms and sea-sickness.

Saturday, a very strong wind, but not much for us. This day the sea was very rough, and we saw the truth of that Scripture, Psalm 107. Some were very seasick ; but none could stand or go upon the deck, because of the tossing and tumbling of the ship. This day we lost sight of the Angel Gabriel, sailing slowly behind us, and we never saw her again any more.

The second Sabbath from Milford Haven, and the

CHAP.
XXII.

1 6 3 5.
June
29.

30.

July
1.

2.

3.

4.

5.

seventh on ship.    This day God was very gracious

unto us, in giving a fair, calm, sunshiny day, that we

might above, upon the deck, exercise ourselves in his
worship.    For if this day had been as the former for
wind and rain, we could not have known how to
have sanctified the Sabbath in any comfortable manner.    I was exercised in the forenoon, and Mr. Maud
in the afternoon.

6.    Monday, wind north and north-east ; good for us,
had it been strong enough ; but being but weak, we
could not despatch much way.    A fair day, and our
people were most of them hearty and cheerful.    This
morning Mathew Michell and I spake to our master,
desiring him that we might not stay for the Angel,
because we doubted our hay for our cattle would not
hold out, and many casks of water were leaked and
spent.    To which request he gave free assent, and
caused the sailors to make all the sail they possibly
could ; and so we went that day as the soft wind
could drive us.

7.    Tuesday, a fair day, but soft wind at south.    Our
people cheerful, and in good health.

8.    Wednesday, wind westerly; yet by tacking southward and northward, we gained, as the seamen conceived, twenty or twenty-one leagues.

9.    Thursday, a strong wind at north-west, which
made the sea somewhat rough.    Yet the passengers,
by the mercy of God, were few of them seasick.
This day and two days before we saw following the
ship a little bird like a swallow, called a *pitterill*,[1]

---

[1] The Stormy Petrel, or Mother    Ornithol. Biog. iii. 486 ; Nuttall's
Carey's Chicken.    See Wilson's    Ornithology, Water Birds, p. 322.
Am. Ornithol. vii. 90 ; Audubon's

which they say doth follow ships against foul weather; CHAP. XXII. and we saw also this afternoon by the ship side a great grampus, as big as an ox. July 9.

Friday, wind westerly, so that we could gain lit- 10. tle. A fair day, and our people generally in good health.

Saturday, much like. 11.

The third Sabbath from Milford, and the eighth 12. on shipboard. A very fair day, so that we had liberty to serve God without distraction and disturbance from weather. Mr. Maud was exercised in the forenoon, and I in the afternoon. Wind southward.

Monday, a foggy, misty day ; but a good gale of 13. wind at south and by east, which carried us apace, after ten leagues a watch.

Tuesday, also very foggy and misty. Wind south- 14. erly, but about noon became calm.

Wednesday, a strong wind northerly, which made 15. the sea rough ; yet we went about eight or nine leagues a watch. Few of us were seasick ; though a wind not so strong and sea not so rough would, in the beginning of our journey, have wrought more upon us. But now we were better used unto it.

Thursday, a fair day ; though the wind being 16. westerly, carried us more to the southward than else we desired. This day we saw with wonder and delight an innumerable multitude of porpoises leaping and playing about the ship. Towards evening the wind was little.

Friday, calm in the morning. But afore noon, the 17. wind waxed strong at north, and so continued all day, and carried us a good speed in our course.

CHAP.
XXII.

July
18.

Saturday, wind north-west, a fair, cool day. We saw this morning a great many of bonitoes[1] leaping and playing about the ship. Bonito is a fish somewhat bigger than a cod, but less than a porpoise.

19. Sabbath, a fair forenoon ; but at noon the wind became stiff westward, which was against us. In the afternoon it blew so hard and loud, that my voice could scarce be heard, though I extended it to the furthest that I could.

20. Monday, a foggy and misty day; wind about north-west. We saw this day divers dolphins playing about the ship, and many sea-fowl, hagbats,[2] and others.

21. Tuesday morning a great calm after a hot night. This morning our seamen took a bonito, and opened him upon the deck ; of which, being dressed, our master sent Mathew Michel and me part, as good fish in eating as could be desired. About noon the wind became north-east, good for our purpose, so that we went that afternoon nine or ten leagues a watch.

22. Wednesday, wind still about north-east, but not so strong as the day before. Now we saw every day abundance of sea-fowl, as pitterels, hagbats, &c.

23. Thursday morning, a fine gale of wind at north and by east. Now we saw this morning abundance of porpoises and grampuses, leaping, and spewing up water about the ship. About eight or nine of the clock the wind blew more stiffly, and we went about

---

[1] " Or Spanish dolphins, a fish about the size of a large mackerel, beautified with admirable variety of glittering colors in the water." Josselyn's Two Voyages to New-England, p. 7, in Mass. Hist. Coll. xxiii. 217.

[2] Higginson, in his Journal, calls them *hag-birds*. See page 229.

eight or nine leagues a watch. Towards evening, our seamen deemed that we were near to some land, because the color of the water was changed. But sounding with a line of a hundred and sixty fathom, they could find no bottom. It was a very cold wind, like as if it had been winter, which made some to wish for more clothes.

Friday, wind still northerly, but very faint. It was a great foggy mist, and exceeding cold, as it had been December. One would have wondered to have seen the innumerable numbers of fowl, which we saw swimming on every side of the ship,[1] and mighty fishes rolling and tumbling in the waters, twice as long and big as an ox. In the afternoon we saw mighty whales spewing up water in the air, like the smoke of a chimney, and making the sea about them white and hoary, as it is said in Job ; of such incred- ible bigness that I will never wonder that the body of Jonas could be in the belly of a whale. At evening our seamen sounded, and found ground at fifty fathom.

Saturday morning, they sounded again, and found no bottom, conceiving thereby that we were the day before on Newfoundland Bank, on the end of it nearer to New-England. This day, about nine of the clock, the wind turned from being northerly, and came about by the east unto the south, and the great fog vanished away, and it became a clear, sunshiny day. This day Mathew Michel and I, taking notice that our hay and water waxed scarce, went to our master, entreating him to tell us how far he conceived

---

[1] They were now near the Grand Bank of Newfoundland. See pages 228 and 229.

us to want of our journey's end, that so we might better know how to order our water and provisions for our cattle, which yet were all alive and in good liking; and he thereupon summed up all the passages of our journey past, and conceived two hundred and fifty leagues to be yet remaining unfinished.

On Friday, in the evening, we had an hour or two of marvellous delightful recreation, which also was a feast unto us for many days after, while we fed upon the flesh of three huge porpoises, like to as many fat hogs, striked by our seamen, and hauled with ropes into the ship. The flesh of them was good meat, with salt, pepper and vinegar; the fat like fat bacon, the lean like bull-beef; and on Saturday evening they took another also.

26.    The fifth Sabbath from Milford Haven, and the tenth on shipboard; a fair, sunshiny summer day, and would have been very hot, had not God allayed the heat with a good gale of southerly wind; by which also we were carried on in our journey after seven leagues a watch. I was exercised in the forenoon, and Mr. Maud in the afternoon. In the afternoon the wind grew stronger, and it was a rough night for wind and rain, and some had our beds that night ill wet with rain beating in through the sides of the ship.

27.    Monday, wind still strong at south. This day we spent much time in filling divers tuns of emptied cask with salt water; which was needful, because much beer, fresh water, beef, and other provisions being spent, the ship went not so well, being too light for want of ballast. When this work was done, we set forth more sail, and went that evening and all the night following with good speed in our journey.

Tuesday morning, a great calm, and very hot all the forenoon ; our people and cattle being much afflicted with faintness, sweating, and heat. But (lo ! the goodness of our God,) about noon the wind blew at north and by east, which called us from our heat, and holp us forward in our way. This afternoon there came and light upon our ship a little land-bird, with blue-colored feathers, about the bigness of a sparrow ; by which some conceived we were not far from land.

Wednesday, not extremely hot, but a good gale of cooling wind. But yet, being at the west and by north, it was against us in our way ; so that we were forced to tack northward and southward, and gained little.

Thursday, wind still westerly, against us, all the forenoon. But about one of the clock the Lord remembered us in mercy, and sent us a fresh gale at south ; which, though weak and soft, yet did not only much mitigate the heat, but also holp us something forward in our way. In the evening, about sun-setting, we saw with admiration and delight, innumerable multitudes of huge grampuses, rolling and tumbling about the sides of the ship, spewing and puffing up water as they went, and pursuing great numbers of bonitoes and lesser fishes ; — so marvellous to behold are the works and wonders of the Almighty in the deep.

## 30

Friday, a great foggy mist all the forenoon, and the wind west-northwest, which was against us. In the afternoon the mist vanished, and the day cleared up ; but the wind still against us, so that we gained little, being forced to run a by-course, viz. north and by east, and at night to run southward.

CHAP.
XXII.

1635.
Aug.
1.

Saturday morning, a cool wind at north, whereby we went on in our course an hour or two, though very slowly, because of the weakness of the wind. Afterwards it became a great calm, and our seamen sounded about one of the clock, and found ground at sixty fathom.[1] Presently after, another little land-bird came and light upon the sails of the ship. In the cool of the evening, the calm still continuing, our seamen fished with hook and line, and took cod as fast as they could haul them up into the ship.

2.

The sixth Sabbath from Milford, and the eleventh on shipboard. This day was a day of great refreshing to us ; not only because of preaching and prayers, which we enjoyed for the good of our souls, but also by reason of abundance of fowl which we saw swimming in the sea, as a token of nearness of land. Besides, our bodies fed sweetly on the fresh cod taken the day before, of which our master sent Mr. Maud and me good store. And the wind blew with a cool and comfortable gale at south all day, which carried us away with great speed towards our journey's end ; — so good was our loving God unto us, as always, so also this day. Mr. Maud was exercised in the forenoon and I in the afternoon.

3.

But lest we should grow secure, and neglect the Lord through abundance of prosperity, our wise and loving God was pleased on Monday morning, about three of the clock, when we were upon the coast of land, to exercise us with a sore storm and tempest of wind and rain ; so that many of us passengers, with wind and rain were raised out of our beds, and our seamen were forced to let down all the sails ;

[1] See note [3] on page 229.

and the ship was so tossed with fearful mountains
and valleys of water, as if we should have been overwhelmed and swallowed up. But this lasted not
long ; for at our poor prayers the Lord was pleased
to magnify his mercy in assuaging the winds and seas
again about sunrising. But the wind was become
west, against us, so that we floated upon the coast,
making no despatch of way all that day and the night
following. And besides, there was a great fog and
mist all that day, so that we could not see to make
land, but kept in all sail and lay still, rather losing
than gaining, but taking abundance of cod and hali-
but, wherewith our bodies were abundantly refreshed after they had been tossed with the storm.

Tuesday, the fog continued still all the forenoon.
About noon, the day cleared up, and the wind blew
with a soft gale at south, and we set sail again, going on in our course, though very slowly, because of
the smallness of the wind. At night it was a calm,
and abundance of rain.

Wednesday morning, we had a little wind at north,
but a foggy forenoon. In the afternoon, the day
somewhat cleared ; but it became a calm again.
Thus the Lord was pleased, with foggy mists and
want of winds, to exercise our patience and waiting
upon his good leisure, still keeping us from sight of
land, when our seamen conceived us to be upon the
coast. This day, in the afternoon, we saw multitudes of great whales ; which now was grown ordinary and usual to behold.

Thursday, a foggy morning; afterward a very hot
day, and great calm, so that we could make no way,
but lay still, floating upon the coast, and could not
come to any sight of land.

CHAP.
XXII.

1635.
Aug.
7.

8.

Friday morning, a great fog still, and a slender soft wind at west-southwest. In the afternoon the wind wakened, and we went forward with good speed, though too far northward, because the wind was so much on the west.

Saturday morning, we had a good gale of wind at west-southwest ; and this morning our seamen took abundance of mackerel ;[1] and about eight of the clock we all had a clear and comfortable sight of America, and made land again at an island called Menhiggin,[2] an island without inhabitants, about thirty-nine leagues northward or northeast short of Cape Ann. A little from this island we saw, more northward, divers other islands, called St. George Islands,[3] and the main land of New-England all along, northward and eastward, as we sailed. This mercy of our God we had cause more highly to esteem of, because when we first saw land this morning, there was a great fog, and afterward, when the day cleared up, we saw many rocks and islands almost on every side us, as Menhiggin, St. George Islands, Pemmaquid, &c. Yet, in the midst of these dangers our God preserved us ; though, because of the thick fog, we could not see far about us to look unto ourselves. In the afternoon, the wind continuing still westward, against us, we lay off again to the sea southward, and our seamen and many passengers delighted themselves in taking abundance of mackerel.

---

[1] See note [2] on page 232.
[2] See Chronicles of Plymouth, note [4] on p. 182, and Williamson's History of Maine, i. 61.
[3] St. George's Islands are a cluster of islands, about twenty in number, on the coast of Maine, situated about the mouth of St. George's river eastwardly, and on the east margin of Broad or Muscongus Bay. See them described in Williamson, i. 59, 60.

The seventh Sabbath from Milford, and the twelfth on shipboard. This day was a fair, clear, and comfortable day, though the wind was directly against us, so that we were forced to tack to and again, southward and northward, gaining little, but were all day still in sight of land. Mr. Maud in the forenoon ; I in the afternoon.

Monday morning, the wind still continuing against us, we came to anchor at Richmond's Island,[1] in the east part of New-England ; the Bay of Massachusetts, whither we were bound, lying thirty leagues distant from us to the west. Our seamen were willing here to cast anchor, partly because the wind was against us, and partly because of necessity they must come to anchor to take in a pilot somewhere before we came to the Bay, by reason that our pilot knew the harbours no further but to the Isle of Shoals. When we came within sight of the island, the planters there, (or rather fishers, for their chief employment was fishing,) being but two families, and about forty persons, were sore afraid of us, doubting lest we had been French, come to pillage the island, as Penobscots had been served by them about ten days before.[2]

CHAP.
XXII.

1635.
Aug.
9.

10.

[1] Richmond's (or Richman's) Island is on the coast of Maine, near Cape Elizabeth. It is three miles in circumference, and is only half a mile from the main ; the strait being fordable at low water. This island is frequently mentioned in the early history of the country See Williamson's Maine, i. 30.

[2] " At this time (Aug. 1635,)" says Winthrop, " a French ship came with commission from the king of France, (as they pretended,) and took Penobscott, a Plymouth trading house, and sent away the men which were in it, but kept their goods, and gave them bills for them, and bade them tell all the plantations they would come with eight ships next year and displant them all. But, by a letter which the captain wrote to the Governor of Plymouth, it appeared that they had commission from Mons. Rossillon, commander at the fort near Cape Breton, called La Heve, to displant the English as far as Pemaquid ; and by it they professed all courtesy to us here." See Winthrop, i. 166 ; Hubbard, p. 161 ; Williamson's Maine, i. 262 ; Hutchinson's Mass. i. 46 ; Holmes's Annals, i. 230.

CHAP. XXII. When we were come to anchor, and their fear was past, they came some of them aboard to us in their 1635. shallops, and we went some of us ashore into the isl- Aug. 10. and, to look for fresh water and grass for our cattle; and the planters bade us welcome, and gave some of us courteous entertainment in their houses.

11. Tuesday, we lay still at anchor at Richmond's Island, the wind being still against us.

12. Wednesday morning, the wind serving with a fresh gale at north and by east, we set sail from Richmond's Island for Massachusetts Bay, and went along the coast by Cape Porpus,¹ still within sight of land. This day the wind was soft and gentle; and as we went along, our seamen and passengers took abundance of mackerel. Towards night it became a calm, so that then we could despatch little way.

13. Thursday morning, the wind was against us, at south-southwest, and so had been all night before, so that we tacked to and fro, gaining little, but con- tinuing on the coast towards Cape Ann, within sight of land for the most part, passing by Boon Islands,² Agamenticus,³ &c. This evening our seamen desir- ed to have anchored at Hog Island,⁴ or the Isle of Shoals, being seven leagues short of Cape Ann, and thirteen or fourteen leagues from the Isle of Rich- mond. But the wind being strong at south-south- west, they could not attain their purpose, and so were forced to lie off again to sea all night.

---

¹ Cape Porpoise is near Kenne- bunk harbour.

² Boon Island is an island of rocks a quarter of a mile in length, situa- ted six or seven miles southeast from York harbour.

³ This mountain is about eight miles northwesterly from York har- bour. It is a noted landmark for mariners, being the first height seen by them from the sea. See Wil- liamson's Maine, i. 96, 231.

⁴ Hog island is the largest of the Isles of Shoals, containing about 350 acres.

Friday morning, the wind was strong at south-
southwest, and so continued till towards evening,
and then was somewhat milder. This day we tacked
to and again all day, one while west and by north
towards Isles of Shoals, another while east-southeast
to sea again; Cape Ann, whither our way was, lying
from us south-southwest, directly in the eye of the
wind, so that we could not come near unto it. But
this evening, by moonlight, about ten of the clock,
we came to anchor at the Isles of Shoals,[1] which are
seven or eight islands and other great rocks, and
there slept sweetly that night till break of day.

But yet the Lord had not done with us, nor yet
had let us see all his power and goodness, which he
would have us to take knowledge of; and therefore,
on Saturday morning, about break of day, the Lord
sent forth a most terrible storm of rain and easterly
wind, whereby we were in as much danger as, I
think, ever people were. For we lost in that morning three great anchors and cables ; of which cables
one, having cost £50, never had been in any water
before ; two were broken by the violence of the
waves, and the third cut by the seamen in extremity
and distress, to save the ship and their and our lives.
And when our cables and anchors were all lost, we
had no outward means of deliverance but by loosing
sail, if so be we might get to the sea from amongst
the islands and rocks where we anchored. But the
Lord let us see that our sails could not save us
neither, no more than our cables and anchors. For,
by the force of the wind and rain, the sails were rent

CHAP.
XXII.

1635.
Aug.
14

15.

---

[1] See a topographical and histor-  Mass. Hist. Coll. vii. 242-261 ;
ical account of these islands in  Williamson's Maine, i. 23.

in sunder and split in pieces, as if they had been but rotten rags, so that of the foresail and spritsail there was scarce left so much as a hand-breadth that was not rent in pieces and blown away into the sea. So that at this time all hope that we should be saved, in regard of any outward appearance, was utterly taken away ; and the rather, because we seemed to drive with full force of wind and rain directly upon a mighty rock,[1] standing out in sight above the water ; so that we did but continually wait when we should hear and feel the doleful rushing and crashing of the ship upon the rock. In this extremity and appearance of death, as distress and distraction would suffer us, we cried unto the Lord, and he was pleased to have compassion and pity upon us ; for by his overruling providence and his own immediate good hand, he guided the ship past the rock, assuaged the violence of the sea and of the wind and rain, and gave us a little respite to fit the ship with other sails, and sent us a fresh gale of wind at [blank], by which we went on that day in our course south-west and by west towards Cape Ann. It was a day much to be remembered, because on that day the Lord granted us as wonderful a deliverance as, I think, ever people had, out of as apparent danger as I think ever people felt. I am sure our seamen confessed they never knew the like.[2] The Lord so imprint the memory of it on our hearts, that we may be the better for it, and be more careful to please him and to walk uprightly before him as long as we live ; and I hope

---

[1] At Piscataqua, says Winthrop, i. 165.

[2] For a further account of this storm, see Winthrop, i. 164 ; Morton's Memorial, p. 179 ; Hubbard, pp. 199–201 ; Mather's Magnalia, i. 406 ; Scottow's Narrative, p. 14.

we shall not forget the passages of that morning until our dying day.

In the storm, one Mr. Willett,[1] of New Plymouth, and other three men with him, having been turned out of all their havings at Penobscot about a fortnight before,[2] and coming along with us in our ship from Richmond's Island, with his boat and goods in it made fast at the stern of our ship, lost his boat with all that was therein, the violence of the waves breaking the boat in pieces, and sinking the bottom of it into the bottom of the sea. And Richard Becon, lending his help to the seamen at the hauling of a cable, had the cable catched about his arm, whereby his arm was crushed in pieces, and his right hand pulled away, and himself brought into doleful and grievous pain and misery.

But in all this grievous storm, my fear was the less, when I considered the clearness of my calling from God this way;[3] and in some measure (the Lord's holy name be blessed for it,) he gave us hearts contented and willing that he should do with us and ours what he pleased, and what might be most for the glory of his name ; and in that we rested ourselves. But when news was brought unto us into the gunroom, that the danger was past, O how our hearts did then relent and melt within us ! and how we burst out into tears of joy amongst ourselves, in love unto our gracious God, and admiration of his

---

[1] Thomas Willett was an Assistant of Plymouth Colony from 1651 to 1664, fourteen years. Farmer says he was the first mayor of New York after its conquest from the Dutch by the English in 1664, and that he died at Barrington, in Rhode Island, Aug. 4, 1674, aged 64. See Morton's Memorial, pp. 250, 304 ; Mass. Hist. Coll. xiv. 100, 293.

[2] See page 471.

[3] That is, his call to come to New-England.

CHAP.
XXII.

1635.

Aug.

16.

kindness, in granting to his poor servants such an extraordinary and miraculous deliverance ! His holy name be blessed forever !

This day we went on towards Cape Ann, as the wind would suffer, and our poor sails further, and came within sight thereof the other[1] morning ; which Sabbath, being the thirteenth we kept on shipboard, was a marvellous pleasant day, for a fresh gale of wind, and clear sunshiny weather. This day we went directly before the wind, and had delight all along the coast, as we went, in viewing Cape Ann, the Bay of Saugust, the Bay of Salem, Marvil head, Pullin Point,[2] and other places ; and came to anchor, at low tide, in the evening, at Nantascot, in a most pleasant harbour, like to which I had never seen, amongst a great many of islands on every side. I was exercised on shipboard both ends of the day. After the evening's exercise, when it was flowing tide again, we set sail again, and came that night to anchor again before Boston, and so rested that night with glad and thankful hearts that God had put an end to our long journey, being a thousand leagues, that is, three thousand miles English, over one of the greatest seas in the world.[3]

Now this our journey, by the goodness of our God, was very prosperous unto us, every manner of way. First of all, it was very safe, and healthful to us ; for though we were in the ship a hundred passengers,[4] besides twenty-three seamen, and twenty-three cows and heifers, three sucking calves, and eight mares,

[1] That is, the *next* morning ; a peculiar use of the word.
[2] See page 405–410.
[3] Higginson uses almost precisely the same words in his Journal. See page 235.
[4] Winthrop, i. 164, adds, " honest people of Yorkshire."

yet not one of all these died by the way, neither CHAP.
person nor cattle, but came all alive to land, and ⌒⌒
many of the cattle in better liking than when we first 1635.
entered the ship ; and most of the passengers in as Aug.
good health as ever, and none better than mine own
family ; and my weak wife,[1] and little Joseph,[2] as
well as any other. Fevers, calentures, small pox,
and such diseases as have afflicted other passengers,
the Lord kept from among us, and put upon us no
grief in our bodies, but a little seasickness in the
beginning of the voyage ; saving that two or three
seamen had the flux, and Richard Becon lost his
right hand in the last storm, and one woman, and a
little child of hers, towards the end of the journey,
had the scurvy. The means of which infirmity in
her we all conceived to be the want of walking and
stirring of her body upon the deck ; her manner being to sit much, between the decks, upon her bed.
And a special means of the healthfulness of the passengers, by the blessing of God, we all conceived to
be much walking in the open air, and the comfortable variety of our food. For seeing we were not
tied to the ship's diet, but did victual ourselves, we
had no want of good and wholesome beer and bread ;
and as our land stomachs grew weary of ship diet, of
salt fish and salt beef, and the like, we had liberty to
change for other food, which might sort better with
our healths and stomachs ; and therefore sometimes
we used bacon and buttered pease, sometimes but-

---

[1] Sept. 29, 1624, he married Ka-
tharine, daughter of Edmund Holt,
Esq., of Bury in Lancashire, by
whom he had six children, all sons.
She died in Feb. 1655, and he married the widow of John Cotton, Aug.
26, 1656.
[2] Joseph was the fourth son, and
the last born in England.

CHAP.
XXII.

1635.
Aug.

tered bag-pudding, made with currants and raisins; and sometimes drinked pottage of beer and oatmeal, and sometimes water pottage, well buttered.

And though we had two storms by the way, the one upon Monday, the 3d of August, the other on Saturday, the 15th of the same, yet our gracious God (blessed and forever blessed be his name!) did save us all alive in them both, and speedily assuaged them again. Indeed, the latter of them was very terrible and grievous; insomuch, that when we came to land, we found many mighty trees rent in pieces in the midst of the bole, and others turned up by the roots, by the fierceness thereof.[1] And a bark going from the Bay to Marvil head, with planters and seamen therein, to the number of about twenty-three, was cast away in the storm, and all the people therein perished, except one man[2] and his wife, that were spared to report the news. And the Angel Gabriel, being then at anchor at Pemmaquid, was burst in pieces and cast away in this storm, and most of the cattle and other goods, with one seaman and three or four passengers, did also perish therein, besides two of the passengers that died by the way, the rest having their lives given them for a prey.[3] But the James, and we that were therein, with our cattle

---

[1] Morton, describing the effects of this storm in his New-England's Memorial, p. 180, says, " It blew down many hundred thousands of trees, turning up the stronger by the roots, and breaking the high pine trees, and such like, in the midst; and the tall young oaks, and walnut trees of good bigness, were wound as a withe by it, very strange and fearful to behold."

[2] Anthony Thacher. See his Narrative of the Shipwreck in the next chapter.

[3] Scottow says that "the ship and whole cargo perished, but not one soul of seamen or passengers miscarried." Hubbard too declares, that " the passengers were all preserved alive, losing only their goods." Yet Mather probably has the truth. See Winthrop, i. 165; Scottow, p. 14; Hubbard, p. 199.

and goods, were all preserved alive. The Lord's name be blessed forever !

Secondly, it was very delightful, while we took pleasure and instruction in beholding the works and wonders of the Almighty in the deep ; the sea sometimes being rough with mighty mountains and deep valleys, sometimes again plain and smooth like a level meadow, and sometimes painted with variety of yellow weeds.[1] Besides it was a pleasant thing to behold the variety of fowls and mighty fishes, swimming and living in the waters.

Thirdly, it was comfortable to us, by means of the fellowship of divers godly Christians in the ship, and by means of our constant serving God morning and evening every day, the daily duties being performed one day by Mr. Maud, another by myself, and the Sabbath's exercises divided, (for the most part,) equally betwixt us too.

True it is, our journey was somewhat long. For though from Monday, the 22d of June, when we lost sight of our Old English coast, until Saturday, the 8th of August, when we made land again, at Menhiggin, it was but six weeks and five days, yet from our first entering the ship in King Road, on Saturday, the 23d of May, till our landing at Boston, in New-England, on Monday, the 17th of August, it was twelve weeks and two days. For we lay at anchor in King Road eleven days, before we ever set sail, and three days at Lundy, and twelve days at Milford, and spent three days in tacking between King Road and Lundy, one day between Lundy and

---

[1] Higginson also mentions these yellow flowers. See pp. 232, 233.

CHAP.
XXII.

1635.
Aug.

Milford, and eight days between Menhiggin and Boston. Nevertheless, our God preserved us all the while, and we had opportunity by these often delays to take in more hay, oats, and fresh water, and arrived in a good condition. Again let our gracious God be blessed forevermore! Amen.[1]

---

[1] RICHARD MATHER, the writer of the preceding Journal, and the progenitor of all the Mathers in New-England, was born in 1596, at the village of Lowton, in the parish of Winwick, two miles from Warrington, in Lancashire. His parents, Thomas and Margaret Mather, were of ancient families in that village, but in reduced circumstances. So great was his proficiency in his studies at Winwick School, that in 1611, at the early age of fifteen, he was invited to take charge of a public school at Toxteth Park, near Liverpool. Having spent seven years in this occupation, and fitted several scholars for the University, he removed there himself, and was entered a student of Brazen Nose College, May 9, 1618, at the age of 22. But he had been here but a few months before he was invited by the people of Toxteth to return and become their minister. This invitation he accepted, preached his first sermon Nov. 30, 1618, and was soon after ordained by Dr. Morton, Bishop of Chester. After his marriage in 1624, he removed his habitation to Much-Woolton, three miles from Toxteth, but continued to preach at Toxteth. Having thus spent fifteen years, he was suspended from his ministry in August, 1633, for Nonconformity to the ceremonies, but in November following was restored through the intercession of some gentlemen in Lancashire. This restored liberty, however, continued not long; for in 1634, Neal, Archbishop of York, sent his visitors into Lancashire, who suspended Mr. Mather again, chiefly for not wearing the surplice. Being thus silenced,

and seeing no chance of resuming his ministry, and apprehending further persecution, he meditated a removal to New-England; and he was confirmed in this purpose by urgent letters received from Cotton and Hooker. On his arrival, he remained for some months in Boston, and was admitted to the church there Oct. 25, 1635, with his wife, and Daniel Maud, his fellow-passenger. He immediately received invitations to settle at Plymouth, Roxbury, and Dorchester. By the advice of his friends Cotton and Hooker, he chose the last place, where a new church was formed Aug. 23, 1636, (the former church, with its pastor, Mr. Warham, having removed to Windsor, in Connecticut,) and he was ordained their teacher. Here he spent the remainder of his days, and died April 22, 1669, in the 73d year of his age, and was buried in Dorchester burying-ground. Of six sons, all by his first wife, four, Samuel, Timothy, Nathaniel, and Joseph, were born in England, and two, Eleazar and Increase, in New-England. Four of them were settled in the ministry,—Eleazar at Northampton, in Massachusetts; Samuel at Dublin, in Ireland; Nathaniel at Barnstable in Devonshire, at Rotterdam in Holland, and in London; and Increase, President of Harvard College and father of Cotton Mather, in Boston. Richard Mather had begun a Memoir of himself, which he had brought down to the 39th year of his age, being the year in which he came to New-England, but left it unfinished. It was never printed, and is probably lost. Extracts from it are contained in his

Life, which has usually been ascribed to his son, Increase Mather, but which, as appears from his son's Preface to it, was written by some other person who was "not willing that his name should be published. But it is done by one who hath had the viewing of my father's manuscripts; from whence, as well as from personal and intimate acquaintance of many years' continuance, and other ways, he hath been truly furnished with the knowledge of what is here reported." One of the Public Grammar Schools of Boston, situated in that part of the city which was formerly Dorchester Neck, is called the *Mather School*, in honor of this patriarch. See the Life of Richard Mather, printed at Cambridge, N. E., in 1670, (42 pages, small 4to.); Mather's Magnalia, i. 401–414; Wood's Athen. Oxon. iii. 832 (ed. Bliss); Blake's Annals of Dorchester, pp. 14, 24.

The MS. of the preceding Journal, which is now printed for the first time, was discovered in Dorchester in November, 1844, in a box of old papers, which had not been examined for twenty-five years.

The author of the Life of Richard Mather, mentioned above, had this Journal, for on page 21 he quotes at length the description of the storm. The manuscript, which is the original, in the handwriting of the author, is in excellent condition, considering its age, 211 years, except that two pages at the beginning are a little torn in the margin. It probably once belonged to James Blake, the author of the Annals of Dorchester, who died in 1750, and from him descended to the Rev. James Blake Howe, of Claremont, N. H., whose son, William B. W. Howe, of St. John's, Berkley, S. C. found it in the box of papers left at Dorchester by his father, and presented it to the Dorchester Antiquarian and Historical Society. By the kindness of that Society, I have been permitted to copy and insert it among these Chronicles. The accuracy of my copy has been secured by its careful collation with another copy, which had also been collated with the original and corrected by my friend the Hon. James Savage, the editor of Winthrop's History, and President of the Massachusetts Historical Society.

# ANTHONY THACHER'S

# NARRATIVE OF HIS SHIPWRECK.

# CHAPTER XXIII.

## THACHER'S NARRATIVE OF HIS SHIPWRECK.

I MUST turn my drowned pen and shaking hand to indite the story of such sad news as never before this happened in New-England.

There was a league of perpetual friendship between my cousin Avery[1] and myself, never to forsake each other to the death, but to be partakers of each other's misery or welfare, as also of habitation, in the same place. Now upon our arrival in New-England,[2] there was an offer made unto us. My cousin Avery was invited to Marble-head,[3] to be their pastor in due time ; there being no church planted there as yet, but a town appointed to set up the trade of fishing. Because many there (the most being fishermen,) were something loose and remiss

---

[1] " This Mr. Avery was a precious, holy minister, who came out of England with Mr. Anthony Thacher." Increase Mather's note. His baptismal name was John. Winthrop calls him " a minister in Wiltshire, a godly man." See Winthrop, i. 165.

[2] They came in the James, from Southampton, which arrived at Boston, June 3. See Winthrop, i. 161 ; Mass. Hist. Coll. xxviii. 319.

[3] Marblehead was not set off from Salem till 1649. See note [4] on page 244, and page 410.

in their behaviour, my cousin Avery was unwilling
to go thither ; and so refusing, we went to New-
berry,[1] intending there to sit down.  But being solicited so often both by the men of the place, and by
the magistrates, and by Mr. Cotton, and most of the
ministers, who alleged what a benefit we might be
to the people there, and also to the country and
commonwealth, at length we embraced it, and thither
consented to go.  They of Marble-head forthwith
sent a pinnace[2] for us and our goods.

11.          We embarked at Ipswich August 11, 1635, with
our families and substance, bound for Marble-head,
we being in all twenty-three souls, viz., eleven[3] in
my cousin's family, seven[4] in mine, and one Mr.
William Eliot, sometimes of New Sarum, and four
12.     mariners.  The next morning, having commended
ourselves to God, with cheerful hearts, we hoisted
sail.  But the Lord suddenly turned our cheerfulness into mourning and lamentations.  For on the
14.     14th of this August, 1635, about ten at night, having a fresh gale of wind, our sails being old and
done, were split.  The mariners, because that it
was night, would not put to new sails, but resolved
15.     to cast anchor till the morning.  But before daylight,
it pleased the Lord to send so mighty a storm, as
the like was never known in New-England since the

---

[1] See note [1] on page 411.
[2] Winthrop, i. 165, says that this was " a bark of Mr. Aller-ton's." Isaac Allerton was one of the Pilgrims who landed at Plymouth in the Mayflower.  Moses Maverick, of Marblehead, married his daughter Sarah.  See Chronicles of Plymouth, p. 195, and Mass. Hist. Coll. xxvii. 243–249, 301–304.

[3] Mr. Avery, his wife, a maid-servant, and " six small children," according to Winthrop, i. 165.
[4] Besides himself and his wife, and his four children, there was probably his servant, or journeyman, Peter Higden, who came over with him from England.  See Mass. Hist. Coll. xxviii. 319.

English came, nor in the memory of any of the In- CHAP.
dians.[1] It was so furious, that our anchor came
home. Whereupon the mariners let out more cable, 1635.
which at last slipped away. Then our sailors knew Aug. 15.
not what to do ; but we were driven before the
wind and waves.

My cousin and I perceived our danger, [and] solemnly recommended ourselves to God, the Lord both of
earth and seas, expecting with every wave to be swallowed up and drenched in the deeps. And as my
cousin, his wife, and my tender babes, sat comforting
and cheering one the other in the Lord against ghast-
ly death, which every moment stared us in the face
and sat triumphing upon each one's forehead, we
were by the violence of the waves and fury of the
winds, (by the Lord's permission,) lifted up upon a
rock between two high rocks, yet all was one rock.
But it raged with the stroke, which came into the pinnace, so as we were presently up to our middles in
water, as we sat. The waves came furiously and violently over us, and against us, but, by reason of the
rock's proportion, could not lift us off, but beat her
all to pieces. Now look with me upon our distress,
and consider of my misery, who beheld the ship broken, the water in her, and violently overwhelming us,
my goods and provisions swimming in the seas, my
friends almost drowned, and mine own poor children
so untimely (if I may so term it without offence,) before mine eyes drowned, and ready to be swallowed
up and dashed to pieces against the rocks by the merciless waves, and myself ready to accompany them.
But I must go on to an end of this woful relation.

[1] See note [1] on page 473.

In the same room whereas he sat, the master of the pinnace, not knowing what to do, our foremast was cut down, our mainmast broken in three pieces, the fore part of the pinnace beat away, our goods swimming about the seas, my children bewailing me, as not pitying themselves, and myself bemoaning them, poor souls, whom I had occasioned to such an end in their tender years, whenas they could scarce be sensible of death. And so likewise my cousin, his wife, and his children ; and both of us bewailing each other in our Lord and only Saviour Jesus Christ, in whom only we had comfort and cheerfulness ; insomuch that, from the greatest to the least of us, there was not one screech or outcry made ; but all, as silent sheep, were contentedly resolved to die together lovingly, as since our acquaintance we had lived together friendly.

Now as I was sitting in the cabin room door, with my body in the room, when lo ! one of the sailors, by a wave being washed out of the pinnace, was gotten in again, and coming into the cabin room over my back, cried out, " We are all cast away. The Lord have mercy upon us ! I have been washed overboard into the sea, and am gotten in again." His speeches made me look forth. And looking towards the sea, and seeing how we were, I turned myself to my cousin, and the rest, and spake these words ; " O cousin, it hath pleased God to cast us here between two rocks, the shore not far from us, for I saw the tops of trees, when I looked forth." Whereupon the master of the pinnace, looking up at the scuttle hole of the quarter deck, went out at it ; but I never saw him afterwards. Then he that had

been in the sea, went out again by me, and leaped
overboard towards the rocks, whom afterwards also
I could not see.

Now none were left in the bark, that I knew or
saw, but my cousin, his wife and children, myself
and mine, and his maid-servant. But my cousin
thought I would have fled from him, and said unto
me, " O cousin, leave us not, let us die together ;"
and reached forth his hand unto me. Then I, letting
go my son Peter's hand, took him by the hand, and
said, " Cousin, I purpose it not. Whither shall I
go ? I am willing and ready here to die with you
and my poor children. God be merciful to us, and
receive us to himself ;" adding these words, " the
Lord is able to help and deliver us." He replied,
saying, " Truth, cousin ; but what his pleasure is,
we know not. I fear we have been too unthankful
for former deliverances. But he hath promised to
deliver us from sin and condemnation, and to bring
us safe to heaven through the all-sufficient satisfaction of Jesus Christ. This therefore we may challenge of Him." To which I replying, said, " That
is all the deliverance I now desire and expect."

Which words I had no sooner spoken, but by a
mighty wave I was, with the piece of the bark, washed out upon part of the rock, where the wave left
me almost drowned. But recovering my feet, I saw
above me, on the rock, my daughter Mary. To
whom I had no sooner gotten, but my cousin Avery
and his eldest son came to us ; being all four of us
washed out by one and the same wave. We went
all into a small hole on the top of the rock, whence
we called to those in the pinnace to come unto us,

supposing we had been in more safety than they were in. My wife, seeing us there, was crept up into the scuttle of the quarter deck, to come unto us. But presently came another wave, and dashing the pinnace all to pieces, carried my wife away in the scuttle, as she was, with the greater part of the quarter deck, unto the shore ; where she was cast safely, but her legs were something bruised. And much timber of the vessel being there also cast, she was some time before she could get away, being washed by the waves. All the rest that were in the bark were drowned in the merciless seas. We four by that wave were clean swept away from off the rock also into the sea ; the Lord, in one instant of time, disposing of fifteen souls of us according to his good pleasure and will.

His pleasure and wonderful great mercy to me was thus. Standing on the rock, as before you heard, with my eldest daughter, my cousin, and his eldest son, looking upon and talking to them in the bark, whenas we were by that merciless wave washed off the rock, as before you heard, God, in his mercy, caused me to fall, by the stroke of the wave, flat on my face ; for my face was toward the sea. Insomuch, that as I was sliding off the rock into the sea, the Lord directed my toes into a joint in the rock's side, as also the tops of some of my fingers, with my right hand, by means whereof, the wave leaving me, I remained so, hanging on the rock, only my head above the water ; when on the left hand I espied a board or plank of the pinnace. And as I was reaching out my left hand to lay hold on it, by another coming over the top of the rock I was washed away

from the rock, and by the violence of the waves was CHAP. XXIII.
driven hither and thither in the seas a great while,
and had many dashes against the rocks. At length, 1635. Aug. 15.
past hopes of life, and wearied in body and spirits, I
even gave over to nature ; and being ready to receive
in the waters of death, I lifted up both my heart and
hands to the God of heaven. For note, I had my
senses remaining perfect with me all the time that I
was under and in water, who at that instant lifted
my head above the top of the water, that so I might
breathe without any hindrance by the waters. I
stood bolt upright, as if I had stood upon my feet ;
but I felt no bottom, nor had any footing for to stand
upon but the waters.

While I was thus above the water, I saw by me a
piece of the mast, as I suppose, about three foot
long, which I labored to catch into my arms. But
suddenly I was overwhelmed with water, and driven
to and fro again, and at last I felt the ground with
my right foot. When immediately, whilst I was
thus grovelling on my face, I presently recovering
my feet, was in the water up to my breast, and
through God's great mercy had my face unto the
shore, and not to the sea. I made haste to get out ;
but was thrown down on my hands with the waves,
and so with safety crept to the dry shore. Where,
blessing God, I turned about to look for my children
and friends, but saw neither, nor any part of the
pinnace, where I left them, as I supposed. But I
saw my wife about a butt length from me, getting
herself forth from amongst the timber of the broken
bark ; but before I could get unto her, she was gotten to the shore. I was in the water, after I was

CHAP.
XXIII. washed from the rock, before I came to the shore, a
quarter of an hour at least.

1635. When we were come each to other, we went and
Aug.
15. sat under the bank. But fear of the seas roaring,
and our coldness, would not suffer us there to remain.
But we went up into the land, and sat us down under
a cedar tree, which the wind had thrown down,
where we sat about an hour, almost dead with cold.
But now the storm was broken up, and the wind was
calm ; but the sea remained rough and fearful to us.
My legs were much bruised, and so was my head.
Other hurt had I none, neither had I taken in much
quantity of water. But my heart would not let me
sit still any longer ; but I would go to see if any
more were gotten to the land in safety, especially
hoping to have met with some of my own poor children ; but I could find none, neither dead, nor yet
living.

You condole with me my miseries, who now began
to consider of my losses. Now came to my remembrance the time and manner how and when I last
saw and left my children and friends. One was sev-
ered from me sitting on the rock at my feet, the
other three in the pinnace ; my little babe (ah, poor
Peter !) sitting in his sister Edith's arms, who to the
uttermost of her power sheltered him from the waters ; my poor William standing close unto them,
all three of them looking ruefully on me on the rock,
their very countenances calling unto me to help them;
whom I could not go unto, neither could they come
at me, neither would the merciless waves afford me
space or time to use any means at all, either to help
them or myself. Oh I yet see their cheeks, poor

silent lambs, pleading pity and help at my hands. CHAP. XXIII.
Then, on the other side, to consider the loss of my dear
friends, with the spoiling and loss of all our goods and 1635.
provisions, myself cast upon an unknown land, in a 15.
wilderness, I knew not where, nor how to get thence.
Then it came to my mind how I had occasioned the
death of my children,[1] who caused them to leave
their native land, who might have left them there,
yea, and might have sent some of them back again,
and cost me nothing. These and such like thoughts
do press down my heavy heart very much.

But I must let this pass, and will proceed on in
the relation of God's goodness unto me in that desolate island, on which I was cast. I and my wife
were almost naked, both of us, and wet and cold
even unto death. I found a snapsack cast on the
shore, in which I had a steel, and flint, and powder-
horn. Going further, I found a drowned goat; then
I found a hat, and my son William's coat, both which
I put on.[2] My wife found one of her petticoats,
which she put on. I found also two cheeses and
some butter, driven ashore. Thus the Lord sent us
some clothes to put on, and food to sustain our new
lives, which we had lately given unto us, and means
also to make fire; for in a horn I had some gunpowder, which, to mine own, and since to other men's
admiration, was dry. So taking a piece of my wife's
neckcloth, which I dried in the sun, I struck fire,
and so dried and warmed our wet bodies; and then
skinned the goat, and having found a small brass pot,

---

[1] His children were four in number, William, Mary, Edith, and
Peter.

[2] We may infer from this that
his son William was a full-grown
youth.

CHAP.
XXIII.

1635.
Aug.
17.

18.

we boiled some of her. Our drink was brackish water. Bread we had none.

There we remained until the Monday following; when, about three of the clock in the afternoon, in a boat that came that way, we went off that desolate island, which I named after my name, *Thacher's Woe*,[1] and the rock, *Avery his Fall*,[2] to the end that their fall and loss, and mine own, might be had in perpetual remembrance. In the isle lieth buried the body of my cousin's eldest daughter, whom I found dead on the shore. On the Tuesday following, in the afternoon, we arrived at Marblehead.[3]

[1] Now called Thacher's Island. It lies about two miles east of the south-east point of Cape Ann.

[2] Now called Avery's Rock.

[3] ANTHONY THACHER, the writer of this heart-rending Narrative, was a tailor, from Salisbury, in Wiltshire, where his brother Peter was the rector of the church of St. Edmund as early as 1622. It was written in a letter to his brother, as Increase Mather says, "within a few days after that eminent providence happened to him, when matters were fresh in his memory." Anthony Thacher sailed from Southampton in April, 1635, in the James, of London, and arrived at Boston June 3. With him came his brother's son, Thomas, then a youth of fifteen, his parents intending soon to follow with the rest of the family; which intention, however, was prevented by the death of his mother. Cotton Mather says that "a day or two before that fatal voyage from Newbury to Marblehead, our young Thacher had such a strong and sad impression upon his mind about the issue of the voyage, that he, with another, would needs go the journey by land, and so he escaped perishing with some of his pious and precious friends by sea." He was educated for the ministry under the

Rev. Charles Chauncy, afterwards President of Harvard College, married, May 11, 1643, a daughter of the Rev. Ralph Partridge, of Duxbury, was ordained pastor of the church at Weymouth Jan. 2, 1645, and installed the first pastor of the Third, or Old South Church, in Boston, Feb. 16, 1670, where he continued till he died, Oct. 16, 1678, aged 58. He was the progenitor of the long line of clergymen who have illustrated the name of Thacher, the last of whom was my young friend and parishioner, the Rev. William Vincent Thacher, the amiable and accomplished pastor of the Unitarian Church at Savannah, in Georgia, who died July 16, 1839, aged 24.

After this sad catastrophe, by which he lost all his children, Anthony Thacher resided at Marshfield; and "the General Court," says Winthrop, "gave him £26 13s. 4d. towards his losses, and divers good people gave him besides." In Jan. 1639, he removed to Yarmouth, on Cape Cod, being one of the three original grantees of land in that town, where he resided till his death in 1668, aged about 80. He left two sons and one daughter, born after the disastrous shipwreck, John, Judah, and Bethiah, who, tradition says, were the children of a second wife, named Elizabeth Jones, whom he married about six weeks before he left England. A long line of descendants, the children of John, perpetuate the name at Yarmouth, Boston, and elsewhere. The late Dr. James Thacher, of Plymouth, was a descendant from Anthony in the sixth generation. Winthrop mentions among the articles saved from the wreck "a truss of bedding;" and Dr. Thacher states that "a cradle coverlet, of scarlet broadcloth, and some articles of clothing, said to have been saved from the shipwreck, are now in the possession of Mr. Peter Thacher, and such is the veneration for these relics, that every child of Thacher families that has been baptized in Yarmouth, has been carried to the baptismal font enwrapped in them." See Increase Mather's Illustrious Providences, pages 2–14; Winthrop, i. 161, 165; Mather's Magnalia, i. 441–448; Mass. Hist. Coll. viii. 277, xxviii. 317, 319; N. Eng. Magazine, vii. 1–16.

CHAP.
XXIII.

1635.

# THOMAS SHEPARD'S

# MEMOIR OF HIS OWN LIFE.

# CHAPTER XXIV.

T. { MY BIRTH AND LIFE. } S.

In the year of Christ 1604,[1] upon the 5th day of November, called the Powder Treason day, and that very hour of the day wherein the Parliament should have been blown up by Popish priests, I was then born; which occasioned my father to give me this name, Thomas; because, he said, I would hardly *believe*[2] that ever any such wickedness should be attempted by men against so religious and good [a] Parliament.

My father's name was William Shepard, born in a little poor town in Northamptonshire, called Fosse-cut, near Towcester; and being a 'prentice to one Mr. Bland, a grocer, he married one of his daugh-ters, of whom he begat many children, three sons, John, William, and Thomas, and six daughters, Ann, Margaret, Mary, Elizabeth, Hester, Sarah; of all

CHAP.
XXIV.

1604.
Nov.
5.

---

[1] This is a singular anachronism, antedating the Powder Plot a whole year. It is well known that it was in 1605 that this plot was contrived.

[2] An allusion to the skepticism of the Apostle Thomas, recorded in the Gospel of John, xx. 25.

which only John, Thomas, Anna, and Margaret, are
still living in the town where I was born, viz. Towcester,[1] in Northamptonshire, six miles distant from
the town of Northampton, in Old England.

I do well remember my father, and have some
little remembrance of my mother. My father was a
wise, prudent man, the peacemaker of the place ;
and toward his latter end much blessed of God in his
estate and in his soul. For there being no good ministry in the town, he was resolved to go and live at
Banbury,[2] in Oxfordshire, under a stirring ministry,
having bought a house there for that end. My mother was a woman much afflicted in conscience, sometimes even unto distraction of mind; yet was sweetly
recovered again before she died. I being the youngest, she did bear exceeding great love to me, and
made many prayers for me; but she died when I was
1608. about four years old, and my father lived, and married a second wife, now dwelling in the same town,
of whom he begat two children, Samuel and Eliza-
1614. beth, and died when I was about ten years of age.

But while my father and mother lived, when I was
1607. about three years old, there was a great plague in the
town of Towcester, which swept away many in my
father's family, both sisters and servants. I being
the youngest, and best beloved of my mother, was
sent away the day the plague brake out, to live with
my aged grandfather and grandmother in Fossecut,
a most blind town and corner, and those I lived with
also being very well to live, yet very ignorant. And

---

[1] Towcester is a market town,
eight miles from Northampton. Population in 1841, 2749.

[2] Banbury is a borough and market town, 69 miles northwest from
London. Population in 1841, 7366.

there was I put to keep geese, and other such country CHAP.
XXIV.
work, all that time much neglected of them; and afterward sent from them unto Adthrop, a little blind 1607.
town adjoining, to my uncle, where I had more content, but did learn to sing and sport, as children do
in those parts, and dance at their Whitson Ales;[1]
until the plague was removed, and my dear mother
dead, who died not of the plague, but of some other
disease, after it. And being come home, my sister
Ann married to one Mr. Farmer, and my sister Margaret loved me much, who afterward married to my
father's 'prentice, viz. Mr. Mapler, and my father
married again to another woman, who did let me see
the difference between my own mother and a stepmother. She did seem not to love me, but incens-
ed my father often against me; it may be that it
was justly also, for my childishness. And having
lived thus for a time, my father sent me to school to
a Welshman, one Mr. Rice, who kept the free school
in the town of Towcester. But he was exceeding
curst[2] and cruel, and would deal roughly with me,
and so discouraged me wholly from desire of learning, that I remember I wished oftentimes myself in
any condition, to keep hogs or beasts, rather than to
go to school and learn.

But my father at last was visited with sickness,
having taken some cold upon some pills he took, and
so had the hickets[3] with his sickness a week together;

[1] These were the sports and dances usual in the country at Whit-suntide. · They were attended with ludicrous gestures and acts of foole-ry and buffoonery, and commonly ended in drunkenness and debauch-ery; and of course were discounte-nanced by the grave Puritans. See the description of them in Brand's Popular Antiquities, i. 157, (Ellis's edit. 1841); Hone's Every-Day Book, i. 685; Strutt's Sports and Pastimes, pp. 358, 367.
[2] Crusty, peevish, snarling.
[3] Hickups, hiccoughs.

CHAP.
XXIV. in which time I do remember I did pray very strongly
and heartily for the life of my father, and made some
covenant, if God would do it, to serve Him the better, as knowing I should be left alone if he was gone.
Yet the Lord took him away by death, and so I was
1614. left fatherless and motherless, when I was about ten
years old ; and was committed to my stepmother to
be educated, who therefore had my portion, which
was a £100, which my father left me.  But she neglecting my education very much, my brother John,
who was my only brother alive, desired to have me
out of her hands, and to have me with him, and he
would bring me up for the use of my portion ; and
so at last it was granted.  And so I lived with this
my eldest brother, who showed much love unto me,
and unto whom I owe much ; for him God made to
be both father and mother unto me.  And it happened that the cruel schoolmaster died, and another
came into his room, to be a preacher also in the
town ; who was an eminent preacher in those days,
and accounted holy, but afterward turned a great
apostate, and enemy to all righteousness, and I fear
did commit the unpardonable sin.  Yet it so fell out,
by God's good providence, that this man stirred up
in my heart a love and desire of the honor of learning, and therefore I told my friends I would be a
scholar ; and so the Lord blessed me in my studies,
and gave me some knowledge of the Latin and Greek
tongues, but much ungrounded in both.  But I was
studious, because I was ambitious of learning and being a scholar; and hence when I could not take notes
of the sermon, I remember I was troubled at it, and
prayed the Lord earnestly that he would help me to

note sermons ; and I see cause of wondering at the CHAP. XXIV. Lord's providence therein ; for as soon as ever I had prayed (after my best fashion) Him for it, I presently, the next Sabbath, was able to take notes, who the precedent Sabbath could do nothing at all that way.

So I continued till I was about fifteen years of age, 1619. and then was conceived to be ripe for the University; and it pleased the Lord to put it into my brother's heart to provide and to seek to prepare a place for me there ; which was done in this manner. One Mr. Cockerill, Fellow of Emmanuel College in Cambridge, being a Northamptonshire man, came down into the country to Northampton, and so sent for me ; who, upon examination of me, gave my brother encouragement to send me up to Cambridge. And so I came up; and though I was very raw and young, yet it pleased God to open the hearts of others to admit me into the College a pensioner ; and so Mr. Cockerill became my tutor. But I do here wonder, and, I hope, shall bless the Lord forever in heaven, that the Lord did so graciously provide for me ; for I have oft thought what a woful estate I had been left in, if the Lord had left me in that profane, ignorant town of Towcester, where I was born ; that the Lord should pluck me out of that sink and Sodom, who was the least in my father's house, forsaken of father and mother, yet that the Lord should fetch me out from thence, by such a secret hand.

The first two years I spent in Cambridge was in 1620. studying, and in much neglect of God and private prayer, which I had sometime used ; and I did not regard the Lord at all, unless it were at some fits. The third year, wherein I was Sophister, I began to 1621.

CHAP.
XXIV.

be foolish and proud, and to show myself in the Public Schools, and there to be a disputer about things which now I see I did not know then at all, but only prated about them. And toward the end of this year, when I was most vile, (after I had been next unto the gates of death by the small pox the year before,) the Lord began to call me home to the fellowship of his grace ; which was in this manner.

1. I do remember that I had many good affections, but blind and unconstant, oft cast into me since my father's sickness, by the spirit of God wrestling with me ; and hence I would pray in secret, and hence, when I was at Cambridge, I heard old Doctor Chadderton,[1] the master of the College when I came.

1619. And the first year I was there, to hear him, upon a sacrament day, my heart was much affected ; but I did break loose from the Lord again. And half a

1620. year after, I heard Mr. Dickinson common-place in the Chapel upon those words, " I will not destroy it for ten's sake," and then again was much affected ; but I shook this off also, and fell from God to loose and lewd company, to lust, and pride, and gaming,

Gen.
xviii.32.

---

[1] Laurence Chadderton was born at Chadderton, in Lancashire, in 1537, of an ancient and wealthy family. His parents, who were Papists, intended him for the Law, and sent him to the Inns of Court. But he soon became a Protestant, forsook the study of the Law, and entered Christ's College, Cambridge, in 1564, of which he was chosen a Fellow three years afterwards. In 1584, when Sir Walter Mildmay founded Emmanuel College, he was chosen by him its first Master, in which office he continued thirty-eight years, till 1622. In 1603 he was one of the four Puritan divines selected by James I. to at- tend the Conference at Hampton Court, and was also appointed by him the same year one of the Translators of the Bible He was a man of great abilities and learning, a decided but moderate Puritan, and " a grave, pious, and excellent preacher." He lived to see three successors in the mastership of his College, and died Nov. 13, 1640, in the 103d year of his age. See Vita Chaddertoni, a Gul. Dillinghamo ; Samuel Clarke's Lives, p. 145, (fol. 1677) ; Fuller's Worthies, i. 550 ; Brook's Lives of the Puritans, ii. 445 ; Dyer's Hist. of Univ. of Cambridge, ii. 351.

and bowling, and drinking. And yet the Lord left CHAP.
me not ; but a godly scholar, walking with me, fell XXIV.
to discourse about the misery of every man out of 1620.
Christ, viz. that whatever they did was sin ; and
this did much affect me.  And, at another time, when
I did light in godly company, I heard them discourse
about the wrath of God, and the terror of it, and
how intolerable it was ; which they did present by
fire, how intolerable the torment of that was for a
time ; what then would eternity be ?  And this did
much awaken me, and I began to pray again.  But
then, by loose company, I came to dispute in the
Schools, and there to join to loose scholars of other
Colleges, and was fearfully left of God, and fell to
drink with them.  And I drank so much one day,
that I was dead drunk, and that upon a Saturday
night ; and so was carried from the place I had
drinked at and did feast at, unto a scholar's chamber,
one Bassett, of Christ's College, and knew not where
I was until I awakened late on that Sabbath, and sick
with my beastly carriage.  And when I awakened, I
went from him in shame and confusion, and went out
into the fields, and there spent that Sabbath lying hid
in the cornfields ; where the Lord, who might justly
have cut me off in the midst of my sin, did meet me
with much sadness of heart, and troubled my soul for
this and other my sins, which then I had cause and
leisure to think of.  And note, when I was worst,
He began to be best unto me, and made me resolve
to set upon a course of daily meditation about the
evil of sin and my own ways.  Yet although I was
troubled for this sin, I did not know my sinful nature
all this while.

2. The Lord therefore sent Dr. Preston[1] to be Master of the College ; and Mr. Stone[2] and others commending his preaching to be most spiritual and excellent, I began to listen unto what he said. The first sermon he preached was Romans xii. " Be renewed in the spirit of your mind." In opening which point, viz. the change of heart in a Christian, the Lord so bored my ears, as that I understood what he spake, and the secrets of my soul were laid open before me, the hypocrisy of all my good things I thought I had in me ; as if one had told him of all that ever I did, of all the turnings and deceits of my heart ; insomuch as that I thought he was the most searching preacher in the world, and I began to love

[1] John Preston was born at Heyford, in Northamptonshire, in 1587, and was admitted to King's College, Cambridge, in 1604, and in 1609 was chosen a Fellow of Queen's. At this time he was a very ambitious and aspiring student ; but hearing a sermon preached at St. Mary's by our John Cotton, of Boston, he was seriously impressed, and directed all his studies to a preparation for the ministry. He was appointed chaplain to the Prince of Wales, and preacher at Lincoln's Inn, and on the resignation of Dr. Chadderton in 1622 was chosen Master of Emmanuel College. He was in great favor with the Duke of Buckingham, and might have had the bishoprick of Gloucester, but he preferred the Lectureship of Trinity Church, Cambridge. On the accession of Charles I. the Duke offered him the Great Seal, which he prudently declined, though he had abilities enough to manage it. He died July 20, 1628, being only 41 years of age. Fuller, who classes him among the learned writers of Queen's College, says " he was all judgment and gravity, an excellent preacher,

a subtle disputant, and a perfect politician." Echard styles him " the most celebrated of the Puritans." See page 422 ; his Life by Thomas Ball in Clarke's Lives, pp. 75–114 ; Fuller's Worthies, ii. 171, Hist. Cambridge, pp. 121, 206, Church Hist. iii. 355 ; Brook's Puritans, ii. 352 ; Neal's Puritans, ii. 219 ; Echard's Hist. of Eng. ii. 72.

[2] Samuel Stone was born at Hertford, in Hertfordshire, and was educated at Emmanuel College, where he took the degree of A. B. in 1623, and of A. M. in 1627. To escape persecution, he came over to New-England in Sept. 1633, in the same ship with Cotton and Hooker, was settled as colleague with the latter at Cambridge Oct. 11, 1633, and in 1636 removed with him to Hartford, on Connecticut river, which received its name from his birthplace. He died July 20, 1663, being probably about 60 years old. He accompanied Mason's expedition in the Pequot War, as chaplain. See Mather's Magnalia, i. 392 ; Winthrop, i. 108 ; Morton's Memorial, p. 301 ; Mass. Hist. Coll. xviii. 134, xxviii. 248.

him much, and to bless God I did see my frame, and CHAP.
XXIV.
my hypocrisy, and self and secret sins, although I
found a hard heart, and could not be affected with 1624.
them.

3. I did therefore set more constantly upon the May
3.
work of daily meditation, sometimes every morning,
but constantly every evening before supper; and my
chief meditation was about the evil of sin, the terror
of God's wrath, day of death, beauty of Christ, the
deceitfulness of the heart, &c. But principally I
found this my misery; sin was not my greatest evil,
did lie light upon me as yet; yet I was much afraid
of death and the flames of God's wrath. And this I
remember, I never went out to meditate in the fields
but I did find the Lord teaching me somewhat of myself, or Himself, or the vanity of the world, I never
saw before. And hence I took out a little book I
have every day into the fields, and writ down what
God taught me, lest I should forget them; and so
the Lord encouraged me, and I grew much. But, in
my observation of myself, I did see my atheism. I
questioned whether there were a God, and my unbelief whether Christ was the Messiah; whether the
Scriptures were God's word, or no. I felt all manner of temptations to all kind of religions, not knowing which I should choose; whether education might
not make me believe what I had believed, and
whether, if I had been educated up among the Papists, I should not have been as verily persuaded
that Popery is the truth, or Turcisme is the truth.
And at last I heard of Grindleton, and I did question whether that glorious estate of perfection might
not be the truth, and whether old Mr. Rogers's Seven

CHAP.
XXIV.
——
1624.

Treatises,[1] and the Practice of Christianity, the book which did first work upon my heart, whether these men were not all legal men, and their books so. But the Lord delivered me at last from them, and in the conclusion, after many prayers, meditations, duties, the Lord let me see three main wounds in my soul. (1.) I could not feel sin as my greatest evil. (2.) I could do nothing but I did seek myself in it, and was imprisoned there ; and though I desired to be a preacher, yet it was honor I did look to, like a vile wretch, in the use of God's gifts I desired to have. (3.) I felt a depth of atheism and unbelief in the main matters of salvation, and whether the Scriptures were God's word. These things did much trouble me, and in the conclusion did so far trouble me, that I could not read the Scriptures, or hear them read, without secret and hellish blasphemy, calling all into question, and all Christ's miracles. And hereupon I fell to doubt whether I had not committed the unpardonable sin ; and because I did question whether Christ did not cast out devils from Beelzebub, &c., I did think and fear I had. And now the terrors of God began to break in, like floods of fire, into my soul.

For three quarters of a year this temptation did last, and I had some strong temptations to run my head against walls, and brain and kill myself. And so I did see, as I thought, God's eternal reprobation of me ; a fruit of which was this dereliction to these

[1] Richard Rogers was settled in the ministry at Weathersfield, in Essex, and was twice suspended and silenced by Archbishop Whitgift. He was the father of Daniel and Ezekiel Rogers, both eminent Puritan divines, and the latter of whom came over to New-England, and was the first minister of Rowley. See Brook's Puritans, ii. 231.

doubts and darkness, and I did see God like a con- CHAP. XXIV.
suming fire and an everlasting burning, and myself
like a poor prisoner leading to that fire ; and the 1624.
thoughts of eternal reprobation and torment did
amaze my spirits, especially at one time upon a Sabbath day at evening.  And when I knew not what
to do, (for I went to no Christian, and was ashamed
to speak of these things,) it came to my mind that
I should do as Christ, when he was in an agony.  He
prayed earnestly ; and so I fell down to prayer.
And being in prayer, I saw myself so unholy, and
God so holy, that my spirits began to sink.  Yet the
Lord recovered me, and poured out a spirit of prayer
upon me for free mercy and pity ; and in the conclusion of the prayer, I found the Lord helping me
to see my unworthiness of any mercy, and that I was
worthy to be cast out of his sight, and to leave myself with him to do with me what he would ; and
then, and never until then, I found rest, and so my
heart was humbled, and cast down, and I went with
a stayed heart unto supper late that night, and so
rested here, and the terrors of the Lord began to
assuage sweetly.  Yet when these were gone, I felt
my senselessness of sin, and bondage to self, and
unconstancy, and losing what the Lord had wrought,
and my heartlessness to any good, and loathing of
God's ways.  Whereupon, walking in the fields, the
Lord dropped this meditation into me, " Be not discouraged, therefore, because thou art so vile, but
make this double use of it ; first, loathe thyself the
more ; secondly, feel a greater need and put a greater
price upon Jesus Christ, who only can redeem thee
from all sin."  And this I found of wonderful use to

me in all my course; whereby I was kept from sink- ings of heart, and did beat Satan, as it were, with his own weapons. And I saw Christ teaching me this before any man preached any such thing unto me. And so the Lord did help me to loathe myself in some measure, and to say oft, Why shall I seek the glory and good of myself, who am the greatest enemy, worse than the Devil can be, against myself; which self ruins me, and blinds me, &c. And thus God kept my heart exercised, and here I began to forsake my loose company wholly, and to do what I could to work upon the hearts of other scholars, and to humble them, and to come into a way of holy walking in our speeches and otherwise. But yet I had no assurance Christ was mine.

4. The Lord therefore brought Dr. Preston to preach upon that text, 1 Cor. i. 30, " Christ is made unto us wisdom, righteousness, sanctification, and redemption." And when he had opened how all the good I had, all the redemption I had, it was from Jesus Christ, I did then begin to prize him, and he became very sweet unto me, although I had heard, many a time, Christ freely offered by his ministry, if I would come in, and receive him as Lord, and Sa- viour, and husband. But I found my heart ever un- willing to accept of Christ upon these terms. I found them impossible for me to keep [on] that con- dition; and Christ was not so sweet as my lust. But now the Lord made himself sweet to me, and to embrace him, and to give up myself unto him. But yet, after this, I had many fears and doubts.

5. I found, therefore, the Lord revealing free mercy, and that all my help was in that to give me

Christ, and to enable me to believe in Christ, and CHAP. XXIV. accept of him ; and here I did rest.

1624.

6. The Lord also letting me see my own constant vileness in everything, put me to this question, Why did the Lord Jesus keep the law, had no guile in his heart, had no unbrokenness, but holiness there ? Was it not for them that did want it ? And here I saw Christ Jesus's righteousness for a poor sinner's ungodliness ; but yet questioned whether ever the Lord would apply this and give this unto me.

7. The Lord made me see that so many as receive him, he gives power to be the sons of God. And I saw the Lord gave me a heart to receive Christ with a naked hand, even naked Christ ; and so the Lord gave me peace.

John, i. 12.

And thus I continued till I was six years' standing ; and then went, half a year before I was Master of Arts, to Mr. Weld's house,[1] at Tarling, in Es-

1625.

---

[1] Thomas Welde was educated at Trinity College, Cambridge, where he received the degree of A. B. in 1613, and of A. M. in 1618. He arrived at Boston June 5, 1632, and in July was ordained the first minister of the church in Roxbury. In November following, John Eliot was settled as his colleague. In 1639 he assisted his colleague and Richard Mather in making the New-England Version of the Psalms ; and in 1641 was sent with Hugh Peters to England as an agent of the Colony. In 1646, when Edward Winslow was sent out to answer Gorton's complaint, Peters and Weld were dismissed from the agency, and desired to return home. But they both preferred to remain in England. Weld was afterwards settled in the ministry at Gateshead, in the bishoprick of Durham, opposite Newcastle. Hutchinson says he went to Ireland with Lord Forbes, but came back to England, and was ejected from his living in 1662. Whilst in New-England he took an active part in the proceeding against Mrs. Hutchinson, and in 1664 published in London a book entitled " A Short Story of the Rise, Reign and Ruin of the Antinomians, Familists, and Libertines, that infected the Churches of New-England," and the same year a Vindication of the New-England Churches. His son Edmund graduated at Harvard College in 1650, and was settled in Ireland. Another son, John, was a minister at Riton, in the county of Durham. A third son, Thomas, remained in New-England, whose son Thomas graduated at Harvard College in 1671, and was the first minister of Dunstable, N. H. See notes on pages 135 and 365 ; Newcourt's Reperto-

CHAP.
XXIV.

1626.

sex; where I enjoyed the blessing of his and Mr.
Hooker's[1] ministry at Chelmesfoord.[2] But before I
came there, I was very solicitous what would become
of me when I was Master of Arts; for then my time
and portion would be spent. But when I came

rium, ii. 578; Calamy's Noncon.
Mem. ii. 181; Winthrop, i. 77, 82,
258, ii. 25; Hutchinson's Mass. i.
98, 149, ii. 492, 504; Mass. Hist.
Coll. xxviii. 248.

[1] Thomas Hooker, "the Light of
the Western Churches," as Cotton
Mather calls him, and "the father
and pillar of the churches of Connecticut," according to Trumbull,
was born at Marefield, in Leicestershire, about the year 1586. He
was educated at Emmanuel College,
Cambridge, where he took the degree of A. B. in 1607, and of A. M.
in 1611, and was elected to a fellowship. In 1626 he was chosen lecturer at Chelmsford, in Essex. After preaching here four years with
great acceptance, he was obliged,
on account of his Nonconformity, to
relinquish his ministry, and set up a
grammar school at Little Baddow,
near Chelmsford, where he had John
Eliot, afterwards the Indian Apostle,
for his usher. Having been cited
before the spiritual court sitting at
Chelmsford, and bound over to appear before the High Commission,
he judged it prudent to retire into
Holland, where he preached as a
colleague to the celebrated Dr. Ames
of Rotterdam. But hearing that
many of his friends in Essex were
about emigrating to New-England,
he accepted their invitation to accompany them as their pastor. For
this purpose he returned to England,
and narrowly escaped arrest by the
pursuivants, and went on board the
ship at the Downs in disguise. In
company with Cotton, Stone, and
Haynes, he arrived at Boston Sept.
4, 1633, and on the 11th of October
was chosen pastor of the church at
Newtown, (Cambridge,) Mr. Stone
being chosen teacher. In May, 1636,

he removed with his colleague and
most of his congregation to Hartford, on Connecticut river, where he
remained till he died of an epidemic
disease, July 7, 1647. Winthrop,
speaking of the ravages of this epidemic, says, "But that which made
the stroke more sensible and grievous both to them (at Connecticut,)
and to all the country, was the death
of that faithful servant of the Lord,
Mr. Thomas Hooker, pastor of the
church in Hartford, who, for piety,
prudence, wisdom, zeal, learning,
and what else might make him serviceable in the place and time he
lived in, might be compared with
men of greatest note; and he shall
need no other praise; the fruits of
his labors in both Englands shall
preserve an honorable and happy remembrance of him forever." He
left a widow, Susan. His son Samuel was the second minister of
Farmington, in Connecticut, and
three of his daughters, Joanna, Mary, and Sarah, married Rev. Thomas Shepard, of Cambridge, Rev.
Roger Newton, the first minister of
Farmington, and Rev. John Wilson, of Medfield. See Mather, i.
302; Winthrop, i. 88, 108, 115,
187, ii. 310; Morton's Memorial,
p. 237; Trumbull's Conn. i. 293;
Mass. Hist. Coll. xxviii. 248.

[2] Chelmsford, so called from an
ancient ford on the river Chelmer,
near its junction with the Can, is a
county-town near the centre of Essex, 29 miles east-northeast of London. It is the great thoroughfare
between London and the towns of
Colchester, Harwich and Braintree,
and the county of Suffolk, and many
parts of Norfolk. Population in
1841, 6789. See Camden's Britannia, p. 346.

thither, and had been there some little season, until
I was ready to be Master of Arts, one Dr. Wilson[1]
had purposed to set up a Lecture,[2] and given £30
per annum to the maintenance of it. And when I
was among those worthies in Essex, where we had
monthly fasts, they did propound it unto me to take
the Lecture, and to set it up at a great town in Essex, called Cogshall ;[3] and so Mr. Weld especially
pressed me unto it, and wished me to seek God
about it. And after fasting and prayer, the ministers in those parts of Essex had a day of humiliation,
and they did seek the Lord for direction where to
place the Lecture ; and toward the evening of that
day they began to consider whether I should go to
Cogshall, or no. Most of the ministers were for it,
because it was a great town, and they did not know
any place [that] did desire it but they. Mr. Hooker
only did object against my going thither ; for being
but young and unexperienced, and there being an
old, yet sly and malicious minister in the town, who
did seem to give way to it to have it there, did
therefore say it was dangerous and uncomfortable for
little birds to build under the nests of old ravens and
kites.

But while they were thus debating it, the town of

---

[1] Perhaps Dr. Edmund Wilson, a physician, who was brother of our John Wilson, of the First Church. See note on page 326, and Wood's Fasti Oxon. i. 360, (ed. Bliss.)

[2] These Lectures, says Carlyle, were set up by the wealthy Puritans in those parts of the country which were insufficiently supplied with preachers. The lecturers were generally persons who were not in priests' orders, having scruples about the ceremonies, and they lectured on market-days and Sunday afternoons, as supplemental to the regular priest, when he might happen to be idle, or given to black and white surplices. They were greatly followed by the serious part of the community. See note [3] on page 70, and Carlyle's Cromwell, i. 50, 86–88.

[3] Coggeshall (Great) is a market town in Essex, six miles from Braintree. Population in 1841, 3408.

Earles-Colne,[1] being three miles off from Essex,
hearing that there was such a Lecture to be given
freely, and considering that the Lecture might enrich
that poor town, they did therefore, just at this time
of the day, come to the place where the ministers
met, viz. at Tarling,[2] in Essex, and desired that it
might be settled there for three years; (for no longer
was it to continue in any place, because it was conceived if any good was done, it would be within such
a time; and then, if it went away from them, the
people in a populous town would be glad to maintain
the man themselves; or if no good was done, it was
pity they should have it any longer.) And when
they thus came for it, the ministers, with one joint
consent, advised me to accept of the people's call,
and to stay among them if I found, upon my preaching a little season with them, that they still continued in their desires for my continuance there.

And thus I, who was so young, so weak, and unexperienced, and unfit for so great a work, was called
out by twelve or sixteen ministers of Christ to the
work; which did much encourage my heart; and
for the Lord's goodness herein I shall, I hope, never
forget his love. For I might have been cast away
upon a blind place, without the help of any ministry
about me. I might have been sent to some gentleman's house, to have been corrupted with the sins

[1] There are four parishes in the
archdeaconry of Colchester known by
the name of Colne, so called from
their situation on or near the river
Colne, distinguished by the several
additional names of their respective
lords. The first of these is Colne-
Comitis, or Earls-Colne, so called
from the sepulture there of the earls
of Oxford, lords of this manor. It
is about 35 miles north-east from
London, and seven north-west from
Colchester. Population in 1841,
1385. See Newcourt's Repertorium, ii. 182; Camden's Britannia,
pp. 350, 358.

[2] Terling is a parish four miles
from Witham. Population in 1841,
921.

in it. But this I have found ; the Lord was not con- CHAP.<br>XXIV.
tent to take me from one town to another, but from
the worst town I think in the world to the best place 1626.
for knowledge and learning, viz. to Cambridge.
And there the Lord was not content to give me good
means, but the best means, and ministry, and help of
private Christians ; for Dr. Preston and Mr. Goodwin[1] were the most able men for preaching Christ in
this latter age. And when I came from thence, the
Lord sent me to the best country in England, viz.
to Essex, and set me in the midst of the best ministry in the country ; by whose monthly fasts and con-
ferences I found much of God ; and thus the Lord
Jesus provided for me of all things of the best.

So being resolved to go unto Earles-Colne, in Essex, after my commencing Master of Arts, and my 1627.
sinful taking of orders, about a fortnight after, of the
Bishop of Peterborough, viz. B. Dove,[2] I came to the

---

[1] Thomas Goodwin was an eminent Puritan divine, born at Rollesby,
in Norfolk, Oct. 5, 1600. He was
educated in Christ's College, Cambridge, and was a Fellow of Catharine Hall. In 1628, he was chosen
to succeed Dr. Preston, of whom he
was a great admirer, in the lectureship at Trinity Church, Cambridge,
which he held till 1634, when he
left the University and relinquished
all his preferments, from unwilling-
ness to conform. He remained in
retirement till 1638, when he removed to Holland, and became pastor of a congregation at Arnheim.
At the beginning of the Long Parliament in 1640, he returned to
England, and became one of the
Assembly of Divines at Westminster, being one of the five Dissent-
ing Brethren, or Congregationalists.
He was a favorite of Cromwell,
who in 1650 appointed him President of Magdalen College, Oxford.
In 1653 he was appointed one of the
Triers of preachers, and at the Restoration in 1660 was removed from
his presidency. Whereupon he retired to London, and died there Feb.
23, 1680, in his 81st year. See
Wood's Fasti Oxon. ii. 179, (ed.
Bliss) ; Calamy's Nonconformists'
Memorial, i. 236 ; Fuller's Church
Hist. iii. 447, 461-467.

[2] Dr. Thomas Dove was educated
in Pembroke Hall, Cambridge. He
was chaplain to Queen Elizabeth,
Dean of Norwich, and in 1600 was
made Bishop of Peterborough. He
was a very ornate and florid preacher ; and Queen Elizabeth, when she
first heard him, profanely said " she
thought the Holy Ghost was descended again in this *Dove*." He
died in 1631. See Harington's
Nugæ Antiquæ, ii. 206, (ed. Park);
Fuller's Ch. Hist. iii. 368.

town, and boarded in Mr. Cosins his house, an aged,
but godly and cheerful Christian, and schoolmaster
in the town, and by whose society I was much refreshed, there being not one man else in all the town
that had any godliness but him that I could understand. So having preached upon the Sabbath day
out of 2 Cor. v. 19, all the town gave me a call, and
set to their hands in writing; and so I saw God
would have me to be there; but how to be there,
and continue there, I could not tell. Yet I sinfully
got a license to officiate the cure, of the Bishop of
London's register,[1] before my name was known, and
by virtue of that I had much help.

But when I had been here a while, and the Lord
had blessed my labors to divers in and out of the
town, especially to the chief house in the town, the
Priory,[2] to Mr. Harlakenden's children, where the
Lord wrought mightily upon his eldest son, Mr.
Richard,[3] (now dwelling there,) and afterward on

---

[1] The diocese of London includes
Essex. Mountain was at this time
Bishop of the diocese.

[2] In the time of William the Con-
queror, Aubrey de Vere, and Beat-
rice his wife, sister of the Conquer-
or, founded in the parish of Earls-
Colne a small convent or priory,
which he dedicated to St. Andrew.
Weever, whose book was published
in 1631, says that the house was
standing in his time, converted into
a private dwelling-place, as also the
old chapel, in which had been buried
thirteen earls of Oxford. See Newcourt's Repertorium, ii. 183; Weever's Funeral Monuments, p. 614;
Dugdale's Monasticon Anglicanum,
i. 436.

[3] Richard Harlakenden was the
eldest son of Richard Harlakenden,
a gentleman of ancient family and
good estate, who was the second

son of Roger Harlakenden, Esq.,
who in Sept. 1583, purchased of the
Earl of Oxford, for the sum of
£2000, the manor and park of
Earls-Colne, containing 1800 acres
of land. Richard was born Dec. 21,
1600, married in May, 1630, Alice,
daughter of Henry Mildmay, of
Graces, Essex, who was a cousin
of our Gov. Winthrop, and died
Sept. 4, 1677. His name is mentioned in the records of the proprietors of Cambridge under the date of
1632, as one of "Mr. Hooker's or
the Braintree company," the first
settlers of that town. Whatever
rights he may have thus acquired,
he forfeited by not coming over.
Being the eldest son and heir, he
probably felt it his duty to remain
on his paternal estate, in which resolution he was doubtless confirmed
by his brother's early death in the

Mr. Roger,[1] who came over with me to New-England, and died here, Satan then began to rage, and
the commissaries, registers, and others, began to
pursue me, and to threaten me, as thinking I was a
non-conformable man, when, for the most of that
time, I was not resolved either way, but was dark in
those things. Yet the Lord, having work to do in
the place, kept me, a poor, ignorant thing, against
them all, until such time as my work was done, by
strange and wonderful means. Notwithstanding all
the malice of the ministers round about me, the Lord
had one way or other to deliver me.

The course I took in my preaching was, first, to
show the people their misery; secondly, the reme-
dy, Christ Jesus; thirdly, how they should walk
answerable to his mercy, being redeemed by Christ.
And so I found the Lord putting forth his strength
in my extreme weakness, and not forsaking of me
when I was so foolish, as I have wondered since why
the Lord hath done any good to me and by me.

Colony. See Morant's Hist. of Essex, ii. 211; Mass. Hist. Coll. vii.
10, xxviii. 314, 315.

[1] Roger Harlakenden, the second
son, was born Oct. 1, 1611, and
married Elizabeth, daughter of God-
frey Bosseville, Esq., of Gunth-
wayte, in Yorkshire, June 4, 1635,
two months before he embarked for
New-England. He came with Shepard in the Defence, in Aug. 1635,
bringing with him his wife and his
sister Mabell, born Sept. 27, 1614,
and who afterwards married John
Haynes, Governor of Connecticut,
who had large estates in Essex, and
had come over two years before.
Roger Harlakenden was chosen an
Assistant in May, 1636, and was re-
elected the two following years.
He settled with his friend and

pastor at Newtown, (Cambridge,)
where he purchased Deputy-Governor Dudley's estate. He died
Nov. 17, 1638, of the small pox,
aged 27. In his will, which is in
the Probate Records of Suffolk, i.
13, he mentions his estate in England, "Colne Park, or the Little
Lodge." Winthrop says "he was
a very godly man, and of good use
both in the commonwealth and in the
church. He was buried with military honor, because he was lieutenant colonel. He left behind a vir-
tuous gentlewoman and two daughters. He died in great peace, and
left a sweet memorial behind him of
his piety and virtue." See Winthrop, i. 278; Mass. Hist. Coll.
xxviii. 268, 315; Newell's Cambridge Church-Gath. in 1636, p. 49.

CHAP.
XXIV.

1630.

So the time of three years being expired, the people would not let me go, but gathered about £40 yearly for me ; and so I was intended to stay there, if the Lord would, and prevailed to set up the Lecture in the town of Towcester, where I was born, as knowing no greater love I could express to my poor friends than thus; and so Mr. Stone, (Dr. Wilson giving way thereto,) had the Lecture, and went to Towcester with it, where the Lord was with him. And thus I saw the Lord's mercy following me to make me a poor instrument of sending the Gospel to the place of my nativity.

So when I had preached a while at Earles-Colne, about half a year, the Lord saw me unfit and unworthy to continue me there any longer ; and so the Bishop of London, Mountain, being removed to York, and Bishop Laud,[1] (now Archbishop,) coming in his place, a fierce enemy to all righteousness, and a man fitted of God to be a scourge to his people, he pre-

Dec.
16.

sently, (having been not long in the place,) sent for me up to London ; and there, never asking me whether I would subscribe, (as I remember,) but what I had to do to preach in his diocese, chiding also Dr. Wilson for setting up this Lecture in his diocese, after many railing speeches against me, forbade me to preach; and not only so, but if I went to preach any where else, his hand would reach me. And so God put me to silence there, which did somewhat humble me ; for I did think it was for my sins the Lord set him thus against me.

[I was inhibited from preaching in the diocese of

---

[1] " Our great enemy," as Winthrop calls him, ii. 31.   See note [1] on page 426.   See Fuller's Church Hist. iii. 292, 471–477.

London by Dr. Laud, bishop of that diocese. As
soon as I came in the morning, about eight of the
clock, falling into a fit of rage, he asked me what
degree I had taken in the University. I answered
him I was a Master of Arts. He asked, Of what College ? I answered, Of Emmanuel. He asked, how
long I had lived in his diocese. I answered, Three
years and upwards. He asked, who maintained me
all this while, charging me to deal plainly with him ;
adding withal, that he had been more cheated and
equivocated with by some of my malignant faction,
than ever was man by Jesuit. At the speaking of
which words he looked as though blood would have
gushed out of his face, and did shake as if he had
been haunted with an ague fit, to my apprehen-
sion, by reason of his extreme malice and secret
venom. I desired him to excuse me. He fell then
to threaten me, and withal to bitter railing, calling
me all to naught, saying, "You prating coxcomb,
do you think all the learning is in your brain ?" He
pronounced his sentence thus, "I charge you that
you neither preach, read, marry, bury, or exercise
any ministerial function in any part of my diocese ;
for if you do, and I hear of it, I'll be upon your back,
and follow you wherever you go, in any part of the
kingdom, and so everlastingly disenable you." I
besought him not to deal so in regard of a poor town.
And here he stopped me in what I was going on to
say. "A poor town ! You have made a company of
seditious, factious bedlams. And what do you prate
to me of a poor town ?" I prayed him to suffer me
to catechize in the Sabbath days in the afternoon.
He replied, "Spare your breath. I'll have no such

fellows prate in my diocese. Get you gone ; and
now make your complaints to whom you will." So
away I went ; and blessed be God that I may go to
Him.]¹

Yet when I was thus silenced, the Lord stirred me
up friends. The house of the Harlakendens were so
many fathers and mothers to me ; and they and the
people would have me live there, though I did nothing but stay in the place. But remaining about
1631. half a year, after this silencing, among them, the
Lord let me see into the evil of the English ceremonies, cross, surplice, and kneeling. And the Bishop
of London, viz. Laud, coming down to visit, he cited
me to appear before him at the Court at Reldon ;²
where I appearing, he asked me what I did in the
place ; and I told him I studied. He asked me,
What ? I told him the Fathers. He replied, I might
thank him for that ; yet charged me to depart the
place. I asked him, Whither should I go ? To the
University, said he. I told him I had no means to
subsist there. Yet he charged me to depart the
place.

Now, about this time, I had great desire to change
my estate by marriage ; and I had been praying
three years before, that the Lord would carry me to
such a place where I might have a meet yoke-fellow.

---

¹ This passage included in brack-
ets, is inserted from Prince, page
338, who says, " I have by me a
manuscript of Mr. Shepard's, written with his own hand, in which are
these words." Prince adds, "Thus
did this bishop, a professed disciple
of the meek and lowly Jesus, treat
one of the most pious, humble, diligent and faithful young ministers in
the Church of England in this day."
See Laud's character portrayed in
Hallam's Const. Hist. i. 450, (4th
ed. London, 1842,) and Macaulay's
Essays, i. 241, (Phila. 1843.)

² So in the manuscript, and in
Jacie's Letter, *Keldon;* both undoubtedly errors for *Peldon,* which
is a parish in Essex, five miles south
by west of Colchester.

And I had a call at this time to go to Yorkshire, to
preach there in a gentleman's house. But I did not
desire to stir till the Bishop tired me out of this
place. For the Bishop having thus charged me to
depart, and being two days after to visit at Dunmow,[1] in Essex, Mr. Weld, Mr. Daniel Rogers,[2]
Mr. Ward,[3] Mr. Marshall,[4] Mr. Wharton, consulted
together whether it was best to let such a swine to
root up God's plants in Essex, and not to give him
some check. Whereupon it was agreed upon privately at Braintry,[5] that some should speak to him,
and give him a check.

So Mr. Weld and I, travelling together, had some
thoughts of going to New-England. But we did think
it best to go first unto Ireland, and preach there,
and to go by Scotland thither. But when we came
to the church, Mr. Weld stood and heard without,
being excommunicated by him. I being more free,
went within. And after sermon, Mr. Weld went up
to hear the Bishop's speech ; and being seen to follow the Bishop, the first thing he did was to examine Mr. Weld what he did to follow him, and to
stand upon holy ground. Thereupon he was committed to the pursuivant, and bound over to answer

---

[1] Dunmow (Great) is a market-town on the western bank of the Chelmer, 12 miles from Chelmsford and 38 miles from London. Population in 1841, 2792.

[2] Daniel Rogers was the son of Richard Rogers, of Weathersfield, mentioned on page 508, and brother of Ezekiel Rogers, of Rowley. See Brook's Lives of the Puritans, iii. 149.

[3] Either old Mr. John Ward, of Haverhill, or his son Samuel, of Ipswich, or Nathaniel, of Standon

Massey. See note [5] on page 112, and note [2] on page 426.

[4] Stephen Marshall was a celebra-ted Puritan minister, at Weathers-field, in Essex, and afterwards at Finchingfield, in the same county. See Brook's Lives of the Puritans, iii. 241–254 ; Neal's Puritans, iv. 169 ; Fuller's Worthies, i. 473 ; Newcourt's Repertorium, ii. 265.

[5] Braintree is a market-town in Essex, forty miles north-east of London, and eight east of Dunmow. Population in 1841, 3670.

CHAP.
XXIV.
1631.
it at the High Commission. But when Mr. Weld was pleading for himself, and that it was ignorance that made him come in, the Bishop asked him whither he intended to go, whether to New-England, and if so, whether I would go with him. While he was thus speaking, I came into the crowd, and heard the words. Others bid me go away. But neglecting to do it, a godly man pulled me away with violence out of the crowd ; and as soon as ever I was gone, the apparitor calls for Mr. Shepard, and the pursuivant was sent presently after to find me out. But he that pulled me away, Mr. Holbeech by name, a schoolmaster at Felsted, in Essex, hastened our horses, and away we rid, as fast as we could ; and so the Lord delivered me out of the hand of that lion a third time.[1]

And now I perceived I could not stay in Colne without danger ; and hereupon receiving a letter from Mr. Ezekiel Rogers,[2] then living at Rowly, in

---

[1] The preceding account is incidentally confirmed by a letter dated Jan 9, 1632, written to John Winthrop, Jr. by Henry Jacie, a celebrated Puritan divine, mentioned by Wood, in his Fasti Oxon. i. 435, (ed. Bliss.) He says, "The plague having been lately at Colchester, the Bishop's visit was *propriâ personâ* at Keldon. There he excommunicated Mr. Weld, who had been suspended about a month, and requiring Mr. Rogers, of Dedham, to subscribe there, he refused ; so he suspended him. Mr. Shepard he charged to be gone out of his diocese, as one that kept conventicles. Mr. Weld, after excommunication, coming into a church where the Bishop was visiting, the Bishop spied him, and called him, and asked him if he were on this side New-England, and if he were not excommunicated. He answered, Yes. ' And why here then ?' He hoped he had not offended. ' But he would make him an example to all such. Take him, pursuivant.' The pursuivant called Mr. Shepard, and said he would rather have Shepard ; but he escaped, and Mr. Weld, by a bond of 100 marks, (others bound with him) and so fled to Bergen." See Mass. Hist. Coll. xxi. 236–238.

[2] Ezekiel Rogers was the second son of the venerable Richard Rogers, the minister of Weathersfield, in Essex, and brother of Daniel Rogers, mentioned on page 501, who succeeded his father in the same parish. He was born in 1590, and at the early age of thirteen was sent to Cambridge, where took the degree of A. B. at Bennet College in 1604, and of A. M. at Christ's in 1608. On leaving the University

Yorkshire, to encourage me to come to the knight's CHAP.
XXIV.
house, called Sir Richard Darley, dwelling at a town
called Buttercrambe,[1] and the knight's two sons, 1631.
viz. Mr. Henry and Mr. Richard Darley, promising
me £20 a year for their part, and the knight promising me my table, and the letters sent to me crying
with that voice of the man of Macedonia, " Come
and help us," hereupon I resolved to follow the
Lord to so remote and strange a place ; the rather
because I might be far from the hearing of the malicious Bishop Laud, who had threatened me, if I
preached any where. So when I was determined to
go, the gentleman sent a man to me to be my guide
in my journey ; who coming for me, with much grief
of heart I forsook Essex and Earles-Colne, and they
me, going, as it were, now I knew not whither.

he spent five or six years as chaplain in the family of Sir Francis Barrington, by whom he was presented
to the benefice of Rowley, in Yorkshire. Here he remained twenty
years, till he was suspended, as he
says, for refusing to read the Book
of Sports. He came to New-England in 1638, with some twenty families of good estate, from Yorkshire, and though earnestly solicited
to settle at New Haven, he commenced a new plantation between
Ipswich and Newbury, to which
was given the name of Rowley,
from the former place of his residence and ministry. Johnson says,
that these Yorkshiremen " were the
first people that set upon making of
cloth in the western world ; for
which end they built a fulling-mill,
and caused their little ones to be
very diligent in spinning cotton
wool, many of them having been
clothiers in England." He preached the Election Sermon in 1643,
and also preached before the Synod
at Cambridge in 1647. Having
met with many misfortunes in losing
two wives and all his children, having his house burnt with his furniture and library, and by a fall from
his horse losing the use of his right
arm, he died Jan. 23, 1661, aged 70.
He was a cousin of the Rev. Nathaniel Rogers, of Ipswich, and he
married for his second wife the
daughter of the Rev. John Wilson,
of Boston. Winthrop speaks of him
as " a man of special note in England for his zeal, piety, and other
parts, a very wise man, a worthy
son of a worthy father." In his
will he left to Harvard College a
reversionary interest in his real estate, from which the College has
derived $5000 of its funds. See
Winthrop, i. 278, 294, 324, ii. 99,
308 ; Mather, i. 369 ; Brook's Puritans, iii. 341 ; Gage's Hist. of Rowley, pp. 55–67, 120–134 ; Mass.
Hist. Coll. xxvii. 13, xviii. 248.

[1] Buttercrambe is a township in
the parish of Bossall, in the north
riding of Yorkshire, twelve miles
north-east of York, pleasantly situated on the Derwent.

So as we travelled, (which was five or six days together, near unto winter,) the Lord sent much rain and ill weather, insomuch as the floods were up when we came near Yorkshire, and hardly passable. At last we came to a town called Ferrybridge,[1] where the waters were up and ran over the bridge, for half a mile together, and more. So we hired a guide to lead us. But when he had gone a little way, the violence of the water was such, that he first fell in, and after him another man, who was near drowning before my eyes. Whereupon my heart was so smitten with fear of the danger, and my head so dizzied with the running of the water, that had not the Lord immediately upheld me, and my horse also, and so guided it, I had certainly perished that bout. But the Lord was strong in my weakness ; and we went on, by some little direction, upon the bridge, and at last I fell in ; yet in a place where the waters were not so violent, but I sat upon my horse ; which, being a very good horse, clambered up upon the bridge again. But Mr. Darley's man, for fear of me, fell in also, but came out safe again ; and so we came to the dry land, where we had a house, and shifted ourselves, and went to prayer, and blessed God for this wonderful preservation of us. And the Lord made me then to profess that I looked now upon my life as a new life given unto me ; which I saw good reason to give up unto him and his service. And truly, about this time, the Lord, that had dealt only gently with me before, began to afflict me, and to let me taste how good it was to be under his tutoring. So I came to York late upon Saturday night ; and

[1] Ferrybridge is 20 miles south-southwest of York, on the river Aire.

having refreshed ourselves there, I came to Buttercrambe, to Sir Richard's house, that night, very
wet and late, which is about seven miles off from
York.

Now as soon as I came into the house, I found
divers of them at dice and tables ; and Mr. Richard
Darley, one of the brothers, being to return to London the Monday after, and being desirous to hear me
preach, sent me speedily to my lodging, (the best in
the house,) and so I preached the day after once ;
and then he departed the day after, having carefully
desired my comfortable abode there. But I do remember I never was so low sunk in my spirit as
about this time. For, first, I was now far from all
friends. Secondly, I was, I saw, in a profane house,
not any sincerely good. Thirdly, I was in a vile,
wicked town and country. Fourthly, I was unknown, and exposed to all wrongs. Fifthly, I was
unsufficient to do any work, and my sins were upon
me, &c. ; and hereupon I was very low, and sunk
deep. Yet the Lord did not leave me comfortless ;
for though the lady was churlish, yet Sir Richard
was ingenious, and I found in the house three servants, (viz. Thomas Fugill,[1] Mrs. Margaret Toute-
ville,[2] the knight's kinswoman, that was afterward
my wife, and Ruth Bushell, who married to Edward

[1] Thomas Fugill was one of the principal settlers of New-Haven, in 1638, one of the seven pillars of the church there, and the first secretary of the Colony, with the title of "public notary." Bacon says that "in the year 1645, he fell under censure for having made an incorrect record for his own advantage. He was very sternly dealt with, turned out of office, and excommunicated from the Church. Soon afterwards he returned, it is believed, to London." See Trumbull's Conn. i. 99, 106 ; Bacon's Historical Disc. pp. 24, 317 ; Kingsley's Hist. Disc. pp. 83; 163.

[2] She was at this time 27 years old. See Mass. Hist. Coll. xxviii. 268.

Michelson,[1]) very careful of me ; which somewhat refreshed me.

But it happened, that when I had been there a little while, there was a marriage of one Mr. Allured,[2] a most profane young gentleman, to Sir Richard's daughter ; and I was desired to preach at their marriage. At which sermon the Lord first touched the heart of Mistress Margaret with very great terrors for sin and her Christ-less estate. Whereupon others began to look about them, especially the gentlewoman lately married, Mrs. Allured ; and the Lord brake both their hearts very kindly. Then others in the family, viz. Mr. Allured, he fell to fasting and prayer and great reformation. Others also were reformed, and their hearts changed ; the whole family brought to external duties, but I remember none in the town or about it brought home. And thus the Lord was with me, and gave me favor, and friends and respect of all in the family; and the Lord taught me much of his goodness and sweetness. And when he had fitted a wife for me, he then gave me her, who was a most sweet, humble woman, full of Christ, and a very discerning Christian, a wife who was most incomparably loving to me, and every way amiable and holy, and endued with a very sweet spirit of prayer. And thus the Lord answered my desires. When my adversaries intended most hurt

---

[1] Edward Mitchenson and Ruth his wife both came over to New-England, and were members of the Church in Cambridge. Their children were Ruth, Bethia, Edward, and Elizabeth. See Newell's Cambridge Ch. Gathering in 1636, p. 56.

[2] There was a Colonel Alured, and some others of the name, from Yorkshire, who were somewhat conspicuous in the Civil Wars. See Carlyle's Cromwell, i. 57, ii. 79, 80.

to me, the Lord was then best unto me, and used me
the more kindly in every place. For the Lord turned all the sons, and Sir Richard, and Mr. Allured,
so unto me, that they not only gave her freely to be
my wife, but enlarged her portion also ; and thus I
did marry the best and fittest woman in the world
unto me, after I had preached in this place about a
twelvemonth. For which mercy to me in my exiled
condition in a strange place, I did promise the Lord
that this mercy should knit my heart the nearer to
Him, and that his love should constrain me. But I
have ill requited the Lord since that time, and forgot
myself, and my promise also.

1632.

But now when we were married, in the year 1632,
she was unwilling to stay at Buttercrambe, and I
saw no means or likelihood of abode there. For
Bishop Neale[1] coming up to York, no friends could
procure my liberty of him, without subscription.
And hereupon the Lord gave me a call to Northumberland, to a town called Heddon, five miles beyond
Newcastle.[2] Which when I had considered of, and
saw no place but that to go unto, and saw the people
very desirous of it, and that I might preach there in
peace, being far from any Bishops, I did resolve to
depart thither. And so being accompanied with Mr.
Allured to the place, I came not without many fears
of enemies, and my poor wife full of fears. It was
not a place of subsistence with any comfort to me

---

[1] "Bishop Neile and Bishop
Laud were a frightfully ceremonial
pair of Bishops ; the fountain they
of innumerable tendencies to Papis-
try and the old clothes of Babylon !" See Carlyle's Cromwell, i. 61.

[2] Newcastle is the county-town
of Northumberland, situated on the
left bank of the Tyne, ten miles
from the sea, and 273 from London.
Population in 1841, 49,860.

CHAP.
XXIV.

1632.

1633.

there.    But the good Lord, who all my life followed me, made this place the fittest for me ; and I found many sweet friends and Christian acquaintance, Mrs. Sherbourne maintaining me, and Mrs. Fenwick lending us the use of her house ; and so God comforted us in our solitary, and yet married condition, many ways.

Now when I was here, the Lord blessed my poor labors both to the saints, and to sundry others about and in Newcastle ; and I came here to read and know more of the ceremonies, church government and estate, and the unlawful standing of Bishops than in any other place.    I lived at Mrs. Fenwick's house for a time, about a twelvemonth or half a year, and then we went and dwelt alone in a town near Heddon, called [blank], in a house which we found haunted with the Devil, as we conceived.    For when we came into it, a known witch went out of it ; and being troubled with noises four or five nights together, we sought God by prayer to remove so sore a trial ; and the Lord heard and blessed us there, and removed the trouble.    But after we were settled, the Bishop put in a priest, who would not suffer me to preach publicly any more.    Hereupon the means was used to the Bishop of Durham, Bishop Morton ; and he professed he durst not give me liberty, because Laud had taken notice of me.    So I preached up and down in the country, and at last privately in Mr. Fenwick's house.    And there I stayed till Mr. Cotton, Mr. Hooker, Stone, Weld, went to New-England ; and hereupon most of the godly in England were awakened, and intended much to go to New-England.    And I having a call by divers friends in

New-England to come over, and many in Old England desiring me to go over, and promising to go
with me, I did hereupon resolve to go thither, especially considering the season. And thus the Lord
blessed me in this dark country, and gave me a son,
called Thomas, anno 1633; my poor wife being in
sore extremities four days, by reason she had an unskilful midwife. But as the affliction was very bitter,
so the Lord did teach me much by it, and I had need
of it; for I began to grow secretly proud, and full of
sensuality, delighting my soul in my dear wife more
than in my God, whom I had promised better unto;
and my spirit grew fierce in some things, and secretly
mindless of the souls of the people. But the Lord,
by this affliction of my wife, learnt me to desire to
fear him more, and to keep his dread in my heart.
And so, seeing I had been tossed from the south to
the north of England, and now could go no farther,
I then began to listen to a call to New-England.

The reasons which swayed me to come to New-
England were many. 1. I saw no call to any other
place in Old England, nor way of subsistence in
peace and comfort to me and my family. 2. Divers
people in Old England of my dear friends, desired
me to go to New-England, there to live together;
and some went before, and writ to me of providing a
place for a company of us; one of which was John
Bridge;[1] and I saw divers families of my Christian
friends who were resolved thither to go with me.
3. I saw the Lord departing from England when Mr.

---

[1] John Bridge was at Cambridge in 1632, admitted a freeman March 4, 1635, a representative in 1637, and a deacon of the church. He had a son Matthew. See Winthrop, ii. 347, 365; Farmer's Genealogical Register; Newell's Church-Gathering at Cambridge, p. 53.

CHAP.
XXIV.
~~~~
1633.

Hooker and Mr. Cotton were gone, and I saw the hearts of most of the godly set and bent that way; and I did think I should feel many miseries if I stayed behind.  4. My judgment was then convinced not only of the evil of ceremonies, but of mixed communion, and joining with such in sacraments ; though I ever judged it lawful to join with them in preaching. 5. I saw it my duty to desire the fruition of all God's ordinances, which I could not enjoy in Old England. 6. My dear wife did much long to see me settled there in peace, and so put me on to it.  7. Although it was true I should stay and suffer for Christ, yet I saw no rule for it now the Lord had opened a door of escape.   Otherwise, I did incline much to stay and suffer, especially after our sea-storms.  8. Though my ends were mixed, and I looked much to my own quiet, yet the Lord let me see the glory of those liberties in New-England, and made me purpose, if ever I should come over, to live among God's people, as one come out from the dead, to his praise. Though since I have seen, as the Lord's goodness, so my own exceeding weakness to be as good as I thought to have been.

And although they did desire me to stay in the north, and preach privately, yet, 1. I saw that this time could not be long without trouble from King Charles.  2. I saw no reason to spend my time privately, when I might possibly exercise my talent publicly in New-England.  3. I did hope my going over might make them to follow me.  4. I considered how sad a thing it would be for me to leave my wife and child (if I should die) in that rude place of the north, where was nothing but barbarous wickedness generally, and how sweet it would be to leave CHAP.<br>XXIV. them among God's people, though poor. 5. My lib- erty in private was daily threatened ; and I thought 1634. it wisdom to depart before the pursuivants came out, for so I might depart with more peace and lesser trouble and danger to me and my friends. And I knew not whether God would have me to hazard my person, and comfort of me and all mine, for a disorderly manner of preaching privately (as it was reputed,) in those parts.

So after I had preached my farewell sermon at Newcastle, I departed from the north in a ship laden with coals for Ipswich, about the beginning of June, June. after I had been about a year in the north, the Lord having blessed some few sermons and notes to divers in Newcastle, from whom I parted, filled with their love. And so the Lord gave us a speedy voyage from thence to Ipswich,[1] in Old England, whither I came in a disguised manner,[2] with my wife and child and maid; and stayed a while at Mr. Russell's[3] house, another while at Mr. Collins[4] his house, and then went down to Essex, to the town where I had preached, viz. Earles-Colne, to Mr. Richard Harlakenden's house, where I lived privately, but with much love from them all, as also from Mr. Joseph Cooke,[5] and also with friends at London and North-

---

[1] Ipswich, an inland port, and the capital of Suffolk, is situated on the north-eastern banks of the united rivers Gipping and Orwell, 69 miles north-east of London. Population in 1841, 24,940.

[2] See note [5] on page 260.

[3] Perhaps John Russell, who was admitted a freeman at the same time with Shepard and Harlakenden, and was a prominent citizen of Cambridge. See Newell's Cambridge Church-Gathering, pp. 47, 50.

[4] Perhaps Edward Collins, who was admitted a freeman May 13, 1640, and was deacon of the church at Cambridge. See Mather's Magnalia, ii. 116 ; Newell's Cam. Ch. Gath. p. 53 ; Winthrop, ii. 370 ; Farmer's Genealogical Register.

[5] Joseph Cooke came to New-England in 1635 in the same ship

CHAP.
XXIV. amptonshire. And truly I found this time of my life,

1634. wherein I was so tossed up and down, and had no place of settling, but kept secret in regard of the Bishops, the most uncomfortable and fruitless time, to my own soul especially, that ever I had in my life. And therefore I did long to be in New-England, as soon as might be ; and the rather because my wife, having weaned her first son, Thomas, had conceived again, and was breeding ; and I knew no place in England where she could lie in, without discovery of myself, danger to myself and all my friends that should receive me, and where we could not but give offence to many, if I should have my child not baptized. And, therefore, there being divers godly Christians resolved to go toward the latter end of the year, if I would go, I did therefore resolve to go that year, the end of that summer I came from the north. And the time appointed for the ship to go out was about a month or fortnight

Sept. before Michaelmas, (as they there call it.) The ship
29. was called the Hope, of Ipswich. The master of it, a very able seaman, was Mr. Gurling, who professed much love to me, who had got this ship, of 400 tons, from the Danes, and, as some report, it was by some fraud. But he denied it ; and being a man very loving and full of fair promises of going at the time

with Shepard, being at that time 27 years old, and settled with his pastor at Newtown. He and his brother George, and Samuel Shepard, are registered, in the list of passengers, under the disguised character of servants to Roger Harlakenden. He was admitted a freeman of the Colony March 3, 1636, with others of the same company. He was a person of note in Cambridge, and represented that town in the General Court for five years, from 1636 to 1640. His wife's name was Elizabeth, and his children were Joseph, Elizabeth, Mary, Grace, and Ruth. See Newell's Cam. Church Gath. pp. 47, 49, 52 ; Mass. Hist. Coll. xxviii. 268 ; Farmer's Geneal. Register.

appointed, and an able seaman, hence we resolved to adventure that time, though dangerous in regard of the approaching winter.[1]

Now here the Lord's wonderful terror and mercy to us did appear. For being come to Ipswich with my family, at the time appointed, the ship was not ready, and we stayed six or eight weeks longer than the time promised for her going ; and so it was very late in the year, and very dangerous to go to sea.[2] And, indeed, if we had gone, doubtless we had all perished upon the seas, it being so extreme cold and tempestuous winter. But yet we could not go back, when we had gone so far ; and the Lord saw it good to chastise us for rushing onward too soon, and hazarding ourselves in that manner ; and I had many fears, and much darkness, I remember, overspread my soul, doubting of our way. Yet, I say, we could not now go back. Only I learnt from that time never to go about a sad business in the dark, unless God's call within as well as that without be very strong, and clear, and comfortable.

So that in the year 1634, about the beginning of the winter, we set sail from Harwich.[3] And having gone some few leagues on to the sea, the wind stopped us that night, and so we cast anchor in a dangerous place, and on the morning the wind grew fierce,

[1] " Now one cause of our going at this time of winter was, because we were persecuted in Old England for the truth of Christ, which we profess here. We durst not stay to make ourselves known, which would have been at the baptizing of the child. Hence we hastened for New-England." Shepard's Preface to this Memoir.

[2] Edward Johnson says, that whilst they were waiting for the ship to sail, plots were laid to entrap and apprehend Shepard and Norton. See the account at length in his Hist. of New-England, ch. 29. [3] Harwich is a seaport in Essex, at the mouth of the Stour, having a spacious and safe harbour. Population in 1841, 3289.

and rough against us full, and drave us toward the
sands. But the vessel being laden too heavy at the
head, would not stir for all that which the seamen
could do, but drave us full upon the sands near Harwich harbour; and the ship did grate upon the sands,
and was in great danger. But the Lord directed one
man to cut some cable or rope in the ship, and so
she was turned about, and was beaten quite backward toward Yarmouth,[1] quite out of our way.

But while the ship was in this great danger, a
wonderful miraculous providence did appear to us.
For one of the seamen, that he might save the vessel, fell in when it was in that danger, and so was
carried out a mile or more from the ship, and given
for dead and gone. The ship was then in such danger, that none could attend to follow him; and when
it was out of the danger, it was a very great hazard
to the lives of any that should take the skiff to seek
to find him. Yet it pleased the Lord, that being
discerned afar off floating upon the waters, three of
the seamen adventured out upon the rough waters,
and at last, about an hour after he fell into the sea,
(as we conjectured,) they came and found him float-
ing upon the waters, never able to swim, but supported by a divine hand all this while. When the
men came to him, they were glad to find him, but
concluded he was dead, and so got him into the skiff,
and when he was there, tumbled him down as one
dead. Yet one of them said to the rest, "Let us
use what means we can, if there be life, to preserve
it;" and thereupon turned his head downward for

---

[1] Yarmouth (Great) is a seaport
in the county of Norfolk, at the
mouth of the Yare. Population in
1841, 24,086.

the water to run out. And having done so, the fellow began to gasp and breathe. Then they applied
other means they had ; and so he began at last to
move, and then to speak, and by that time he came
to the ship, he was pretty well, and able to walk.
And so the Lord showed us his great power. Whereupon a godly man in the ship then said, "This man's
danger and deliverance is a type of ours ; for he did
fear dangers were near unto us, and that yet the
Lord's power should be shown in saving of us."

For so, indeed, it was. For the wind did drive
us quite backward out of our way, and gave us no
place to anchor at until we came unto Yarmouth
roads — an open place at sea, yet fit for anchorage, but otherwise a very dangerous place. And so
we came thither through many uncomfortable hazards, within thirty hours, and cast anchor in Yarmouth roads. Which when we had done, upon a
Saturday morning, the Lord sent a most dreadful and
terrible storm of wind from the west, so dreadful that
to this day the seamen call it *Windy Saturday;* that
it also scattered many ships on divers coasts at that
time, and divers ships were cast away. One among
the rest, which was the seaman's ship who came
with us from Newcastle, was cast away, and he and
all his men perished. But when the wind thus
arose, the master cast all his anchors ; but the storm
was so terrible, that the anchors broke, and the ship
drave toward the sands, where we could not but be
cast away. Whereupon the master cries out that we
were dead men, and thereupon the whole company
go to prayer. But the vessel still drave so near to
the sands, that the master shot off two pieces of ord-

nance to the town, for help to save the passengers.
The town perceived it, and thousands came upon
the walls of Yarmouth, and looked upon us, hearing
we were New-England men, and pitied much, and
gave us for gone, because they saw other ships perishing near unto us at that time ; but could not send
any help unto us, though much money was offered
by some to hazard themselves for us.

So the master not knowing what to do, it pleased
the Lord that there was one Mr. Cock, a drunken
fellow, but no seaman, yet one that had been at sea
often, and would come in a humor unto New-England with us ; whether it was to see the country, or
no, I cannot tell. But sure I am, God intended it
for good unto us, to make him an instrument to save
all our lives ; for he persuaded the master to cut
down his mainmast. The master was unwilling to it,
and besotted, not sensible of ours and his own loss.[1]
At last this Cock calls for hatchets, tells the master,
" If you be a man, save the lives of your passengers,
cut down your mainmast." Hereupon he encouraged all the company, who were forlorn and hopeless
of life ; and the seamen presently cut down the mast
aboard, just at that very time wherein we all gave
ourselves for gone, to see neither Old nor New England, nor faces of friends any more, there being near
upon two hundred passengers in the ship. And so
when the mast was down, the master had one little
anchor left, and cast it out. But the ship was driven

---

[1] Edward Johnson, in his Hist. of New-England, chap. 29, says that " the master and other seamen made a strange construction of the sore storm they met withal, saying the ship was bewitched, and therefore made use of the common charm ig-norant people use, nailing two red-hot horse-shoes to their mainmast." See Mass. Hist. Coll. xiii. 141.

away toward the sands still ; and the seamen came CHAP·<br>XXIV.
to us, and bid us look, pointing to the place, where
our graves should shortly be, conceiving also that 1634.
the wind had broke off this anchor also. So the Oct.<br>18.
master professed he had done what he could, and
therefore now desired us to go to prayer. So Mr.
Norton[1] in one place, and myself in another part of
the ship, he with the passengers, and myself with the
mariners above decks, went to prayer, and committed
our souls and bodies unto the Lord that gave them.
Immediately after prayer, the wind began to abate,
and the ship stayed. For the last anchor was not
broke, as we conceived, but only rent up with the
wind, and so drave, and was drawn along, plough-

---

[1] John Norton was born at Starford, in Hertfordshire, May 6, 1606,
and was educated at Peter House,
Cambridge, where he took the degree of A. B. in 1623, and of A.
M. in 1627. He was for a time curate of the church at Starford, and
afterwards chaplain to Sir William
Masham, at High Lever, in Essex.
But, like the other non-conformists
of that day, he was so harassed by
the bishops and the pursuivants, that
he resolved to emigrate to America.
After escaping, with his wife, from
the storm mentioned in the text, he
returned to his friends in Essex, and
the next year embarked again, in
the same ship with Edward Winslow, and arrived at Plymouth in
October, 1635. Here he preached
through the winter, and the church
were very desirous of retaining him.
But he preferred to settle in the
Massachusetts Colony, and in 1636
was ordained the second minister of
Ipswich. On the death of John
Cotton he was chosen to succeed
him as teacher of the church in Boston, and was installed colleague
with Wilson July 23, 1656. In
Feb. 1662, he was sent to England,
with Simon Bradstreet, as an agent
for the Colony, returned in September, and died very suddenly on Sunday, April 5, 1663, in his 57th year.
He was an accomplished scholar
and theologian, as his writings
show. He wrote a Life of his predecessor, John Cotton ; a treatise
against the doctrines of the Quakers,
entitled The Heart of New-England
Rent ; an Answer to the heretical
book of Pynchon, mentioned on page
283, and several other works, both
in English and Latin. In reference
to one of the latter, Fuller, the
English Church historian says, "Of
all the authors I have perused concerning the opinions of these dis-
senting brethren, (the Congregationalists,) none to me was more in-
formative than Mr. John Norton,
one of no less learning than modes-
ty, minister in New-England, in his
Answer to Apollonius, pastor in the
church of Middleburgh." He left
a widow, Mary, but no children.
See Winthrop, i. 175 ; Mather, i.
261–275 ; Morton's Memorial, page
298 ; Hutchinson's Mass. i. 219–
223 ; Emerson's Hist. of the First
Church in Boston, pp. 88–98 ; Felt's
Ipswich, p. 221 ; Mass. Hist. Coll.
xxviii. 248 ; Fuller, iii. 467.

ing the sands with the violence of the wind ; which abating after prayer, though still very terrible, the ship was stopped just when it was ready to be swallowed up of the sands, a very little way off from it. And so we rid it out ; yet not without fear of our lives, though the anchor stopped the ship ; because the cable was let out so far, that a little rope held the cable, and the cable the little anchor, and the little anchor the great ship, in this great storm. But when one of the company perceived that we were so strangely preserved, had these words, " That thread we hang by will save us ;" for so we accounted of the rope fastened to the anchor in comparison of the fierce storm. And so indeed it did, the Lord showing his dreadful power towards us, and yet his unspeakable rich mercy to us, who, in depths of mercy, heard, nay helped us, when we could not cry through the disconsolate fears we had, out of these depths of seas, and miseries.

This deliverance was so great, that I then did think, if ever the Lord did bring me to shore again, I should live like one come and risen from the dead. This is one of those living mercies the Lord hath shown me, a mercy to myself, to my wife and child then living, and to my second son, Thomas, who was in this storm, but in the womb of his dear mother, who might then have perished, and been cut off from all hope of means and mercy ; and unto my dear friends then with me, viz. brother Champney,[1]

[1] Richard Champney came to New-England, and was at Cambridge in 1635, was admitted a freeman May 25, 1636, and was a ruling-elder of the church in Cambridge in February, 1637. He died Nov. 26, 1669. His wife's name was Jane, and his children were Esther, Samuel, Lydia, and Daniel, See Newell's Cambridge Church-Gathering, pp. 48, 50, 52 ; Farmer's Genealogical Register.

Frost,[1] Goff,[2] and divers others, most dear saints; CHAP.<br>XXIV. and also to all with me. And how would the name of the Lord [have] suffered, if we had so perished. 1634. That the Lord Jesus should have respect to me, so Oct.<br>18. vile, and one at that time full of many temptations and weaknesses, amazed [me] much, and deeply afraid of God's terror, yet supported. I desire this mercy may be remembered of my children, and their children's children, when I am dead, and cannot praise the Lord in the land of the living any more.

And so we continued that night, many sick, many weak and discouraged, many sad hearts. Yet upon the Sabbath morning we departed and went out of 19. the ship; I fear a little too soon, for we should have spent that day in praising of Him. Yet we were afraid of neglecting a season of providence in going out while we had a calm; and many sick folk were unfit for that work, and had need of refreshing at shore. So, upon the Sabbath-day morning, boats came to our vessel from the town; and so my dear wife and child went in the first boat. But here the Lord saw that these waters were not sufficient to wash away my filth and sinfulness, and therefore he cast me into the fire, as soon as ever I was upon the sea, in the boat; for there my first-born child, very precious to my soul, and dearly beloved of me, was

---

[1] Edmund Frost was admitted a freeman with Shepard's company March 3, 1636, and was a ruling-elder of the church in Cambridge. He died in 1672. His wife's name was Thomasine, and his children were John, Samuel, Joseph, James, Mary, Ephraim, Thomas, and Sarah. See Newell, pp. 47, 48, 50, 52.

[2] Edward Goffe was made a free-man May 25, 1626, was a represent-ative in 1646 and 1650, and died Dec. 26, 1658. His children by his first wife, Joyce, were Samuel and Lydia, and by his second wife, Margaret, were Deborah, Hannah, and Abiah. See Newell, pp. 48, 49, 50, 54; Farmer's Gen. Reg.

smitten with sickness. The Lord sent a vomiting upon it, whereby it grew faint ; and nothing that we could use could stop its vomiting, although we had many helps at Yarmouth. And this was a very bitter affliction to me ; and the Lord now showed me my weak faith, want of fear, pride, carnal content, immoderate love of creatures, and of my child especially, and begat in me some desires and purposes to fear his name. But yet the Lord would not be entreated for the life of it, and after a fortnight's sickness, at last it gave up the ghost, when its mother had given it up to the Lord, and was buried at Yarmouth ; where I durst not be present, lest the pursuivants should apprehend me and I should be discovered ;[1] which was a great affliction, and very bitter to me and my dear wife. And hereby I saw the Lord did come near to me, and I did verily fear the Lord would take away my wife also, if not myself, not long after.

And these afflictions, together with the Lord's crossing us and being so directly against our voyage, made me secretly willing to stay and suffer in England ; and my heart was not so much toward New-England. Yet this satisfied me, that seeing there was a door opened of escape, why should I suffer, and I considered how unfit I was to go to such a good land, with such an unmortified, hard, dark, formal, hypocritical heart ; and therefore no wonder if

---

[1] Scottow, in his " Narrative of the Planting of the Massachusetts Colony," after describing the above storm, says, page 15, " The next day they all landed safe ; and as soon as ashore, two vipers designed not only to leap upon the hands of them both, (Shepard and Norton,) but to seize their persons. But how strangely preserved, is not unknown to *some of us ;* though the house was beset by them, whenas they were at a pious meeting, then called a conventicle."

the Lord did thus cross me. And the Lord made me fear my affliction came in part for running too far in a way of separation from the mixed assemblies in England ; though I bless God I have ever believed that there are true churches in many parishes in England, where the Lord sets up able men and ministers of his Gospel, and I have abhorred to refuse to hear any able minister in England.

So that now, I having buried my first-born, and being in great sadness, and not knowing where to go nor what to do, the Lord sent Mr. Roger Harlakenden and my brother, Samuel Shepard,[1] to visit me after they had heard of our escape at sea ; who much refreshed us, and clave to me in my sorrows. And being casting about where to go and live, Mr. Bridge, then minister in Norwich, sent for me to come and live with him ; and being come, one Mrs. Corbet, who lived five miles off Norwich, an aged, eminent, godly gentlewoman, hearing of my coming, and that by being with Mr. Bridge might hazard his liberty by countenancing of me, she did therefore freely offer to me a great house of hers, standing empty, at a town called Bastwick ;[2] and there the Lord stirred up her heart to show all love to me, which did much lighten and sweeten my sorrows. And I saw the Lord Jesus' care herein to me, and saw cause of trusting him in times of straits, who set me in such a

---

[1] Samuel Shepard came over with his brother, being at that time 22 years old, and settled at Cambridge. In 1639 he was one of the superintendents for erecting the first college-building at Cambridge. He returned to England after 1645, and in 1658 was a major, and living in Ireland. His wife's name was Hannah, and his daughter Jane remained here. See Newell, pp. 47, 50, 54 ; Farmer's Genealog. Reg. ; Mass. Hist. Coll. xxviii. 268.

[2] Bastwick, a hamlet in the parish of Repps, in the county of Norfolk.

CHAP.
XXIV.
~~~
1634.

place ; where I lived for half a year, all the winter long, among and with my friends, (Mr. Harlakenden dwelling with me, and bearing all the charge of housekeeping,) and far from the notice of my enemies ; where we enjoyed sweet fellowship one with another, and also with God, in a house which was fit to entertain any prince for fairness, greatness and pleasantness.

1635.

Here the Lord hid us all the winter long ; and when it was fit to travel in the spring, we went up to London, Mr. Harlakenden not forsaking me all this while ; for he was a father and mother to me. And when we came to London, to Mrs. Sherborne, not knowing what to do nor where to live privately, the Lord provided a very private place for us ; where my wife was brought to bed and delivered of my second son, Thomas, and none but our friends did know of it. And so, by this means, my son was not baptized until we came to New-England, the winter

April
5.

following, being born in London, April 5, 1635. One remarkable deliverance my wife had when we were coming up to London. Mr. Burrowes, the minister, kindly entertained us about a fortnight in the way ; and when my wife was there, being great with child, she fell down from the top of a pair of stairs to the bottom. Yet the Lord kept her, and the child also, safe from that deadly danger.

When we had been also at London for a time, and began to be known in the place, my wife was brought to bed. The Lord put it into our hearts to remove to another place in Mr. Eldred's[1] house, in London,

---

[1] Alured, called also Alred or Aldred. See page 526, and Carlyle's Cromwell, i. 57.

which stood empty; and the very night we were all
come away, then came the pursuivants and others to
search after us.  But the Lord delivered us out of
their hands.  And so, when the Lord had recovered
my wife, we began to prepare for a removal once
again to New-England.  And the Lord seemed to
make our way plain.  1. Because I had no other
call to any place in England.  2. Many more of
God's people resolved to go with me, as Mr. Roger
Harlakenden and Mr. Champney, &c.  3. The Lord
saw our unfitness and the unfitness of our going the
year before.  And therefore giving us good friends
to accompany us, and good company in the ship, we
set forward about the 10th of August, 1635, with
myself, wife, and my little son Thomas, and other
precious friends, having tasted much of God's mercy
in England, and lamenting the loss of our native
country, when we took our last view of it.[1]

In our voyage upon the sea, the Lord was very
tender of me, and kept me from the violence of sea-
sickness.  In our coming we were refreshed with
the society of Mr. Wilson,[2] [and] Mr. Jones,[3] by their
faith, and prayers, and preaching.  The ship[4] we
came in was very rotten, and unfit for such a voyage;

---

[1] He embarked in disguise, under the assumed name of his brother "John Shepard, husbandman." — See Mass. Hist. Coll. xxviii. 268, 276.

[2] Rev. John Wilson, of Boston. See note [3] on page 325.

[3] Rev. John Jones, who was colleague with Peter Bulkley at Concord about eight years, having been ordained pastor April 6, 1637, and then removed with part of his church to Fairfield, in Connecticut, where he died about 1664, being over 70 years of age.  His son John graduated at Harvard College in 1643, and a daughter married Thomas, son of Rev. Peter Bulkley, went with her father to Fairfield, and died about 1652.  See Winthrop, i. 169, 189, 217; Shattuck's History of Concord, pp. 153, 160 ; Trumbull's Conn. i. 280.

[4] Her name was the Defence, of London, Capt. Thomas Bostock.— See Mass. Hist. Coll. xxviii. 268.

and therefore the first storm we had, we had a very
great leak, which did much appall and affect us. Yet
the Lord discovered it unto us when we were thinking of returning back again, and much comforted our
hearts. We had many storms; in one of which my
dear wife took such a cold, and got such weakness,
as that she fell into a consumption, of which she
afterward died. And also the Lord preserved her,
with the child in her arms, from imminent and apparent death. For by the shaking of the ship in a
violent storm, her head was pitched against an iron
bolt, and the Lord miraculously preserved the child
and recovered my wife. This was a great affliction
to me, and was a cause of many sad thoughts in the
ship, how to behave myself when I came to New-
England. My resolutions I have written down in my
little book.

And so the Lord, after many sad storms and wea-
risome days, and many longings to see the shore,
the Lord brought us to the sight of it upon October
Oct.
3.
2, anno 1635; and upon October the 3d, we arrived, with my wife, child, brother Samuel,[1] Mr. Harlakenden, Mr. Cookes,[2] &c. at Boston, with rejoicing
in our God after a longsome voyage;[3] my dear wife's
great desire being now fulfilled, which was to leave
me in safety from the hand of my enemies, and

---

[1] His younger brother, mentioned
on page 500, who was at this time
22 years of age, and who, as well
as the Cookes, came in the assumed
character of servants to Roger Harlakenden. See Mass. Hist. Coll.
xxviii. 268, 273.

[2] Joseph Cooke, mentioned in note
[5] on page 531, had a brother George,
who accompanied him, and who settled in Cambridge. He was a cap-

tain, and commanded the troops sent
to arrest Gorton and his company in
1643, was speaker of the House of
Deputies in 1645, and was afterwards a colonel under Cromwell, in
Ireland. See Newell's Cam. Ch.
Gath. pp. 47, 50; Winthrop, ii.
53, 137, 142; Mass. Hist. Coll.
xvii. 55, xxviii. 268.

[3] Their passage was fifty-four
days, from Aug. 10.

among God's people, and also the child under God's CHAP. XXIV. precious ordinances.[1]

Now when we came upon shore, we were kindly 1635. Oct. saluted and entertained by many friends, and were the first three days in the house of Mr. Cottington,[2] being Treasurer at that time, and that with much love.

When we had been here two days, upon the Monday, October 5, we came, (being sent for by friends 5. at Newtown,) to them, to my brother Mr. Stone's house. And that congregation being upon their removal to Hartford, at Connecticut, myself and those that came with me, found many houses empty, and many persons willing to sell ; and hence our company bought off their houses to dwell in, until we should see another place fit to remove unto. But having been here some time, divers of our brethren did desire to sit still, and not to remove farther ; partly, because of the fellowship of the churches ; partly, because they thought their lives were short, and removals to new plantations full of troubles ; partly, because they found sufficient for themselves and their company. Hereupon there was a purpose to enter into church fellowship, which we did the 1636. year after, about the end of the winter ;[3] a fortnight Feb. 1. after which my dear wife Margaret died, being first 15. received into church fellowship ; which as she much

---

[1] The child was baptized February 7, 1636.

[2] William Coddington. See note [1] on page 337.

[3] It was on February 1st, 1636, old style, according to Winthrop, corresponding to Feb. 11th of new style. See a graphic and beautiful description of this transaction in "A Discourse on the Cambridge Church-Gathering in 1636, delivered in the First Church of Cambridge, Feb. 22, 1846, by William Newell, Pastor of the Church." The next year, 1637, Shepard preached the Election Sermon and offered the prayer at the opening of the Synod at Cambridge. See Winthrop, i. 179, 221, 237.

longed for, so the Lord did so sweeten it unto her, that she was hereby exceedingly cheered, and comforted with the sense of God's love, which continued until her last gasp.

No sooner were we thus set down and entered into church fellowship, but the Lord exercised us and the whole country with the opinions of Fami- lists ; begun by Mrs. Hutchinson,[1] raised up to a
great height by Mr. Vane, too suddenly chosen Governor, and maintained too obscurely by Mr. Cotton, and propagated too boldly by the members of Boston, and some in other churches. By means of which division by these opinions, the ancient and received truth came to be darkened, God's name to be blasphemed, the churches' glory diminished, many godly grieved, many wretches hardened, de- ceiving and being deceived, growing worse and worse. The principal opinion and seed of all the rest was this, viz. that a Christian should not take any evidence of God's special grace and love toward him by the sight of any graces, or conditional evan- gelical promises to faith or sanctification, in way of ratiocination, (for this was evidence, and so a way of works,) but it must be without the sight of any grace, faith, holiness, or special change in himself, by immediate revelation in an absolute promise. And because that the whole Scriptures do give such clear, plain, and notable evidences of favor to per- sons called and sanctified, hence they said that a second evidence might be taken from thence, but

---

[1] See note [1] on page 360.

no first evidence. But from hence it arose, that as all error is fruitful, so this opinion did gender above a hundred monstrous opinions in the country. Which the elders perceiving, having used all private brotherly means with Mr. Cotton first, and yet no healing, hereupon, they publicly preached both against opinions publicly and privately maintained. And I account it no small mercy to myself, that the Lord kept me from that contagion, and gave me any heart or light to see through those devices of men's heads; although I found it a most uncomfortable time to live in contention; and the Lord was graciously pleased, by giving witness against them, to keep this poor church spotless and clear from them.

CHAP. XXIV.

1636.

This division in the Church began to trouble the Commonwealth. Mr. Wheelwright, a man of a bold and stiff conceit of his own worth and light, preached (as the Court judged,) a seditious sermon,[1] stirring up all sorts against those that preached a covenant of works; meaning all the elders in the country that preached justification by faith, and assurance of it by sight of faith, and sanctification, being enabled thereto by the spirit. The troubles thus increasing, and all means used for crushing and curing these sores, a Synod was thought of and called, from the example Acts xv.; wherein, by the help of all the elders joined together, those errors,

1637.
Jan.
20.

---

[1] This sermon, the text of which was from Matth. ix. 15, has never been printed; but the larger part of the original manuscript, being the last thirty-three pages, is preserved in the archives of the Massachusetts Historical Society. A comparatively modern hand has written on a blank page, that " it was left in the hands of Mr. John Coggeshall, who was a deacon of the church in Boston." A perfect copy of this sermon is contained in the first volume of the Hutchinson manuscripts, belonging to the same Society. See Winthrop, i. 215.

CHAP.
XXIV. through the grace and power of Christ, were discovered, the defenders of them convinced and ashamed,
1637. the truth stablished, and the consciences of the
saints settled; there being a most wonderful presence of Christ's spirit in that Assembly, held at
Aug. Cambridge anno 1637, about August, and continued
30.
a month together, in public agitations.[1] For the
issue of this Synod was this:

1. The Pekoat Indians were fully discomfited.
For as the opinions arose, wars did arise; and when
these began to be crushed by the ministry of the
elders, and by opposing Mr. Vane, and casting him
and others from being magistrates, the enemies began to be crushed, and were perfectly subdued by
the end of the Synod.

Nov.   2. The magistrates took courage, and exiled Mr.
Wheelwright, Mrs. Hutchinson, and divers Islanders,
whom the Lord did strangely discover, giving most
of them over to all manner of filthy opinions, until
many that held with them before, were ashamed of
them. And so the Lord, within one year, wrought
a great change among us.

At this time I cannot omit the goodness of God
as to myself, so to all the country, in delivering us
from the Pekoat furies. These Indians were the
stoutest, proudest, and most successful in their wars
of all the Indians. Their chief sachem was Sasakus,
a proud, cruel, unhappy, and headstrong prince;
who, not willing to be guided by the persuasions
of his fellow, an aged sachem, Monanattuck, nor
fearing the revenge of the English, having first

---

[1] See Sparks's American Bio-   i. 237–241; Hutchinson's Mass. i.
graphy, xvi. 249–260; Winthrop,   67–69.

sucked the blood of Captain Stone and Mr. Oldham,[1] CHAP. XXIV.
found it so sweet, and his proceedings for one whole
winter so successful, that having besieged and killed 1637.
March.
about four men that kept Seabrook fort, he adventured to fall upon the English up the river at
Wethersfield, where he slew nine or ten men, April
23.
women, and children at unawares, and took two
maids prisoners, carrying them away captive to the
Pekoat country.   Hereupon, those upon the river
first gathered about seventy men, and sent them
into [the] Pekoat country, to make that the seat
of war, and to revenge the death of those innocents,
whom they barbarously and most unnaturally slew.
These men marched two days and nights from the May
24.
way of the Naraganset unto Pekoat, being guided
by those Indians, then the ancient enemies of the
Pekoats.   They intended to assault Sasakus's fort;
but falling short of it the second night, the providence of God guided them to another, nearer, full of
stout men, and their best soldiers, being, as it were,
cooped up there, to the number of three or four
hundred in all, for the divine slaughter by the hand
of the English.   These, therefore, being all night 25.
making merry, and singing the death of the English
the next day, toward break of the day, being very 26.
heavy with sleep, the English drew near within the
sight of the fort, very weary with travel and want
of sleep ; at which time five hundred Naragansets
fled for fear, and only two of the company stood
to it to conduct them to the fort, and the door and
entrance thereof.   The English being come to it,

_____

[1] See pages 363 and 364.

CHAP.  awakened the fort with a peal of muskets, directed
XXIV.
—⁓—   into the midst of their wigwams; and after this,
1637.  some undertaking to compass the fort without, some
May
26.    adventured into the fort, upon the very faces of the
enemy, standing ready with their arrows ready bent
to shoot whoever should adventure.  But the English, casting by their pieces, took their swords in
their hands, (the Lord doubling their strength and
courage,) and fell upon the Indians; when a hot
fight continued about the space of an hour.  At
last, by the direction of one Captain Mason, their
wigwams were set on fire; which being dry, and
contiguous one to another, was most dreadful to the
Indians; some burning, some bleeding to death by
the sword, some resisting till they were cut off;
some flying were beat down by the men without;
until the Lord had utterly consumed the whole
company, except four or five girls they took prisoners, and dealt with them at Seabrooke as they dealt
with ours at Wethersfield.  And 't is verily thought,
scarce one man escaped, unless one or two to carry
forth tidings of the lamentable end of their fellows.
And of the English not one man was killed, but one
by the musket of an Englishman, as was conceived.
Some were wounded much; but all recovered, and
restored again.[1]

Thus the Lord having delivered the country from
war with Indians and Familists, (who arose and fell
1636.  together,) he was pleased to direct the hearts of the
Sept.
8.     magistrates, (then keeping Court ordinarily in our
town, because of these stirs at Boston,) to think of

---

[1] See page 364, and note [2] on page 306.

erecting a School or College, and that speedily, to CHAP. XXIV. be a nursery of knowledge in these deserts, and supply for posterity.[1]  And because this town, 1636. then called Newtown, was, through God's great care and goodness, kept spotless from the contagion of the opinions, therefore, at the desire of some of our town, the Deputies of the Court, having got Mr. Eaton[2] to attend the School, the Court, for that and sundry other reasons, determined to erect the College here.[3]  Which was no sooner done, but the 1637.

---

[1] " After God had carried us safe to New-England, and we had builded our houses, provided necessaries for our livelihood, reared convenient places for God's worship, and settled the civil government, one of the next things we longed for and looked after, was to advance learning, and perpetuate it to posterity; dreading to leave an illiterate ministry to the churches, when our present ministers shall lie in the dust. And as we were thinking and consulting how to effect this great work, it pleased God to stir up the heart of one Mr. Harvard, a godly gentleman and a lover of learning, there living amongst us, to give the one half of his estate, it being in all about £1700, towards the erecting of a College, and all his library. After him another gave £300 ; others after them cast in more ; and the public hand of the State added the rest." New-England's First Fruits, p. 12, (London, 1643.)

[2] Nathaniel Eaton, brother of Theophilus Eaton, of New Haven, was admitted a freeman June 9, 1638. He had been educated under Dr. Ames in Holland, and was known to Mr. Hooker whilst there, who says " he did not approve of his spirit, and feared the issue of his being received here." He was intrusted not only with the education of the students, but with the

management of the funds. For his cruel treatment of his usher, Briscoe, he was dismissed from office, sentenced by the Court to pay a fine of twenty marks, and to pay Briscoe £20. After this sentence, the church at Cambridge excommunicated him. He went first to Piscataqua, afterwards to Virginia, and then to England, where he lived privately till the Restoration, then conformed, and was settled at Bideford, where he persecuted the Nonconformists, and at last died in prison, where he had been put for debt." See Winthrop, i. 308 ; Mather, ii. 8 ; Hutchinson's Mass. i. 91.

[3] Edward Johnson says, "For place, they fix their eye upon Newtown, which, to tell their posterity whence they came, is now named Cambridge ; and withal, to make the whole world understand that spiritual learning was the thing they chiefly desired, to sanctify the other, and make the whole lump holy, and that learning, being set upon its right object, might not contend for error instead of truth, they chose this place, being then under the orthodox and soul-flourishing ministry of Mr. Thomas Shepard ; of whom it may be said, without any wrong to others, the Lord by his ministry hath saved many a hundred souls." Mass. Hist. Coll. xvii. 27.

chief of the magistrates and elders sent to England
to desire help to forward this work. But they all
neglecting us, in a manner, the Lord put it into the
heart of one Mr. HARVARD,[1] who died worth £1600,
to give half his estate to the erecting of the School.
The man was a scholar, and pious in his life, and
enlarged towards the country and the good of it,
in life and death.

But no sooner was this given, but Mr. Eaton,
(professing eminently, yet falsely and most deceit-
fully, the fear of God,) did lavish out a great part
of it, and being for his cruelty to his scholars,
especially to one Briscoe,[2] as also for some other
wantonness in life, not so notoriously known, driven
the country, the Lord, about a year after, graciously
made up the breach by one Mr. Dunstar,[3] a man

[1] Of JOHN HARVARD little is
known. In 1628, he entered Emmanuel College, Cambridge, where
he took the degree of A. B. in 1631,
and of A. M. in 1635. He was
admitted an inhabitant of Charlestown Aug. 6, 1637, " with promise
of such accommodations as we best
can ; " was made a freeman Nov. 2 ;
was admitted, with his wife Anna,
a member of the church at Charlestown Nov. 6 ; and " was sometime
minister of God's word here," as
assistant to the Rev. Zechariah
Symmes. There is no account,
however, of his ordination. The
town records state that he had a
lot of land assigned him in 1637,
and the next year his share in another allotment was a third larger
than Mr. Symmes's. He was appointed, April 26, 1638, one of a
committee " to consider of some
things tending towards a body of
laws," and had a grant of three
and a half feet of ground for a
portal to his house. He died of a
consumption Sept. 14, 1638, aged

not above thirty, supposing he entered college between his seventeenth and twentieth year. Frothingham makes it probable that his
widow married the Rev. Thomas
Allen, of Charlestown. His library
consisted of 260 volumes, a catalogue of which is preserved, though
the books were destroyed in the fire
of 1764. On the 26th of Sept.
1828, a monument of granite, a
solid obelisk, fifteen feet high and
four square at the base, was erected
to the memory of Harvard in the
burying-ground at Charlestown ; on
which occasion an eloquent address
was delivered by Edward Everett,
now President of the College which
he founded. See Winthrop, ii.
88, 342 ; Mather, ii. 7 ; Everett's
Orations, p. 163 ; Frothingham's
Charlestown, p. 74 ; Budington's
Charlestown Church, pp. 44, 182,
247 ; Mass. Hist. Coll. xvii. 16, 28,
xxviii. 248, 249.

[2] See an account of this in Winthrop, i. 308.

[3] Henry Dunster is placed by Cot-

pious, painful, and fit to teach, and very fit to lay CHAP. XXIV. the foundations of the domestical affairs of the College ; whom God hath much honored and blessed. 1640. The sin of Mr. Eaton was at first not so clearly discerned by me. Yet, after more full information, I saw his sin great, and my ignorance, and want of wisdom, and watchfulness over him, very great ; for which I desire to mourn all my life, and for the breach of his family.

ton Mather among the ministers of his " first class," that is, such as were in the actual exercise of the ministry when they left England. But neither he, nor Morton, nor any other writer, mentions the place of his ministry or birth. He was educated at Emmanuel College, Cambridge, where he received the degree of A. B. in 1630, and of A. M. in 1634. He arrived in New-England in 1640, and was admitted a freeman June 2, 1641. The author of New-England's First Fruits (1643) says, " Over the College is Master Dunster placed, as President, a learned, conscionable, and industrious man." Edward Johnson (1652) speaks of him as " one fitted from the Lord for the work, and by those that have skill that way, reported to be an able proficient in both Hebrew, Greek and Latin languages." He remained in office fourteen years, till, as Mather says, " his unhappy entanglement in the snares of Anabaptism filled the Overseers with uneasy fears lest the students by his means should come to be ensnared. Wherefore they labored with an extreme agony either to rescue the good man from his own mistakes, or to restrain him from imposing them upon the hope of the flock. Of both which finding themselves to despair, they did as quietly as they could procure his removal. Their uneasiness was so signified unto him that on Oct. 24,

1654, he resigned his presidentship." On leaving Cambridge, he retired to Scituate, where he was employed in the ministry till his death, Feb. 27, 1659. Mather remarks, that " he died in such harmony of affection with the good men who had been the authors of his removal from Cambridge, that he, by his will, ordered his body to be carried unto Cambridge for its burial, and bequeathed legacies to those very persons." Morton says, that " his body was embalmed, and removed to Cambridge, and there honorably buried." The Corporation of the College have lately taken measures to erect a monument to his memory on the spot where he is supposed to have been buried, as indicated by the ruins of a former monument, on which no traces of an inscription remain. Dunster revised and polished the New-England version of the Psalms, which had been translated in 1640, by Eliot, Weld, and Mather, as mentioned on page 511. His wife Elizabeth was the widow of the Rev. Jesse Glover, who died on his passage to New-England in 1639 ; and he had three sons ; David, born May 16, 1645, Henry, born in 1650, and Jonathan, born in 1653. See Mather, i. 366, ii. 8, 10 ; Morton's Memorial, p. 283 ; Deane's Scituate, p. 179 ; Peirce's Hist. of Harvard Univ. p. 7 ; Mass. Hist. Coll. xvii. 25, 31, xxviii. 248 ; Farmer's Genealogical Register.

But thus the Lord hath been very good unto me,
in planting the place I live in with such a mercy
to myself, such a blessing to my children and the
country, such an opportunity of doing good to many
by doing good to students, as the School is.

After this, I fell sick after Mr. Harlakenden's
death, my most dear friend, and most precious servant of Jesus Christ. And when I was very low,
and my blood much corrupted, the Lord revived me,
and after that took pleasure in me, to bless my
labors, that I was not altogether useless nor fruitless;
and not only to speak by me to his people, but
likewise to print my *Notes upon the Nine Principles*,
I intended to proceed on with in Yorkshire, but
never intended them, or imagined they should be
for the press. Yet six of them being finished in
Old England, and printed, and the other three desired, I finished (the Lord helping,) those at Cambridge; and so sent them to England, where they
also are printed; which I do not glory in, (for I
know my weakness,) that my name is up by this
means, but that the Lord may be pleased to do some
good by them there in my absence. For I have
seen the Lord making improvement of my weak
abilities as far as they could reach, and of myself
to the utmost; which I desire to bless his name
forever for.

The year after those wars in the country, God
having taken away my first wife, the Lord gave me
a second, the eldest daughter of Mr. Hooker,[1] a
blessed store; and the Lord hath made her a great

---

[1] Her name was Joanna. See Farmer's Gen. Reg., art. Shepard.

blessing to me to carry on matters in the family CHAP.<br>XXIV. with much care and wisdom, and to seek the Lord God of her father.

The first child I had by her, being a son, died through the weakness of the midwife, before it saw the sun, even in the very birth. The second, whom 1641. the Lord I bless hath hitherto spared, viz. my little Oct. Samuel,[1] is yet living. The third son, viz. my son John, after sixteen weeks, departed, on the Sabbath day morning, a day of rest, to the bosom of rest, to Him who gave it ; which was no small affliction and heart-breaking to me, that I should provoke the Lord to strike at my innocent children for my sake.

The Lord thus afflicting, yet continued peace to the country, that amazing mercy, when all England and Europe are in a flame. The Lord hath set me and my children aside from the flames of the fires in Yorkshire and Northumberland, whence if we had not been delivered, I had been in great afflictions and temptations, very weak and unfit to be tossed up and down, and to bear violent persecution. The Lord therefore hath showed his tenderness to me and mine, in carrying me to a land of peace, though a place of trial ; where the Lord hath made the savage Indians, (who conspired the death of all the English by Miantinomo upon a sudden, if Uncas 1643. could have been cut off first, who stood in their

---

[1] He was born in October, 1641, and was brought up, I believe, in the family of his grandfather Hooker, at Hartford. In an unpublished letter that I have seen, written by Samuel Stone of Hartford, and dated July 19, 1647, in which he gives a very affecting account of the death of his colleague, he says, "Little Sam. Shepard is well." He was ordained at Rowley Nov. 15, 1665, the third minister of that town, and died April 7, 1668, aged 26. See Gage's History of Rowley, pp. 19, 74.

CHAP.
XXIV.

1645.
Aug.
26.

way,[1] and determined an open war upon us by the
privy suggestions of some neutral English on the
Island,)[2] to seek for peace from us upon our own
terms, without bloodshed, August 26, 1645.

1646.

April
2.

But the Lord hath not been wont to let me live
long without some affliction or other ; and yet ever
mixed with some mercy.   And therefore, April the
2d, 1646, as he gave me another son, John, so he
took away my most dear, precious, meek, and loving
wife, in child-bed, after three weeks' lying-in ; having left behind her two hopeful branches, my dear
children, Samuel and John.   This affliction was very
heavy to me ; for in it the Lord seemed to withdraw his tender care for me and mine, which he
graciously manifested by my dear wife ; also refused
to hear prayer, when I did think he would have
hearkened and let me see his beauty in the land of
the living, in restoring of her to health again ; also,
in taking her away in the prime time of her life,
when she might have lived to have glorified the
Lord long ; also, in threatening me to proceed in
rooting out my family, and that he would not stop,
having begun here, as in Eli, for not being zealous
enough against the sins of his sons.   And I saw that
if I had profited by former afflictions of this nature,
I should not have had this scourge.   But I am the
Lord's, and He may do with me what he will.   He
did teach me to prize a little grace, gained by a
cross, as a sufficient recompense for all outward
losses.

----

¹ See  Winthrop,  ii.  131–134 ;      ² I suppose he means Gorton and
Hutchinson's  Mass.  i.  136,  138 ;   his company.
Hazard's State Papers, ii. 7–9.

But this loss was very great.  She was a woman CHAP.
XXIV.
of incomparable meekness of spirit, toward myself
especially, and very loving ; of great prudence to 1646.
take care for and order my family affairs, being
neither too lavish nor sordid in anything, so that
I knew not what was under her hands.  She had an
excellency to reprove for sin, and discern the evils
of men.  She loved God's people dearly, and [was]
studious to profit by their fellowship, and therefore
loved their company.  She loved God's word exceedingly, and hence was glad she could read my
notes, which she had to muse on every week.  She
had a spirit of prayer, beyond ordinary of her time
and experience.  She was fit to die long before she
did die, even after the death of her first-born, which
was a great affliction to her.  But her work not
being done then, she lived almost nine years with
me, and was the comfort of my life to me ; and the
last sacrament before her lying-in, seemed to be full
of Christ, and thereby fitted for heaven.  She did
oft say she should not outlive this child ; and when
her fever first began, by taking some cold, she told
me so, that we should love exceedingly together,
because we should not live long together.  Her
fever took away her sleep ; want of sleep wrought
much distemper in her head, and filled it with
fantasies and distractions, but without raging.  The
night before she died, she had about six hours'
unquiet sleep.  But that so cooled and settled her
head, that when she knew none else, so as to speak
to them, yet she knew Jesus Christ, and could speak
to him ; and therefore, as soon as she awakened out
of sleep, she brake out into a most heavenly, heart-

CHAP.
XXIV. breaking prayer, after Christ, her dear Redeemer,

~~ for the spirit of life, and so continued praying until

1646. the last hour of her death, "Lord, though I [am]
unworthy, Lord, one word, one word," &c.; and
so gave up the ghost.

Thus God hath visited and scourged me for my
sins, and sought to wean me from this world. But
I have ever found it a difficult thing to profit even
but a little by the sorest and sharpest afflictions.[1]

[1] Shepard remained pastor of the church at Cambridge till his death, Aug. 25, 1649, in the forty-fourth year of his age. He is described as "a poor, weak, pale-complectioned man." Edward Johnson speaks of him as "that gracious, sweet, heavenly-minded and soul-ravishing minister, Mr. Shepard;" and Fuller classes him among "the learned writers of Emmanuel College." After the death of his second wife, he married a third, Margaret Boradel, by whom he had one son, Jeremiah, who became the minister of Lynn, Oct. 6, 1680. After his death, she married his successor in the church at Cambridge, the Rev. Jonathan Mitchell. Shepard's eldest son, Thomas, was ordained pastor of the church in Charlestown, April 13, 1659, in which place he was succeeded by his son Thomas, May 5, 1680. Samuel, as has been already stated on page 555, was settled in the ministry at Rowley, Nov. 15, 1665. Anna, the daughter of the first Thomas Shepard, of Charlestown, was married, in 1682, to Daniel Quincy. They had one son, named John Quincy, born July 21, 1689, whose daughter Elizabeth married William Smith, the minister of Weymouth, and his daughter, Abigail, married the first President Adams, and was the mother of John Quincy Adams, who is thus a descendant, in the sixth generation,

from Thomas Shepard, of Cambridge. See Mather, i. 343-357, ii. 75, 100, 118, 125; Fuller's Hist. Cambridge, p. 206; Hazard's State Papers, ii. 17; Budington's Hist. of Charlestown Church, pp. 54, 81, 219; Lewis's Lynn, p. 194; Mass. Hist. Coll. xiii. 152, xxviii. 248, 268.

The preceding Memoir is printed from the original manuscript, in the hand-writing of Thomas Shepard. It is evident that it was used by Mather in writing the Life of him in the Magnalia. In 1750, it was in the possession of Samuel Blake, and, in 1768, of James Blake, the author of the Annals of Dorchester; from whom it descended to the Rev. James Blake Howe, of Claremont, N. H., who presented it to the Shepard Congregational Society in Cambridge, for whose use it was transcribed and printed in 1832. By the kindness of the Rev. John A. Albro, the minister of that Society, I have been favored with the loan of the manuscript, and been permitted to reprint it, in a much more accurate and attractive form. Although the spelling has been modernized, and the punctuation corrected, not a single word of the original has been altered or omitted, whilst several passages, left out in the first publication of the Memoir, are now inserted.

# INDEX.

566

Shipwrights sent to the, 161. No "idle drone" to be permitted in the, 188. Justice to be impartially administered in the, 188. Swearers to be punished, 189. Powers of the government of the, 196. Oaths of office for the Governor and Council of the, 201 – 203. Better provided with cattle than the Colony of New Plymouth, 216. Alleged innovations in the government of the, 290. Mortality in the, 314. Gardiner's attempts to injure the, 321, 335. Edmund Wilson, a benefactor of the, 326. Magistrates of the, 356; and ministers, 356, 357. Morton's attempts to injure the, 362. Letters of thanks to be sent to the benefactors of the, 415.

Massachusetts Company, patent of, confirmed by Charles I., 13, 372. First emigration under the authority of the, 13. Second emigration under the authority of the, 14. Condition of the members of the, 14. Third emigration under the authority of the, 15. Their patent, 60. Meetings of the, in London, 66, 68, 74, 78, 99. Instructions of the, to Endicott, 68, 132, 138, 139, – 191, 146, 153. Officers of the, chosen, 70, 71, 105, 106. Courts of Assistants of the, 73, 76, 98, 107, 125, 127. Letters of the, to Endicott, 77, 78, 136 ; to Higginson, Skelton, and Endicott, 99, 283 – 292. Orders of the, 77, 78. General Courts of the, in London, 78; 79, 82, 86, 87, 88, 90, 94, 101, 109, 113, 119, 120, 192. Accounts of the, to be audited, 81. Chalmers's assertions with regard to the, 89, 288. Joint stock of the, 95, 98, 110, 113, 114, 116, 125. Chaplains of the General Court of the, chosen, 112. Common stock of the, 120, 121, 125. Agreement of, with the ministers, 143, 207 – 212, 263. Endeavour to prevent immoral characters from going to their plantation, 189. Careful not to render themselves obnoxious to the government at home, 289, 291. See Brereton.

Massachusetts Fields, 305, 395. See Mount Wollaston.

Mather, Cotton, Rev., 142. On attempts of the English to settle certain parts of New-England, 6. On the origin and signification of the name, Naumkeag, 12. On Blackstone, 170. Cited, 164, 221, 303, 318, 365, 385, 419, 430, 448, 454, 553.

Mather, Increase, Rev., 16, 364.

Mather, Richard, Rev., 16, 260, 357, 419, 422, 438, 511. Account of, and of his family, 480. His Journal, 445 – 480, 481. At Bristol; goes aboard the James, 448. See Massachusetts Colonists.

Mathewes, Andrew, 53.

Maud, Daniel, Rev., 450, 451, 452, 454, 455, 456, 460, 462, 463, 466, 468, 471, 479. Notice of him, 449.

Maverick, John, Rev., 123, 260, 314, 347, 356, 357, 380, 386. Account of him, 348. He removes to Dorchester, 380.

Monmouth, England, noted for the manufacture of caps, 41.

Maverick, Samuel, 150, 306. Account of him, 322.

Mayflower, the, 39, 78, 107, 125, 154, 175, 184, 186, 216, 217, 242, 249, 261, 311. Alleged treachery of the captain of the, 4, 308. No Pilgrim returns in the, 315. See Jones, and Peirce.

Mayhew, ——, 161.

Mayo, ——, 62.

Meare, ——, 220.

Medford, settlement of, 313. Described, 402. See Mistick.

Meech, John, 375.

Meetinghouse, a modern term, 121.

Merrimack, described, 411.

Meyrick, Sir Samuel R., cited, 44.

Miantinomo, 555.

Michell, Barnard, 43.

Michelson, or Michenson, Edward, notice of, and of his family, 526.

Milburne, ——, 83, 92.

Mildmay, Sir Walter, founder of Emmanuel College, 421, 504. His conversation with Queen Elizabeth, 421.

Milk Island, 22.

Miller, Sydrach, 47.

Milton, John, cited, 127.

Ministers, 42, 96, 134, 142, 148, 187, 205, 263. Letters to the, 99, 286–289. Appointed referees, 120. Of the Massachusetts Colony, 356, 357.

Mistick, plantation at, 137, 313, 374, 402. Described, 404. See Medford.

Mitchell, Matthew, 456, 457, 460, 462, 464, 465. Account of him, 454.

Monanattuck, sachem of the Pequods, 548.

Money, raised, 80, 93, 110. To be paid, 107. Monhegan, fishing at, 22. Purchased by Aldworth and Elbridge, 362. The James arrives at, 470.

Monish, Lieutenant, 358.

Montowompate, or Sagamore James, 307.

Morell, William, Rev., 394.

Morley, Robert, 53.

Mortality, of the Colonists, 319, 325, 378, 379. At Charlestown, 314. Causes of the, 325. In England, 331, 500. See Indians.

Morton, Nathaniel, Secretary, on the treachery of the captain of the Mayflower, 4. His New-England's Memorial, 287. On the great storm, 478.

Morton, Thomas, 150, 151, 156. The first to sell guns and ammunition to the Indians, 83. His insinuation respecting the physician of New Plymouth, 131. Sent prisoner to England, account of him, 321. His attempts to injure the Colony, 362. Cited, 334.

Morton's Point, in Charlestown, 161.

Mosquitoes, 255.

Mott, ——, 264.

Moulton, Robert, 94, 180. Account of him, 161.

Mount Wollaston, 83, 150, 156, 305, 309, 395. See Quincy.

Mountain, Bishop of London, 516, 518.

Moxon, George, Rev., 283.

N.

Nahant, description of, 406.

Nantasket, 393. A habitation set up at, 19.

THE END.